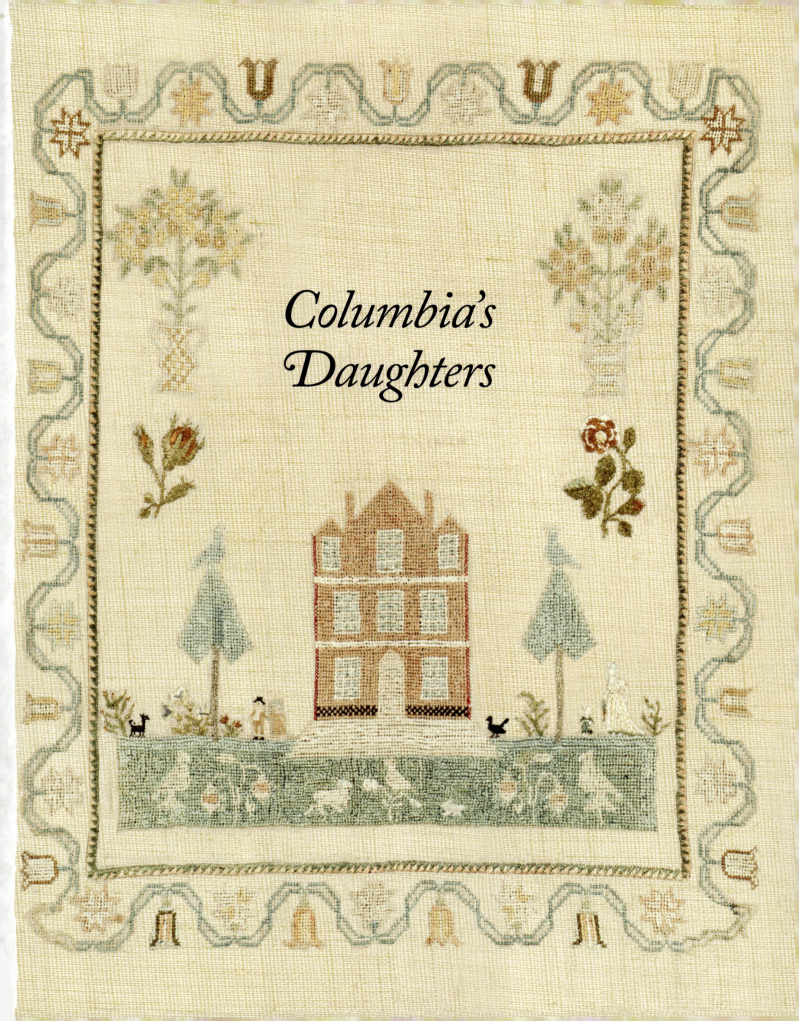

Columbia's Daughters

Rebecca Lauck, ca.1801, by Charles Peale Polk. Oil on canvas, 36 x 27 ½ in.
Image courtesy of the Museum of Early Southern Decorative Arts (MESDA) at Old Salem

Rebecca (1787-1854), a daughter of Peter and Amelia Heiskell Lauck of Winchester, Virginia, is shown seated at her tambour frame embroidering the left side of a man's waistcoat. She may have learned to use a tambour hook while studying with Mrs. Tennent who conducted a Tambouring School in Alexandria, 1797-1798. Rebecca's interest in needlework most likely came from her mother, whose elaborate quilts stitched for each of her four surviving children are treasured today in museum collections.

Charles Peale Polk (1767-1822), son of an Annapolis needlework teacher and nephew of Charles Willson Peale, was a portrait painter who found it necessary to supplement his income as an artist by working for the government as a clerk-copyist. He was living in Washington City in 1801 at the time he probably received his commission to paint Rebecca.

Columbia's Daughters

Girlhood Embroidery from the District of Columbia

Gloria Seaman Allen

Edited by Lynne Anderson

Chesapeake Book Company • Sampler Consortium

2012

Design for half title and part title pages (i, ix, 5, 69, 139, 189, 215) is based on:
Sampler worked by Julia Ann Crowley. Washington City, 1810.
Inscribed: "Julia Ann Crowley. / Aged 10 years. th' 14th / of Decr 1809. / Washington Navy Yard February th' 10th 1810."
Silk and silk chenille on linen ground, 30 by 27 threads per in.
21 ⅜ x 17 ¾ in.

The Colonial Williamsburg Foundation, Museum Purchase, 1991-25

ISBN 978-0-9823049-5-2

© 2012 Gloria Seaman Allen

All rights reserved.

Designed by James F. Brisson
Williamsville, Vermont

Printed in China

*This book is dedicated to
the memory of needlework scholars
Sue Swan
and
Sue Studebaker*

CONTENTS

FOREWORD — *Lynne Anderson*   XI

PREFACE   XIII

ACKNOWLEDGMENTS   XV

OVERVIEW: The District of Columbia   1

PART I Alexandria

1 Introduction to Alexandria and Its Teachers   7

2 Alexandria Samplers   15

3 Alexandria Pictorial Embroideries and Maps   49

PART II Georgetown

4 Introduction to Georgetown and Its Teachers   71

5 Georgetown Samplers   79

6 Young Ladies' Academy, Georgetown — *Gloria Seaman Allen and Susi B. Slocum*   101

PART III Washington City

7 Introduction to Washington City and Its Schools   141

8 Washington City Samplers   151

9 Navy Yard Architectural Samplers   167

PART IV Teaching Needlework in the District of Columbia –
Sheryl De Jong

10 The Teachers and Schools 191

11 The Teaching and Learning Enterprise:
THREE VIGNETTES 203

AFTERWORD: Some Reflections on Samplers from the District of Columbia 213

Appendices

I. Samplers and Embroidered Pictures from the District of Columbia — *Susi B. Slocum* 217

>ALEXANDRIA 220
>
>GEORGETOWN 222
>
>WASHINGTON CITY 224
>
>WORKED BY DISTRICT OF COLUMBIA GIRLS IN OUT-OF-TOWN SCHOOLS 228

II. Needlework Teachers and Schools in the District of Columbia — *Sheryl De Jong* 231

>ALEXANDRIA 232
>
>GEORGETOWN 234
>
>WASHINGTON CITY 238

III. Young Ladies' Academy, Georgetown, Student Records — *Susi B. Slocum* 251

SELECT BIBLIOGRAPHY 259

INDEX 265

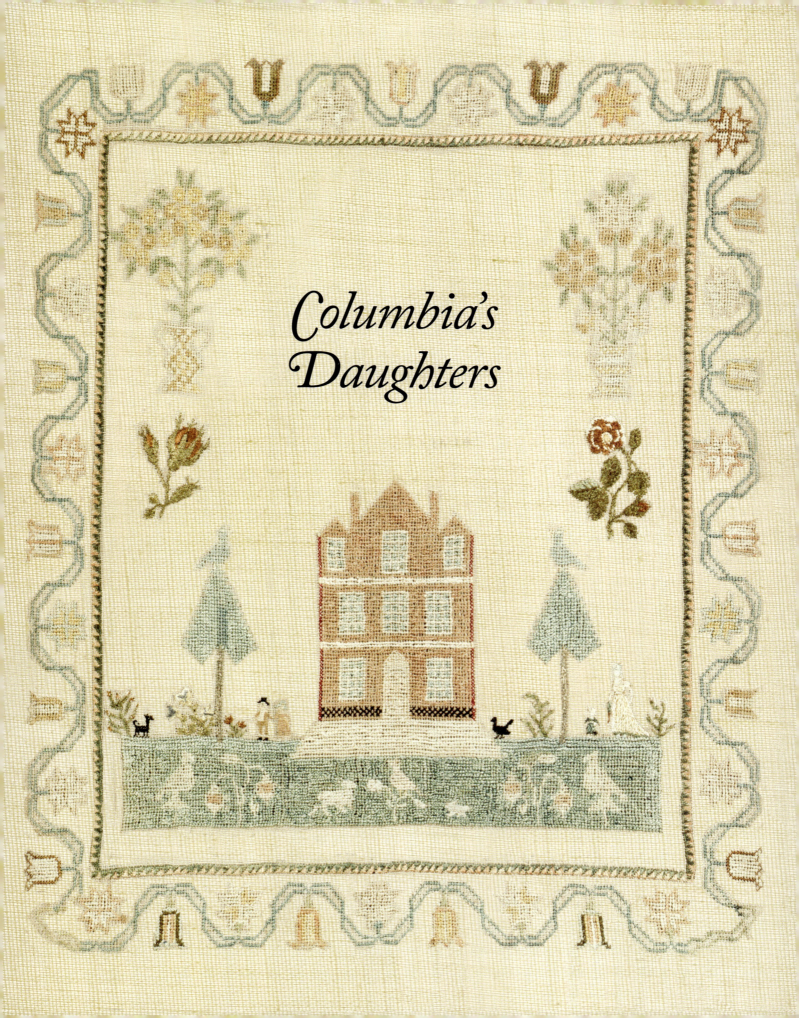

Columbia's Daughters

Embroidery attributed to Julietta Marie Massoletti. Washington City, 1835–1840.
Inscribed on reverse: "J M M."
Silk and silk chenille on silk ground.
7 x 5 in.
Collection of Julia Parish

Julietta (1825–1895) was a daughter of Vincent Massoletti and sampler maker Sarah Horwell of Alexandria. Around 1822 the Massolettis moved to the Navy Yard area of Washington City and that is where Julietta probably stitched her embroidery using a combination of satin and outline stitches. She married John C. Metcalfe in 1851, and they relocated to Wisconsin.

FOREWORD

SAMPLERS tend to be elusive. Often small enough to bury in a drawer or slip into an envelope, they may go undetected in family collections for decades, passed from one generation to the next without notice. Other samplers may be carefully stored in private or public collections but remain silent about their true origins, disconnected from the larger familial, historical, and geographical contexts in which they were created. Unappreciated for what they might tell us, samplers' stories are often lost over time, or garbled by faulty memories and inaccurate assumptions.

Fortunately, scholarship that focuses on revealing the stories of historic samplers and other schoolgirl embroideries is flourishing. Spurred by national interest in material culture, historic needlework, women's studies, the history of education, and the artistic endeavors of children, the study of girlhood needlework has increased in prominence and popularity. When that scholarship focuses on a specific geographic region, then the interactive effects of key variables (e.g., settlement patterns, economics, politics, religion, race, etc.) on educational opportunity begin to emerge.

Samplers are among the most personal of all historic objects. Stitched in endless variety by girls and young women well into the middle of the nineteenth century, samplers and their makers reach out to us from the past, introducing us to a time, a place, and, most importantly, a young person on the path to adulthood. Through carefully stitched personal details, we often learn the sampler maker's name, her age, and the year in which she received needlework instruction. Sometimes the stitches also reveal where she lived, or where she went to school, or who spent time teaching her to embroider. Occasionally a sampler will even provide a glimpse of the entire family—parents and siblings—their names, and the dates on which they were born, married, and even died. Advances in sampler scholarship rely on scholars' abilities to use these clues to unlock the stories that samplers have to tell, and then interpret those stories within the socio-economic, historic, and geographic contexts in which the samplers were created.

Columbia's Daughters: Girlhood Embroidery from the District of Columbia is a regional study of the samplers and pictorial embroideries wrought by girls in the late eighteenth to mid-nineteenth centuries in three urban communities: Alexandria, Georgetown, and the new federal entity called Washington City. Although the three cities were merged to form the District of Columbia, their political, economic, and social dynamics varied greatly. This in turn affected the education available to girls and young women living in the District, and their access to needlework instruction "plain and ornamental."

To the task of unraveling the genealogical and historical contexts associated with District of Columbia needlework, Dr. Gloria Seaman Allen brought three decades of experience studying and writing about women's material culture. In her earlier research, Dr. Allen investigated the textiles and needlework of the Chesapeake Bay region and the surrounding states of Virginia and Maryland. Narrowing her focus to the District of Columbia resulted in challenges and opportunities, and we are in her debt that she surmounted the challenges and took advantage of the opportunities.

Dr. Allen and her research team have successfully located and documented nearly 130 schoolgirl embroideries stitched by girls living in the District of Columbia, spread more or less equally across the District's three major cities. This endeavor proved to be more difficult, and resulted in fewer examples, than anticipated. Although geographically restricted to a relatively small area, the District's population was diverse and much of it itinerant.

Local newspapers advertised the instructional offerings for nearly 250 teachers and schools, but remarkably few needlework examples could be tied directly to a specific instructor. Schools were often short-lived, and teachers moved in and out of the District with astounding frequency. The same was true for many families, who were drawn to the District for its political and economic opportunities but moved on, or back home, as circumstances dictated, taking samplers and sampler makers with them. The resulting pool of samplers and related girlhood embroideries is therefore stylistically diverse and geographically dispersed.

Columbia's Daughters reflects the best of twenty-first-century scholarship in material culture. Dr. Allen allows each sampler or needlework picture to tell its own story. Without over interpretation, she highlights important elements, draws comparisons with other known examples, and connects the embroidered work to the historical, social, and educational contexts from which it emerged. Each piece of needlework is seen as a reflection of the educational opportunities afforded girls and young women of the time, and therefore its story is embedded in a careful examination of the schools and teachers who dedicated their energies to preparing the youth of our nation's capital for adulthood. Recognizing the social and economic implications of educational opportunity, Dr. Allen is careful to document the institutions and teachers whose instructional offerings were available to girls from families rich and poor, black and white, free and enslaved.

Columbia's Daughters is the most recent volume in a growing body of work surveying regional needlework styles and sampler-making traditions. In this century alone, we have benefited from books such as *This Have I Done: Samplers and Embroideries from Charleston and the Lowcountry* by Jan Hiester and Kathleen Staples (2001); *Ohio Is My Dwelling Place: Schoolgirl Embroideries 1800–1850* by Sue Studebaker (2002); *Virtue Leads and Grace Reveals: Embroideries and Education in Antebellum South Carolina* by Patricia V. Veasey (2003); *A Maryland Sampling: Girlhood Embroidery 1738–1860* by Gloria Seaman Allen (2007); *Connecticut Needlework: Women, Art and Family, 1740–1840* by Susan P. Schoelwer (2010); and *With Needle and Brush: Schoolgirl Embroidery from the Connecticut River Valley, 1740–1840* by Carol and Stephen Huber, Susan P. Schoelwer, and Amy Kurtz Lansing (2011). Characteristic of all these initiatives is an emphasis on identifying regional nuances and interpreting regional needlework in the contexts of female education, familial relationships, and locally relevant historical events.

Gloria Seaman Allen's *Columbia's Daughters: Girlhood Embroidery from the District of Columbia* is a welcome addition to the literature examining our country's regional needlework. The book not only documents what is known to date about schoolgirl embroideries from the District of Columbia, but also demonstrates the power of online technologies to support investigations into material culture, and sets the parameters for future scholarship and interpretation.

Lynne Anderson, Ph.D.
Director, *Sampler Archive Project*
http://samplerarchive.org

PREFACE

My interest in girlhood embroidery from the District of Columbia—Alexandria, Georgetown, and Washington City—dates to my years with the Daughters of the American Revolution (DAR) Museum in Washington, D.C., during which I worked with their outstanding collection of American needlework. My predecessor, Elisabeth Donaghy Garrett, had made the fascinating connection between the DAR's 1813 Julia Ann Crowley sampler and one other known at the time (Martha Ensey) by establishing these girls lived in the vicinity of the Washington Navy Yard. Thus, she identified the first District of Columbia needlework group.[1]

After years of collecting data and writing about textile production in the Chesapeake region and needlework from Maryland, it was relatively easy to narrow my geographic focus to the District of Columbia, where many of the residents traditionally had kinship and socio-economic connections to Maryland and Virginia. My collected data have evolved continually as research on new discoveries confirmed or disproved the origin of an embroidery or the identity of a teacher.

I had three objectives in writing this survey of the District of Columbia's girlhood embroidery. The first was to explore the regional differences within this small geographical area by tracing the history of needlework instruction and attempting to identify stylistic groups unique to the District of Columbia. My second objective was to uncover and present as much information as possible about the young embroiderers and their families. Although some of the young women have been frustratingly elusive, existing documentation has revealed interesting and sometimes tragic stories for many of the other girls. The third objective was to place both the embroiderers and their teachers in geographical and historical context.

From the beginning I had two valuable research allies: Ethel Stanwood Bolton and Eva Johnston Coe. In their 1921 survey of American schoolgirl needlework, Bolton and Coe included thirteen District of Columbia samplers, the majority from Alexandria.[2] Although only three of these have since been located, Bolton and Coe provided helpful information about the samplers' appearance, stitches, and verses, along with some images. In a similar manner, other examples of

---

1 Elisabeth Donaghy Garrett, "American Samplers and Needlework Pictures in the DAR Museum, Part II: 1806–1840," *The Magazine Antiques*, 107, no. 4 (April, 1975), 688–701.

2 Ethel Stanwood Bolton and Eva Johnston Coe, *American Samplers* (1921; New York: Dover Publications, 1973).

needlework from the District of Columbia are known only from early published notations and rarely with an accompanying image.

The Craftsman Database in the archives at the Museum of Early Southern Decorative Arts (MESDA)—part of Old Salem Museums and Gardens in Winston-Salem, North Carolina—provided the bulk of the documentation for approximately seventy-four needlework teachers active in the District of Columbia prior to 1821. Data from District of Columbia directories, histories, and contemporary newspapers yielded more information on educators and their institutions, expanding the book's scope to 1860 and beyond.

The museum collections of the Colonial Williamsburg Foundation, the Smithsonian Institution's National Museum of American History, and the DAR Museum include a number of fine and well-documented needlework examples from the District of Columbia. And the Georgetown Visitation Monastery Archives has a specialized collection of needlework stitched at their Young Ladies' Academy, accompanied by valuable archival documentation for their schoolgirl embroiderers.

Over the course of this project, information about a District of Columbia sampler seen at auction, discovered in a collection, or owned by a friend came to me sporadically via the mail or Internet, resulting in archival and online research to firmly locate the embroiderer in one of the District's three jurisdictions. These efforts led to uncovering nearly 130 girlhood embroideries, all of which have been researched, documented, and entered into a database of schoolgirl needlework from the District of Columbia.* The samplers, maps, and pictorial embroideries in this database are physically scattered across the United States (and the United Kingdom), many residing in private and small public collections. I have, however, studied firsthand most of the samplers and pictorial embroideries included in this volume and, with the assistance of dedicated colleagues, analyzed their physical characteristics.

For those who enjoy reading footnotes, I have included stories and facts from my research that did not fit the flow of the main narrative but seemed too interesting to leave out. Forgive me for this indulgence.

Finally, my hope is that this volume will lead to the discovery of other samplers and pictorial embroideries marked or attributed to Alexandria, Georgetown, and Washington City. Some of these may relate stylistically to groups or individual examples illustrated here and provide additional clues to the identity and/or location of the embroiderers and their teachers. Others may be unlike any examples seen before, further attesting to the fascinating needlework diversity found within the ten-mile square of the District of Columbia.

* Available online at www.dcneedlework.com

ACKNOWLEDGMENTS

For more than thirty years I have been collecting information about samplers and pictorial embroideries from the District of Columbia, researching their historical and genealogical context, and locating extant pieces. During this time, many people have given their time and knowledge to this project. I would especially like to thank my collaborators.

Dr. Lynne Anderson's expertise as an editor and educator set the tone of this book. Her skillful editing and her vast knowledge have enriched and vastly improved the text. She contributed extensive research and her enthusiasm for the project has been unwavering. In addition, Dr. Anderson made possible the sponsorship of the Sampler Consortium, with its access to an international public of scholars and needlework enthusiasts.

Deborah Cooney, with whom I had worked on Maryland quilts, read an early draft and keenly noted inconsistencies.

Rita Holtz, an Alexandria genealogist, delved into the lives of elusive sampler makers, leading to the discovery of current owners of "lost" samplers.

Susi Slocum, a collector of needlework and native Washingtonian, provided genealogical and historical research assistance that served to solve problematic connections. Her work in the archives of the Georgetown Visitation Monastery has resulted in the first in-depth study of samplers and pictorial embroideries from their school.

Sheryl De Jong brought to the project her skill in doing genealogical research and her knowledge of embroidery from many years volunteering in the Textile Division of the National Museum of American History. She built upon Joan Stephens' list of documented needlework teachers and schools (Appendix II) and expanded that work in an essay on teachers in the District of Columbia. Her husband John was invaluable at our photo sessions.

Barbara Hutson, a talented embroiderer, designer, and teacher, identified stitches and counted threads on numerous samplers with the assistance of her husband Jim and colleague Cynthia Steinhoff. Katherine Franetovich, another skilled embroiderer and teacher, analyzed additional samplers.

I would also like to thank Kristin B. Lloyd, Curator at the Lyceum, Alexandria's History Museum, John Henry Loomis, Corporate Administrator at the National Theatre in Washington, D. C., and Sister Mada-anne Gell, Archivist at the Georgetown Visitation Monastery, for hosting sampler identification and photography days.

Conservation of two important Georgetown Visitation needleworks was generously funded by the Swan Sampler Guild, Salt

Lake City, Utah, and the Loudoun Sampler Guild, Leesburg, Virginia.

Many knowledgeable people, who have published books, catalogues, and articles on girlhood embroidery, have been very generous with their expertise and in leading me to additional samplers. They include Betty Ring, Betsy Garrett Widmer, Trish Herr, Kim Ivey, Olive Graffam, and the late Joan Stephens and Betty Flemming. Needlework dealers Amy Finkel, Stephen and Carol Huber, Ruth Van Tassel, and Christopher Jones also brought District of Columbia examples to my attention, and shared their research.

Independent scholars and collectors scouted out District of Columbia samplers in their localities, shared their research, or mined the Internet and library collections for genealogical and historical information. They include Betty-Anne Stokes, Anna Marie Witmer, Paul Turczynski, Wendy White, Kathy Moyer, Patsy Hall, Mary Brooks, and Gary Parks.

Numerous museums and archives were contacted in my search for District of Columbia needlework. As always, their capable staffs were helpful and offered valuable assistance. It is impossible to mention here everyone with whom I have exchanged e-mails, letters, phone calls, or visited, and I apologize to those whose names I have omitted. My special thanks go to Sister Mada-anne Gell, Archivist at the Georgetown Visitation Monastery; Kimberly Smith Ivey, Associate Curator, Textiles & Historic Interiors at The Colonial Williamsburg Foundation; Linda Eaton, Director of Museum Collections & Senior Curator of Textiles and Susan Newton, Coordinator of Photo Services at the Winterthur Museum, Garden & Library; Kristin B. Lloyd, Curator, and Jim McKay, Director, of the Lyceum; Martha Rowe, Research Associate, and Johanna Brown, Curator of Moravian Decorative Arts & Director of Collections at the Museum of Early Southern Decorative Arts; Olive Graffam, Curator of Collections, Alden O'Brien, Curator of Costume, Textiles, and Toys, and Anne Ruta, Registrar, at the National Society Daughters of the American Revolution Museum; Doris Bowman, Curator, Textile Division, National Museum of American History, Smithsonian Institution; Susan P. Schoelwer, Curator, George Washington's Mount Vernon Estate, Museum & Gardens; and S. Scott Scholz, Museum Curator at Dumbarton House, The National Society of The Colonial Dames of America.

The success of the District of Columbia needlework book depended on numerous people, but especially the owners of samplers and pictorial embroideries who allowed their needlework to be studied and photographed. Many also shared their considerable research. For those who wished to be identified, their individual names or their affiliations are indicated in the captions.

As always, I have enjoyed working with Ric Cottom at the Chesapeake Book Company and Jim Brisson. They have patiently attended to my many detailed requests and have brought consistency in text and design to this work.

Finally, this book would have continued to languish without the help, once again, of my dearest friend, Vince Hovanec, who provided encouragement, transportation, editing expertise, and numerous "scholar support services."

Gloria Seaman Allen
Rock Hall, Maryland
May 2012

OVERVIEW

The District of Columbia

HISTORICALLY, the District of Columbia consisted of three separate communities—Alexandria, Georgetown, and Washington City—each founded at different times and by different groups of people. The port of Alexandria was established around 1749 in northern Virginia, an area settled primarily by Scots. In the late eighteenth century, members of the Religious Society of Friends moved to Alexandria from Pennsylvania and Maryland. Georgetown, originally part of the Province of Maryland, was incorporated in 1751 at the fall line of the Potomac River and flourished as a tobacco port. Members of the Roman Catholic faith were drawn to the area by the establishment of the first Catholic college on the western edge of town.

In 1791, Washington City was created out of swamp, farmland, and wilderness at the confluence of two rivers and within the new special district designated to serve as the permanent national capital.[1] Beginning in 1800, federal government employees and others seeking their patronage relocated from Philadelphia to the District of Columbia. At the turn of the nineteenth century the combined population of the District of Columbia stood at barely eleven thousand, unevenly divided with 4,971 persons in

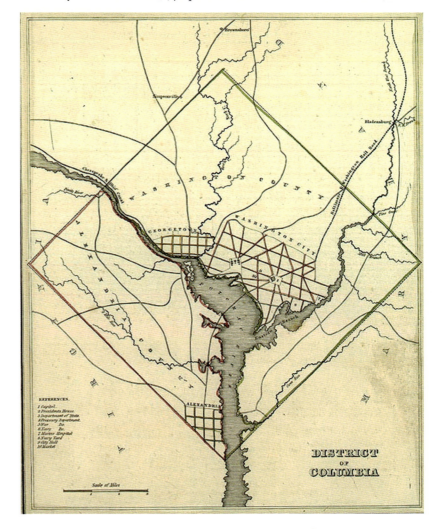

Figure 1.
District of Columbia, 1835.
Published by T. G. Bradford, Boston.

---

[1] The Residence Act, passed July 16, 1790, established a "Permanent Seat of the Government of the United States" on the Potomac River. All federal offices would be removed from their temporary location in Philadelphia to this site in 1800.

Alexandria, 3,210 in Washington City, and 2,993 in Georgetown.² Only a decade later the population had increased significantly, and the size of Washington City exceeded that of the more established communities within the District.

In the eighteenth century, Alexandria and Georgetown had settled populations that derived their growth and mercantile wealth from flourishing tobacco ports. The Potomac River brought the towns together and provided a conduit for trade goods and people. Later, the river created a natural barrier, especially when Georgetown became enveloped in the movement of people, commerce, and influence toward the adjacent federal city. By the nineteenth century Alexandria and Georgetown had become economic and philosophical rivals, leading up to the 1847 severing of the area originally ceded by Virginia—Alexandria and Alexandria County.

Alexandria and Georgetown had stable merchant and artisan classes that could adequately provide their children with a proper education. The towns also attracted, usually as boarding students, sons and daughters of the landed gentry from rural areas where populations were too small to support schools. Quakers from northern Virginia and from across the Potomac River joined their urban cousins in attending Alexandria schools. Wealthy Catholic families in southern Maryland patronized schools in Georgetown. The service industry necessary to provision the seasonal, transient,

---

2 Campbell Gibson, "Population of 33 Urban Places, 1800," in *Population of the 100 Largest Cities and Other Urban Places in the United States: 1790 to 1990* (Washington, D.C.: U.S. Census Bureau, 1998). The consensus estimate of the District's population in 1800 is 14,093. See W. B. Bryan, "Beginnings of the Presbyterian Church in the District of Columbia," *Records of the Columbia Historical Society* 8 (1905): 59; Charles E. Howe, "The Financial Institutions of Washington City in Its Early Days," ibid., 25.

Figure 2. "Prospect of Georgetown from the Tenleytown Road," painted by Rebecca Wistar Morris Nourse. Georgetown, ca. 1820. Watercolor on paper. 6 ¼ x 7 ½ in.
Dumbarton House, The National Society of The Colonial Dames of America, Washington, D.C., DH92.4.

Figure 3. "A Glimpse of the Capitol," painted by William Douglas MacLeod, ca. 1844. Oil on canvas. 21 ¾ x 29 ½ in. Diplomatic Reception Rooms, U.S. Department of State, Washington D.C. Photography by Will Brown.

and predominantly male society of federal Washington soon required schools of its own. One observer commented:

> *No monotony here, every season, nay every week and month brings change and variety. New faces, new interests, new objects of every kind, in politics, fashions, works of art and nature. . . . When lo, Congress adjourns, the curtain drops, the drama is over, all is quiet, not to say solitary. . . . In April we retire from all bustle and society [and] go into the country.*[3]

Although the District of Columbia is a small geographic area—conceived as a ten-mile square and depicted on maps up until 1847 as a diamond on point—the population was diverse, and teachers of needlework within the District drew on several different sampler traditions for their inspiration. Unlike New England with its deep-rooted families, early town formation, established schools, and needle instruction dating back to the seventeenth century,[4] the District lacked long-standing traditions. But with the new federal era came a growing demand for cultural accomplishments for the area's young ladies. Teachers, newly relocated, taught designs from their own cultural backgrounds or introduced the new classicism popular in Philadelphia or the more formulaic Quaker designs from England, Pennsylvania, and New York.

In the second quarter of the nineteenth century, interest in needlework education for young women in the District gradually waned, as it did elsewhere in the United States. During the 1820s, the components of female education were questioned and debated. With the exception of Catholic schools, instruction in advanced needlework soon gave way to more academic subjects, allowing "Columbia's daughters" to receive an education suitable to their emerging role as women in the New Republic.

---

[3] Margaret Bayard Smith, *The First Forty Years of Washington Society in the Family Letters of Margaret Bayard Smith*, ed. Gaillard Hunt (New York: Frederick Ungar Publishing Co., 1906), 372.

[4] Carol and Stephen Huber, Susan P. Schoelwer, Amy Kurtz Lansing, *With Needle and Brush: Schoolgirl Embroidery from the Connecticut River Valley, 1740–1840* (Hartford: Connecticut Historical Society, 2011), 1–2.

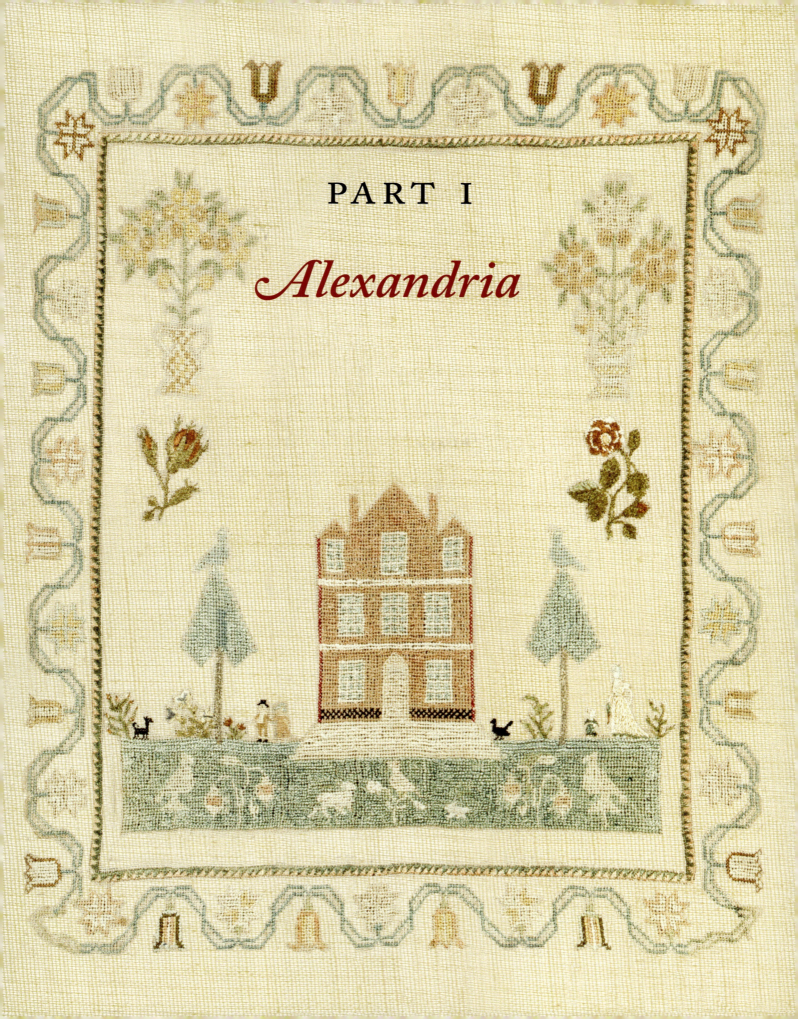

PART I

Alexandria

Painting by Edward Savage, "The Washington Family," ca. 1798.
Oil on wood.
18 ¼ x 24 ¼ in.
Winterthur Museum, bequest of Henry Francis du Pont, 1961.0708

George Washington was a Virginian with many ties to Alexandria. He represented the town in the House of Burgesses before the American Revolution and built a house on Cameron Street in the 1760s to avoid the hazards of traveling back and forth between Alexandria and Mount Vernon, some eight miles distant. He is shown here with Martha Washington, two of her grandchildren, George Washington Parke Custis and Eleanor Parke Custis, and an unidentified enslaved servant.

Martha points with her fan to the future location of the Capitol on the official plan of the City of Washington. This plan was replicated in embroidery on silk by several Alexandria school girls.

CHAPTER 1

Introduction to Alexandria and Its Teachers

The town of Alexandria was laid out along the Potomac River and Hunting Creek in 1749, on land acquired from the Alexander and West families. It soon became the focal point for political and economic life in northern Virginia.¹ The attractions of this vibrant seaport, mercantile hub and artisanal center were enhanced by its proximity to George Washington's extensive landholdings along the Potomac. In 1791 Alexandria was included in the area President Washington selected as the location for the nation's new Federal District. Alexandria became part of the District of Columbia in 1801 and remained part of the District until the area was ceded back to Virginia in 1847 (Figure 1-1).²

In 1810, upon viewing Alexandria for the first time, a New England teacher observed:

*Alexandria is situated on the river Potomac, one of the largest, handsomest, and most commercial cities in Virginia. The situation is pleasant and elevated, the city is built on the plan of Philadelphia, the streets are as wide if not wider than those of that city. The trade of Alexandria is very considerable; ships of almost any burthen can ride in the river.*³

Visitors to Alexandria frequently noted the city's orderly plan and river front prosperity. At least one recorded his impressions of Alexandria's inhabitants, especially the city's young women:

*Females amongst them uncommonly intelligent, uncommonly courteous and polite in their behavior with each other and especially with strangers. Polite and courteous conduct does much credit to parents, to the teachers, to the clergy and to human nature itself.*⁴

---

1 Lots were available for sale by July 1749, but the town of Alexandria was not incorporated until 1779.

2 A portion of the town and surrounding area were ceded by Virginia to the United States government when the District of Columbia was established in 1791, but Alexandria did not officially become a part of the District until Congress formally accepted it on February 27, 1801. In 1800 the population of Alexandria was approximately five thousand.

3 Martha von Briesen, ed., *The Letters of Elijah Fletcher* (Charlottesville: The University Press of Virginia, 1965), October 1, 1810.

4 Quoted by T. Michael Miller from an 1823 advertisement in *Portrait of a Town: Alexandria 1820–1830* (Bowie, Md.: Heritage Books, 1995), vii.

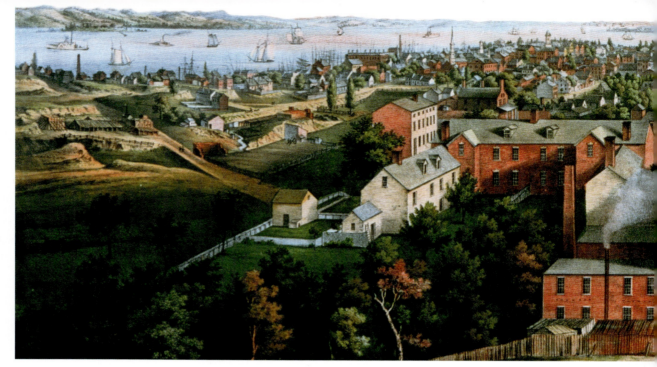

Figure 1-1.
View of Alexandria drawn by James T. Palmatary. Alexandria, 1845. Inscribed: "View of Alexandria, Va." Lithographed and printed by Edward Sachse and Company, Baltimore, 1853. 20 ½ x 31 in.
Alexandria Library, Special Collections Branch

Educational Opportunities in Alexandria

Girls and young women of Alexandria had many and diverse opportunities to acquire the attributes of polite society, including skills in needlework, plain and fancy. Young girls whose parents could afford to pay tuition attended private schools conducted by women in their homes or rented rooms, where they received basic instruction in reading, needlework, and moral values. Teachers with more advanced education added writing and arithmetic to the curriculum. In the antebellum period (the years between the American Revolution and the Civil War), a large number of schoolmistresses resided in Alexandria, teaching independently or in the city's female academies and seminaries. They offered instruction in a wide range of subjects, both useful (e.g., reading, writing, arithmetic, geography) and ornamental (drawing, painting, and embroidery).

Documentary evidence from newspaper advertisements confirms that ample opportunities existed for local girls to acquire advanced needlework skills.[5] Moreover, parents in Alexandria, many of whom had benefited from the city's commercial prosperity, considered proficiency with a needle an essential component of their daughters' genteel education. One advice book proclaimed that:

> *Amongst the accomplishments necessary to the female character . . . needle work may claim first place, it having so close a connection with neatness which is indisputably requisite to render you comfortable to yourself, or amiable in the esteem of others.*[6]

For girls whose parents lacked the financial resources to send their daughters to a private school, or to a specialized needlework instructor, there were also opportunities to become proficient in sewing, at least sufficient to obtain employment as seamstresses or skilled servants.

---

5 A rare mention of needlework in legal documents lists "1 piece of framed needlework" in the debt record of James Card and Elizabeth Downey Card, Alexandria, December 27, 1802. I am grateful to Jean Taylor Federico, former director of the Office of Historic Alexandria, for supplying this reference from her database.

6 Cornelia, "Letters from a Mother to her Daughters," in Erasmus Darwin, *A Plan for the Conduct of Female Education in Boarding Schools, Private Families, and Public Seminaries* (Philadelphia: John Ormrod, 1798), 40.

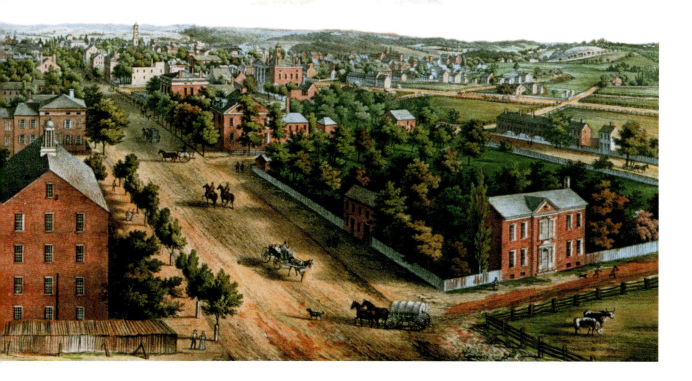

Mr. and Mrs. Winter offered such an opportunity to less fortunate girls in Alexandria when they advertised "Cheap Schooling" in their establishment on Wilkes Street.

> *Young Misses will be improved in Reading, Grammar, and Writing: and particular attention will be paid to such whose abilities entitle them to become complete sempstresses [sic]. A part of the day will be taken up for that purpose.*
> *Price Two Dollars per Quarter.*[7]

An opportunity for free education was available from the Female Lancasterian School, established in Alexandria in 1812 with an endowment by Elizabeth Foote Washington,[8] childless widow of Lund Washington, a distant cousin of George Washington.[9] Elizabeth Washington, who had lost two daughters in infancy, directed in her will that the annual income from her bequest be used to

> *rescue from poverty, and the sinks of shameless immorality those sweet tho' wild blossoms which under their fostering care and virtuous inculcations, may add much to the store of human happiness. I confine this donation to my own sex, because I believe that human happiness has material dependence upon our moral and religious worth.*[10]

The Female Lancasterian School, also known as the Alexandria Free School for Girls, was located in the 200 block of North Columbus Street.[11] It was organized according

---

7 *Alexandria Herald*, September 6, 1820.

8 During the 1780s, Elizabeth Washington taught her two female slaves to read and write. She noted that "few young ladies ever have the same pain taken with them." Mary Carroll Johansen, "All Useful, Plain Branches of Education: Educating Non-Elite Women in Antebellum Virginia," *Virginia Cavalcade* 49, no. 2 (Spring 2000): 78.

9 Lund Washington managed Mount Vernon in George Washington's absence during the Revolution. See, William Buckner McGroarty, "Elizabeth Washington of Hayfield," *Virginia Magazine of History and Biography* 33 (1925): 154–65.

10 Elizabeth Foote Washington, Fairfax County Wills, 1742–1864, December 16, 1810 (probated June 18, 1812).

11 Male and female schools followed the same Lancasterian curriculum with the exception of needlework. Both were successors to the Washington Free School, endowed by George Washington in 1785 and located on the third floor of the Alexandria Academy at 604 Wolfe Street. The Washington Free School accepted girls, orphans or daughters of indigent parents, on a ratio of one girl to four boys. There is no indication, however, that the Washington Free School offered needlework instruction.

to the monitorial system developed by British educator Joseph Lancaster.[12] Older, more advanced students were taught to be "monitors," each teaching a group of younger students. This system effectively and economically enabled a large number of girls to learn the basics of reading, writing, arithmetic, and sewing because it required only one paid teacher.[13]

Rachel Judge (1790–1867) became the first teacher of the Female Lancasterian School in Alexandria shortly before her older sister, Margaret, took over as head of the female division of the Georgetown Lancasterian School.[14] Rachel belonged to the Religious Society of Friends (commonly known as Quakers), a religion that actively promoted educational opportunities for girls and young women, especially those from lower socio-economic levels.[15] Miss Judge would have followed the course of needlework instruction outlined in several Lancasterian manuals.[16] Every day, student monitors would distribute to each girl in her group a pinafore to wear, as well as a thimble, needle, thread, and materials for work. When a student could neatly reproduce the sewing specimen supplied by the monitor, she was promoted to the next class in difficulty. In the course of ten classes she would learn to hem, fell seams, draw threads, gather cloth, edge buttonholes, sew on buttons, make herringbone stitches, darn holes, tuck pleats, and mark linen. Although early skills such as hemming were practiced on scraps of paper, students would conclude their needlework education by completing marking samplers on linen. These simple samplers were often worked in black cross stitch with upper and lower case alphabets and numbers enclosed by a zig-zag border (Figure 1-2).[17] Although hundreds of young girls attended Lancasterian schools in

---

12 Joseph Lancaster was a London-born Quaker who opened his first school in England—free to the poor—in 1798. To cope with large numbers of students, he devised the system of using older, better students to act as teachers or monitors to the younger children. With financial backing from members of the nobility, Lancaster founded a society in 1808 that became known as the British and Foreign School Society. Through the society, schools were established throughout England and their success led to the adoption of the Lancasterian monitorial system in countries around the world. Lancaster's pedagogical method, disseminated by instruction manuals, employed an elaborate set of rules and routines: learning was by rote and motivated by competition. The system stressed moral values of obedience, subordination, promptness, cleanliness, thrift, and temperance—all calculated to teach a poor child discipline and awareness of his or her proper place in society. For background on Lancasterian schools, see Carl F. Kastle, ed., *Joseph Lancaster and the Monitorial School Movement: A Documentary History* (New York: Columbia University, 1973).

13 The Lancasterian female program of education, with its emphasis on practical or plain sewing, was developed in England by Ann Springmann who established schools for poor girls throughout the country. She successfully convinced parents of the merits of giving up their child's weekly earnings for the advantages of an education. Kastle, *Joseph Lancaster and the Monitorial School Movement: A Documentary History*, 134–36.

14 The Georgetown Lancasterian School had been established in 1811 by an Act of Congress as a co-educational school. The experiences of that school led to the opening a few months later of separate male and female Lancasterian schools in Alexandria.

15 Rachel and Margaret Judge were the daughters of Susannah Hatton and esteemed Quaker minister Hugh Judge of Chester County, Pennsylvania, and Wilmington, Delaware. The Hugh Judge family moved from Wilmington to Purchase, Dutchess County, New York, in 1792. Rachel was educated nearby at the Nine Partners' Boarding School, opened in 1796 by the Religious Society of Friends. In 1813 she married Townshend Waugh, a teacher at the male Lancasterian school in Alexandria, and was disowned by the Alexandria Meeting of the Society of Friends for marriage out of unity. Rachel Judge Waugh opened Waugh's Female Boarding School, a private seminary, in 1827.

16 *An Account of the Lancasterian Method of Teaching Needlework* (Baltimore, ca. 1821) contained instructions and patterns for marking linen. See Davida Tenenbaum Deutsch, "Needlework Patterns and Their Use in America," *The Magazine Antiques*, 139, no. 2 (February 1991): 372–73.

17 See Deutsch, "Needlework Patterns," 373, fig. 5.

the District of Columbia, to date no samplers associated with either the Alexandria or Georgetown Lancasterian schools can be attributed to one or the other school with certainty.[18]

Other young women in Alexandria may have acquired sewing skills at little or no cost through educational programs in their churches. Saint Paul's Episcopal Church, for example, formed a "Sewing Society" during the tenure of the Reverend William Wilmer (1812–1826), and in 1823 started a Sunday School where reading, writing, religion, and sewing were taught in the female department.[19]

Educational opportunities for free blacks in antebellum Alexandria were closely tied to the city's political situation. Prior to 1831, Virginia's largest cities, including Alexandria, openly tolerated schools taught by black teachers for African American students. One such teacher was Sylvia Morris, whose primary school was located on Washington Street for about twenty years.[20] At least two white women also ran schools for black children. In an 1871 special report by the District of Columbia's commissioner of education, Henry Barnard wrote that by the year 1809, "Mrs. Cameron, a white Virginia lady . . . had for some years a primary school for coloured boys and girls on the corner of Duke and Fairfax streets. . . . Mrs. Tutten, a white Virginia lady, also had a school about that period."[21] In these schools, young girls of color studied religion, the rudiments of reading and writing, sewing, and housekeeping in preparation for becoming servants, needlewomen, or teachers. The prevailing view was that education would mold them into obedient workers and Christian women, but not lift them out of the class to which they had been born.[22]

Figure 1-2. Joseph Lancaster, *An Account of the Lancasterian Method of Teaching Needlework*. Baltimore, ca. 1821. Maryland Historical Society

---

18 The closing date of the Female Lancasterian School is uncertain. It did not prosper as well as the boys' school and eventually lost its property. Around 1847, the school became part of the Female Orphan Asylum in Alexandria.

19 Margery Arden Hall, *History of Saint Paul's Church, Fairfax Parish, Alexandria, Virginia, 1810–1932* (Alexandria, Va.: Kate Waller Barrett Chapter NSDAR, 1933), 5, 19.

20 Mary Carroll Johansen, "'Intelligence, Though Overlooked': Education for Black Women in the Upper South, 1800–1840," *Maryland Historical Magazine* 93 (1998): 447–50, and Johansen, "All Useful, Plain Branches of Education," 78. Henry Barnard, *Special Report of the Commissioner of Education on the Condition and Improvement of Public Schools in the District of Columbia* (Washington, D.C.: Government Printing Office, 1871), 283–84.

21 Barnard, *Special Report*, 283–84. Barnard also mentions a school for African American students founded by an association of free colored people after the War of 1812 and located in the building formerly occupied by the Washington Free School. The school, under the direction of a white Methodist Episcopal minister and conducted on the Lancasterian system, averaged about 300 students. Unfortunately it is not known if the school instructed female students.

22 Johansen, "All Useful, Plain Branches of Education," 78.

Educational opportunities for African American students were significantly reduced after 1831, when Nat Turner, a literate slave, led a fierce rebellion in Virginia's Southampton County that was only put down after much bloodshed. Nervous about future uprisings, the Commonwealth of Virginia made it illegal to openly teach African Americans to read or write. With the retrocession of the city and county of Alexandria to Virginia in 1847, all schools serving black students had to be closed.

THE TEACHERS

Elizabeth Hannah was one of the first women to open a school for girls in Alexandria. In 1784 she instructed ten young female students in writing and needlework at thirty pounds per year.[23] Christian Smith, formerly of Charleston, South Carolina, was teaching in Alexandria at about the same time. She advertised in 1786 that she would teach reading, writing, and needlework, and "that young ladies from the country will be accommodated as boarders."[24] Another transplanted Charleston resident, Mrs. Bell, taught in Norfolk and Richmond before coming to Alexandria in 1795. She offered a more varied needlework curriculum of plain work, marking, open work, and embroidery, along with reading and writing.[25]

Mrs. Simson was a teacher who, like Mrs. Bell, frequently relocated her school. She advertised in Baltimore in 1792, Alexandria in 1793, Richmond in 1794, and Fredericksburg in 1795. In addition to darning and plain sewing, she provided instruction in fancy needlework, tambouring, and embroidery in silk and worsted. Mrs. Simson was also an artist and taught drawing and painting and executed the designs on her students' needlework canvases, thus saving parents that additional expense.[26] Mrs. Tennent, formerly of Norfolk, opened her needlework school in Alexandria in 1797. Under her tutelage, girls learned to do plain sewing, marking, open work, tambouring, and embroidery. Her students copied embroidery designs from a pattern book supplied by their teacher.[27]

Girls living in Alexandria frequently continued their needlework education beyond the learning of basic stitches. Daughters of affluent parents had the opportunity to take advanced instruction from an expert needlewoman capable of teaching many of the diverse branches of needlework. Alternatively, they could attend a school or academy where several teachers provided instruction in the subjects of an English curriculum—reading, writing, arithmetic, history, geography, and astronomy, plus the ornamental subjects of French, music, dancing, drawing, painting, and needlework. Alexandria students pursuing more advanced needlework instruction were responsible for the fine embroidered pictures and maps discussed in Chapter 3.

During the first quarter of the nineteenth century, a number of women in Alexandria advertised instruction in fancy needlework, either as the only subject offered or as part of a broader curriculum. One teacher who specialized was Mrs. Cooke. She opened her Embroidery School in 1801 "for those young ladies who having attained other branches of education" are interested in expanding their needlework expertise. Her school, which was still operating at the corner of Prince and Washington Streets in 1803, was also

---

23 *Virginia Journal and Alexandria Advertiser*, October 28, 1784.

24 Ibid., March 23, 1786.

25 *Columbia Mirror and Alexandria Gazette*, July 4, 1795.

26 Prior to coming to Baltimore, Mrs. Simson had taught in Philadelphia, New York, and Charleston.

To supplement her income as a teacher she worked ladies' gowns, muffs, and shawls in gold, silver, and silk. She boasted that her gentlemen's vest patterns were "equal to any imported." *Columbia Mirror and Alexandria Gazette*, July 23, 1793.

27 *Alexandria Advertiser*, September 28, 1797.

advertised to young matrons who wished to learn the latest fashions in fancy needlework.[28] Mrs. Cooke may have called upon the talents of itinerant painter Frederick Kemmelmeyer to supply her students with embroidery patterns.[29] Kemmelmeyer, who also resided in Alexandria in 1803, was a highly versatile painter and offered a range of artistic services beyond the more usual sign painting. He noted that he would "punctually attend on ladies who wish patterns drawn for Tambouring, Embroidery, Toilet Tables & other Needle Work."[30] In the same year, gilder S. Thomee opened his shop and provided elegant framing for the needlework efforts of Alexandria's young ladies.

> GILDING
> And Enameling on Glass
> Looking Glass and Picture
> Frames Made and
> REGILT.
> NEEDLEWORK
> framed in a handsome manner.
> And NAMES done on Glass.[31]

One of the more accomplished needlework teachers to advertise in Alexandria newspapers may have been Mrs. Robert O'Reilly [O'Riley]. In November 1804, she and her husband announced plans to relocate from Baltimore, where they had conducted a school since 1799, and open a Young Ladies' Boarding and Day School in Alexandria.[32] While Robert O'Reilly would take responsibility for teaching the useful branches, Mrs. O'Reilly proposed to teach an extensive list of ornamental subjects. Her curriculum emphasized elegant and advanced needlework:

> *Embroidery in chenilles, gold, silver, silks, &c. comprising figures, historical and ornamental, landscapes, flowers, fruit, birds, &c. maps wrought in silks, chenilles, gold, &c. print work in figures or landscapes . . . with many other accomplishments to [sic] numerous to mention.*[33]

It is uncertain whether the O'Reillys actually opened their Alexandria school. A January 1, 1805, advertisement referred to a delayed opening due to Mrs. O'Reilly being ill, but a May 15 notice assured parents that she was ready to commence instruction.[34] Later that year, an advertisement almost identical to those placed by the O'Reillys in Alexandria papers appeared in a Richmond newspaper announcing their opening of a Young Ladies' Academy in that city.[35]

Five years later, in 1810, Mrs. Edmund Edmonds opened a school on Prince Street and advertised a fancy work curriculum that curiously echoed that of Mrs. O'Reilly's (Figure 1-3). She listed "Embroidery in chenilles, gold, silver and silk. Maps wrought in do. Print work in figures, or landscapes. Tambour, and Needle work, plain and fanciful. Fringe, and Netting, in all its variety."[36] Her school met with success,

---

28 Ibid., November 3, 1801 and June 10, 1803.

29 Frederick Kemmelmeyer emigrated from Europe to Maryland in 1788. He is best known for his paintings of George Washington and other historic subjects, but his artistic services included everything from portraits, to sign painting, to decorating Masonic aprons. Before coming to Alexandria, Kemmelmeyer painted and taught in Baltimore; later he moved on to western Maryland and the Valley of Virginia. See John Bivins and Forsyth Alexander, *The Regional Arts of the Early South* (Winston-Salem, N.C.: MESDA, 1991), 159–60.

30 *Alexandria Advertiser*, June 27, 1803.

31 Ibid., December 30, 1803.

32 *Alexandria Advertiser and Commercial Intelligencer*, November 20, 1804.

33 Ibid.

34 *Washington Federalist*, May 15, 1805.

35 *Virginia Gazette and General Advertiser*, November 20, 1805.

36 *Alexandria Daily Gazette*, March 6, 1810. Edmund Edmonds, a teacher in Alexandria since 1785, assisted his wife with teaching the useful or academic subjects. Sarah Edmonds, wife of Edmund, is sometimes confused with Julia F. Edmonds, a needlework instructor in Norfolk, Virginia, and later in Wadesboro, North Carolina. Julia Edmonds was the wife of Robert Edmonds, also a teacher.

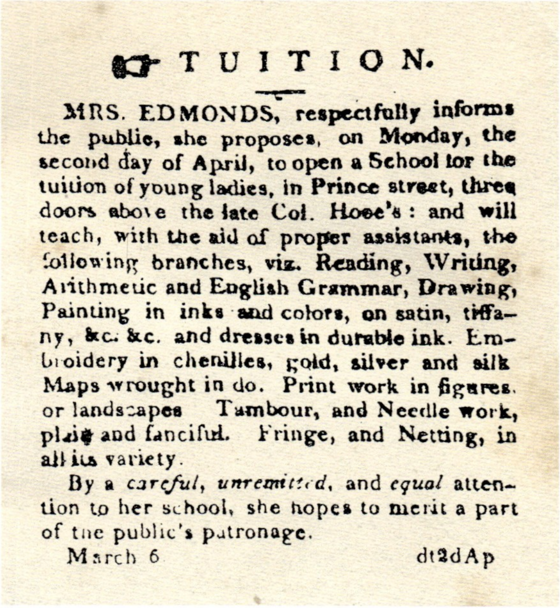

Figure 1-3. Advertisement published in the *Alexandria Daily Gazette*, March 6, 1810.

TUITION.

MRS. EDMONDS, respectfully informs the public, she proposes, on Monday, the second day of April, to open a School for the tuition of young ladies, in Prince street, three doors above the late Col. Hooe's: and will teach, with the aid of proper assistants, the following branches, viz. Reading, Writing, Arithmetic and English Grammar, Drawing, Painting in inks and colors, on satin, tiffany, &c. &c. and dresses in durable ink. Embroidery in chenilles, gold, silver and silk Maps wrought in do. Print work in figures, or landscapes Tambour, and Needle work, plain and fanciful. Fringe, and Netting, in all its variety.

By a *careful, unremitted,* and *equal* attention to her school, she hopes to merit a part of the public's patronage.

March 6   dt2dAp

and she received public acclaim for "enabling the citizens of Alexandria to educate their females at home with every advantage that could derive from similar institutions abroad."[37] When Mrs. (Sarah Allison) Edmonds held the annual examination and exhibition of her students' work in December 1813 "before a large assembly of Ladies and several Gentlemen," the *Alexandria Daily Gazette* observed that:

> *The proficiency of the young ladies reflects equal honor on the teacher and her pupils.— They read with propriety, emphasis & spirit; they discovered an acquaintance with grammar far beyond what is common; their attainments in Geography are great; they are familiar with the common rules of Arithmetic, and write a legible and elegant hand. Specimens of drawing and needle-work were pronounced excellent.*[38]

In 1823 Mrs. Edmonds still held annual examinations, and the public responded enthusiastically, as "the pupils acquitted themselves in a manner creditable to themselves and to their instructors."[39]

After 1830, needlework instruction in Alexandria began to wane in importance. Newly organized female seminaries were "established upon the most liberal and enlightened views of female consequence, and the necessity and advantages of devoting more attention and more extensive means to the education of females [had] become a popular subject of discussion."[40] Former teachers of sewing and embroidery opened seminaries that placed emphasis on the higher branches of learning.

Quaker educator Margaret Judge, for example, advertised in 1826 that her girls had "the privilege of attending lectures delivered by [scholars] on natural philosophy and chemistry, illustrated by experiments with suitable apparatus." Several years later, her sister Rachel Judge Waugh added Latin and bookkeeping to her school's curriculum "to afford young ladies an opportunity of acquiring either a common English [education] or one more scientific and Classical."[41] Advanced skill with a needle was no longer seen as a high educational priority, and gradually it disappeared from the curriculum.

---

37 *Alexandria Daily Gazette*, December 25, 1812.

38 Ibid., December 22, 1813.

39 The school was described as "large" and the students excelled in grammar, geography, and penmanship; needlework was not mentioned. *Alexandria Gazette & Advertiser*, December 30, 1823.

40 Mrs. Porter, *Phenix Gazette*, August 19, 1828.

41 *Alexandria Daily Gazette*, April 4, 1826, and March 4, 1829.

CHAPTER 2

Alexandria Samplers

EIGHTEENTH-CENTURY SAMPLERS

During the last decades of the eighteenth century, the thriving town of Alexandria provided a variety of educational opportunities for young girls, including instruction in needlework. Unfortunately, relatively little of the needlework stitched during this period has come to light. Teachers were clearly seeking patronage, but only a small number of their students' samplers have been located. Some are known only from a photograph or mention in an early publication.

The Janney Sisters

Two late eighteenth-century samplers can be attributed to the Janney sisters of Alexandria. Hannah (1774–1846) and Rebecah (1776–1817) were the daughters of Hannah Jones and Joseph Janney, Quakers of Alexandria and Loudoun County, Virginia.[1] Hannah (age eleven) and Rebecah (age nine) worked their samplers in 1785 and 1786, respectively. Because of the many similarities on their samplers, it is probable that the girls received instruction from the same teacher. Hannah and Joseph Janney may have arranged for the girls to study with either Elizabeth Hannah or Christian Smith, although the latter seems more likely. Miss Smith advertised her day and boarding school as "located next door to Mr. Joseph Janney's on Fairfax St."[2] That was the business location of the girls' father, a wholesale merchant who in 1784 advertised a "large and general assortment of European goods."[3]

---

1 The Janneys, originally from Pennsylvania, settled in northern Virginia in the mid-eighteenth century and were members of the Fairfax Monthly Meeting at Waterford in Loudoun County. According to Hinshaw, "The Janney families lived largely in Alexandria, Virginia, . . . [and] had organized Alexandria Preparative Meeting almost amongst themselves about 1765; but until 1802 their records were kept by Fairfax Monthly Meeting." William Wade Hinshaw, *The Encyclopedia of American Quaker Genealogy, 1750–1930*, vol. 6 (Baltimore: Genealogical Publishing Co., Inc., 1973, 1993), 516.

2 *Virginia Journal and Alexandria Advertiser*, March 23, 1786.

3 Ibid. June 24, 1784. Other business transactions put Joseph Janney in Alexandria in 1784 and 1785.

Figure 2-1. Sampler worked by Hannah Janney. Alexandria, 1785. Inscribed: "Hannah Janney / 1785." Silk on linen ground. Location unknown

Hannah Janney's 1785 sampler was described and illustrated in a 1921 survey of American samplers conducted by Ethel Stanwood Bolton and Eva Johnston Coe for The National Society of The Colonial Dames of America (Figure 2-1).[4] The sampler (current location unknown) includes two alphabets, large numbers 1–12, and scattered motifs surrounded by an arcaded floral border emerging from two jardinières. Hannah skillfully used a combination of stitches in her work, including eyelet, chain, tent, and cross stitch. Her sampler also features a seven-line verse entitled "On Education."

Tis Education forms the youthful mind
Just as the twig is bent the trees inclin'd
As Diamonds rough no Luster can impart
Till polish d and improv'd by aiding Art
So untaught youth we very rarely find
Display the dazling Beauties of the mind
Till art and science are with Nature Joind

Although presented as one verse, the text is composed of lines from two different sources. The first two lines were extracted from an essay by the English poet Alexander Pope (1688–1744),[5] written in the mid-1730s as an epistle to Sir Richard Temple, discussing, "Of the Knowledge and Characters of Men." In Pope's original version the first line reads: *Tis education forms the common mind*. The remaining five lines of Hannah's verse are unattributed but appear to have been used in the late eighteenth century as a copying exercise for students attending writing school.[6] The lines were also frequently included in late eighteenth-century collections of quotations.[7]

In 1792, Hannah married Samuel Hopkins in Anne Arundel County, Maryland, and spent her married life there. The second of their eleven children, Johns Hopkins (1795–1874), became a well-known financier and philanthropist, founding the university in Baltimore that bears his name.

Hannah's sister Rebecah stitched her sampler in 1786, also using a combination of

---

4 Ethel Stanwood Bolton and Eva Johnston Coe, *American Samplers* (New York: Dover Publications, 1973), Plate xxxii, 55, 93. Bolton and Coe illustrated Hannah's sampler and described it as, "Rose and vine border rising out of vases at lower corners. Strawberry cross-borders, also vine and small blossoms, small figures of children and animals and insects. Verses 94, 96."

5 Alexander Pope, *Moral Essays*, Epistle 1, Line 149. Published in Cassell, *An Essay on Man: Moral Essays and Satires* (London, 1891), 65. Available online at: http://www.archive.org/details/essayonmanmoraleoopopeuoft.

6 Copied by Benjamin Larcom into his copybook (page 23) on January 15, 1789 at the age of 12, Beverly Historical Society, Beverly, Mass.

7 At least one of these mistakenly attributes the verse to Percy Bysshe Shelley, which is impossible as Shelley was not born until 1792 and Hannah included the verse on her sampler in 1785.

stitches: cross, eyelet, hem, outline, queen, and satin stitches (Figure 2-2). She scattered small motifs of men, women, animals, birds, angels, and flowers around her design, many identical to the motifs on Hannah's sampler. The arcaded floral, berry, and vine border is

Figure 2-2. Sampler worked by Rebecah Janney. Alexandria, 1786.
Inscribed: "Rebecah Janney / in her tenth year / 1786."
Silk and wool on linen ground, 25 by 25 threads per in. 18 ½ x 17 ⅞ in.
The Colonial Williamsburg Foundation, purchased with gift funds from Mr. and Mrs. Charles T. Freeman, 1998-160

ALEXANDRIA SAMPLERS 17

worked entirely in wool—a fiber not usually found on Alexandria samplers. A related sampler was stitched by Christiana Copper (1774–1815) of Alexandria in 1785 or 1786. The condition of the sampler is poor and the date cannot be verified, but the arrangement of motifs and use of multiple rows of queen stitch is similar.[8]

Like her sister, Rebecah stitched two verses on her sampler, both written by Scottish poet Michael Bruce (1746–1767). The lines are two stanzas from a fourteen-stanza poem entitled "Complaint of Nature" that paraphrases Job 14:1–15. Rebecah's text reads:

> *FEW are thy days and full of woe*
> *o man of woman born*
> *thy doom is writen dust thou art*
> *and shall to dust return*
> *Determin'd are the days that fly*
> *Successive o'er thy head*
> *the number'd hour is on the wing*
> *that lays thee with the dead*

The carefully stitched lines are set within a stunning reserve composed of three rows of queen stitch, embellished at the corners with flowers and leaves in satin stitch.

In 1798, Rebecah married John Lloyd (1775–1854). Because her husband was not a Quaker, Rebecah was disowned by the Religious Society of Friends for marrying out of unity. Evidently the marriage did not disrupt family relations, for by 1803 John Lloyd had joined Joseph Janney in the business of importing European goods.[9] In 1809, Rebecah was reinstated to the Fairfax Monthly Meeting. She died in 1817 after giving birth to her eighth child.

Betsy Green

In 1798, twelve-year-old Elizabeth (Betsy) Green stitched another late eighteenth-century Alexandria sampler. Recorded by Bolton and Coe in 1921, the sampler is described as having six alphabets a "Great variety of stitches. Border, festoons of eyelets and bunches of strawberries."[10] Betsy's sampler included the first portion of a poem written in 1704 by Dr. Isaac Watts (1674–1748) entitled "The Life of Souls."[11] It is possible that Betsy Green was a student of Betsey Lunt, who advertised in 1798 that she would teach "reading, writing, plain needlework, fancy work and drawing" at several different locations in the vicinity of Queen Street.[12] Betsy Green may have been the Elizabeth Green who married Zachariah Baker in Alexandria on July 30, 1805.[13]

---

8 Christiana Davis Copper was a daughter of Elizabeth Arell and Cyrus Copper of Alexandria. She married Phillip G. Marsteller in 1792, and they had eleven children. Her sampler is in the Marsteller Collection, #1986.782.009, Manassas Museum System. Although the sampler has some areas worked in wool thread, they may have been added later.

9 T. Michael Miller, *Artisans and Merchants of Alexandria, Virginia, 1780–1820* (2 vols.; Bowie, Md. : Heritage Books, 1991–1992), 1:236.

10 Bolton and Coe, *American Samplers*, 49. Bolton and Coe list this sampler as being from Alexandria but it is unclear from their entry if Betsy Green's sampler was marked "Alexandria." In 1921 the sampler was owned by Virginia L. Maury, but its location is currently unknown.

11 Bolton and Coe, *American Samplers*, 49, 280. They indicate Betsy's 1798 sampler contains a variant of the first quatrain of verse number 202, first recorded on a sampler in 1771: *Swift as the Sun Revolves the Day / we hasten to the Dead / Slaves to the wind we Puff away / and to the ground we tread.*

12 *Alexandria Advertiser*, February 2, 1798. Betsey, daughter of Ezra Lunt, may have continued teaching until her 1804 marriage to Heppel Brough.

13 Marriage record for Elizabeth Green and Zachariah Baker, July 30, 1805. T. Michael Miller, *Alexandria . . . Marriage Bonds, 1801–1852* (Bowie, Md.: Heritage Books, 1987), 49.

Ann Leap

Ann Leap (1789–1831) stitched her sampler in 1799 (Figure 2-3), most likely in Alexandria, for her family had strong ties with the Alexandria community. Ann used a combination of cross, eyelet, satin, and four-sided stitches to create her alphabets and stylized motifs, including flowers, birds, animals, and a basket of fruit. Two of the motifs on Ann's sampler reappear in later Alexandria samplers, suggesting a common design source, a shared teacher, or a regional preference. The first is a bird sitting on a tiny hillock wreathed on both sides with inward facing vines. Ann included two of these wreathed birds, placed opposite each other just under her verse. The second motif is an oversized basket filled with many layers of round fruit and trimmed with large spiky leaves. Ann's short verse is from the New Testament and is commonly known as the "Golden Rule" (Matthew 7:12). *What so ever ye would that men should / Do unto you do ye also unto them.*

Ann was the daughter of Ann (died after 1831) and Jacob Leap (ca. 1754–1820). Jacob, a native of Prussia, was a grocer and tavern keeper with a business and dwelling on Union Street in Alexandria. It is possible that ten-year-old Ann learned how to sew from her mother or someone else in the Leap household. Alexandria apprenticeship indentures recorded that six-year-old Elizabeth Reardon was bound over to Jacob Leap "to learn the mystery of house keeper and seamstress,"[14] suggesting there was someone in the Leap household with the necessary expertise to teach Elizabeth the "mystery" of sewing. It is also possible that Ann was a student of Mrs.

Figure 2-3. Sampler worked by Ann Leap. Alexandria, 1799. Inscribed: "Ann Leap 1799." Silk on linen ground, 33 by 36 threads per in. 18 ⅜ x 11 ¾ in. Private collection Image courtesy of the Colonial Williamsburg Foundation

---

14 Although this apprenticeship was arranged in 1803, Leap may have taken other young girls into his household for the purpose of training them in housewifery skills. Presumably Mrs. Leap or a housekeeper provided instruction for apprentices and could have taught Ann to sew as well. T. Michael Miller, *Portrait of a Town, Alexandria, District of Columbia 1820–1830* (Bowie, Md.: Heritage Books, 1995), 409.

ALEXANDRIA SAMPLERS   19

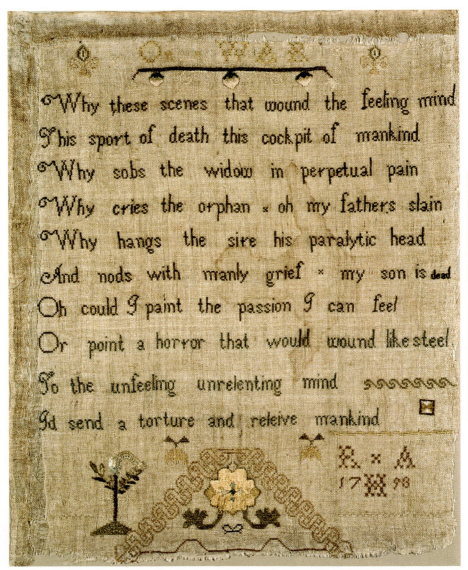

Figure 2-4. Sampler worked by Ann May Horwell. Alexandria, 1798. Inscribed: "R x A / 17 H 98." Silk on linen ground, 34 by 34 threads per in. 21 ¾ x 17 in. The Colonial Williamsburg Foundation, Museum Purchase, 1985-90

Andrew Ford, who advertised in 1799 that she would teach the "various branches of needle work" at her husband's school on Prince Street, a few blocks from the Leap residence.[15]

On February 26, 1806, Ann married William Nelson Mills (1783–1852), an Alexandria wheat merchant who also ran a grocery and tavern. Ann and William were married at the Old Presbyterian Meeting House in Alexandria, and their first child was baptized there in 1807. Mills served as a ward councilman and was appointed Justice of the Peace of Alexandria by Presidents Van Buren and Polk. Between 1836 and his death in 1852 he was the city's superintendent of police. Ann and William had at least six children: Adaline, Jacob, William, Thomas, Albert, and John, the first two dying young. Ann died unexpectedly on February 6, 1831, in Alexandria. Her obituary stated:

> Mrs. ANN MILLS, wife of William N. Mills, of this place, in the 42nd year of her age. Mrs. Mills was in the enjoyment of her usual health up to the time of herself and family retiring to rest, on the preceding evening—when death came at a little past the midnight hour, and, almost in one moment, separated her spirit from its earthly tabernacle. By this sudden death and unexpected bereavement, a disconsolate and afflicted husband and four children, and her aged and afflicted mother, have met with an earthly loss.[16]

Ann May Horwell

Ann May (ca. 1780–1814) was a daughter of Sarah Isabel Butler (born 1747) and Edward Arthur May (1751–1810), an Alexandria merchant. In 1797, Ann opened a school for young girls in a "commodious room" in her father's house on Prince Street, between Union and Water Streets. The advertisement for "Miss May's School" stated her intent "to teach young ladies reading and the different branches of needlework and [to] give the greatest attention to their morals."[17] Some time after the opening of her school, probably in 1798, Ann May married Richard Horwell (born 1766), a tailor from Cornwall, England.

In their 1921 survey of American samplers, Bolton and Coe included four samplers owned by a Horwell descendant.[18] The earliest, dated 1798, is worked in cross, double cross, eyelet, outline, queen, and satin stitches, and is attributed to needlework

---

15 *Alexandria Times*, August 1, 1799.
16 Alexandria *Phenix Gazette*, February 6, 1831.
17 *Alexandria Advertiser*, August 16, 1797.
18 Bolton and Coe, *American Samplers*, 53, 175.

teacher Ann May Horwell (Figure 2-4). The initials R and A over H are believed to signify Ann and her husband Richard.¹⁹ The maker of this sampler included a verse on the suffering caused by war, drawn from an eight-stanza poem written by Thomas Paine in 1778 entitled "An Address to Lord Howe."²⁰ General William Howe commanded British forces from 1775 to 1778 during the American Revolution.

If the sampler was indeed worked by Ann May Horwell, it is possible that she originally stitched it to serve as a model for her students, possibly when she opened her school in 1797. The initials and date of her marriage may have been added later to commemorate the marriage. At the time of her death in 1814, Ann was described as "an affectionate wife, tender parent, kind friend."²¹ Left a widower with small children, Richard married Susan Sleigh in 1817.

Nineteenth-Century Samplers

Several examples of Alexandria needlework are known from the first quarter of the nineteenth century, but identifying the girls' teachers or the schools they attended is difficult. Three of the samplers were stitched by sisters and may have been worked under the instruction of the same teacher. Another pair of samplers shares multiple motifs, a common verse, and a distinctive border—also suggesting the girls had the same, as yet unknown, Alexandria teacher.

The Horwell Sisters

Three samplers are attributed to the children of Ann May and Richard Horwell. The first was stitched in 1807 by eight-year-old Sarah May Horwell (ca. 1799–1884), the oldest of Ann and Richard's five daughters. Sarah worked a multiple alphabet and verse sampler with arcaded strawberry cross band using tapestry, four-sided, rope, star, queen, and cross stitches (Figure 2-5). Her short verse was stitched to read:

Figure 2-5. Sampler worked by Sarah May Horwell. Alexandria, 1807. Inscribed: "Sarah M Horwell / Aged 8 Alexandria 1807." Silk on linen ground. 15 x 9 in. Collection of Brad L. Myers Image courtesy of *The Magazine Antiques*

---

19 I am grateful to Kimberly Smith Ivey, Associate Curator, Textiles & Historic Interiors at Colonial Williamsburg, for sharing her research on the May and Horwell families and for correcting my previously published misinterpretation of their relationship. She has determined from records of Saint Paul's Episcopal Church in Alexandria that Richard and Ann May Horwell had at least five daughters, including sampler makers Sarah and Ann.

20 Ivey, in her worksheet for this sampler, writes that though the sampler was worked twenty years after Paine's 1778 address, Ann's feelings may have been provoked by the 1798–1800 Quasi-War with France, and the X Y Z Affair.

21 Wesley E. Pippenger, *Marriage and Death Notices from Alexandria, Virginia Newspapers*, vol. 1, *1784–1838* (Arlington, Va.: W. E. Pippenger, 2005), 62

Figure 2-6. Unattributed memorial sampler. Alexandria, 1803. Inscribed: "Respectfully Addressed, to Mrs Brown, / On the death of an Infant." Silk on linen ground, 62 by 62 threads per in. 17 ¾ x 15 ¾ in. The Lyceum, Alexandria, Virginia Image courtesy of *The Magazine Antiques*

Merit Should be for Ever plac'd
In Knowledge judgement wit and taste.

Notice that young Sarah ran out of space for the last two letters in the word "taste" but tucked them in above the line. Authored by Jonathan Swift (1667–1745) in 1713 at Windsor, these two lines are part of a very long poem entitled *Cadanus and Vanessa*, written for Esther Vanhomrigh, a young woman who was very much in love with Swift.[22]

A second sampler in the group is also attributed to Sarah May Horwell but is unsigned and undated. Described in 1921 by Bolton and Coe as containing trees, flowers, vines, and baskets within a tulip border, this sampler was considerably larger and more complex than Sarah's 1807 effort.[23] Bolton and Coe were unable to estimate the year in which the sampler was made, indicating only that the sampler was stitched prior to 1819. In all likelihood, Sarah completed this second sampler within a couple of years of her first, probably around the age of ten or eleven. It was not uncommon for young girls to complete more than one sampler, each more accomplished than the last. In 1818, Sarah Horwell married Vincent Massoletti, a recent immigrant from Genoa, Italy, and the purveyor of historical and landscape paper hangings.[24] At the time of the 1850 census, Sarah Massoletti was a wealthy widow living in Washington, D.C. Included in her household was a daughter, Julietta (age twenty-four), and Sarah's father Richard Horwell (see embroidery on page x).

The last sampler in this group is also attributed to a Horwell daughter, although the estimated date is more than a decade later. Based on information from the owner and descendant, Bolton and Coe attributed this unsigned sampler to Ann and Richard's daughter, Ann Horwell (died ca. 1833), made for her sister Sarah May Horwell on the occasion of her marriage.[25] This sampler is described as having a tulip and strawberry

---

22 First published in Britain in 1726 (http://www.luminarium.org/editions/cadenusvanessa.htm), four lines of the poem have been frequently quoted: *Merit should be forever plac'd / In Knowledge, judgement, wit, and taste; / For these, tis own'd without dispute / Alone distinguish man from Brute.*

23 Sarah's 1807 sampler is 15 x 9 inches. Her second sampler was recorded as 16 x 19 inches and composed of stem, tent, satin, and cross stitches.

24 In Alexandria documents Massoletti was spelled Massolette, Masselitte and Masoleth, suggesting the novelty of an Italian immigrant in the city. All four May/Horwell samplers were owned by Miss Frances (Fannie) Horwell Massoletti (born 1859), Sarah and Vincent's granddaughter, at the time Bolton and Coe recorded them, circa 1920.

25 Bolton and Coe ascribed the sampler to Ann Horwell, made for Sarah Horwell on the occasion of her marriage in 1819. However, Sarah's marriage to Vincent Massoletti was actually in 1818.

border, cross and trefoil borders at the top and bottom, and scattered motifs including flowers, hearts, and baskets. At least one of the motifs was labeled "An emblem of love," a phrase more common to Quaker samplers.

Memorial to William Templeman Brown

One of the earliest nineteenth-century pieces stitched in Alexandria is an 1803 sampler with a long memorial verse worked entirely in black (Figure 2-6). The maker of the sampler remains unknown, but the initials "S E" may serve as a clue to her identity.[26] The verse, "Respectfully Addressed to Mrs. Brown On the death of an Infant," laments the death of William Templeman Brown (1802–1803), a death that apparently occurred during his father's absence. Little William was the third child of William Brown, an Alexandria merchant, and his first wife Sarah Hammond. He was only ten months and seven days old when he succumbed to "complications of the bowel."[27]

The unknown needle worker used a combination of cross, long and short, and stem stitches. She personalized the verse with William's name and concluded with his vital statistics and final resting place. The first wife, Sarah Hammond, had three surviving children. However, according to the manuscript journal of Florida governor Thomas Brown, brother of William, they also had a son who did not survive. "She lost her third child, a fine boy, less than a year old, and his cup and spoon was put aside as sacred and never used for any purpose during her life" (49). The governor's memoirs further stated, "my brother William entered into co-partnership with a Quaker with the name of [David] Smedley in the flour and shipping business in Alexandria and moved with his family to that place in 1802" (57). My thanks to Brown descendants Larry Brown and David Pratt for sharing this information.

Figure 2-7.
Sampler worked by Elizabeth Barton. Alexandria, ca. 1809. Inscribed: "Elizabeth Barton Aged 11 years."
Silk on linen ground.
14 ½ x 14 ½ in.
Private collection
Image courtesy of *The Magazine Antiques*

---

26 The initials also may refer to the author of the verse, which appears to be original and has not been found in online anthologies of poetry, hymns, Psalms, and so forth.

27 William Templeman Brown was born September 8, 1802, and died July 15, 1803. His burial was recorded in early documents of the Presbyterian Church. "First Presbyterian Church, Alexandria, Virginia Register of Baptisms, Marriages and Funerals," typescript compiled by Anita Howard, n.d. Margaret Templeman became the second wife of William Brown in Westmoreland County, Virginia, in 1768. They had thirteen children including his father's namesake, William Brown (1770–1855). The younger William Brown and his

Figure 2-8. Sampler worked by Margaret Fleming. Alexandria, ca. 1810 Inscribed: "Margaret Fleming Aged 9 years." Silk on linen ground, 28 by 34 threads per in. 17 ¾ x 16 in. Private collection

identification of the "Alex^a Prisbyterian [sic] Church yard" as the place of the child's interment ties this sampler to one of Alexandria's most venerable landmarks.[28] Surrounding the poem that laments William's death is a striking flower and vine border, also stitched entirely in black. Black is the traditional color for mourning in many western cultures, a custom that dates to ancient Greece and Rome.

"Advice to a Lady" Samplers

Two early nineteenth-century samplers share multiple motifs, a four-line verse, and a tulip border, indicating they were stitched under the instruction of the same Alexandria teacher. Around 1809, eleven-year-old Elizabeth (Betsey) Barton (1798–1844) worked a charming and colorful motif sampler (Figure 2-7), and family history ties this sampler to Alexandria. Elizabeth Barton was born in Yorkshire, England, in 1798, the first daughter of Mary Goodall (1769–1858) and Benjamin Barton Sr. (1764–1816). Her family emigrated to the United States in 1801, and Benjamin Barton established a successful business in Alexandria as a clock maker and silversmith.[29] An early chronicler of Alexandria history noted that the Barton "family led a very secluded life, but were people of culture and taste, and the best class of literature was to be found on Mr. Barton's library table."[30]

Elizabeth's sampler displays a similar sense of culture and taste. Centered at the top is an elegant basket of flowers, balanced at the bottom by a three-story country home flanked by fruit trees. In the middle is a verse and inscription, elegantly surrounded by a leafy vine that reaches out to other parts of the sampler. The four-line verse is drawn from a much longer poem entitled "Advice to a Lady" written in 1732 by British statesman and writer George Lord Lyttleton (1709–1773).[31]

Do you my fair endeavour to possess
An elegance of mind as well as dress
Be that your ornament and Know to please
By graceful natures unaffected ease

Two of the motifs on Elizabeth's sampler also appear on the one stitched by Ann Leap (Figure 2-3) ten years earlier—birds perched

---

28 The Presbyterian Church was established in Alexandria in 1772, and the meeting house erected in 1774–1775. The elders called the Reverend Doctor James Muir to be their pastor in 1789. He remained in that position until his death in 1820. In 1817 a group of parishioners seceded to form the Second Presbyterian Church. William Buckner McGroarty, *The Old Presbyterian Meeting House at Alexandria Virginia 1774–1874* (Richmond: Wm. Byrd Press, 1940), 44–50.

29 The Barton family was one of several in Alexandria who carried on a successful trade in the various branches of silversmithing. Benjamin Barton's sons, Thomas and Benjamin Jr., succeeded him in business. See Catherine B. Hollan, *In the Neatest, Most Fashionable Manner: Three Centuries of Alexandria Silver* (Alexandria: The Lyceum, 1994).

30 Mary G. Powell, *The History of Old Alexandria, Virginia* (Westminster, Md.: Family Line Publications, 1995), 347.

31 George Lyttleton *The Poetical Works of George Lord Lyttleton: With Additions to Which Prefixed an Account of his Life* (London, 1801), 56–57.

within wreaths and very large baskets with many layers of fruit and spiky leaves.

On February 9, 1828, the Reverend Elias Harrison officiated at the marriage of Elizabeth Barton and Alexander MacKenzie (ca. 1765–1834), a successful Alexandria merchant originally from Scotland.[32] Elizabeth died on January 25, 1844, almost exactly ten years after her husband's death on January 30, 1834.[33] There is no record of any children.

The second "Advice to a Lady" sampler (Figure 2-8) was stitched by nine-year-old Margaret Fleming (1801–1852). Margaret was the eldest daughter of Catherine Steele and Andrew Fleming, who were married in 1793 at the Presbyterian Meeting House by the Reverend James Muir. Margaret worked a simplified version of Elizabeth Barton's sampler, but very likely under the direction of the same Alexandria teacher. While Elizabeth's sampler includes the front and gable end of a blue-roofed house with side porch, rear wing, and multiple doors, Margaret stitched a more conventional view of a three-bay brick house but also with an atypical blue roof.[34] Both girls flanked their buildings with fruit trees and framed their compositions with the same arcaded tulip border. In addition, they both stitched the same four lines from Lyttelton's "Advice to a Lady." Other motifs found on both samplers include an elegant flower basket, birds perched on wreaths, and fruit baskets with large flat spiky leaves, motifs that recall earlier Alexandria samplers.

On November 11, 1825, Margaret Fleming married James Douglass Jr. (ca. 1795–1828) a partner in an Alexandria grocery concern.

They resided on King Street. Within three years Margaret was left a widow with three infants: twin daughters Catherine and Sarah, and a son James. She later lived with her widowed mother and siblings. At the time of the 1850 census Margaret was living in the household of her younger brother A. J. Fleming, along with her children, three sisters, a brother-in-law, a niece, and a nephew.[35] The three men in the household, including Margaret's twenty-two-year-old son, listed their occupations as merchant. Margaret Fleming Douglass died in 1852 in her fifty-second year and is buried in the cemetery of the First Presbyterian Church.

The teacher who provided needlework instruction to Elizabeth Barton and Margaret Fleming has not been identified. No advertisements specifying needlework instruction appeared in Alexandria newspapers in 1809 and 1810, the years Elizabeth and Margaret respectively stitched their samplers. However, teachers who had advertised in previous years may have continued in business. Ann Jacks, for example, opened a day and boarding school in the 300 block of King Street in 1806 and offered "plain Sewing, Marking, Netting, Tambouring, Embroidery," along with reading, writing, and arithmetic. Both the Barton and Fleming families had residences or shops on King Street.[36]

Ann Tottington Rudd

Ann Tottington Rudd was born in England in 1804 but demonstrated American patriotism at an early age. In 1817, Ann used

---

32 Elizabeth was the second wife of widower Alexander MacKenzie. His first wife, Ann Symburn, had died in 1815.

33 Pippenger, *Marriage and Death Notices from Alexandria, Virginia Newspapers*, 2:7.

34 The blue color may represent a slate roof that was waterproof, fireproof, and very long lasting. There is a Slaters Lane in Alexandria, and Virginia "Buckingham" slate (from the county of that name) has a blue-gray-black color.

35 U.S. Census Record for 1850

36 *Alexandria Daily Advertiser*, March 28, 1806. Jacks advertised again in 1807. Her location on King Street, near Market Square, was less than two blocks from where Benjamin Barton Sr. is known to have resided in 1810. Information courtesy of T. Michael Miller.

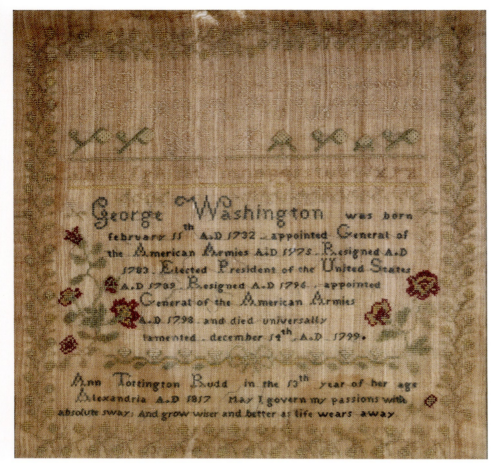

Figure 2-9. Sampler worked by Ann Tottington Rudd. Alexandria, 1817. Inscribed: "Ann Tottington Rudd in the 13th year of her age / Alexandria A.D 1817." Silk on linen ground, 30 by 30 threads per in. 16 x 16 ¼ in.
The Lyceum, Alexandria, Virginia
Image courtesy of *The Magazine Antiques*

cross, queen, and rice stitches to write the highlights of George Washington's career on her sampler (Figure 2-9).[37]

George Washington was born
february 11th A.D. 1732. appointed General of
the American Armies A.D. 1775. Resigned A.D.
1783. Elected President of the United States
A.D. 1789. Resigned A.D. 1796. appointed
General of the American Armies
A.D. 1798 and died universally
lamented december 14th A.D. 1799.

Ann Tottington Rudd in the 13th year of her age
Alexandria A.D. 1817 May I govern my passions with
absolute sway and grow wiser and better as life wears away

George Washington was a Virginian with many ties to Alexandria. He represented the town in the House of Burgesses before the American Revolution and built a house on Cameron Street in the 1760s to avoid the hazards of traveling back and forth between Alexandria and Mount Vernon, some eight miles distant. Alexandrians delighted in Washington's close association with their town and greatly mourned his death in 1799. Throughout the nineteenth century, the city's residents memorialized his accomplishments with parades and the annual Washington Birthnight Ball, a tradition that continues today.

The verse on Ann's sampler was drawn from an English poem and song entitled "The Old Man's Wish," written by English astronomer and poet Walter Pope (1627–1714).[38] Ann's two lines are part of the song's chorus, sung after every verse, and somewhat modified from the original, which reads:

May I govern my passions with absolute sway,
And grow wiser and better as strength wears away,
Without gout or stone, by a gentle decay.

Born to Mary Anderson and William Rudd (1775–1821), Ann was the sixth of their eight children (five of whom shared her middle name of Tottington, their paternal grandmother's maiden name). Ann was christened October 14, 1804, in Saint Mary's Church in Nottingham, England.[39] In January 1807, the family emigrated to the

---

37 Even though Ann stitched her sampler in 1817, long after the provisions of the Gregorian calendar had been implemented in Britain and her colonies [1752], she used Old Style or the Julian calendar dating for Washington's birth—February 11 instead of February 22.

38 Walter Pope, *The Wish* (London, 1697). Available online at: http://www.readbookonline.net/readOnLine/24176/. Also published as a song of five verses, entitled "The Old Man's Wish" in Playford's *Theory of Musick*, 1685.

39 Parish records for Saint Mary's Church, Nottingham, England.

United States where William leased a three-story brick dwelling and shop on Prince Street in Alexandria.⁴⁰ Ann probably was enrolled in a nearby school, possibly that of Miss Moulton, who offered an English curriculum including needlework in her location at Prince and Alfred Streets. In 1820, sixteen-year-old Ann was living with her parents, siblings, and five slaves on the family farm in Truro Parish, Fairfax, Virginia, just outside Alexandria.⁴¹ Ann married Jedson (Judson) King (born ca. 1800) on August 6, 1822, in Fairfax County. Ann and Judson settled in Alexandria, where the 1850 census listed his occupation as farmer and gardener. Interestingly, forty-six-year-old Ann was recorded as head of the household, with real estate worth $500. Living with them were six of their children, ages five to twenty.

Rebecca Ann Fifield

In September 1823 seven-year-old Rebecca Ann Fifield used cross and reversible cross stitches to complete a simple alphabet sampler in a horizontal format (Figure 2-10). Rebecca Ann was born in 1816 to Ann Green Gough (died 1875) and Ebenezer O. Fifield (1781–1859), originally of Boston. She was the oldest of their three surviving daughters. Ebenezer Fifield was educated at Dartmouth College. He studied medicine and then practiced law with Daniel Webster in Boston. A ship's surgeon during the War of 1812, he was captured by the British and held for eight months. In poor health after his imprisonment, he relocated to Alexandria to teach grammar, mathematics, surveying, and other subjects at the Alexandria Academy, a prestigious school for boys.⁴² In 1820 he opened Mechanic's Hall Academy, also for boys, and in 1822 moved the school to his home at the corner of Prince and Alfred Streets.

Although Rebecca Ann's needlework teacher is unknown, it is unlikely that she attended Mechanic's Hall Academy since the school enrolled only boys. It is possible that Rebecca Ann studied with Miss Moulton, whose school for girls was located at the corner of Prince and Alfred in 1818, very close to the Fifield home. However, it is not known whether Miss Moulton was still teaching in 1823 and, if so, whether she remained at that location. Some time after 1823 the Fifield family returned to Boston, where Rebecca Ann died May 29, 1828, at the age of twelve.

Williamina Robertson

In 1827, Williamina Robertson stitched an alphabet sampler plus six verses of an Anglican hymn, clearly identifying the location of her school as Alexandria (Figure 2-11). Records suggest that nine-year-old Williamina was the daughter of James Robertson of nearby Truro Parish in Fairfax

Figure 2-10. Sampler worked by Rebecca Ann Fifield. Alexandria, 1823. Inscribed: "Rebecca Ann Fifield aged 7 years / Alexandria September 18, 1823." Silk on linen ground, 28 by 26 threads per in. 7 ½ x 16 ¾ in. Collection of Anna Marie Witmer

---

40 Immigration record for January 18, 1807. Ann's two younger brothers, James Tottington Rudd and William Tottington Rudd, were both born in Alexandria: James in 1807 and William in 1809 (U.S. Census records for 1850, 1860, and 1870). Miller, *Artisans and Merchants*, 2:184.

41 U.S. Census record for 1820.

42 The Alexandria Academy only admitted boys. A free school with a male division run on the Lancasterian system was located on the third floor of the same building.

ALEXANDRIA SAMPLERS

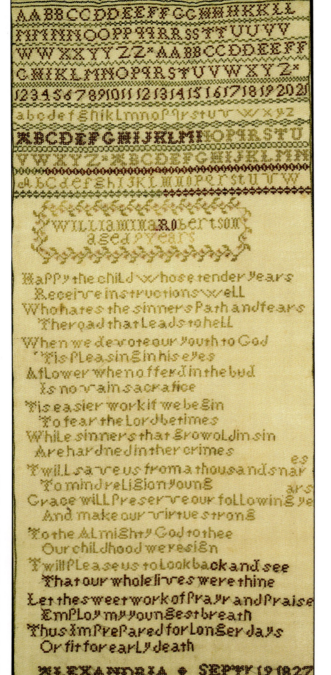

Figure 2-11. Sampler worked by Williamina Robertson. Alexandria, 1827. Inscribed: "Williamina Robertson / aged 9 years / Alexandria * Sept[r] 19 1827." Silk on linen ground. 20 x 8 ½ in. Collection of Brad L. Myers. Image courtesy of *The Magazine Antiques*

County and so may have been among those students who came to Alexandria for an education and boarded at the school or with relatives.[43] Many Alexandria schools provided accommodation for boarding as well as day students. For girls living in southern Maryland, Alexandria was but a ferry ride across the Potomac River. Others came by land from neighboring Virginia counties.

If Williamina boarded at a school in Alexandria, she probably would have brought her own bedstead, mattress, bedding, and towels, as well as a silver tablespoon, teaspoon, and tumbler.[44] Or she may have shared a bed with another student, since practical advice of the day advocated placing younger girls in beds with older girls.

> *The feet and knees and hands of weaker children are liable to become cold in bed in winter, on which account it is more salutary for them to sleep with a bed-fellow, rather than alone; as they naturally put their cold knees or hands to their companion in bed, and thus frequently prevent rheumatic, and other inflammatory diseases of fatal event.*[45]

The identity of the school where Williamina completed her carefully cross-stitched sampler is unknown. By 1827, Alexandria parents had several schools and teachers to choose from. Although fancy needlework instruction was on the decline, teachers with basic sewing skills could have guided Williamina in planning and stitching her lengthy verse—a hymn written by Dr. Isaac Watts, an English theologian and hymnist.[46] Watts wrote more than 750 hymns

---

43 Williamina Robertson may have been one of four female children under the age of ten in the 1820 household of James Robertson of Fairfax County (U.S. Census 1820). This may be the same James Robertson who owned a schooner docked in the port of Alexandria during the 1820s. Miller, *Portrait of a Town*, 303. Unfortunately, detailed information on Williamina Robertson has been difficult to locate. She remains one of the more elusive sampler makers attending school in Alexandria.

44 These items were mentioned in an advertisement placed by Mrs. Porter for her seminary. *Phenix Gazette*, August 19, 1827.

45 Darwin, *A Plan for the Conduct of Female Education in Boarding Schools . . .*, 153.

during his lifetime, many especially for children.

QUAKER SAMPLERS

During the American Revolution, members of the Religious Society of Friends, or Quakers, began migrating to Alexandria from northern cities to escape persecution for their pacifist views. The city's Quakers were part of the Fairfax Monthly Meeting but congregated locally in a modest meeting house built in the mid-1780s. In 1802 the Alexandria Monthly Meeting's growth led to its being set off from the Fairfax Monthly Meeting. Nine years later, in 1811, the Quakers of Alexandria erected a new two-story meeting house at a cost of nearly $4,000 to accommodate their increasing numbers.

Not until 1815, however, did the daughters of Alexandria's prominent Quakers have the opportunity to attend a local school organized by members of the Society of Friends. Prior to that time they attended Quaker boarding schools—Westtown in southeastern Pennsylvania, Nine Partners' in New York, or smaller schools closer to home in Montgomery County, Maryland.[47] Strong kinship ties among Quakers on both sides of the Potomac River enabled Alexandria girls to board with relatives and attend school with their Maryland cousins.[48] In 1815 the Alexandria Meeting addressed the problem of inadequate female education in Alexandria and proposed a select school that would educate young women in a manner consistent with the Friends' religious principles.[49] The Meeting selected Rachel Painter (1792–1863), a former Westtown Boarding School student, to conduct a girls' school in Alexandria at $500 per annum.[50] The school prospered and one year later had obtained all necessary articles: "1 stove & pipe, benches, 4 chairs, and maps."[51]

Samplers stitched by girls from Quaker families are not usually distinguishable from other samplers stitched in the same region at the same time, unless the girls attended a school run by the Society of Friends or were taught by a teacher who had trained at such a

---

46 The six verses of this hymn were published in such educational books as *Introduction to the English Reader . . . Calculated to Improve the Younger Classes of Learners . . .*, compiled by Lindley Murray, 1816.

47 The Westtown Boarding School, in Westtown, Pennsylvania, was established as a co-educational boarding school in 1799 and soon became one of the most respected boarding schools within the Quaker community. Five Alexandria girls are known to have attended Westtown between 1799 and 1803. Female students received an academic education as well as a practical education in needlework, and many Westtown samplers are known. One worked in 1803 and marked "H I" is attributed to Hannah Irwin from Alexandria, who entered school during the third month of that year. Hannah (1792–1875) was the eldest of twelve children born to Elizabeth Janney and Thomas Irwin, charter members of the Alexandria Monthly Meeting.

48 Northern Virginia and central Maryland Quakers shared numerous geographic, familial, and social connections in the establishment and later set off of their Preparative and Monthly Meetings. See Gloria Seaman Allen, *A Maryland Sampling: Girlhood Embroidery 1738–1860* (Baltimore: Maryland Historical Society, 2007), 125–26, 149.

49 Minutes of the Alexandria Monthly Meeting, November 11, 1815–April 22, 1819, abstracts from Quaker records compiled by Lora Anderberg, Alexandria Archaeology Center, 1988.

50 Rachel Painter entered Westtown as a student in 1812. While there she would have acquired considerable knowledge of needlework, as well as encouragement to pursue a teaching career. Quaker boarding schools "provided special teacher training and often teaching experience. . . . they provided places where young female teachers could pursue further education with access to libraries, equipment, and tutoring from older teachers." Joan M. Jensen, "'Not Only Ours but Others': The Quaker Teaching Daughters of the Mid-Atlantic, 1790–1850," *History of Education* 24 (1984): 10. Rachel Painter continued to teach in Alexandria until 1830 when she turned the school over to Mary Anna Talbott. *Phenix Gazette*, March 3, 1830.

51 Minutes. The Alexandria Monthly Meeting did not authorize hiring a teacher to conduct a boys' school until 1819.

Figure 2-12. Sampler worked by Ann Plummer. Alexandria, 1800. Inscribed: "An Emblem / Of love. / Alexandria / 1800 / Ann Plummer Aged 9." Silk on linen ground. 18 ½ x 19 ¾ in. Washington State Historical Society

school. By the beginning of the nineteenth century, needlework teachers at the larger Quaker schools on both sides of the Atlantic had developed design preferences that spread quickly to other schools where Quaker teachers taught needlework. Betty Ring noted this stylistic dissemination.

> Suddenly between 1800 and 1803, almost identical alphabets and designs were being worked at Quaker schools in widely divided places. No specific records or surviving patterns explain how these consistent styles were introduced or maintained. There was, however, much travel between Quaker communities, and it is evident that America's most prominent Quakers were acquainted with each other.[52]

Today, samplers stitched under the instruction of a Quaker-trained teacher can often be recognized by the inclusion of a Roman-style block alphabet, the presence of ligatures (letter combinations presented as a single letter), and a variety of identifiable motifs. The latter include geometric medallions or half medallions, bellflower pendants, paired doves in a wreath, natural looking sprays of identifiable flowers, and octagon shaped emblems, sometimes with the words "An Emblem of Love" or "An Emblem of Innocence."[53]

---

52 Betty Ring, *Girlhood Embroidery: American Samplers & Pictorial Needlework, 1650–1850* (2 vols.; New York: Alfred A. Knopf, 1993), 290.

53 Carol Humphrey, *Quaker School Girl Samplers from Ackworth* (England: Needleprint, 2006), 71 and Ring, *Girlhood Embroidery*, 290-292.

Ann Plummer

The earliest Alexandria sampler to show the influence of Quaker teaching is the 1800 sampler of nine-year-old Ann Plummer (Figure 2-12). The sampler is an interesting one and suggests a blending of contemporary local traditions with newly emerging Quaker traditions. Characteristic of local contemporary samplers is the array of alphabets, her arcaded carnation border, and a prominent cross band of strawberries on an arcaded vine. An identical band appears on Sarah M. Horwell's 1807 sampler (see Figure 2-5), although Ann used the more difficult Queen stitch. Typical of Quaker samplers is the phrase "An Emblem of Love" enclosed in an octagonal cartouche, the paired birds, and sprays of naturalistic flowers. Motifs identical to Ann's cross-stitched cluster of rose buds and the cornucopia can be found on samplers from Ackworth School in Yorkshire, England, and Westtown School in Pennsylvania, which was established only a year earlier, in 1799.[54]

Ann Plummer clearly marked her sampler with the place name "Alexandria," which almost always signifies where the sampler maker attended school. Ann, unfortunately, has not yet been identified as the daughter of any one of the several Plummer families living in Alexandria during the first two decades of the nineteenth century.[55] Possibly her family resided outside Alexandria and Ann came into the city for her education.[56] No women from Quaker families are recorded in Alexandria Monthly Meeting minutes, or in newspaper advertisements as teaching needlework in Alexandria until about 1805, when a Mary Janney and a Miss Janney advertised instruction in "plain Sewing, Marking, and in all kinds of useful Needlework."[57] Another possibility is that Ann studied needlework in Alexandria informally, perhaps with a relative who had gone to school at Westtown or had Ackworth School connections.

Stabler/Leadbeater Family

Elizabeth Stabler (1797–1843) was the oldest daughter of Alexandria apothecary and abolitionist Edward Stabler (1769–1831) and his first wife, Mary Pleasants. Edward Stabler was a prominent member of the Quaker community. Appointed as an elder in the Fairfax Monthly Meeting in 1798, he helped to establish the Alexandria Meeting in 1802. After the death of her mother in 1806, Elizabeth went to live with her aunt, Deborah Brooke Pleasants Stabler, in Sandy Spring, Maryland, where she attended the school conducted in Deborah's home.[58] Elizabeth's unfinished sampler includes the school location "Sandy Spring" (Figure 2-13).

---

54 Ring, *Girlhood Embroidery*, figure 314. See also Humphrey, *Quaker School Girl Samplers from Ackworth*, 151.

55 The several Plummers active in the Alexandria mercantile community, Jerome, Gerald, Joseph, Jeremiah, and Benjamin, arrived in the town after 1800, and none were old enough to have had a daughter born ca. 1791.

56 Ann may have been the Ann Plummer born June 1, 1790, to Mary Taylor and Joseph West Plummer of Frederick County, Maryland. Her paternal aunt, Ann[a] Plummer Janney, was a member of the Fairfax Monthly Meeting, from which the Alexandria Monthly Meeting was set off in 1802.

57 *Alexandria Daily Advertiser*, August 8, 1805. Janney is usually recognized as a Quaker surname in Virginia and Maryland. Although two girls, Sarah and Hannah Janney from Alexandria, were students at Westtown in 1800 and 1803 respectively, no connection to Mary Janney, teacher, has yet been determined.

58 Deborah Stabler was the older sister of Mary Pleasants Stabler and widow of William Stabler, Edward's older brother. Since members of the Society of Friends generally married within their meeting, it was not uncommon for two sisters to marry two brothers.

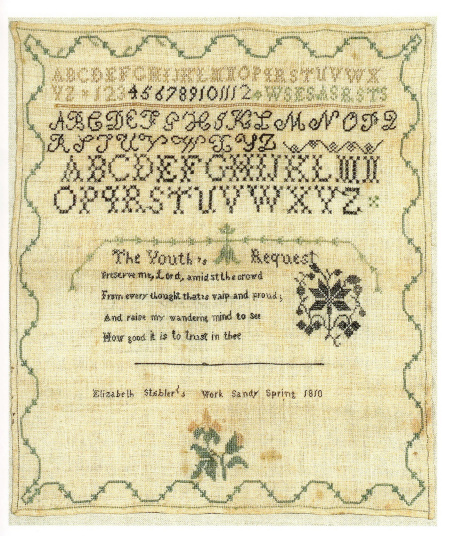

Figure 2-13. Sampler worked by Elizabeth Stabler. Sandy Spring, Maryland, 1810. Inscribed: "Elizabeth Stabler's Work Sandy Spring 1810." Silk on linen ground, 35 by 30 threads per in. 17 x 14 ½ in. Sandy Spring Museum

Well-known Quaker educator Margaret Judge (1783–1872)[59] taught at Deborah Stabler's Sandy Spring school from 1808 to 1812 and most likely supervised the needlework of thirteen-year-old Elizabeth Stabler when she worked her sampler in 1810. Typical of nineteenth-century Quaker schoolgirl embroidery is its centrally located bellflower pendant on a leafy vine. The two floral motifs, one more geometric than the other, are both found on Quaker samplers. Elizabeth included a four-line verse entitled "The Youth's Request." These lines are drawn from a longer poem written by Adam Clarke (1760–1832), a Methodist theologian and biblical scholar. The verse has appeared on other English and American samplers, one as late as 1832, sometimes under the title "Petition."[60]

Elizabeth became the third wife of Joseph Bond on October 2, 1828, in Alexandria, and they settled in Maryland. In the 1840 census for Montgomery County, the Joseph Bond household included fifteen people, ten free whites and five free blacks. Elizabeth and Joseph were the parents of five of the children (two girls and three boys). The household engaged in farming as well as the manufacture and selling of goods. Elizabeth Stabler Bond died on March 7, 1843.

On July 28, 1808, Elizabeth Stabler's father married Mary Hartshorne (ca. 1783–1852) in Alexandria. Their oldest daughter (and half sister to Elizabeth) was Mary Pleasants Stabler[61] (1809–1863) who stitched a simple alphabet sampler when she was eleven years old (Figure 2-14). Mary enrolled in the Quaker school run by Rachel Painter a few years after it opened in 1815. Her marking

---

59 Margaret Judge was a Quaker educator and minister who headed the female division of the Georgetown Lancasterian School and later opened her own school in Alexandria, near the Quaker Meeting House, in the spring of 1825. She was joined the next year by Mary Hallowell, who had previously taught at Westtown and the Fair Hill Boarding School in Montgomery County, Maryland.

Judge also conducted a female school at Woodlawn in Montgomery County between 1816 and 1818. An acquaintance described in a letter her scholars as "20 to 24 nice looking girls from Washington and George Town, they appear like daughters of the first rate families, very few of them belong to the society of Friends." (Sarah Painter to her brother, Ziba Darlington, June 27, 1817, Chester County, Pa. Historical Society.) The Judge/Hallowell school in Alexandria offered instruction in "plain sewing" and a range of academic subjects.

Quaker educator, Benjamin Hallowell, praised Margaret Judge for her "ardent temperament, warm-heartedness, and great physical energy and endurance" as well as "her great powers of observation, and remarkable mental activity, combined with her good judgment and sensibility." *Memoir of Margaret [Judge] Brown* (Philadelphia: Merrihew & Son, 1872), 8–9.

60 In 1823, twelve-year-old Phoebe P. Sneden, New York, stitched all twelve lines of Adam Clarke's poem under the title *Petition*. Information courtesy of Gary D. Putnam.

61 Mary Pleasants Stabler was named after Edward's first wife, Mary Pleasants, an uncommon but not unheard of naming practice in Quaker families.

sampler, with six alphabets worked in black, names Alexandria as its place of origin. Mary stitched her age as eleven, thus dating the sampler to around 1820. Although she was the daughter of a prominent Quaker family and attended a school taught by a Quaker teacher, no features on her sampler suggest Quaker stylistic influences.

In 1835, Mary Pleasants Stabler resigned from the Alexandria Meeting to marry John Leadbeater (died 1860), an Englishman and Anglican who worked in the family-run apothecary shop.[62] Mary and John had eight children, one of whom was Anna Leadbeater (1842–1906), who stitched two samplers in 1852 (Figures 2-15 and 2-16). Both are alphabet samplers with rows of letters and numbers worked in four-sided, rice, Algerian eye, and cross stitches and bear a resemblance to the sampler stitched by her mother more than thirty years earlier (Figure 2-14).

Anna's first sampler is smaller and was stitched when she was nine. It is marked with the place name "Alexandria Va.," which accurately reflects the fact that in 1852 Alexandria was no longer part of the District of Columbia. Anna worked her second sampler after her tenth birthday and dedicated it to her father. She used the Quaker style of dating, where months are referred to by number, not by name.[63] Anna may have stitched her two samplers under the tutelage of her mother, or possibly another female member of her extended Quaker family.[64] Given the use of Quaker dating conventions, it is unlikely that Anna stitched her samplers at one of the few schools in Alexandria that still included the ornamental branches in its curriculum.

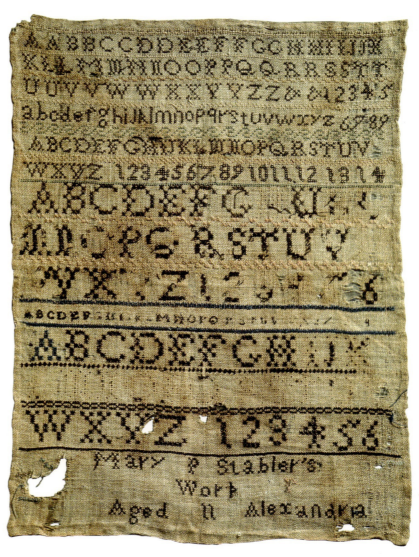

In 1853, a year after completing her two samplers, Anna Leadbeater entered the Alexandria Female Seminary, where she received instruction in natural philosophy, astronomy, and chemistry from noted Quaker educator and scientist, James Hallowell. Nine-year-old Mollie Gregory, who attended Hallowell's Seminary about the same time, regretted the lack of ornamental subjects and recalled years later that James Hallowell indicates she signed her sampler on the twenty-eighth day of the eighth month, or August 28, 1852.

Figure 2-14. Sampler worked by Mary Pleasants Stabler. Alexandria, ca. 1820. Inscribed: "Mary P Stabler's / Work / Aged 11 Alexandria." Silk and cotton on linen ground, 28 by 29 threads per in. 17 x 12 ¼ in. National Museum of American History, Smithsonian Institution, T12610

---

62 The location of the family business is now the Stabler Leadbeater Apothecary Shop Museum at 105–107 South Fairfax Street in Alexandria.

63 Beginning in the seventeenth century, Quakers adopted naming conventions for days and months that eliminated any reference to pagan gods and traditions. So, after the Gregorian reform, January was referred to as the "First Month" and August as "Eighth Month." Anna's inscription of "8 mo 28"

64 Anna's sister Lucy (1838–1917), older by four years, also worked an alphabet sampler in 1852, which she marked, "Alex. Va." Most likely the sisters stitched their samplers together and under the guidance of the same person. This sampler is in the collection of The Lyceum, Alexandria.

RIGHT:
Figure 2-16. Sampler by Anna Leadbeater. Alexandria, 1852. Inscribed: "Anna Leadbeater / to her Father / 8 mo 28th. / 1852. / Age. 10." Cotton on cotton ground, 25 by 25 threads per in. 16 ⅜ x 12 ½ in. National Museum of American History, Smithsonian Institution, T12612

ABOVE:
Figure 2-15. Sampler worked by Anna Leadbeater. Alexandria, 1852. Inscribed: "Anna Leadbeater's / Work / Aged 9 Alexandria Va / 1852." Cotton on linen ground, 23 by 32 threads per in. 13 ⅜ x 8 in. National Museum of American History, Smithsonian Institution, T12611

was a fine teacher of mathematics and chemistry and his girls were well taught in these lines, also in map drawing and penmanship. . . . He was not, however, a man of any polish or manner nor could he teach the nicer branches which were considered necessary for a girl of that day.[65]

In 1866, Anna Leadbeater married Henry C. Slaymaker of Pennsylvania, a dry goods merchant in Alexandria. The couple had three children: Isabell (born 1871), Henry C. Jr. (born December 1873), and Frank Lee (born May 1876). By 1880, Anna's husband had died, and her younger brother Thomas (age thirty-two and also widowed) was living with her, along with his two daughters.[66] In 1900 Anna's two sons were still living with her, as was her youngest niece and namesake, Anna Leadbeater, a schoolteacher. Anna Leadbeater Slaymaker died in 1906.[67]

Quivering Trees and Cornucopias

A group of six Alexandria schoolgirl samplers is identified by bold architectural forms, extravagant cornucopias, a verse entitled "Religion," and a signature executed entirely in four-sided stitch. While some of the decorative elements vary, a distinctive arcaded border with strawberries worked in queen stitch encloses the composition of each sampler in the group. Four of the samplers include a house with blue columns flanked by quivering trees; a fifth displays a pair of lush pineapples and large opposing cornucopias. Two of the quivering tree samplers have prominent cornucopias. A sixth, although lacking an architectural motif, quivering trees, and cornucopias, has the same verse entitled "Religion," the same four-sided stitch signature line, and the same queen stitch border. All six of the samplers were embroidered by Alexandria girls over a period of twelve years, from 1818 to 1830.

---

[65] Mary Gregory Powell, "Scenes of Childhood," with introduction by T. Michael Miller, *The Fireside Sentinel* 4, no. 2 (1990): 21.

[66] U.S. Census Record for 1880

[67] U.S. Census Record for 1900

34   COLUMBIA'S DAUGHTERS

Mary Muir, Marian Wood, Ann Carson, Rebecca Suter

The four earliest samplers in the group were stitched in 1818 and 1819. The three samplers stitched in 1818 by Mary Muir (Figure 2-17), Marian Wood (Figure 2-18), and Ann Carson[68] are the most closely related and were undoubtedly stitched under the direction of the same teacher. The Muir and Carson samplers feature an imposing house flanked by quivering trees and surmounting a large double cornucopia. The Wood sampler

[68] The location of ten-year-old Ann Carson's sampler is currently unknown. Bolton and Coe recorded it and described the design on page 136: "Strawberry border. Colonial house, and two cornucopias filled with flowers." Bolton and Coe also recorded another Alexandria sampler and described it in words remarkably similar to the Carson description: "Strawberry border. At bottom, house with trees and cornucopia of flowers." This sampler by Hester Dashiell Taylor of Alexandria is dated 1800—too early to have been part of the Muir-Carson-Wood group. Genealogical research confirms that Hester or Esther was born to George Taylor and Esther Dashiell about 1790.

ABOVE: Figure 2-17.
Sampler worked by Mary Muir.
Alexandria, 1818.
Inscribed: "Mary Muir Aged twelve years / Alexandria June the 8 1818."
Silk on linen ground, 28 by 28 threads per in.
25 ½ x 17 ½ in.
The Lyceum, Alexandria, Virginia, purchased in tribute of Mr. & Mrs. Harry A. Councilor
Image courtesy of *The Magazine Antiques*

Figure 2-18.
Sampler worked by Marian Wood, Alexandria, 1818.
Inscribed: "Marian Wood May the 13 1818."
Silk on linen ground, 32 by 32 threads per in.
17 x 17 3/16 in.
The Colonial Williamsburg Foundation, funded in part by donations from "Jeannine's Sampler Seminar," 1995-86

ALEXANDRIA SAMPLERS   35

Figure 2-19.
Sampler worked by
Rebecca Suter.
Alexandria, 1819.
Inscribed: "Rebecc[a]
Suter / aged 10 / years /
April the 30 / 1819 /
Alexandria District
of Columbia."
Silk on linen ground,
28 by 28 threads per in.
25 ¼ x 17 in.
Collection of
Anna Marie Witmer

also displays a house with blue columns and roof flanked by quivering trees, but it sits above a large basket of flowers. Rebecca Suter stitched her sampler a year later, dating it "April the 30 1819" (Figure 2-19). Although Rebecca's sampler lacks a large house and quivering trees, it displays the same lavish cornucopias found on the Muir and Carson samplers. In the lower third of her

36 COLUMBIA'S DAUGHTERS

sampler she added two large pineapples—a motif not found on any other District of Columbia needlework.

Of this earlier closely related group, two samplers include a verse entitled "Religion," attributed to Mary Masters (1694–1771), an eighteenth-century English poet. The poem was first published in 1733 in her book entitled *Poems on Several Occasions*.[69]

> *Tis religion that can give*
> *Sweetest pleasures while we live*
> *Tis religion must supply*
> *Solid comfort when we die*
>
> *After death its joys will be*
> *Lasting as eternity*
> *Let me then make God my friend*
> *And on all his ways attend*

The samplers created by Mary Muir and Rebecca Suter share a second verse, consisting of the first and last stanzas of a four-stanza poem, also written by Mary Masters.[70] The first four lines celebrate spring, the last four lines celebrate the God who "such wonders could raise." Why the last line Mary stitched differs from Rebecca's last line remains unexplained.[71]

Inscriptions on the Muir and Suter samplers share the same information and format, but differ in significant ways. Both include the girl's full name and age, along with a date that includes month, day, and year. The format for dating the samplers is somewhat unusual, with each girl stitching the word "the" in between the month and day. Mary Muir's signature is unusual in that it is the only one in this early group worked entirely in four-sided stitch. Rebecca's signature is unique in that she inscribed her 1819 sampler at the bottom with "Alexandria District of Columbia." This is the earliest known inclusion of the words "District of Columbia" or "D.C." on a sampler. The Muir sampler only states "Alexandria" as the place of origin.

Mary Muir (1805-1881) was the daughter of Alexandria cabinetmaker John Muir (1770–1815) and his wife, Mary Lang (1780–1841), who were married by the Reverend Doctor James Muir in the Presbyterian Church of Alexandria in 1800. Mary was born on November 2, 1805, and would have been twelve years old, as stated on her sampler, when she dated her work on June 8, 1818. In 1826, Mary Muir married English-born Stephen Shinn (ca. 1801–ca. 1862), an Alexandria merchant. They lived comfortably and raised five children, the youngest of which, Mary Jane, was born in 1846. Three sons followed their father in the mercantile trade. Mary Muir Shinn died in 1881, "an old and esteemed lady . . . an invalid for twenty years having been confined to the house a major part of that time."[72]

Marian Wood was born in 1805 to Eliza Parsons and William Wood, an Alexandria

---

69 Mary Masters' 1733 collection of poems, entitled *Poems on Several Occasions*, was published by subscription, the first time a volume of English poetry was published this way by a woman. The poem was also published in an anthology of hymns in 1815 entitled *A New Collection of 700 Evangelical Hymns*.

70 Masters' poem was also published as a hymn by Boston area Unitarian churches in 1789 and 1803, before Mary and Rebecca stitched their samplers, e.g., *A Collection of Psalms and Hymns for Publick Worship* (Salem: Dabney & Cushing, 1789) and *A Collection of Hymns, More Particularly Designed for the Use of the West Society in Boston* (Boston: J&T Fleet, 1803).

71 An unattributed version of the poem labeled "Gratitude to the Supreme Being" was published by Lindley Murray in 1816 in his anthology of English literature designed for children entitled *Introduction to the English Reader* (page 143). It is likely that Mary and Rebecca's teacher copied the verse from this source, then newly published in the United States. Lindley's publication uses the version of the last line that appears on Rebecca Suter's sampler.

72 *Alexandria Gazette*, August 6, 1881.

storekeeper with a residence on South Water Street. In 1828 she married grocer/ship chandler Thomas M. White. They had at least five children, the second youngest of whom, Charles Henry White, died in 1845 after one year and twenty-nine days. In 1849, forty-four-year-old Marian Wood White followed her son in death.

Ann Carson, a daughter of Irish immigrants James (1774–1855) and Ursula Brown Carson (died 1835), was born in Alexandria in 1808, the oldest of six children. She married English-born Edward Green, an accountant, in 1827 and had nine children before 1850. Ann Carson Green continued to maintain a household in Alexandria that included five of her children in the 1870s. She died in 1880 at the age of seventy-two.

Rebecca Suter (1809-after 1860) was born in 1809 in Havre de Grace, Harford County, Maryland, to Sarah Dorsey (1787–1853) and John T. Suter (1787–1826), a carriage maker. Suter moved around Maryland and Virginia in search of work, finally settling in Alexandria around 1814 where he operated a coach and harness shop. Through the years, the Suters maintained contact with family in Havre de Grace. In 1827, Rebecca married Alexander K. Myers (1804–1871) from Harford County and returned there to raise seven children and live out her life.[73] Her strong connection to Harford County may explain the presence of the pineapple motif on her Alexandria sampler. Pairs of large pineapples are present in the border designs of a distinctive group of Maryland embroideries known as the "Fruit and Flower" samplers, made by students of Ann Barclay Cloud in Bel Air, Harford County, from 1818 to 1819.[74]

Mary Ann Bontz, Mary Harrison

The remaining two samplers in this distinctive group were stitched a decade later, one by Mary Ann Bontz in 1828 and one by Mary Harrison in 1830. Both have the deeply arcaded border with queen-stitched strawberries seen on the Muir, Wood, Carson, and Suter samplers. In addition to the strawberry border, the sampler stitched by Mary Ann Bontz can be assigned to this Alexandria group on the basis of similarities to the Muir sampler, including the same verse entitled "Religion" and identically formatted place and date inscriptions worked in four-sided stitch: "Alexandria June the 8 1818" on

Figure 2-20. Sampler worked by Mary Ann Bontz. Alexandria, 1828. Inscribed: "Mary Ann Bontz / Aged 9 years 6 months / Alexandria June the 19 1828." Silk on linen ground. 18 ½ x 19 in. Location unknown

---

73 Alexander K. Myers had a blemished background. He fathered a male child with Anne Bartol in 1826. The court awarded her support, and Nicholas Suter Jr., a cousin of Rebecca, signed to assure Alexander Myers would provide maintenance for the child and to take on the liability if he did not. With the family involvement, it seems likely that Rebecca knew about her husband's bastard child. Henry C. Peden, Jr., *Bastardy Cases in Harford County, Maryland, 1774–1844* (Bowie Md.: Willow Bend Books, 2001), 10–11.

74 See Allen, *A Maryland Sampling*, 105–12. Mrs. Cloud, who taught the sampler design, was from Wilmington, Delaware, and later Philadelphia where student Susanna Holland may have been the first to stitch pineapples in the border design of her 1816 sampler. The "Fruit and Flower" motif continued to be taught in the Bel Air area after 1819, probably by other teachers. One may have carried the design to Loudoun County, Virginia, where Lucy Ann Bradfield stitched an 1826 sampler almost identical to those in Harford County.

the sampler stitched by Mary Muir and "Alexandria June the 19 1828" on the sampler stitched ten years later by Mary Ann Bontz (Figure 2-20). Mary Ann also stitched a somewhat modified version of the first stanza of a seven-stanza hymn entitled "Children of the Heavenly King," written by John Cennick (1718–1755), British teacher, itinerant evangelist, and prolific writer of hymns.[75] It reads:

> *Children of the heavenly King*
> *As we journey let us sing*
> *Sing our saviours worthy Praise*
> *Glorious in his works and ways*

This verse does not appear on any of the other known samplers in this group.

The 1830 sampler by eleven-year-old Mary Harrison (Figure 2-21) is also clearly related to those of Mary Muir and Marian Wood. The central motif in the lower register is a building that replicates the one found on Mary Muir's sampler, with its portico, blue columns, and four tall windows.[76] As with the Muir and Wood samplers, Mary Harrison's building is flanked by a row of quivering trees, albeit on only one side. The scene in the upper register includes a well-dressed man and woman standing by a flowering tree, a scene that does not appear on any of the other known samplers in this group. Mary Harrison stitched two verses on her sampler. The first appears to be compiled from multiple poems by Robert Dodsley (1703–1774), English bookseller, author, and playwright.[77] It reads:

What is the blooming fair
And tincture of the skin
to Peace of mind from c[are]
And harmony within.
Sickn[ess an]d age will blast
All outward charmes away
Virtue will sooth at last
in deaths tremendous day.

Mary's second verse is the first stanza of a four-stanza poem written by an anonymous British poet or hymnist.

Figure 2-21. Sampler worked by Mary Harrison. Alexandria, 1830. Inscribed: "Mary Harrison Aged Eleven Years / Alexandria July 1830." Silk on linen ground, 29 by 31 threads per in. 19 ½ x 16 ⅝ in. National Museum of American History, Smithsonian Institution, T14710

---

75 The hymn was first published by Cennick in 1741 in a collection of hymns entitled *Sacred Hymns, for the Children of God in the Days of their Pilgrimage*.

76 The design of the building on the Muir and Harrison samplers, with its portico and four tall windows, bears a slight resemblance to the central block of Benjamin Dulany's country house built on Shuter's Hill, just outside of Alexandria, around 1781. The building on the Wood sampler has a different window arrangement on the lower floors, but it does have a row of windows in the attic that resembles those on the Dulany house. The Dulany house burned to the ground in 1842 and is known only from sketches. See Junior League of Washington, *The City of Washington* (New York: Alfred A. Knopf, 1977), 33.

77 A variation of this verse was published in America in the 1804 edition of Nathanael Low's *Almanack*, Other variations are known to have been stitched on both English and American samplers, 1808–1830. A version was also published in *The Ariel: A Literary Gazette*, Philadelphia, March 23, 1828. In that publication it was called "Beauty" from Elizabeth Rowe's *Art of Charming*.

*See the kind shepherd Jesus stands
With all engaging charmes
Hark how he calls his tender lambs
And folds them in his arms.*

Although the poem's authorship is unclear, it appears to have been first published about 1795 in England as a hymn in Rebecca Wilkinson's *Short Sermons to Children, To which are added Short Hymns suited to the Subject*.[78] Mary Harrison's use of the four-sided stitch to record her city (Alexandria) and a date (July 1830) also helps to place her sampler within this distinctive group.

Mary Ann Bontz (1818–1893) and Mary Harrison (1819–1906) were first cousins. Mary Ann was a daughter of Sarah Carlin and Jacob Bontz (born ca. 1784), a grocer with a shop at the corner of Patrick and Prince Streets. Mary Harrison was a daughter of Elizabeth Carlin and Alexandria merchant John D. Harrison.[79] Sarah Carlin Bontz and Elizabeth Carlin Harrison were sisters.[80] Although their daughters were the same age and most likely received needlework instruction from the same teacher, they completed their samplers two years apart. This may help to explain the simpler composition in the sampler stitched by Mary Ann Bontz, who was two years younger when she completed her needlework.

Both girls married and continued to live and raise families in the District of Columbia. In 1841 Mary Harrison married Isaac Kell Jr., a successful coppersmith and tin plate maker in Alexandria. They had at least five children, three boys and two girls. At the time of the 1870 census, Mary was a widowed head of a large household that included four of her children, her brother-in-law, and six additional relatives.[81] Mary Harrison Kell died in 1906 and is buried in the Methodist Protestant Cemetery in Alexandria.

Mary Ann Bontz married George Roszel Adams of Alexandria. By 1850 her husband had a governmental appointment, and the family was living in Washington City.[82] The household included three of their four children, her four siblings, and her parents. By 1870 the family had returned to Alexandria where George Adams listed his occupation as farmer.[83] Mary Ann Bontz Adams died on February 12, 1893, in Alexandria.

Searching for the Teacher

Considerable research has been conducted to uncover the teacher or teachers responsible for this identifiable group of six related samplers from Alexandria. It is likely that the teacher responsible for the design of the early (1818–1819) samplers was a member of one of two Muir families who were engaged in

---

78 In 1814 the verse was included, anonymously, as No. 15 in J. Benson's *Hymns for Children, selected chiefly from the publications of the Rev. John and Charles Wesley and Dr. Watts, &c*. It subsequently was included in a large number of hymnals, at least two of which were published in the U.S. for the Unitarian church in Philadelphia prior to 1820.

79 Mary Harrison, the sampler maker, does not appear to have been related to the Reverend Elias Harrison, identified in the following pages as a prominent Alexandria theologian and educator. The Reverend Harrison's daughter, Mary, had previously been credited as the Mary Harrison who stitched the 1830 Alexandria sampler in this group. Mary was born March 8, 1821, to Elizabeth Veitch and Elias Harrison; in 1830, she would have been nine years old, not "eleven," as stated on the sampler. On April 2, 1849, Mary married William H. Clagget at the First Presbyterian Church. *Register of Baptisms, Marriages and Funerals During the Ministry of the Revd Doctr James Muir in the Presbyterian Church of Alexandria, D.C.* [DAR GRC VA S1 V66], 41, 46.

80 In 1821, Jacob Bontz and J. D. Harrison were executors of the estate of William Carlin and presumably sons-in-law of the decedent. Miller, *Portrait of a Town*, 50.

81 U.S. Census Records for 1870

82 U.S. Census Records for 1850

83 U.S. Census Records for 1870.

educating Alexandria's female youth. The first was the Reverend Doctor James Muir (1757–1820) and his wife, Elizabeth Welman (1766–1830), formerly of Bermuda. Doctor Muir, a pastor of the Presbyterian Church in Alexandria, opened an academy in 1790 that had as its objective "the cultivation of the [female] mind."[84] Muir's school proposed to follow a challenging academic curriculum, but he assured his patrons that he would not neglect the ornamental subjects. He advertised that "a person shall be engaged capable of teaching the branches *peculiar* to the Female Education."[85] The length of Reverend Muir's association with his female academy is uncertain. He brought the Reverend Elias Harrison, a tutor at Princeton College, to Alexandria to take charge of the Alexandria Academy (for boys) in 1817. Harrison then succeeded Muir as pastor of the Alexandria Presbyterian Church after Muir's death in 1820.

Elizabeth Welman Muir conducted a school for girls at the old parsonage at the edge of the churchyard and carried on at that location for several years after her husband's death.[86] With the assistance of her daughters Jane, Mary,[87] and Elizabeth, the school continued from their residence at Prince and Washington Streets. The Muir school closed briefly when Elizabeth Muir died in March 1830, but soon reopened under the direction of the three Muir daughters as the Misses Muir's Boarding and Day School for Young Ladies. The sisters taught all branches "generally deemed important to the solid, useful, polite and ornamental education,"[88] and their students also had "the privileges of attending the lectures of Mr. [James] Hallowell on Astronomy and Chemistry."[89] The Reverend Elias Harrison served as general superintendent of the Misses Muir's school, where he oversaw the "higher branches of study."[90] The Muir sisters remained unmarried

---

84 The Reverend Doctor Muir was president of the board of trustees of the Alexandria Academy from 1792 to 1820 and active in its administration. He founded and directed a number of local religious, educational, and charitable organizations. "Installed Clergy at the Old Presbyterian Meeting House, 1772 to Present," http://www.opmh.org/content/view/488/131/. Gay Montague Moore, *Seaport in Virginia: George Washington's Alexandria* (Richmond: Garrett and Massie, Inc., 1949), 141–42.

85 *Virginia Gazette and Alexandria Advertiser*, August 5, 1790.

86 Although Reverend James Muir died in 1820, Elizabeth Welman Muir may have taken up teaching as a means of support around 1817 when her husband's health was noticeably failing. During that year Reverend Elias Harrison began to assist Reverend Muir with his pastoral duties. Muir's death notice reported that he died "of a painful and distressing sickness, which he endured with the most unshaken fortitude and Christian resignation."

87 It was initially tempting to assume that the Reverend and Elizabeth Muir's daughter Mary was Mary Muir the sampler maker. Growing up in an academic and religious household and later becoming a teacher, she had opportunities to become proficient in needlework. Although

Mary's birth date is uncertain, it is clear that she was born too early to have been twelve years old in 1818. She was the second of three surviving Muir daughters, probably born in the mid-1790s. An analysis of birth records reveals that James and Elizabeth Muir had seven children. Samuel Muir was born in 1785 and Jane Wardlaw Muir was born in 1788 or early 1789, before their parents moved to Alexandria. Frances Wardlaw Muir was born in 1790 or 1791 and died at age seven months. Elizabeth Muir was born in 1798 and died in 1799, and Elizabeth Love Muir was born in 1801. Mary Wardlaw Muir and an unidentified son, who did not survive infancy, were probably born during the 1792–1797 period. *Register of Baptisms, Marriages and Funerals During the Ministry of the Revd Doct^r James Muir in the Presbyterian Church of Alexandria, D.C.* [DAR GRC VA S1 V66] 23, 25. Wesley E. Pippenger, *Tombstone Inscriptions of Alexandria, Virginia*, Vol. I (Westminster, Md,: Family Line Publications, 1992, rev. 1993), 106. "Installed Clergy at the Old Presbyterian Meeting House, 1772 to Present."

88 *Alexandria Gazette*, August 14, 1835.

89 Quoted from an 1831 issue of the *Alexandria Gazette* by Moore, *Seaport in Virginia*, 141.

90 *Alexandria Gazette*, August 14, 1835.

and conducted their school into the 1840s. Mollie Gregory unkindly described their appearance when they attended the Presbyterian Church: "How well I recall the three Misses Muir—their red noses, the black velvet bands worn on their foreheads to keep their wigs in place, and their antiquated bonnets and hoopless black dresses."[91]

Also engaged in educating girls and young women of Alexandria was Mary Lang Muir, wife of Scottish-born John Muir, a successful Alexandria cabinetmaker, who immigrated to Alexandria in 1790 and formed a partnership with William Buckland II as cabinet and chair manufacturers between 1794 and 1797. In 1800 he married Mary Lang, a native of Scotland, then residing in Philadelphia. John Muir does not appear to have been related to the Reverend James Muir, but he and Mary were members of his Presbyterian Church, where four of their children were baptized between 1802 and 1812.

After her husband's death in 1815, Mary Lang Muir was left a widow with five young children to support.[92] It is known that from 1815 to 1817 she continued his cabinet-making business, but her occupation between 1817 and the close of 1820 has not been documented.[93] This is the period, however, in which at least four young girls in Alexandria, including her daughter Mary Muir, completed four of the known samplers in this group. It is also a time when Elizabeth Muir may have required someone to assist at her school due to the failing health of her husband, Reverend James Muir.

In late December 1820, Mary Lang Muir opened her house on Royal Street to boarding students "from the age of six to fourteen."[94] By April 1821 she was able to "take a few more scholars, in addition to those she [had]" and provide instruction in "the various branches of needle-work and tamboring in particular."[95] She immodestly advertised her qualifications:

> *having acquired the knowledge in Scotland by devoting much of the early part of her life to it, there is doubtless none to excel her in the United States. Samples of her work will be shown to any person who may call on her at her residence on the mall.*[96]

It is possible that Mary Lang Muir started teaching needlework as early as 1817, either as an independent teacher or at the nearby Muir academy or parsonage school where she was well known to the minister and his family. Mary Lang Muir was apparently a highly capable businesswoman, a skilled needle worker, and a member of Reverend Muir's congregation. She therefore had a network of contacts from which to draw patronage for a needlework school.

Mary Lang Muir may have instructed her daughter and other young girls in pictorial sampler work from 1817 to 1819, which would account for the four Alexandria samplers from this period.[97] With two sons still at home in

---

91 Powell, *The History of Old Alexandria, Virginia*, 104.

92 The John Muirs had three surviving sons and two daughters—Jane, born in 1804 and Mary, born in 1805. Jane married Alexandria cabinetmaker James Green in 1825.

93 *Alexandria Gazette*, February 2, 1815.

94 *Alexandria Gazette*, January 1, 1821. Though published in 1821, the Muir advertisement is dated December 28, 1820.

95 The 1820 Alexandria, D.C. census listing for Mary Lang Muir indicates that two girls, one 10–15 (Mary) and one 16–25 (Jane), and two boys were living at home. At that point she did not have boarding students.

96 *Alexandria Gazette*, April 30, 1821. No connection between teachers Elizabeth Muir and Mary Lang Muir has been found, but since the latter did not teach academic subjects, her students may have attended Elizabeth's Muir's parsonage school for their "solid" education. Additionally, Mary Muir may have provided room and board for several of the parsonage students who lived at a distance. The parsonage school was on Royal Street, a few blocks from Mary Lang Muir's home.

97 From her advertisement, we know that by 1821, if not before, Mary Lang Muir was conducting a school in her residence on Royal Street between King and Prince Streets. Sampler maker Marian Wood lived within a block of Mary Muir's house. Ann Carson, daughter of merchant James Carson, also lived within a block of Mrs. Muir's.

1830, she would have had good reason to continue teaching needle skills to support her family. Therefore, she may also have been responsible for the later samplers stitched by Mary Ann Bontz and Mary Harrison. If Mary Lang Muir did teach needlework for more than a decade, it is likely that other samplers will come to light to fill in the gap between 1819 and 1828.[98]

Based on known examples, this distinctive group of samplers, all with a similar queen-stitched strawberry border, as well as shared motifs and verses, shows the enduring preference for a local design and its adaptations by one or more of Alexandria's talented teachers over a number of years.

THE DECLINE OF NEEDLEWORK INSTRUCTION IN ALEXANDRIA

Needlework instruction in Alexandria began to decline in the 1830s, as increased emphasis was being placed on providing girls and young women with a more academically oriented education. Nonetheless, a few established Alexandria schools continued to offer instruction in the needle arts. The Muir sisters advertised "Needle Work" in 1834 and carried on their school into the 1840s.[99] Mrs. Porter, however, limited teaching of "Plain and Ornamental Sewing in all their varieties" to the primary class in her seminary.[100] Many of the known samplers from this period are relatively simple marking samplers, where students demonstrated their ability to replicate the alphabet in different sizes and scripts using various stitches.

Mary Stewart Vowell

In 1831, eight-year-old Mary Stewart Vowell (1823–1894) stitched an alphabet sampler on which she clearly named Alexandria as the location of her school (Figure 2-22). Mary's sampler includes eight complete alphabets and at least three sets of consecutive numerals. Her sampler fits into a long tradition of alphabet or marking samplers, designed to prepare girls to stitch personal or family initials on clothes and household linens. Other samplers with a similar style include those of Mary Pleasants Stabler, stitched in 1820 (Figure 2-14), Rebecca Ann Fifield, stitched in 1823 (Figure 2-10) and Anna Leadbeater, stitched in 1852 (Figures 2-15 and 2-16).[101]

Mary Stewart Vowell was born in Alexandria on August 19, 1823, to Margaretta Brown (1798–1857) and druggist John Dick Vowell (1795–1862), the third of their nine

Figure 2-22. Sampler worked by Mary Stewart Vowell. Alexandria, 1831. Inscribed: "Mary Stewart Vowell Aged 8 years 1831 Alexandria." Silk on linen ground. 17 x 17 in. Cohasset Historical Society, 1990.001.366

---

98 It is possible that after 1817 the two Muir families collaborated to provide educational opportunities to young girls in Alexandria, with Elizabeth Muir and her daughters responsible for academic subjects and Mary Lang Muir responsible for needlework instruction. Since their school can be documented as having continued into the 1840s, it is possible that the Muir sisters adopted and adapted earlier sampler formats and features developed by Mary Lang Muir.

99 Alexandria *Daily National Intelligencer*, September 3, 1834. The 1840 census for East of Washington Street, Alexandria, recorded Jane Muir, her two sisters, and four girls between ten and fourteen. Under the Academies and Grammar Schools column of the census, forty scholars were noted.

100 *Richmond Enquirer*, August 24, 1832. Mrs. Porter advertised her seminary in Alexandria, Washington, and Richmond newspapers between 1827 and 1834.

101 Mary Vowell's first cousin, Elizabeth Mankin (1819–1876), daughter of Polly Mary Vowell and Charles Mankin, stitched an alphabet sampler with an arcaded strawberry border in 1832.

children. On December 17, 1845, she married Richard Sears McCulloch (McCulloh) (1818–1894) from Baltimore, a college-educated scientist and civil engineer. Beginning shortly after their marriage Richard worked for the U.S. Mint in Philadelphia (1846–1849), and during that time their only child, Margaretta Grace Brown McCulloch (1847–1941), was born. From 1849 to 1863 McCulloch was a university professor, first at Princeton in New Jersey and then at Columbia in New York City.

During the Civil War McCulloch left Columbia to become a consulting chemist for the Confederate Nitre and Mining Bureau in Richmond, where he led the development of weapons for biological warfare using lethal gas. With the fall of Richmond to the Union army, he was captured and spent two years in a federal prison. After his release Richard was appointed professor of experimental philosophy and applied mathematics at Washington and Lee University in Lexington, Virginia.[102] By the 1880 census Richard and Mary and their adult daughter Margaretta, were back in Baltimore, where Richard listed his occupation as mining engineer. Mary died at the age of seventy on July 1, 1894, in Pass Christian, Mississippi. Richard died a few months later in Baltimore.

RIGHT: Figure 2-23. Advertisement published in the *Alexandria Gazette*, June 25, 1832.

Saint Francis Xavier's Academy

In 1832, four Sisters of Charity from Saint Joseph's Academy in Emmitsburg, Maryland, established Saint Francis Xavier's Academy in Alexandria.[103] This school, like others organized by Catholic orders with their tradition of ecclesiastical needlework, offered ornamental subjects long after most schools had removed them from their curricula. Academy girls could take lessons in "Plain and Fancy Needle-work" and for a fee of ten dollars, embroidery (Figure 2-23). Unfortunately there are no known samplers or other items of embroidery that can be associated with this school. In a manner similar to other Catholic schools for young women, Saint Francis Xavier's Academy also responded to the "spirit of improvement" in female education and offered a course of instruction that included such subjects as natural philosophy, chemistry, and bookkeeping.

ACADEMY FOR YOUNG LADIES
UNDER THE DIRECTION OF
The Sisters of Charity

THIS institution is located at the corner of Fairfax and Duke streets, Alexandria, D. C. And will commence on Monday the 19th inst. The class rooms are spacious and airy, and will be kept neat and clean for the benefit of the pupils.

Besides the usual branches of female education, lessons will be given in French, Music, Drawing, Painting, &c. The Sister who will attend to the French department, will use every exertion to communicate to the pupils, an accurate and correct pronunciation of the language, and introduce the practice of speaking the language, during class and recreation.

The Sisters will endeavor to impart that useful knowledge, and inculate those correct principles of literature and morality, which are the brightest gems in the female character. The inhabitants of the principal cities of the Union are witnesses of the general benefit resulting to society since the commencement of the Institution in the United States. In the year 1809 a Society of pious ladies located themselves in the vicinity of Emitsburgh, Frederick County, Maryland, known to the public by the name of Sisters of Charity, and incorporated by the General Assembly of Maryland in 1816; since that period, these Ladies have dedicated themselves to the service of God, and Education of Females, of which this is a branch.

The course of instruction embraces the English and French languages, Orthography, Grammar, Composition, Writing, Rational Arithmetic, Geography, Ancient and Modern History, Conversations on Natural Philosophy and Chemistry, Book Keeping, Plain and Fancy Needle-work.

CHARGES:

The Common Branches of English, per quarter,	$5 00
French,	7 00
Music and use of Instruments,	10 00
Drawing and Painting,	5 00
Oil Painting on Velvet,	10 00
Embroidery,	10 00
Fancy Work,	5 00

Hours of Attendance, from 8 to 12 A. M., and from 2 to 5 P. M. Apply at the Academy, or to the Rev. J. Smith, Pastor of St. Mary's Church.

Alexandria Gazette, June 25, 1832.

---

102 Milton Halsey Thomas, *Professor McCulloh of Princeton, Columbia, and points south*. (Princeton, N.J., 1847). Wikipedia entry for Richard Sears McCulloh, online at: http://en.wikipedia.org/wiki/Richard_Sears_McCulloh.

103 Saint Francis Xavier's Academy was in existence from 1832 to 1839. For a study of needlework from Saint Joseph's Academy, see Allen, *A Maryland Sampling*, 165–83.

Flower Basket Samplers

Another exception to the gradual decline in needlework instruction is the appearance of two attractive samplers from the early 1830s, probably stitched under the direction of the same unidentified teacher. Both feature a large overflowing basket of flowers with distinctive tulips, roses, and oak leaves, all worked in cross stitch. Both samplers also include verses entitled "A Prayer." The first sampler was stitched by Margreter (Margaret) McFarlane (ca. 1823–1866) in 1831 and included the place name of Alexandria (Figure 2-24).[104] Her vertical format recalls the Alexandria samplers worked by Mary Muir (Figure 2-17) and Rebecca Suter (Figure 2-19). Margaret included eight lines of a prayer whose author remains unidentified.

> *Jesus lover of mankind*
> *Shine upon my youthful mind*
> *Teach me wisdom from above*
> *Fill my so[ul] w[ith] purest love*
> *In the slipry [sic] paths of youth*
> *Guide me in the way of truth*
> *And if bless'd with length of days*
> *Let my life be spent in praise.*

Margaret was the daughter of Suky Mills and John McFarlane (born 1789), an immigrant from Ireland. Her parents were married in 1819 in Alexandria, where her father had established a successful business as a boot and shoe manufacturer and dealer. On November 17, 1841, Margaret married Samuel A. Munson (died 1873), a sea captain from New Haven, Connecticut. They raised four sons, the youngest born in 1852. Margaret McFarlane Munson died on July 25, 1866, in Baltimore, and her husband died seven years later in Rio de Janeiro.

The second sampler was stitched by Ann Maria Wood in a more traditional square format. Although she did not include a date, she did give her age as seven and her location as Alexandria (Figure 2-25). Ann Maria Wood was most likely the Ann M. Wood who was born in 1825 to John (born 1782) and Elizabeth (born 1790) Wood of Alexandria. If this is the correct identification, Ann Maria stitched her sampler in 1832, a year after Margaret

Figure 2-24. Sampler worked by Margaret McFarlane. Alexandria, 1831. Inscribed: "Margreter McFarlane / Alexandria / 1831." Silk on linen ground, 28 by 28 threads per in. 25 ¼ x 17 ⅝ in. Collection of A. E. Steidel

---

104 Margaret stitched her name as "Margreter," but documents give her name as Margaret. Her younger sister, Elizabeth (born about 1834), stitched an alphabet sampler, using cross, herringbone, and eyelet stitches, in 1840.

Figure 2-25. Sampler worked by Ann Maria Wood. Alexandria, ca. 1832. Inscribed: "Ann Maria Wood / Aged 7 Years / Alexandria." Silk on linen ground. 16 x 15 ⅞ in. Image courtesy of Sloans & Kenyon.

McFarlane stitched her strikingly similar work. John Wood, originally from New Jersey, was a successful cooper, with three black assistants living in his household in 1850. Ann was the third of at least five children born to John and Elizabeth and was still living with her parents in 1860. The poem on Ann's sampler is also entitled "A Prayer," but this one can be attributed to Alexander Pope, a well-known eighteenth-century English poet. Written in 1738, the lines stitched by Ann are the last four lines in a much longer poem entitled "The Universal Prayer."

Sarah E. Atkinson

The latest sampler to be identified with Alexandria was stitched by Sarah (Sallie) Elizabeth Atkinson (1843–1897), oldest daughter of Richard (1812–1855) and Ruth Ann Atkinson (1818–1857). It is probable that Sarah worked her undated sampler (Figure 2-26) in the mid- to late 1850s at a time when Alexandria was no longer part of the District of Columbia.[105] Sarah was born October 1, 1843, in Prince William County, Virginia, and christened at Christ Church, Alexandria May 12, 1844. During much of her childhood the Atkinson family resided at Rippon Lodge in Prince William County but kept ties to Alexandria.[106] After the early deaths of her parents, Sarah and two younger siblings were taken to Alexandria to be raised by relatives. Most likely she attended school in the city.[107]

Sarah used cross stitch to combine a solemn verse on death with a large image of a contented feline. The verse is the first stanza of a four-stanza poem by Isaac Watts, first published in 1707 in *Hymns and Spiritual Songs*.[108] Her stitched cat, seated on a cushion, recalls similar motifs from samplers and wool work compositions from a wide geographic region.[109] On September 29, 1870, Sarah married Milton A. Ish (1836–1890), a physician from Prince William County, Virginia, in the same Alexandria church in which she had been baptized. They had two daughters. Sarah Atkinson Ish died in 1897, at age fifty-three from complications of pneumonia.

---

105 During the 1830s and 1840s the economy of Alexandria stagnated as the town lost trade to the north side of the Potomac River with its port at Georgetown and access to the Chesapeake and Ohio Canal. An abolitionist movement in Congress further threatened the economy of Alexandria and its active slave trade. The petitions of Alexandrians to Congress and the Virginia legislature to retrocede to Virginia were finally approved in 1846 and accepted by the Virginia General Assembly, which welcomed the additional pro-slavery votes, on March 13, 1847.

106 Rippon Lodge, the oldest extant house in Prince William County, Virginia, is now a Virginia Historic Site.

107 Information on the Atkinson family courtesy of Donald L. Wilson, Virginiana Librarian, Prince William Public Library System.

108 For the complete poem, see The Hymnary.org: http://www.hymnary.org/text/o_for_an_overcoming_faith.

109 See Sue Studebaker, *Ohio is My Dwelling Place: Schoolgirl Embroideries, 1800–1850* (Athens: Ohio University Press, 2002), figure 125 for "Miss Puss," Clark County, Ohio, 1837.

Figure 2-26.
Sampler worked by
Sarah E. Atkinson.
Attributed to
Alexandria, ca. 1855.
Inscribed: "Sarah E.
Atkinson."
Silk on linen ground,
28 by 28 threads per in.
15 ⅜ x 16 ½ in.
Collection of A. Newbold
Richardson

In spite of these few interesting exceptions, by the mid-1830s proprietors of Alexandria's female seminaries generally agreed that "the education of young ladies has been too circumscribed, and too much confined to the ornamental branches to the neglect of more important studies."[110] The flowering of Alexandria girlhood embroidery had passed, and "needlework" in Alexandria schools was relegated to the "inferior branches," if it was taught at all.[111]

---

110 Mr. Brashears did concede that "in due course of time" he would introduce into his curriculum several of the "Polite Sciences" including "Music, Drawing, Dancing, Beadwork, etc.," but not needlework. *Phenix Gazette*, May 28, 1830.

111 Alfred Armstrong, *Phenix Gazette*, August 18, 1827.

Detail from Figure 3-3. Embroidered picture worked by Julia Maria Hooff. Alexandria, ca. 1815. Silk, wool, chenille, watercolor, and paper on silk ground over linen foundation. 17 ½ x 22 in.
Collection of Margaret Cheeseman
Photography by Gary Connaughton

CHAPTER 3

Alexandria Pictorial Embroideries and Maps

GIRLS IN ALEXANDRIA acquired and demonstrated their basic needle skills by stitching samplers. After having mastered their stitches, many young women, especially daughters of the affluent merchant class, attended schools that offered advanced embroidery instruction. In addition to tuition, these schools usually required extra fees for the purchase of expensive materials such as silk and the services of a competent artist to lay out the embroidery design. Among examples of needlework from the District of Columbia, two design formats appear to be unique to Alexandria—pictorial embroideries with applied painted faces and embroidered maps replicating the "Plan of the City of Washington."

PICTORIAL EMBROIDERIES

Few examples of pictorial embroidery on silk are known from the District of Columbia. Of the embroideries identified to date, eight can be assigned to students in Alexandria.[1] Alexandria pictorial embroideries can be divided into two groups based on their design sources: (a) patriotic America and (b) stories from literature popular in the nineteenth century, often based on classical or biblical themes.

Patriotic America

At the turn of the nineteenth century, a popular design source for schoolgirl paintings and silk embroideries was the image of "America" surrounded by numerous patriotic symbols and references to leading national figures of the day. Several schoolgirl variations of this design exist in paint or thread and can be traced to

---

1 One exception is an unsigned embroidery in the collection of the DAR Museum of "Wisdom Directing Innocence to the Temple of Virtue," backed with an 1813 Georgetown newspaper. Three others are attributed to the Young Ladies' Academy in Georgetown. In general, embroideries on silk are unsigned, so if an embroidery has lost its original frame and inscribed mat or has been separated from the family of the maker, attribution can be uncertain.

Figure 3-1. Print on glass, "America." England, 1801. Mezzotint, reverse painted glass. Published by P. Conceria. 13 ⅞ x 9 ⅞ in. Winterthur Museum, bequest of Mrs. Waldron Phoenix Belknap, 1960.0293 A

contemporary engravings available in the United States, including an 1801 mezzotint of "America" published by P. Conceria (Figure 3-1).[2]

Ann Leap

In 1801, Ann Leap stitched a silk embroidered picture featuring "America," a popular patriotic image of the new republic. Ann's "Emblem of America" includes a neoclassical figure of Columbia holding an American flag, flanked by two small Native American figures on one side and a "family tree" of portrait medallions on the other (Figure 3-2). Identified within the medallions are "Columbus," "Hancock," "Franklin," "Montgomery," "Geo Washington," "Burr," and "Jefferson." Ann's design derives from a transfer-printed image found on Liverpool pitchers made for the American market at the turn of the century.[3] Her inclusion of President Thomas Jefferson and Vice President Aaron Burr confirms the 1801 date of her work and reflects an awareness of the national interest in the contested presidential election of 1800 that was not resolved until February 17, 1801.[4]

In this composition, twelve-year-old Ann demonstrated her progress in embroidery since working an alphabet and motif sampler two years earlier (Figure 2-3). In her silk on silk embroidery Ann used a combination of cross, outline, and satin stitches with French knots. Her teacher, possibly Mrs. Cooke who

---

2 See Olive Blair Graffam, *"Youth Is the Time for Progress": The Importance of American Schoolgirl Art, 1780–1860* (Washington, D.C.: DAR Museum, 1998), 52–53, for an embroidery and painting inspired by the Conceria image. M. Finkel & Daughter advertised in *The Magazine Antiques* 176, no. 1 (January/February 2010): 94, a silk embroidered memorial to George Washington with a figure of a young woman holding a Liberty pole and facing two diminutive Native Americans with feather headdresses and weapons.

3 I am grateful to Kimberly Smith Ivey for suggesting this design source. Robert McCauley in his definitive work on transfer-printed pottery notes that around 1785, in a bid for American business, Liverpool potters began printing on creamware pitchers, bowls, etc. portraits of American heroes prominent in the struggle for independence. He describes one version of "Emblem of America" in catalogue entry #170: "To the left of her [Columbia] two stumpy black Indians with weapons. At the right are seven oval portraits entitled "Columbus, Americus (Vespucius), Sir W.

Raleigh, G. Washington, Dr. Franklin, J. Adams and one unnamed, probably Jefferson." Robert McCauley, *Liverpool Transfer Designs on Anglo-American Pottery* (Portland, Me.: The Southworth-Anthoensen Press, 1942).

4 In what is sometimes referred to as the "Revolution of 1800," Democratic-Republican Thomas Jefferson defeated the sitting Federalist president John Adams in the bitter general election. As is still the case, the election was officially decided in the Electoral College. In 1800, each elector could vote for two candidates, and the vice-president was determined by the one who received the second largest number of votes. When the electoral ballots were counted on February 11, 1801, Jefferson and his running mate Aaron Burr tied in the number of votes received and the election was thrown into the House of Representatives for a vote by members from the sixteen states. On February 17, on the thirty-sixth ballot, Jefferson received the required majority of nine votes and was elected president with Burr as his vice-president.

opened her "Embroidery School" in Alexandria in 1801, may have painted the landscape details and the "portraits."

Literary Themes
Julia Maria Hooff

Rarely are southern silk embroideries as well documented as the one stitched by Julia Maria Hooff in 1815 (Figures 3-3, 3-3a, 3-3b. There is no painted inscription on the original églomisé mat, but on the reverse of the embroidery an 1894 handwritten note names the embroiderer and credits her teacher, Sarah Eliza Edmonds, with painting the design.

> *This picture was embroidered by Julia Maria Hooff,*
> *(daughter of, Lawrence Hooff)*
> *a pupil of*
> *Sarah Eliza Edmonds*
> *who did the work*
> *in water colours.*
> *About the year*
> *One thousand eight-*
> *hundred and fifteen.*

Julia was an advanced embroidery student about seventeen years of age when she used wool, silk, and chenille thread in a combination of long and short, straight, trellis, and satin stitches to fill in her teacher's complex design. Julia's embroidery is based on the story of the ill-fated romance between Trojan hero Aeneas and Dido, queen of Carthage, from Virgil's epic poem the *Aeneid*. In this depiction Dido, surrounded by her attendants, is pleading with Aeneas not to sail with his fleet to fulfill his destiny in Italy.[5] Upon completion of the stitching, Julia's instructor, Sarah Eliza Edmonds, applied

Figure 3-2. Embroidered picture worked by Ann Leap. Alexandria, 1801. Inscribed in ink: "An Emblem of America / 1801." Silk, watercolor, and ink on silk ground. 18 ½ x 14 ¾ in.
Private collection
Image courtesy of the Colonial Williamsburg Foundation

---

5 The subject matter is not identified on the reverse of the embroidery, but when an illustration of this work was published in the February 1945 issue of *The Magazine Antiques*, it was captioned "Aeneas Bidding Farewell to Dido." To date, no print source has been found for this image. Perhaps Miss Edmonds used an illustrated copy of the *Aeneid* for reference or inspiration. Carol Huber noted that the Trojan War was a favorite text of female academies in her article, "What Were They Thinking? Silk Embroideries Give Us a Clue," *Antiques & Fine Art* 9, no.2 (Winter–Spring 2009): 245.

ALEXANDRIA PICTORIAL EMBROIDERIES AND MAPS

Figure 3-3.
Embroidered picture worked by Julia Maria Hooff. Alexandria, ca. 1815. Silk, wool, chenille, watercolor, and paper on silk ground over linen foundation. 17 ½ x 22 in.
Collection of Margaret Cheeseman
Photography by Gary Connaughton

Figure 3-3a. Detail of Hooff embroidery.

Figure 3-3b. Reverse of Hooff embroidery showing cutout in linen foundation cloth.

areas of cut paper to correspond to the heads, arms, and feet of the figures outlined on the silk and then drew their features and shaded their forms with watercolors. The sky, an expanse of unworked silk with the linen foundation cut away, also received a wash of watercolor.

Julia Maria Hooff (1798–1863) was the tenth of twelve children of Mary Ann Gretter (1760–1836) and Lawrence Hooff II (1754–1834). Julia's father was a cartwright, farmer, and operator of a slaughterhouse in the west end of Alexandria, as well as senior warden of Saint Paul's Church. In 1823, Julia married Scottish-born Benjamin L. Wallace, a merchant, in Henrico County, Virginia. By 1850, Julia was a widow and living with her daughter, Mary Ann Redfield, and family in Albany, New York, where her son-in-law was principal agent for a line of freight barges on the Hudson River.

Julia Hooff's silk embroidery is noteworthy as a rare example of southern needlework. The presence of three unusual techniques, however, adds additional interest and reveals the inventiveness or unorthodox method of the instructor. The use of applied and painted paper for faces and other figural areas, the stitching of some parts of the design in wool, and the cutting away of the linen foundation behind the section corresponding to the sky are techniques that have not been found elsewhere in combination or singularly on embroideries from the South.[6]

Three additional silk embroidered pictures can be attributed to the Alexandria area on the basis of family history, yet the identities of the embroiderers of these unsigned pieces are uncertain. All examples have a stylistic and/or technical affinity with the Hooff embroidery and were most likely worked under the direction of Julia's teacher, Sarah Eliza Edmonds, between 1810 and 1815.

Anne Campbell

The first of these embroideries may represent the parable of "Palemon and Lavinia" (Figure 3-4), a popular subject during the early decades of the nineteenth century that appears frequently on schoolgirl embroideries from Massachusetts to Virginia (see embroidery that faces the appendix).[7] Kimberly Smith Ivey notes that the story of Palemon and Lavinia, based on "Old Testament themes of unselfish devotion and human kindness over and above conventional duty and the importance of family status," was included in the "Autumn" passage of Scottish poet James Thomson's (1700–1748) widely circulated poem *The Seasons*.[8] Here, Palemon, a gentleman, recognizes that Lavinia, a gleaner in the field, is the long lost daughter of his friend Acasto.[9]

When publicly exhibited in 1956, this embroidery was attributed to Margaret Ann Potter (1820–1900) and dated circa 1835.[10]

---

6 My conclusions have been confirmed by consultation with American and southern embroidery authorities Amy Finkel, Carol Huber, Kimberly Smith Ivey, and Kathleen Staples. Mrs. Ivey has brought to my attention a needlework picture in the Colonial Williamsburg collection that was worked by Ann Culpepper of Fairfax, Virginia, in 1805 and depicts Catherine Fairfax and her servant Chloe in a composition that suggests the "Finding of Moses in the Bulrushes." She described it as "worked in the unusual combination of appliquéd wool and linen fabrics, wool embroidery threads and beads on a wool ground."

7 See Kimberly Smith Ivey, *In the Neatest Manner: The Making of the Virginia Sampler Tradition* (Austin, Tex.: Curious Works Press, 1997), 76-80, for several variations on this theme; Ring, *Girlhood Embroidery*, 439; and Patricia T. Herr, *"The Ornamental Branches": Needlework and Arts from the Lititz Moravian Girls' School* (Lancaster, Pa.: The Heritage Center Museum of Lancaster County, Pennsylvania, 1996), 24. Several students at the Moravian school also stitched compositions based on the "Finding of Moses" discussed below.

8 Ivey, *In the Neatest Manner*, 76; James Thomson, *The Seasons, with the Castle of Indolence Poems* (Philadelphia: Budd & Bartram, 1804).

9 Ring, *Girlhood Embroidery*, 439.

10 *Our Town, 1749–1865: Likenesses of This Place & Its People Taken from Life, by Artists Known and Unknown* (Alexandria, Va.: Alexandria Association, 1956), 88.

Figure 3-4. Embroidered picture attributed to Anne Campbell. Alexandria, 1810–1815. Silk, wool, chenille, watercolor, and paper on silk ground over linen foundation. 16 ½ x 15 ¼ in. Collection of Mr. and Mrs. John E. Roberts. Image courtesy of Julia M. Brennan

Figure 3-4a. Reverse of Campbell embroidery showing cutout in linen foundation cloth.

Stylistically, this piece dates much earlier and therefore may have been stitched by Margaret Ann's mother Anne Campbell some time between 1810 and 1815. Anne was born in Dundee, Scotland, July 8, 1796, to Margaret Taws (born 1781) and Daniel Campbell (born 1773), a tailor. The Campbell family emigrated to Virginia in 1805 or 1807, and by 1808 Daniel was listed on the tax rolls for Alexandria's second ward as a tailor and retailer.[11] In 1815 the Campbells moved to Washington City where Daniel leased space in the marketplace for his tailoring business. After the death of her husband, Margaret found similar employment as a seamstress and *tailoress*.[12] With both parents in the needle trades, Anne Campbell came by her embroidery skill naturally. Her use of a combination of long and short, straight, satin, and herringbone stitches shows the work of an accomplished young needlewoman, while the sophisticated design suggests the influence of a skilled teacher, most likely Sarah Eliza Edmonds. In this composition, like the embroidery worked by Julia Hooff, the faces and hands are composed of applied and painted paper. Wool has been used in foliage and ground areas. Inspection of the reverse of the embroidery reveals that the section of the linen foundation that corresponds to the painted silk sky area has been cut away, using the same technique found on Julia Hooff's embroidery (Figure 3-4a).

In 1815, Anne married John Potter (1789–1823), a silversmith apprenticed to John Adams in Alexandria. The Potters relocated

---

[11] Additional confirmation of the Campbell family in Alexandria comes from Daniel Campbell's name on the 1810 roster of the Saint Andrews Society of Alexandria. Information courtesy of descendant Jean Campbell Roberts Harris; T. Michael Miller, *Artisans and Merchants of Alexandria, Virginia*, 2:341.

[12] Margaret Campbell is listed in the Washington Directory for 1822 as "widow, tailoress, one door west of Strother's hotel."

to Norfolk where John carried on his trade and Anne gave birth to five children. With John's untimely death in 1823 and Anne's in 1825, Margaret Ann Potter, one of their two surviving daughters, returned to Alexandria to live with the family of Thomas Davy, a grocer. In 1842 she married Allen Cobb Harmon, Davy's young business partner, and the embroidery descended in their family. Over time it became attributed to Margaret instead of to her mother.[13]

Martha Bryan McKnight

The third embroidery in this group illustrates "The Finding of Moses in the Bulrushes" (Figure 3-5). As with "Palemon and Lavinia," the biblical story of the finding of baby Moses in the bulrushes was popular as a needlework pattern in female academies at the time and would have been familiar to instructors like Sarah Eliza Edmonds. The scene is described in Exodus, 2:5–6.

> *And the daughter of Pharaoh came down to wash herself at the river and her maidens walked along by the river's side, and when she saw the ark among the flags, sent her maids to fetch it, and when she had opened it she saw a child.*

This embroidery was originally attributed to Catherine (Kitty) Piercy (1780–1867), and it descended in her family.[14] Catherine was the youngest daughter of Mary Smith and Captain Christian Piercy, of the Alexandria earthenware manufacturing family. In 1799 she married John McKnight (1769–1834), a sea captain and member of the Masonic Lodge at Alexandria. On the occasion of their October marriage, the *Alexandria Gazette* described her as, "Miss Kitty Piercy, a young lady possessed of every accomplishment capable of rendering the marriage state truly happy."[15] If Catherine was the embroiderer, she stitched her composition as a young matron a number of years after her 1799 marriage. More likely, this embroidery is the work of her eldest daughter, Martha Bryan McKnight, born May 7, 1802. In the 1810 to 1815 period when Sarah Eliza Edmonds was teaching, Martha Bryan McKnight would have been between eight and thirteen years old. Martha married John Rumney, a Georgetown merchant, in 1824.

The Piercy-McKnight pictorial embroidery was formerly known only from a black-and-white illustration. Recently, it has been located and studied. When visually compared with the embroidery by Julia Maria Hooff, stylistic similarities are apparent. Leafy plants are designed and stitched in the same form, and the figure of one the maids of Pharaoh's daughter replicates the pose of Aeneas. The unusual techniques of applied paper figural

Figure 3-5. Embroidered picture attributed to Martha Bryan McKnight. Alexandria, 1810–1815. Silk, watercolor, and paper on silk ground over linen foundation. 26 x 26 in.
Collection of Richard Howard
Image courtesy of Julia M. Brennan

---

13 Margaret Ann Potter was adopted by Thomas Davy. The embroidery was owned by her granddaughter, Mary Hunt Roberts, at the time it was exhibited.

14 When this piece was exhibited in "Made in Alexandria, 1790–1860" in 1979, it was attributed to Catherine Piercy and owned by Katherine Piercy Howard.

15 *Alexandria Gazette*, November 2, 1799.

areas combined with large sections of linen removed to correspond to the watercolor sky confirm that this embroidery was worked under the tutelage of Sarah Eliza Edmonds (Figure 3-5a). Like her schoolmates, Martha McKnight used silk and some wool thread in a combination of short and long, satin, and straight stitches along with couched chenille to complete her composition.

Figure 3-5a. Reverse of McKnight embroidery showing cutout in linen foundation cloth.

Margaret Fleming

A fourth pictorial embroidery with a literary theme (Figure 3-6) descended in the family of Jonathan Edward Douglass (born 1828) and is attributed to his mother Margaret Fleming Douglass (1801–1852). Margaret Fleming was one of thirteen children and the eldest daughter of Catherine Steele (1773–1846) and Alexandria house joiner/carpenter Andrew Fleming (1759–1820). Margaret married James Douglass Jr., a merchant, on October 26, 1826.

About 1810, when Margaret was nine years old, she stitched a decorative sampler (Figure 2-8). Over time Margaret progressed in her mastery of embroidery skills, enabling her to create a challenging composition of a figure seated by a well in a landscape of ruins using surface embroidery and satin, straight, long and short stitches.[16] Stylistically and technically, Margaret's embroidery can also be attributed to the instruction of Sarah Eliza Edmonds or one of her associates. The composition, though, is not as complex as the other embroideries ascribed to her instruction, the figure is not as graceful, and the drawing is not as delicate. Nonetheless, the applied shaped pieces paper for the head, arms, and feet of the figure, and the delineation of features and shading of forms in watercolors identifies this embroidery as one from the Edmonds school. In addition, Margaret used chenille and wool to work certain areas of her silk composition—the same materials found in the other embroideries. An inspection of the reverse, however, revealed that the linen backing had not been cut away, perhaps due to the large expanse of sky or a change in the instructor's technique.[17]

Southern embroidered pictures are rare, even though a number of teachers advertised advanced instruction in "Embroidery." At present, only a few embroideries on silk have been attributed to schoolgirls in the District of Columbia. With the discovery of four embroidered pictures that are so similar in style and technique, perhaps it will be possible to assign other "anonymous" embroidered compositions with unique stylistic and technical features to Alexandria and the tutelage of Sarah Eliza Edmonds.

---

16 To date, the subject matter of this composition has not been identified. The figure is androgynous and could possibly be Rebekah at the well, the Woman of Samaria, Moses resting at the well, or Jeremiah lamenting the fall of Jerusalem. Or the composition may not represent a biblical scene.

17 The cut out foundation may have made the painted sky more luminous, but the lack of support clearly weakened the silk ground, causing it to sag over time. Perhaps Edmonds came to this conclusion.

Figure 3-6. Embroidered picture attributed to Margaret Fleming. Alexandria, 1810–1815. Silk, wool, chenille, watercolor, and paper on satin-weave silk ground over linen foundation. 16 x 14 in.
Collection of Mrs. James E. Douglass Sr.

Sarah Eliza Edmonds: Teacher of Pictorial Embroideries

Sarah Eliza Edmonds (ca. 1790–1870) was the daughter of Alexandria teachers Edmund Edmonds and the afore-mentioned Sarah Allison Edmonds (ca. 1762–1831). Although Sarah Eliza Edmonds never placed her own advertisements in local newspapers, she probably worked in association with her mother who, in 1812, advertised instruction in

Reading and English Grammar, Writing, Arithmetic, Geography, Embroidery, Fancy Work on Muslin, Cambric, & c. &c.

Drawing and Painting in [ ]ubes and Colours. The former of those branches are taught by Mrs. Edmonds; and Embroidery, Fancy Work, Drawing, &c. jointly by two young Ladies of great genius and acquirements.[18]

Sarah Eliza, about twenty-two at the time and quite likely a lady "of great genius and

---

[18] *Alexandria Daily Gazette, Commercial and Political*, December 25, 1812. For additional information on the Edmonds family, see Gloria Seaman Allen, "Pictorial Embroideries from Antebellum Alexandria," *Sampler & Antique Needlework Quarterly* 17, no. 3 (2011): 40–47.

acquirements," is identified separately from her mother Sarah in estate and property matters. In 1821, the Edmonds family—Edmund, Sarah, and daughter Sarah Eliza—each received a sizable legacy of Alexandria real estate from Captain John Turnpin Brooks, with whom the family had had a long friendship.[19] Even with their expanded quarters and income from their newly acquired rental properties, the Edmonds family continued to teach.[20] In 1827, Sarah Eliza and her widowed mother moved to the Philadelphia area. There Sarah Edmonds, "full of years and Christian grace," conducted a school until her death in 1831.[21] Her daughter Sarah Eliza, teaching on her own, attracted boarding students to her Philadelphia seminary up to and during the 1840s.

EMBROIDERED MAPS

Embroidered maps are another form of silk on silk girlhood embroidery. Although embroidered maps are rare, those that can be attributed to students in the District of Columbia all appear to have an Alexandria provenance.[22] Three elaborate embroidered and painted maps were worked in the first years of the nineteenth century and all are entitled "Plan of the City of Washington." Although Alexandria was then part of the District of Columbia, the design for these embroidered maps includes only the proposed layout of the new federal city and the established community of Georgetown. Alexandria, located several miles down the Potomac River, is not represented on the "Plan for the City of Washington" or its embroidered copies. Of the three embroidered maps, only one is signed, but it is this embroiderer's close ties to Alexandria that help to document the origin of all three known examples.

Printed Maps as Design Sources

In 1791, George Washington commissioned Andrew Ellicott (1754–1820), surveyor and mathematician, to survey the bounds of the ten-mile-square, diamond-shaped tract at the confluence of the Potomac River and the Eastern Branch (Anacostia River) that Congress had authorized as the future site of the federal government. Ellicott was assisted by Benjamin Banneker (1731–1806), a free black man and self-taught astronomer who maintained notes and used celestial calculations to establish base points. Within

---

19 Alexandria, *Will Book*, May 9, 1815–January. 30, 1821. Edmonds and Brooks shared a house in 1806 and Brooks, a mariner who did not have other heirs, may have looked upon the Edmonds as family and Sarah Eliza as a "daughter" he never had.

20 Sarah Edmonds moved her school from 202 Prince Street to another, presumably more spacious, location in 1821. She probably took over one of the buildings inherited earlier that year from Captain Brooks.

21 Obituary, *Alexandria Gazette*, December 23, 1831.

22 Two additional maps from the general region have a more tentative connection with the town of Alexandria, but it is unknown where they were created. Miss H. Potts stitched a silk on linen map of "The State of Maryland" in 1799. Ring, *Girlhood Embroidery*, 503, figure 560. She included the place name of Alexandria beneath her name in a circular cartouche. With only her first initial given, she cannot be positively identified, but stylistically her unembellished map relates to others worked around 1800 in Baltimore, where she may have been a boarding student. Embroidered maps of the state of Maryland were stitched under the direction of at least two teachers in Baltimore between 1797 and the early 1800s. One, stitched in 1816 and possibly in Talbot County, Maryland, relates closely to the earlier examples. Allen, *A Maryland Sampling*, 283–92. A silk on linen map of Virginia worked in 1809 by Helen E. Edmonds (died 1826) of Fauquier County, Virginia, also may have an Alexandria connection. With few select schools for females in rural northern Virginia to choose from, Helen conceivably attended school in Alexandria as a boarding student. A relationship between her parents Captain Elias and Helen M. Edmonds and teachers Edmund and Sarah Edmonds seems unlikely. (The family of the map embroiderer had ancestral Virginia ties, whereas teacher Edmund Edmonds came to Alexandria from Philadelphia in 1785.)

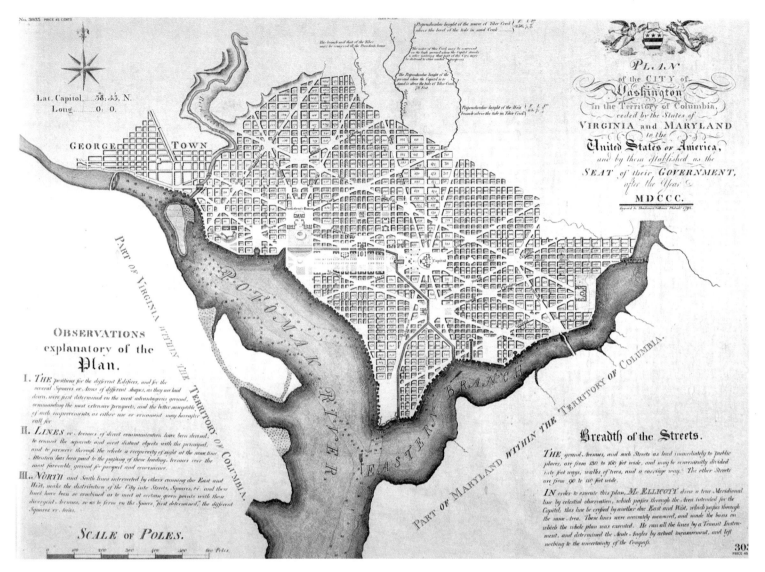

the one-hundred-square-mile area that would be the Territory of Columbia, a small central section of mostly undeveloped land was designated as the federal city and soon known as the City of Washington. Also in 1791, President Washington granted to Pierre (Peter) Charles L'Enfant (1754–1825), a French-born artist and architect who had served with him as military engineer during the Revolutionary War, the commission to design the new city. L'Enfant envisioned a Baroque plan with broad vistas and ceremonial spaces. Taking advantage of the uneven topography, he sited the President's House and the Capitol on elevated land with broad tree-lined avenues radiating outward from the two centers of government. Lesser streets created a grid and left open spaces for parks and monuments.

When Major L'Enfant was dismissed in February 1792 for insubordination and failure to complete his plan in a timely manner, Ellicott took over the project. He made several changes to L'Enfant's plan and produced a map ready for the engravers. Two renderings of the plan were published immediately—one by Samuel Hill in Boston and another by James Thackara and John Vallance in Philadelphia. Thackara and Vallance's second engraving, larger in size and published in November 1792 with street names and lot numbers, became the official plan for the City of Washington and the map used by the government and property speculators (Figure 3-7). Additional adaptations of Ellicott's plan, with changes in the text and location of the title, were

Figure 3-7. Map, "Plan of the City of Washington." Philadelphia, 1792. Engraved and published by James Thackara and John Vallance. Ink on paper. 20 ⅞ x 28 in.

ABOVE: Figure 3-8. Handkerchief, "Plan of the City of Washington," based on Thackara and Vallance map. Attributed United States, 1800–1810. Marked "R. W. G." Ink on cotton. 22 x 24 in. Winterthur Museum, gift of Henry Francis du Pont, 1959.981

published as sheets or in atlases in America and Europe within the decade. Replicas of the plan printed on textiles and ceramics soon found their way into the popular culture (Figure 3-8).

A 1795 map, engraved by William Rollinson and published by John Reid in New York City, closely follows the format of the large Thackara and Vallance plan, while adding "Remarks" on the elevation of various locations and omitting explanatory "Observations" and text on the "Breadth of the Streets." Minor changes include the writing of the plan date in Arabic numbers, 1800, and not MDCCC, and the spelling of the Potomac River as "Potomack" instead of the now equally incorrect "Potomak" (Figure 3-9). These details aid in the determination of the design source for the three embroidered examples of the "Plan of the City of Washington."

Figure 3-9. Map, "Plan of the City of Washington." New York, 1795. Engraved by William Rollinson and published by John Reid. Ink on paper. 16 x 19 ½ in. Winterthur Museum, Museum Purchase, 1974.215

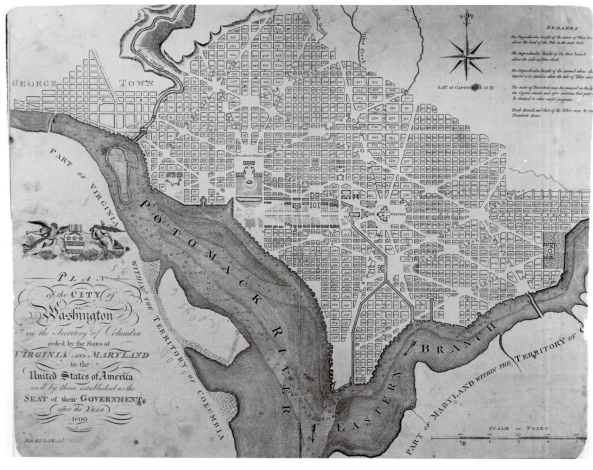

The Maps
Eve Resler

Eve Resler (ca. 1786–1813) of Alexandria marked her name in the lower right corner of a decorative map that was stitched and painted on a silk ground (Figure 3-10). Although Eve's embroidered map is not dated, it was created after George Washington's death in December 1799 (as this date is stitched on the embroidery) and before Eve's marriage in April 1804.[23] Kimberly Smith Ivey, Associate Curator, Textiles & Historic Interiors at Colonial Williamsburg, described Eve's embroidered "Plan of the City of Washington" as "a tour de force of American iconography" and "among the most ambitious of Federal America." Ivey goes on to explain:

> In addition to a detailed map of the city of Washington worked in meticulous backstitches, it features the allegorical figures of "Hope," "La Liberty," and "Justice" at the top. In the bottom left corner is an embroidered and painted portrait bust of George Washington with a tribute to the general and first president.[24]

Eve Resler's embroidered map closely follows the map published by John Reid of New York in 1795. Eve used a combination of black silk backstitches and blue, green, and gold satin stitches to delineate city blocks and name principal buildings, streets, and waterways such as the "Potomack River" and "Eastern Branch." The streets of the adjacent settlement of Georgetown are indicated.[25] The distinctive flourishes and words of the lengthy title "Plan of the City of Washington in the Territory of Columbia ceded by the States of VIRGINIA AND MARYLAND to the United States of America and by them established as the SEAT of their GOVERNMENT after the YEAR 1800" copy the Reid map and are worked entirely in stitches. Eve included other features of the Reid map—an embroidered compass rose, "Scale of Poles," "Lat. of Capitol 38 53 N," and small painted figures of "Fame" and "Liberty" flanking the Washington armorial shield. The map includes Reid's printed "Remarks" on elevations, rendered in ink on the silk ground and now barely visible.

Eve, or her instructor, beautifully embellished her map with a painted swag of roses connecting three oval cartouches with painted and embroidered allegorical figures of

Figure 3-10. Embroidered map worked by Eve Resler. Alexandria, 1800–1804. Inscribed: "Plan of the City of Washington." Silk embroidery threads, watercolor, and ink on silk ground over linen foundation. 19 1/8 x 26 1/4 in. The Colonial Williamsburg Foundation, purchased with partial gift funds from Christy Bennett, Dr. and Mrs. Thomas L. Isaac, and Jeannine's Sampler Seminar, 2006-26.

---

23 The 1800 date on the map, copied from a 1795 engraving, signifies the year of the relocation of the federal government from Philadelphia to the District of Columbia.

24 Colonial Williamsburg Foundation label text for object 2006-26, courtesy of Kimberly Smith Ivey.

25 Since the "Plan of the City of Washington" did not encompass the whole of the ten-mile-square District of Columbia, the embroidered map did not include Alexandria, Eve Resler's hometown, which was some distance south along the Potomac River.

Figure 3-11. Embroidered map attributed to Elizabeth Graham. Alexandria, 1800–1803. Inscribed: "Plan of the City of Washington." Silk embroidery threads, watercolor, and pencil on silk ground over linen foundation. 19 x 28 in. Winterthur Museum, gift of Ruth McClaine and family, 2008.57

"Hope" with an anchor, "La Liberty" with pole and liberty cap, and "Justice" with scales and sword.[26] The painted and embroidered portrait bust of George Washington in a cartouche at the lower left is surmounted by two painted cherubs and inscribed in stitches, "GEORGE WASHINGTON First President of the United States and late LIEUTENANT GENERAL of the American Armies Died at Mount Vernon 14th Dec. 1799 Aged 68 Years."[27]

Eve Resler was the daughter of Mary Stanton (died 1827) and Jacob Resler (died 1803), a tallow-chandler and "old and respectable inhabitant" of Alexandria.[28] After her husband's death in 1803, Mary Resler took over his soap manufacturing business on Prince Street.[29] On April 28, 1804, Eve, with her mother's consent, married James Galt (1779–1847),[30] a clock and watchmaker who later moved his business to Washington City.[31] Eve and James Galt had four children before her

---

26 Davida Deutsch has identified the source for the "Justice" image as a 1797 engraving by Thomas Clark of Philadelphia. Sources for the other figures have not been identified.

27 The image of George Washington is based on a stipple engraving by Benjamin Tanner (1775–1848) of New York.

28 The Reslers were married in New York in 1782 and lived below Wall Street, where Jacob initially carried out his trade as a tallow-chandler.

29 By the time of her death in 1827, widow Mary Resler was a successful business woman. She occupied a two-story brick dwelling and owned extensive property along Prince Street.

30 No birth date for Eve has been discovered, but the marriage bond for James Galt and Eve Resler, issued April 28, 1804, states "Mother Mary Resler consents" and indicates that Eve was not yet twenty-one. Alexandria County, District of Columbia Marriage Bonds 1801–1822 and Minister's Returns (DAR GRC VA S1 V70), 16. Parental or guardian consent was required for a child under age twenty-one to marry in Virginia. Samuel Shepherd, *The Statutes at Large of Virginia, from October Session 1792, to December Session 1806, Inclusive*, 1:130–36.

31 James Galt's Washington shop, known as Galt & Bro. and by variations of that name, became a fashionable jewelry store that continued in business until 2001.

death "after a short illness," probably from the complications of childbirth, on July 17, 1813. Her funeral took place at the family dwelling on Prince Street. Alexandria craftsman John Muir provided a mahogany coffin and hearse services, indicators of the wealth and elevated status of the Resler-Galt family.[32]

Elizabeth Graham

The girl who stitched a related decorative "Plan of the City of Washington" did not stitch her name or otherwise identify herself (Figure 3-11). Her embroidered map is based on the printed map published by Thackara and Vallance in November 1792. The embroiderer stitched in black silk the city plan naming principal avenues, the President's House, the Capitol, and the waterways. Like Eve Resler, she used satin stitches in blues and gold to fill in the rivers and tiny cross stitches to mark the Virginia shoreline. Her spelling of the "Potomak" River further identifies the Thackara and Vallance map as her source. Like Resler, she stitched the title text for the plan and the text for the portrait medallion of George Washington, using shades of blue silk instead of black. The stitched flourishes and date "MDCCC" also correspond to the Thackara and Vallance map. In addition to the other small stitched details found on Resler's map, this young embroiderer replicated in stitches two lengthy blocks of text from the Thackara and Vallance map that were engraved in flowing cursive—"OBSERVATIONS Explanatory of the Plan" and "Breadth of the Streets"—feats of extraordinary needlework skill and patience.

Following the same design concept as Resler, the map is further embellished with embroidered and painted oval cartouches of

Figure 3-11a. Detail of embroidered map attributed to Elizabeth Graham.

George Washington, Justice, Hope, and Liberty (Figure 3-11a). Rather than a garland of roses as a connecting element, the artist adorned each cartouche with painted sprays of flowers or vines of fruit and flowers. Even the embroidered compass rose is enhanced with painted floral decoration.

This needlework descended in a well-documented Maryland family and was probably stitched by Elizabeth Graham (1790–1870), a daughter of Mary Mollen and David Graham (ca. 1758–1803), a merchant in Alexandria.[33] The Grahams had emigrated from Scotland via Ireland to Alexandria some time prior to 1790. Unfortunately, both parents died during the yellow fever outbreak of 1803.[34] After David succumbed on October 7, Mary, possibly in an attempt to escape the fever, took their four children to the City of Washington where she died five days later. Her obituary noted sadly, "They were amiable in their lives, and in their death they were not far divided." The poignant eulogy that followed identified their older daughter Elizabeth as "Eliza."

---

32 Muir Family, Account Books 1807–1888, # 35788, Business Records Collection, Library of Virginia, Richmond.

33 I am grateful to Susi Slocum for tracking the Graham family from Scotland to Alexandria and then Elizabeth to Washington and Baltimore.

34 Outbreaks of yellow fever periodically decimated the coastal towns in the 1790s and early 1800s. Yellow fever, a viral hemorrhagic disease, was carried by mosquitoes and usually flourished after a hot, damp summer. It killed its victims within a few days.

Figure 3-12. Embroidered map attributed to Maria Magdalene Lemoine. Alexandria, 1800–1804. Inscribed: "Plan of the City of Washington." Silk embroidery threads, watercolor, and pencil on silk ground over linen foundation. 19 3/8 x 32 9/16 in. Dumbarton House, The National Society of The Colonial Dames of America, Washington, D.C., 2010.008.0001

Death came! beside her pillow took his stand,
Laid on her fainting form his icy hand;
Nor tarried he, but cut the thread of life,
To take the husband was to take the wife.
Her lovely children, wild with deepest grief,
Whate'er their efforts, yielded no relief;
Tho' live, my mother, live! her WILLIAM cri'd,
For who have we now left alas beside!
Her younger son, her darling daughter too,
Did, all in vain, her cheeks with tears bedew;
Nor could the fair ELIZA's circling arm,
Nor the feeling friends ward off the dire alarm.[35]

If Elizabeth was the map's embroiderer, she probably stitched this magnificent work in Alexandria at about twelve or thirteen years of age, prior to her parents' deaths in 1803 and before relocating to Baltimore to live with her uncle Hamilton Graham.[36] Because some of the map's details remain penciled in but unstitched, it is possible that Elizabeth's efforts to complete the map were interrupted by the death of her parents. This may also explain the lack of a signature.

In 1810, Elizabeth married William Rosensteel at Saint John's Church in Baltimore and remained in Baltimore the rest of her life. According to the 1860 census for Baltimore, the widowed Elizabeth (age sixty-four) was living with her daughter Ann and Ann's husband, Edward A. Wells. Also in the household were four of the Wells's children, including their oldest daughter Elizabeth G. Fowler (presumably Elizabeth Graham's namesake), her husband Edwin C. Fowler, and their eight-month-old daughter Alice. This spectacular embroidered map, now attributed to Elizabeth Graham, came to the Winterthur Museum as a gift from Fowler descendants.

---

35 *Alexandria Daily Advertiser*, October 17, 1803. Jacob Resler, Eve Resler's father, and the Grahams died during the same month and presumably from the same prevailing fever that took the lives of two hundred Alexandria residents in 1803.

36 Colonial Dames of America, *Ancestral Records and Portraits*, vol. 2 (New York: Grafton Press, 1910), 486–87. See page 279 in Allen, *A Maryland Sampling* for a silk memorial to George Washington stitched by Mary Graham, daughter of Hamilton Graham of Baltimore.

64   COLUMBIA'S DAUGHTERS

Maria Magdalene Lemoine

A second unsigned embroidered plan for Washington City has recently become known. This delicate embroidered map with its vibrant colors is based on the same design source as the map attributed above to Elizabeth Graham, Thackara and Vallance's November 1792 plan (Figure 3-12). Somewhat less ambitious, the anonymous embroiderer did not stitch all of the tiny tedious words of the texts (e.g., "Observations Explanatory of the Plan" and the "Breadth of the Streets") but did include all of the other features. Like the other two embroidered maps, this example has painted decoration in the form of neo-classical swags and tassels that connect the three oval medallions of Justice, Liberty, and Hope. The same portrait of Washington is embellished with painted flowers and leaves and surmounted by a pair of oddly drawn angels. Beneath the compass rose the painted figures of Fame and Liberty flank the Washington armorial shield. The layout of streets, their names, and the names of landmarks are clearly delineated in tiny stitches (Figure 3-12a).

This colorful embroidered map descended in the Lemoine/Estave/Spotswood family of Virginia and has been attributed to Maria Magdalene Lemoine (1792–1870). Maria was born in Georgetown, the daughter of Jean Marie Lemoine (Le Moyne) (ca. 1770–1802) and Susanna Margurite Estave (ca. 1771–1859). The Lemoine family moved to Alexandria around 1793, where Maria's father and grandfather, Andrew Estave, conducted various business ventures separately or together as merchant, saddler and harness maker, baker, and broker for real estate and imported goods that included fish, whiskey, wine, sugar, and shoes.[37]

Jean Lemoine experienced ill health and business difficulties and eventually was forced to place all his assets as security against his debts. When his health deteriorated further, he traveled to Cuba with the hope of finding a cure. He died there in 1802, and his estate was settled over the next several years by his widow Susanna, who had remained with her two children in Alexandria. The Lemoine family moved to Petersburg, Virginia, in 1808. By 1860 Maria, age sixty-eight and unmarried, was living in a fine house owned by her brother John, a wealthy Petersburg merchant, along with his wife and some of their children and grandchildren.[38] Maria died in Petersburg in February 1870, having reached the age of seventy-eight.[39]

Figure 3-12a. Detail of embroidered map attributed to Maria Magdalene Lemoine.

---

[37] T. Michael Miller, *Artisans and Merchants*, 1:128, 272, 273.

[38] 1860 census records for Petersburg, Virginia, listed John E. Lemoine (age 62) as head of a household that included his wife Mary (age 59), their sons Paul E. (age 29) and William H. (age 39), William's wife Mary C. and their children Madeline, John, Charlotte, and Edmund. John's estate was valued at $25,000 and his personal estate at $35,000.

[39] United States Federal Mortality Census Schedules, 1850–1880 (formerly in the custody of the Daughters of the American Revolution), and Related Indexes, 1850–1880, T655, 30 rolls. National Archives and Records Administration, Washington D.C. I am grateful to Christopher Jones for sharing the Lemoine family history with me.

Teachers of Embroidered Maps

Identifying the teacher or teachers responsible for providing instruction on embroidered maps to Alexandria's young women has proven to be difficult. Although the known examples are based on different published engravings of the "Plan of the City of Washington" and are decorated with different painted details, there is sufficient similarity in subject matter, type of stitching, and general style of painted decoration to conclude that the three known maps were embroidered under the direction of the same instructor or at the same school. Assuming all three embroideries were created about the same time—between 1800 and 1804—a clue to the teacher's identity may come from information about who was teaching geography through the use of embroidered maps during this period.

The subject of geography was gradually added to the curricula of select female academies in the District of Columbia over a period of years. Although most of the larger schools offered geography, history, and one or more sciences from the middle of the first decade of the nineteenth century, the Reverend Doctor James Muir of Alexandria had proposed as early as 1790 to open an academy where "the cultivation of the mind is immediately in view." His female curriculum was progressive for its time and included "Grammar and Composition; Reading and Writing; Geography and Arithmetic; History, and the easier principles of Moral Philosophy, and Astronomy."[40] Muir and other teachers may have provided their students with more than textbooks as learning aids, but no one in the area advertised teaching "Geography with the use of Globes and Maps" until a Mrs. Hagarty did so in 1828.[41]

Of the more than 240 individual teachers or schools in the District of Columbia that promoted needlework instruction in local newspapers between 1790 and 1860, only three referred to "Working Maps." All three were located in the town of Alexandria, but only Mrs. O'Reilly, advertised in the early 1800s that she would teach in her Young Ladies' Boarding and Day School "maps wrought in silks, chenilles, gold, &c." She also indicated that her students could work embroideries that included figural and historical subjects.[42] Although Mrs. O'Reilly advertised teaching map embroidery in Alexandria in late 1804, it is not certain that O'Reilly's school lasted for more than a few months, if it opened at all.[43] She publicized a similar curriculum in November 1805 for a new school in Richmond, Virginia.[44]

Although two other Alexandria teachers advertised instruction in the making of embroidered maps, their earliest advertisements were published several years later than the estimated dates for known examples illustrating the "Plan of the City of Washington." One of these teachers was Maria Anne Dunlap, who in 1810 placed a single advertisement in the *Alexandria Daily Gazette* claiming that "having been engaged in the tuition of youth for some years past" she would open a school for young ladies and offer academic and ornamental subjects that included "Working Maps."[45] The other teacher was Mrs. Edmund

---

40 *Virginia Gazette and Alexandria Advertiser,* August 5, 1790.

41 *Alexandria Gazette,* August 13, 1828.

42 *Alexandria Advertiser and Commercial Intelligencer,* November 20, 1804.

43 It should be noted that O'Reilly's proposed school opening in November 1804 postdates Eve Resler's marriage and Elizabeth Graham's departure from Alexandria.

44 Richmond, *Virginia Gazette and General Advertiser,* November 20, 1805.

45 *Alexandria Daily Gazette,* October 2, 1810.

Edmonds, who in the same year opened a female school that continued in operation beyond 1823.[46] Her 1810 advertisement, in language similar to that of Mrs. O'Reilly's, indicated that she and her assistants would teach "maps wrought in do [ditto, meaning chenilles, gold, silver, and silks]." She also mentioned instruction in "Drawing, Painting in inks and colors, on satin, tiffany &c. &c.," components of the highly decorative embroidered maps known to exist.[47]

Other teachers in Alexandria provided advanced embroidery instruction, but lessons in map embroidery, if offered, were not publicized.[48] One of these was Mrs. Cooke, who opened her "Embroidery School" in Alexandria in 1801 and aimed to attract "those young ladies who having attained other branches of education" wished to study more advanced or fancy needlework. She further stated that she had on hand from London "a well chosen supply of Silks, Chineals [sic], &c." and would "afford every assistance necessary to her pupils."[49] Mrs. Cooke continued to teach until 1803 and possibly later. According to her advertisements, Cooke changed her teaching location in 1803. In April she was located near the corner of Prince and Washington Streets and in August she was at Mr. Geiger's on Royal Street. Her locations suggest connections with Eve Resler's family. The Reslers owned property on Washington Street near Prince Street, as well as on Royal Street. Jacob Geiger, owner of the property on Royal Street that Mrs. Cooke used for her schoolroom, was named in Jacob Resler's estate and presumably was a close friend. These connections suggest the possibility that Mrs. Cooke was Eve's teacher and therefore the teacher responsible for all three embroidered maps.

Though the identity of the teacher responsible for these three embroidered and painted examples of the "Plan of the City of Washington" is uncertain, their existence attests to the high style of embroidery instruction available to the daughters of Alexandria's merchant class. In combination with the stunning pictorial embroideries attributed to the students of Sarah Eliza Edmunds, it is clear that Alexandria produced some of the most extraordinary examples of girlhood needlework from the American Federal period.

---

46 If Mrs. Edmund Edmonds taught needlework before 1810 in Alexandria where her husband had begun teaching in 1785, she cannot be eliminated as the teacher responsible for the embroideries of the "Plan of the City of Washington." With her first advertisement placed in 1810, there is no way of knowing her activities prior to that time. See Allen, "Pictorial Embroideries from Antebellum Alexandria."

47 *Alexandria Daily Gazette*, March 6, 1810.

48 For example, Mary A. Tyson and her sisters taught in Baltimore, Washington City, and Prince George's County, Maryland, during the 1840s and 1850s. They advertised worsted and ornamental needlework but did not mention working maps. However, Mary M. Bryant identified the Tysons' Washington City school when she stitched a "Map of Asia" there in 1848 (See Figure 11-5).

49 *Alexandria Gazette*, November 8, 1801.

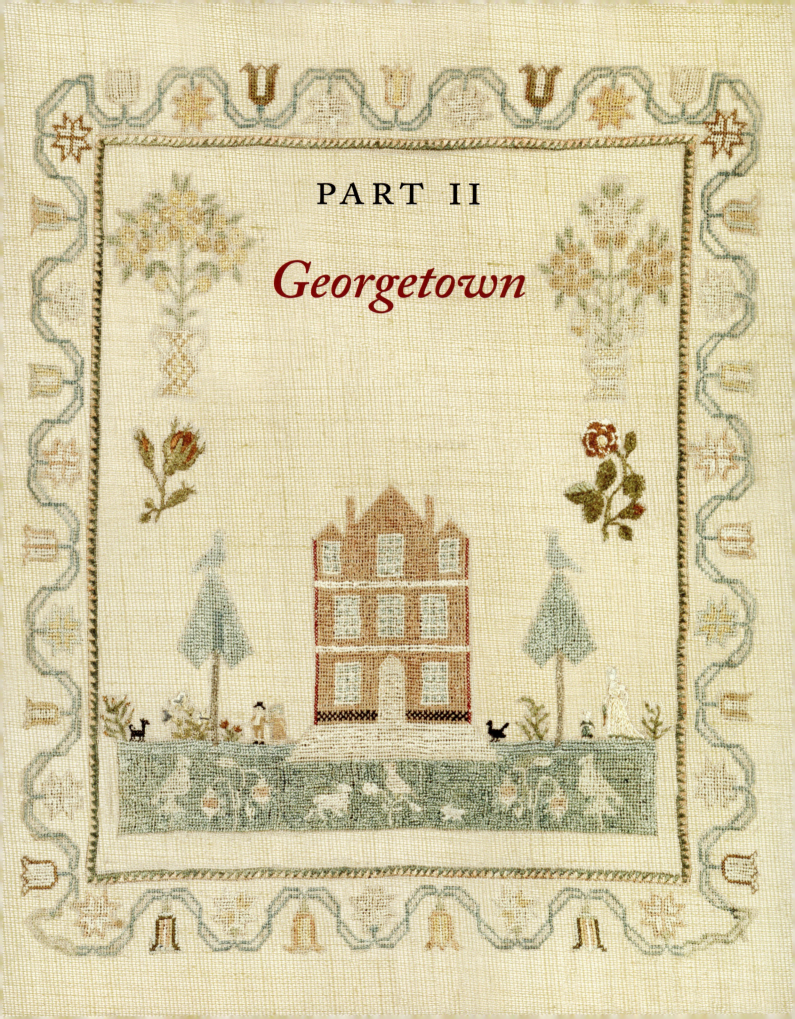

PART II

Georgetown

Figures 4-1 and 4-1a.
"The Benjamin Stoddert Children" painted by Charles Willson Peale. Georgetown, 1789.
Oil on canvas.
40 x 52 in.
Dumbarton House, The National Society of The Colonial Dames of America, Washington, D.C., DH36.50

This detail is the earliest known image of the port of Georgetown and may show the location of Benjamin Stoddert's tobacco export business. Stoddert became the first U. S. Secretary of the Navy.

CHAPTER 4

Introduction to Georgetown and Its Teachers

Before there was a town, a tobacco market developed along the Maryland side of the Potomac River at a point just below the rapids and above where the river connects with the Eastern Branch and widens as it flows into the Chesapeake Bay. A ferry crossing facilitated access from Virginia, and the creation of a tobacco inspection house near the fall line of the Potomac attracted trade and settlers. In 1751, the Maryland Assembly voted to establish a new town on sixty acres of what was then part of Frederick County, and in 1789 the port of Georgetown was incorporated (Figure 4-1a).[1]

While tobacco commerce occupied the busy wharves along the river, houses rose on the highlands overlooking the water. Upper Georgetown had the advantage of being cooler and dryer in the summertime and more sanitary during the rest of the year. Waste from dwellings was carried off by the many streams that drained into the Potomac. When choosing a location for the higher education of young men in the 1780s, Jesuits noted in the prospectus circulated for their new college that "Salubrity of Air, Convenience of Communication, and Cheapness of Living have been principally consulted, and George Town offers these united advantages."[2]

In 1791, Georgetown had a population of about three thousand and was included in the ten-mile-square area selected by George Washington as the new site for the seat of the federal government. By that time Georgetown was an established trading and business center, a crossing point for north-south travel, and a gateway to the Ohio River and western

---

[1] Georgetown was spelled as one or two words or hyphenated until 1871 when Congress enacted the Territorial Act, abolished the Corporation of Georgetown, and created a new territorial government for the entire District. The spelling was then standardized, and not long after, Georgetown street names, in use since 1751, were changed to conform to those of Washington City.

[2] Georgetown University, originally a college with preparatory and elementary schools, dates its founding to 1789. Eleanore C. Sullivan, *Georgetown Visitation Since 1799*, 2nd ed., revised and expanded by Susan Hannan (Washington, D.C.: Georgetown Visitation Monastery, 2004), 31.

Figure 4-2. "View of Georgetown D. C." ca. 1855. Color lithograph published by E. Sachse & Company, Baltimore. 18 ½ x 26 ¾ in. Library of Congress, Prints & Photographs Division

lands. The town had a large number of substantial brick houses, well-equipped inns, and fashionable shops, and it offered amenities not yet available to transients and permanent residents in the newly laid-out Washington City, just across Rock Creek. Writing in 1793, New York jurist James Kent described Georgetown as:

> a pleasant Village situated on the waving Hills on the N. Side of the Potomack. . . . the Hills on the back of the Town which are improved & improving with handsome Country seats . . . command a noble view of the Town, of the City of Washington & of the Potomack quite down to Alexandria. . . . The Houses are exceedingly well built of Brick. The Town may contain between 30 & 40 very good brick Buildings.[3]

In 1824, Anne Royall, Baltimore native and commentator on American society, also found much to admire about Georgetown, now with a population of more than 7,400 and expanding as a coastal trans-shipment center (Figure 4-2).

> *Georgetown has a romantic appearance, being built mostly on hills. It rises up from the water's edge and spreads out in all directions. The streets, which are few and narrow, are paved with stone.*[4]
>
> *The people of Georgetown are polite and hospitable; they form a striking contrast to their neighbours of Washington, their minds being more generally cultivated. It is hardly possible to conceive, how towns so near each other, should differ so widely as they do.*[5]

EDUCATIONAL OPPORTUNITIES IN GEORGETOWN

Education, or cultivation of the mind, had always been an important aspect of life in Georgetown. In 1789 the Jesuits opened the doors of Georgetown College to young Christian men, Catholic and Protestant alike. For pupils at the preparatory levels, local newspapers detailed the professional qualifications of instructors and the curricula available to day and boarding students of both genders. Schools that offered instruction to young ladies focused on the basics of reading, writing, arithmetic, English grammar, and geography, as well as the more genteel accomplishments of speaking a foreign language, playing a

---

3 Quoted in The Junior League of Washington, *The City of Washington: An Illustrated History*, edited by Thomas Froncek (New York: Alfred A. Knopf, 1977), 37.

4 Anne Royall, *Sketches of History, Life, and Manners, in the United States* (New Haven: printed for the author, 1826), 178.

5 Ibid., 181–82.

musical instrument, or acquiring the skills necessary to complete domestic sewing projects or create specimens of ornamental needlework.

Two Georgetown schools are well known for their education of young women over a period of many years. The earliest was the Young Ladies' Academy of Georgetown, now known as Georgetown Visitation. The school was designed to attract affluent young women of the Roman Catholic faith and has been in continuous operation since 1799. From the beginning, and through the nineteenth century, the school offered needlework instruction. A number of needlework samplers and pictorial embroideries survive that either name this school or are closely associated with girls known to have been students at the school. Chapter 6 provides a detailed history of the school, its teachers, and the needlework accomplished by its students.

The other school for young ladies was founded by Lydia Scudder English in 1826. Known as the Female Seminary, the school appealed to affluent families of all religious affiliations and flourished as a large boarding and day school under Lydia English's direction until 1852. Although students at the Female Seminary did not stitch the school's name on their samplers, several can be assigned to the seminary on the basis of student lists. Chapter 5 provides a more detailed look at the Georgetown Female Seminary, its teachers, students, and needlework instruction.

Educational opportunities also existed for children whose parents were unable to pay for private instruction. In November 1811, Georgetown opened a Lancasterian School in order to meet the educational needs of children from the city's less affluent families. Georgetown was experiencing an influx of European immigrants, free blacks, and transients seeking jobs in the newly established federal district. Education and other social services for these and other poor families existed primarily through private and church sponsorship.

Georgetown's Lancasterian School was founded at the initiative of a group of Georgetown gentlemen who requested that a teacher be sent to open a Lancastrian school in their city.[6] Joseph Lancaster (1778–1838), founder of the Lancasterian system in England, sent a former pupil, Robert Ould, to direct the Georgetown school. In a letter to John Laird, one of the trustees, Lancaster wrote,

> *Considering the situation of Georgetown, its increasing prosperity and proximity to Washington and the circumstance of your having the first school-master from me that has been sent to America, . . . you have in Robert Ould, a young man who has the [Lancasterian] plan and love of it in the very grain of his habit.*[7]

The Georgetown Lancasterian School initially intended to enroll a total of 350 male and female students in a thirty-two-by-seventy-foot building built to Lancaster's specifications on land conveyed by Bishop Leonard Neale, former president of Georgetown College, for "the purpose of carrying on a public system of education."[8] It soon became apparent, though, by "the throng daily

---

6   Two of the gentlemen were David English and Samuel Bootes, fathers of young women who would later open female schools in Georgetown, Lydia English's Female Seminary in 1826 and Miss Bootes' Female Academy in 1834. Samuel Yorke Atlee, *History of the Public Schools of the City of Georgetown* (Georgetown, D.C.: Board of Trustees, for the National Centennial Year, 1876), 2.

7   Joseph Lancaster, *The British System of Education: being a complete epitome . . .* (Washington: Joseph Milligan, 1812), 129.

8   Atlee, *History of the Public Schools*, 25.

seeking admission," that an addition was needed to accommodate the female scholars and to discourage "an intercourse of sexes in an assemblage so large and so promiscuous."[9]

In 1814, Margaret Judge, a well-schooled Quaker, took over operation of the female division, shortly after her sister Rachel became the first teacher of the Female Lancasterian School in Alexandria.[10] Advertisements for the Georgetown school indicate that Margaret Judge stressed practical needlework in her curriculum.

> *The school for girls, under the direction of Miss Judge, which has been equally well conducted, consists of 169 scholars, 100 of whom entered within the last year, and 12 have been qualified and left the school. In addition to the customary instruction in this school, useful needle-work has been advantageously taught, and the manufacture of yarn shawls has been introduced as an interesting amusement, that may prove a beneficial employment hereafter, to those who may leave the school.*[11]

In Europe, social services for the poor and destitute were traditionally provided by religious groups. This practice continued in the United States as the Roman Catholic Church recognized new orders and encouraged the opening of schools and asylums. The sisters of the Georgetown monastery, later members of the Visitation Order, operated a Benevolent School for poor girls next to, but separate from, their Young Ladies' Academy on Fayette Street.[12] Little is known about the early years of this school, but correspondence from the monastery dated 1817 indicates that by then the school served, without charge, orphans and children from local families in need.[13] By 1819, at the time a new building had been completed, the school consisted of "about a hundred little girls of the poorer classes [who were being] taught all that is suitable for their condition."[14]

A possibly inflated description in the city directory for 1830 noted that: "A benevolent school is attended by the Sisters where they educate gratuitously three to four hundred females annually, clothe sixty or seventy and afford a subsistence to thirty or forty daily."[15] While it can be documented that the sisters made clothing for the students in the poor school, and one or more sisters taught mantua-making to paying students in the academy, it is presumed that the girls in the poor school also acquired some degree of sewing skills "sufficient for honest Industry" or for gaining employment as dressmakers.[16] Although no needlework is known from the Benevolent School, later called Saint Joseph's, it is assumed that the school followed the practice in other Catholic benevolent schools where students worked alphabet samplers with pious verses while practicing their stitches.[17]

There are relatively few records documenting educational opportunities for African

---

9   Richard P. Jackson, *The Chronicles of Georgetown, D.C. from 1751 to 1878* (Washington: R. O. Polkinhorn, printer, 1878), 245–46. Another source gives enrollment of the Georgetown school between November 1811 and November 1812 as 337 male and 149 female children. "Proceedings of the Royal Lancasterian Institution," *The Scots Magazine and Edinburgh Miscellany*, vol. 75, part 2, 681.

10 The experiences of the co-ed Georgetown school led to the opening a few months later of separate male and female Lancasterian schools in Alexandria. The Georgetown school was maintained by private contribution until 1815. From then on the Georgetown Corporation provided $1,000 annually until the school closed in 1842. Harvey W. Crew, William B. Webb, and John Wooldridge, *Centennial History of the City of Washington D.C.* (Dayton, Ohio: United Brethren Publishing House, 1892), 51.

11 Georgetown, *Federal Republican*, February 16, 1814.

12 Jonathan Elliot, who published his observations in 1830, noted the physical arrangement between the two institutions: "Within the nunnery enclosure, but detached from the academy and approached from a different street, there are upwards of 400 young girls taught gratuitously." Elliot, *Historical Sketches*, 263.

13 Sullivan and Hannan, *Georgetown Visitation*, 106.

14 Ibid., 67.

15 Ibid., 107, and Elliot, *Historical Sketches*, 263.

16 Ibid., 106.

Americans in the federal district, enslaved or free. In Georgetown, Mary Billings, an English-born widow supporting her three children, established a school in a brick house on Dumbarton Street around 1810. Initially she taught black and white pupils, "but prejudice arising, she concluded to devote her energies wholly to colored youth." Billings continued her school at that location until 1821, when she opened a school in Washington City. Unfortunately, her curriculum is unknown.[18]

Maria Becraft, daughter of a former slave, opened a small school for young women of color around 1820. With the assistance of Father Vanlomen (Van Lommel), pastor of Trinity Church, she relocated her school in 1827 to a larger building on Fayette Street across from the convent of the Visitation and instructed between thirty and thirty-five day and boarding students.[19] Sisters at the convent provided advice and encouragement, and Miss Becraft's seminary served an important role in the Georgetown community up until its forced closure in 1831.[20] Becraft then joined the Baltimore religious order of the Oblate Sisters of Providence where she taught embroidery and other subjects in their School for Colored Girls.[21] It is likely that Maria Becraft conducted sewing and embroidery classes in her Georgetown school as well, but this has yet to be documented.

NEEDLEWORK TEACHERS

Private needlework instruction was readily available in Georgetown in a variety of less permanent schools, as well as from teachers instructing small numbers of pupils. From 1798 to 1860, at least fifty individuals advertised their intent to offer one or more of the various branches of needlework instruction for the girls and young women of Georgetown (see Appendix II). Most were active during the first three decades of the nineteenth century. An unidentified citizen of Georgetown noted in his diary on February 14, 1800:

> *I see that there is to be a new school opened April 1 for the education of young ladies. Our Georgetown ladies will be well schooled in reading and sewing, for that is what Mrs. Phillips, late from England, proposed to teach them, while Madame De La Marche a year ago brought a lady into her Academy expressly to teach English grammar and embroidery. Mrs. Phillips, in her school on the north side of Bridge Street opposite the Printing Office, will have her specialty mantua making and millinery. All very practical indeed. And if the young ladies' fingers and eyes tire, their brains at least will not be disturbed.*[22]

---

17 For a sampler stitched by a student at Saint John's Female Benevolent School, operated by the Sisters of Charity in Frederick County, Maryland, see Gloria Seaman Allen, *A Maryland Sampling*, 184.

18 Crew, et al., *Centennial History*, 12

19 The 1870 *Special Report of the Commissioner of Education* suggests that the Visitation sisters may have educated children of color in their benevolent school before Maria Becraft opened her school. "The sisters of the Georgetown convent were the admirers of Miss Becraft, gave her instruction, and extended to her the most heartfelt aid and approbation in all her noble work, as they were in those days wont to do in behalf of the aspiring colored girls, who sought for education, withholding themselves from such work only when a depraved and degenerate public sentiment upon the subject of educating the colored people had compelled them to a more rigid line of demarcation between the races." Barnard, *Special Report of the Commissioner of Education . . .* [1871], 195.

20 Between 1800 and 1820, the number of free blacks in Georgetown increased from two hundred to nine hundred, and by 1830 free blacks outnumbered enslaved in the federal district. However, after the 1831 insurrection led by Nat Turner in Southampton County, Virginia, the education of African Americans became circumscribed.

21 Allen, *A Maryland Sampling*, 250.

22 "Diary of a Georgetowner, Chapter 17," edited by David Roffman, November 2008, http://www.georgetowner.com/archives/11_12_08/diary.shtml.

23 *Centinel of Liberty & Georgetown & Washington Advertiser*, February 14, 1800.

In an advertisement announcing the terms of her school, Mrs. Philips declared that she would teach reading and sewing, both plain and ornamental, and dressmaking "at the very low price of one dollar per month."[23]

Some teachers stayed in the area for less than a year while a number offered a useful and ornamental curriculum over a period of several years. Mrs. Smith and Mrs. Wiley, for example, first advertised their Georgetown school in 1800 and charged thirty dollars per quarter for "Board, English Grammar, Plain and Ornamental Needle work." Drawing, French, writing, arithmetic, geography, and music were offered for additional fees. Parents were also charged three dollars for half a cord of firewood during the winter quarter, and students were advised to supply their own bed, bedding, sheets, and towels.[24] By 1805, Smith and Wiley had relocated to a large brick house "with a good Garden, yard, and excellent spring of water." They continued to offer the same subjects and specified that their needlework curriculum would include "Plain Work, Marking, Embroidery in Lambs Wool, Silks, and Chenille" and be taught in the afternoon.[25]

French-born Madame Du Cherray, who had directed an academy for several years in Moscow, Russia, advertised her intent to open a school in late 1807. By February 1808 she was able to inform the residents of Georgetown that she had taken over the school formerly conducted by Smith and Wiley. She offered a similar course of study with "Embroidery [and] all sorts of Needle work which form part of a Young Lady's education." Her husband, Monsieur Du Cherray, a miniature portrait painter, would provide drawing instruction and perhaps design needlework for her students.[26] Although Madame Du Cherray did not place additional newspaper advertisements, her school appears to have continued into the next decade.[27]

A number of Georgetown teachers advertised needlework instruction during the second decade of the nineteenth century. Mrs. Howard, who stated her intent to open a Ladies' Seminary in Georgetown in 1815, offered the most extensive needle and fancy work curriculum of any teacher in the area. She proposed to teach:

Plain, embossed, and open cotton-works, Netting, and Tetting, Landscape, Flower, and Fancy Crewel Works, Embroidery in Gold, Silver, Silk, and Worsted, Tambour, Artificial Flowers, Fillagree, Mosaic, Beadbasket, Chimney Ornaments, Table Mats, and Hearth Rugs, with other useful and ornamental accomplishments.[28]

Not all teachers promoted their schools through advertisements in the newspaper. Mrs. Simpson, for example, did not advertise and had no listing in city directories. Nonetheless, her teaching made a lasting impression on at least one of her students. Julia Ann Hieronymus Tevis (1799–1879), who established the Science Hill Female Academy in Shelbyville, Kentucky, in 1825, attended Mr. and Mrs. Simpson's school when her family moved to Georgetown around 1813. Julia recorded in her autobiography:

A considerable portion of my time was devoted to music, drawing, and French, with various kinds of embroidery. The girls

---

24 Ibid., October 28, 1800.

25 Georgetown, *Washington Federalist*, May 1, 1805.

26 Ibid., November 28, 1807, February 17, 1808.

27 David Bailie Warden, *A Chorographical and Statistical Description of the District of Columbia* (Paris: Smith, 1816).

28 Mrs. Howard's school did not remain in Georgetown for long. The next year, 1816, a Miss Hawley was occupying her schoolrooms, and Mrs. Howard appears to have relocated to Washington City as early as June, 1815. Georgetown *Daily Federal Republican*, May 6, 1815; Washington *Daily National Intelligencer,* July 14, 1815, and August 26, 1816.

in this school wrought the most elaborate samplers with a variety of stitches, and bordered them with pinks, roses, and morning-glories, and sometimes, when the canvas was large enough, with the name and age of every member of the family. We did not buy French-worked collars then, but embroidered them for ourselves, and some of them were exquisite specimens of the finest needlework; and the skirts of our white muslin dresses were wrought, frequently, half a yard in depth.[29]

During the 1820s and 1830s teachers in Georgetown continued to offer useful and ornamental needlework and other types of fancy work. Many, however, began to place greater emphasis on providing an English or classical education and stated in their advertisements that "Needle-work, if desired, will receive its due share of attention," or "Plain and Fancy Needle Work will be taught [to] those young ladies whose parents may require it."[30]

Rosa M. Nourse was an exception. Her 1845 prospectus for a small, select boarding school in her father's home on the heights of Georgetown was one of the latest published announcements of needlework instruction there. The annual fee of $250 included "Board, bedding, washing, &c.; complete course of tuition in English and French; Useful and Ornamental Needle Work" (Figure 4-3).

Chapter 5 continues with a discussion of needlework attributed to students living in Georgetown, several of whom may have attended Lydia English's Female Seminary.

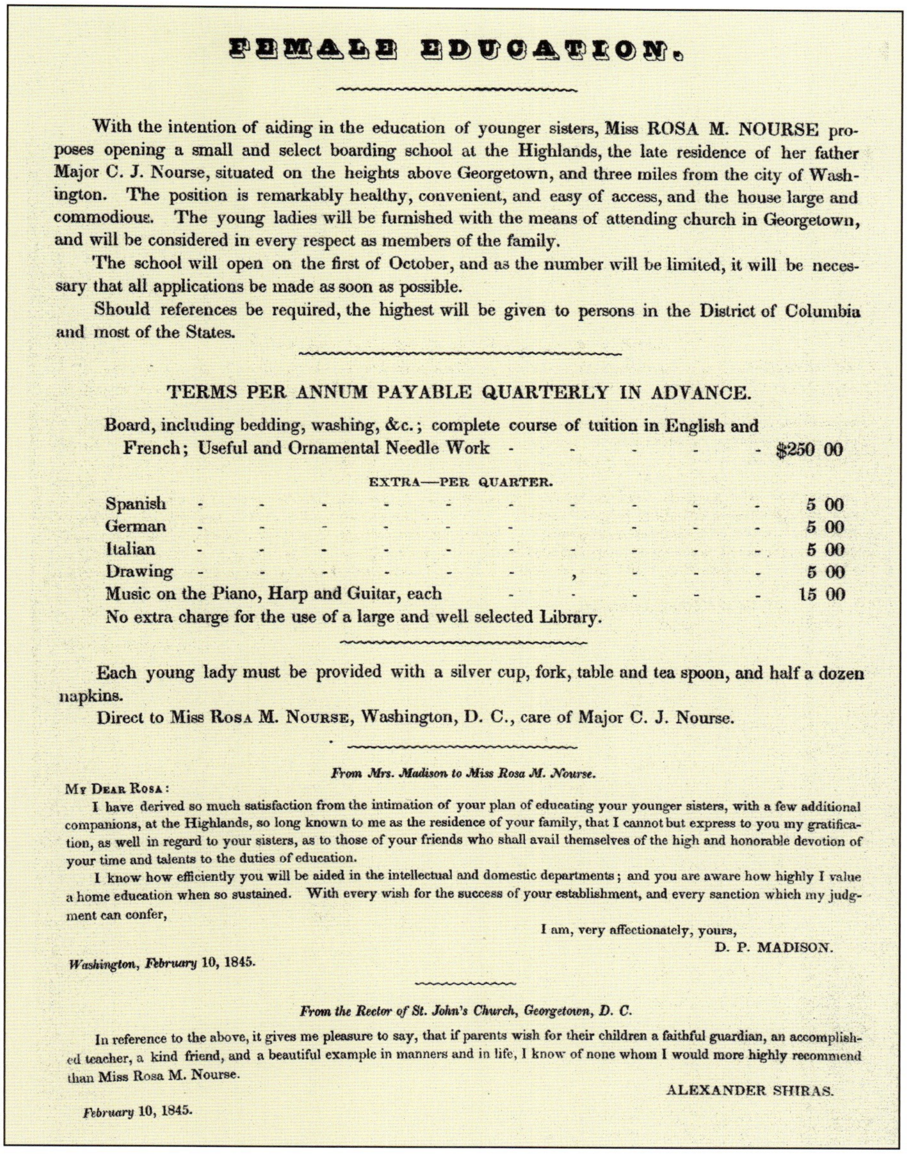

FEMALE EDUCATION.

With the intention of aiding in the education of younger sisters, Miss ROSA M. NOURSE proposes opening a small and select boarding school at the Highlands, the late residence of her father Major C. J. Nourse, situated on the heights above Georgetown, and three miles from the city of Washington. The position is remarkably healthy, convenient, and easy of access, and the house large and commodious. The young ladies will be furnished with the means of attending church in Georgetown, and will be considered in every respect as members of the family.

The school will open on the first of October, and as the number will be limited, it will be necessary that all applications be made as soon as possible.

Should references be required, the highest will be given to persons in the District of Columbia and most of the States.

TERMS PER ANNUM PAYABLE QUARTERLY IN ADVANCE.

Board, including bedding, washing, &c.; complete course of tuition in English and French; Useful and Ornamental Needle Work - - - - - - $250 00

EXTRA—PER QUARTER.

Spanish - - - - - - - - - - 5 00
German - - - - - - - - - - 5 00
Italian - - - - - - - - - - 5 00
Drawing - - - - - - - - - - 5 00
Music on the Piano, Harp and Guitar, each - - - - - 15 00
No extra charge for the use of a large and well selected Library.

Each young lady must be provided with a silver cup, fork, table and tea spoon, and half a dozen napkins.

Direct to Miss ROSA M. NOURSE, Washington, D. C., care of Major C. J. Nourse.

From Mrs. Madison to Miss Rosa M. Nourse.

MY DEAR ROSA:

I have derived so much satisfaction from the intimation of your plan of educating your younger sisters, with a few additional companions, at the Highlands, so long known to me as the residence of your family, that I cannot but express to you my gratification, as well in regard to your sisters, as to those of your friends who shall avail themselves of the high and honorable devotion of your time and talents to the duties of education.

I know how efficiently you will be aided in the intellectual and domestic departments; and you are aware how highly I value a home education when so sustained. With every wish for the success of your establishment, and every sanction which my judgment can confer,

I am, very affectionately, yours,
D. P. MADISON.

Washington, February 10, 1845.

From the Rector of St. John's Church, Georgetown, D. C.

In reference to the above, it gives me pleasure to say, that if parents wish for their children a faithful guardian, an accomplished teacher, a kind friend, and a beautiful example in manners and in life, I know of none whom I would more highly recommend than Miss Rosa M. Nourse.

ALEXANDER SHIRAS.

February 10, 1845.

Although frequently of high quality, the majority of Georgetown samplers were produced under the tutelage of teachers or at schools whose identities remain unknown. Notable exceptions are the samplers that name the Young Ladies' Academy of Georgetown, discussed in Chapter 6.

Figure 4-3. Prospectus. "Female Education," Georgetown, 1845.

---

29 Unfortunately, no District of Columbia genealogical samplers, referred to by Julia Tevis, have been located. Julia A. Tevis, *Sixty years in a School-room: An Autobiography of Mrs. Julia A. Tevis . . .* (Cincinnati: Printed by Western Methodist Book Concern, 1878), 84.

30 Miss Searle, Female Literary Seminary, Washington *Daily National Intelligencer*, December 19, 1823; Mr. and Mrs. Barnard, *Washington Chronicle*, September 11, 1838.

Figure 5-1.
Sampler worked by Sarah Kurtz. Georgetown, 1804.
Inscribed: "Sarah Kurtz" / [in ink] "Worked 1804 age 9."
Silk on linen, 28 by 32 threads per in.
21 1/8 x 17 1/8 in.
National Museum of American History, Smithsonian Institution, T07318

CHAPTER 5

Georgetown Samplers

GEORGETOWN WAS FOUNDED at about the same time as Alexandria, and at least eleven local teachers advertised needlework instruction prior to 1800, but no late eighteenth-century Georgetown samplers have been documented. The number of Georgetown samplers dating from the first half of the nineteenth century is relatively small and stylistically diverse. Most cannot be associated with a specific teacher or school. One exception is needlework that can be attributed to students who attended the Georgetown Female Seminary founded by Lydia English in 1826.

NINETEENTH-CENTURY SAMPLERS

Sarah Kurtz

Sarah Kurtz (1795–1864) worked a sampler with alphabets, verse, and scattered motifs in 1804 when she was nine years old (Figure 5-1). She used a combination of cross, stem, chain, and eyelet stitches to create crowns, baskets of fruit and flowers, birds on trees, and other motifs. Sarah also included a single bird in a wreath—a motif found on early Alexandria samplers—on her otherwise symmetrical composition. Her verse is a variation on lines from John Gay's sixth fable, "The Miser and Plutes."[1] Gay (1685–1732) was an English poet and dramatist, best known for his satirical "The Beggar's Opera."

*But when to virtuous hands is given,
It blesses like the dew of Heaven:
Like Heaven it hears the orphans cries.
And wipes the tears from widows eyes.*

Sarah (Sally) Kurtz was probably the daughter of Maria Elizabeth Gardner (1756–1822) and German-born Christian Kurtz (1751–1808), a pew holder in the Presbyterian Church in Georgetown. On June 2, 1816, the Reverend Stephen Bloomer Balch, founding pastor of the church, conducted Sarah's marriage ceremony to Thomas Orme, a veteran of the War of 1812.* Orme was later employed as a hatter and had a residence on Jefferson Street in Georgetown. Sarah and Thomas had at least five children, one son and four daughters. Their second daughter, Elizabeth Orme (born ca. 1825) may have

*See page 216 facing Appendix I for embroidery by the Reverend Balch's daughter, Jane Whann Balch.

---

1 John Gay, *Fables* (Paris: P. and F. Didot, 1800). Also published by Dr. Samuel Johnson in his *The Works of Poets of Great Britain and Ireland*, vol. 7 (Dublin: Pat. Wogan, 1804). Plutes is a shortened form of "plutocrat" or rich industrialist.

attended Lydia English's Female Seminary in Georgetown and stitched a sampler there around 1833 (Figure 5-15). Three of the Orme daughters continued to live at home, even after marriage. By 1860, Sarah was a widow, but she still had the companionship of Rebecca, who never married, as well as Elizabeth and Anna, both widows, and two grandchildren.

The Laird Sisters

Two Georgetown samplers worked by the Laird sisters were documented and described in *American Samplers* by Bolton and Coe in 1921. Unfortunately, the present location of the samplers is unknown. The Laird girls stitched their samplers around 1807 and 1809.[2] Bolton and Coe described them as having alphabets, verses, baskets of flowers, trees with birds, wreaths, and other motifs. The descriptions suggest a similarity with the sampler stitched by Sarah Kurtz in 1804, perhaps part of the same stylistic tradition set by one of Georgetown's needlework teachers.

Barbara (1795–1872) and Margaret (1797–1858) Laird were the daughters of prominent tobacco merchant John Laird (1768–1833) and his wife Mary Dick. Laird was regarded as one of the wealthiest men in Georgetown and instrumental in bringing the Lancasterian method of teaching and free education to the town in 1811. Like Christian Kurtz, Laird was a pew holder in the Georgetown Presbyterian Church.

Margaret (Miss Peggy) Laird never married and continued to live in the family home bequeathed to her by her father. A Georgetown resident recalled seeing her sitting by her front window "always dressed in Scotch gingham of such fine quality that it seemed like silk."[3] When she died in 1858, "her funeral [was] attended by a numerous retinue of friends of the family."[4]

Barbara Lucinda Laird married James Dunlop, a lawyer, in 1818. At her sister's death she inherited the family mansion, now known as the Laird-Dunlop House. Barbara and James had four children living at home in 1850. James served as secretary of the Municipal Corporation of Georgetown, as a law partner of Francis Scott Key, and after 1855 as chief judge of the United States Circuit Court of the District of Columbia.

Harriet Beall

Some of the most distinctive samplers from the Georgetown area were worked between 1820 and 1840, a period when needlework instruction was beginning to disappear from the schoolgirl curriculum. Harriet Beall (1811–1831) created a pictorial sampler with a densely cross-stitched pastoral landscape in the upper register that anticipates designs found on later woolwork. Below is a large spray of roses with flanking rosevine borders. Above a multicolored chevron band, she stitched "Harriet Beall February 6th 1821" (Figure 5-2).

Like the Laird sisters, Harriet came from one of Georgetown's most prominent families. She was a descendant of Colonel Ninian Beall (1625–1717), who was captured in 1650 at the Battle of Dunbar during the English civil wars and shipped from Scotland to Barbados as a prisoner. Beall was later indentured in Maryland and when freed settled in Prince George's County, where he amassed considerable land holdings. As was the custom, Beall received grants of land from Lord Baltimore in return for transporting immigrants to populate the young colony. Eventually one tract, known as the

---

2 Bolton and Coe, *American Samplers*, 185. The authors note that both Laird daughters were born in Bladensburg, Maryland, but only attribute Barbara's 1807 sampler to Georgetown. Scottish-born John Laird removed his tobacco business from Bladensburg to Georgetown in 1800, so both daughters were probably living in Georgetown at the time they made their samplers.

3 Grace Dunlop Ecker, *A Portrait of Old Georgetown* (Richmond, Va.: The Dietz Press, 1951), 148–49.

4 Washington *National Intelligencer*, October 21, 1858.

Figure 5-2.
Sampler worked by Harriet Beall. Georgetown, 1821. Inscribed: "Harriet Beall / February 6th 1821." Silk on linen.
17 1/8 x 17 in.
Museum of Early Southern Decorative Arts, Old Salem Museums & Gardens

"Rock of Dumbarton," on the eastern side of the Potomac River became part of the future site of Georgetown and later the District of Columbia.[5] Harriet was the second of eleven children born to Rachel H. Grove (1784–1877), a native of Pennsylvania, and Ninian Beall IV (1782–1856), an officer in the War of 1812, Georgetown merchant, and town council member. Harriet died unmarried at the age of twenty.[6]

5 In 1751 by an act of the colonial assembly, Maryland bought some of the Beall land at a discounted rate from Ninian Beall's son, George, and additional land from adjacent landholder George Gordon. In 1752 a plat was laid out for a new settlement to be known as George-Town. In 1791 supplementary Beall property was acquired when the ten-mile-square boundaries were established for the new federal district.

6 Bolton and Coe list an 1801 "Chart of the World" by Harriet Beall of Georgetown. This is obviously a different Harriet, but quite possibly a relative.

The Weschler's auction sale in Washington, D.C. of the 1821 Harriet Beall sampler on May 8, 1999, included an 1829 pictorial sampler by Artridge Priscilla Jackson of Georgetown from the same consignor and descendant of Colonel Ninian Beall (see Figure 5-13). Artridge Jackson's brother's son, William Samuel Jackson, married Martha Beall, daughter of Andrew Beall, Harriet's brother, which may explain how Artridge Jackson's sampler ended up in the Beall family.

GEORGETOWN SAMPLERS 81

Figure 5-3. Sampler worked by Mary Copley. Georgetown, 1830. Inscribed: "Mary Copley 1830 / April 8 / Georgetown D. C. Aged 12 years." Silk on linen. 16 x 16 in. Image courtesy of Adam A. Weschler & Son, Inc.

Mary Copley

In 1830 twelve-year-old Mary Copley (1817–1915) stitched a "Georgetown D. C." house sampler with a distinctive geometric-partitioned front yard (Figure 5-3).[7] The spade-shaped pine trees, baskets of flowers, and tulip border are similar to motifs stitched on samplers in Washington City, just across Rock Creek.

Mary Olive Copley was the daughter of Olive Cole (died 1876) and William Bildad Copley (1786–1846). The 1830 federal census documented a brief period in time when Copley, his wife, three sons, and a daughter between the ages of ten and fourteen resided in Georgetown.[8] Further research confirmed the peripatetic life of the Copley family. Mary's father was born in Connecticut, her mother in Virginia, and they married in Ostego County, New York, in 1810. The Copleys then moved to Oneida, Madison County, New York, where Mary was born on October 7, 1817. At that time, Mary's father was a machinist in the Oneida Manufactory engaged in building power looms for the weaving of cotton cloth. Another move took the family to Watertown in Jefferson County, New York, and then briefly to Georgetown in 1830.[9]

By 1836 the family had relocated to Madison County, Illinois, where Mary married Joshua Parker Delaplaine on October 8, 1836. The Delaplaines had six children and remained in Illinois through most of the 1860s. In 1870 they can be found in Allen County, Kansas, where they lived the rest of their lives.

Ann Lucretia Mayo Scaggs

On March 2 1831, twelve-year-old Ann Lucretia Mayo Scaggs inscribed her sampler with the location of her school, "Georgetown" (Figure 5-4). The sampler is competently worked in a variety of stitches including cross, satin, and Algerian eye. It features a large basket of fruit and flowers flanked by rose vines and bordered above and below with strawberries and hearts. Ann carefully stitched five alphabets and two stanzas of a 1740 hymn by John Wesley (1703–1791), the English theologian and one of the founders of the Methodist movement. Her closely transcribed version of the verse reads:

> *Depth of mercy can there be*
> *Mercy still reserved for me*
> *Can my God his wrath forebear*
> *Me the chief of sinners spare.*
>
> *I have long withstood his grace*
> *Long provoked him to his face*
> *Would not harken to his calls*
> *Grieved him by a thousand Falls*

---

7 Paint has been added to this sampler to highlight the colors. It is unclear from photographs whether the original sampler design included a geometric-partitioned yard. Mary's is the earliest known use of "D.C." on a Georgetown sampler.

8 The Copleys had four sons in all; the eldest no longer resided at home in 1830. The third Copley son was named for his paternal ancestor, John Singleton Copley, artist, and the fourth for George Washington.

9 William Copley's occupation in Georgetown cannot be determined. He did not stay long enough to be listed in city directories. His obituary, published in the December 1846 volume of the *New Jerusalem Magazine* noted, "After living at Watertown about two years, Mr. Copley removed to Georgetown, D.C. He has also resided in various other places in the United States."

Locating Ann Mayo Scaggs proved to be somewhat difficult, complicated in part by her use of two surnames, Mayo and Scaggs. Although Ann clearly identified Georgetown on her sampler, several population centers named "Georgetown" were scattered across the eastern United States at that time, making "Georgetown" an unreliable indicator that a sampler was created in the District of Columbia.[10]

Ann's unusual use of dual surnames has been at least partially explained by carefully examining the Georgetown census records. It is now believed that Ann was born about 1819 (using information from her sampler) to a couple with the last name of Mayo but raised by Susanna Scaggs, probably her grandmother. The 1820 census for Georgetown listed Susanna Scaggs (1762–1850) as the head of a household and over forty-five years old. Living with her were a young man and woman in the sixteen to twenty-five age category (presumably Ann's parents), and a girl under ten years old (Ann would have been about one). In the 1830 census Susanna Scaggs (listed as in her sixties) was still head of a household, and living with her was a woman in her thirties (presumably Ann's mother) and a girl in the ten to fourteen age group (Ann would have been eleven). By 1831, when Ann attended school, Susanna Scaggs may have taken over formal guardianship, thereby explaining the use of two surnames on Ann's sampler.

When Ann married John F. Grimes in the District of Columbia in 1837, she was identified as "Ann Lucretia Mayo." By 1850, Ann L. Grimes and her husband, a shoemaker, were living in the first ward in Washington City, and their household

Figure 5-4. Sampler worked by Ann Lucretia Mayo Scaggs. Georgetown, 1831. Inscribed: "Ann Lucretia Mayo Scaggs. aged 12 Georgetown March 2 1831." Silk on linen, 28 by 32 threads per in. 24 ¼ x 17 in. Collection of Anna Marie Witmer

---

10 "Washington D C" also is not necessarily an indication of a District of Columbia sampler. The place name may signify Washington, Dutchess County, New York.

GEORGETOWN SAMPLERS 83

Figure 5-5. Sampler worked by Julia Ann Dellaway. Georgetown, 1832. Inscribed: "Julia Ann Dellaway George-town October 29th 1832 A·D." Silk on linen. 17 x 16 ½ in. Image courtesy of Christopher H. Jones, American Antiques, Alexandria, Virginia

included ninety-year-old Susanna Scaggs.[11] Although Susanna is listed as illiterate, this evidently did not prevent her from recognizing the importance of education for her granddaughter.

Julia Ann Dellaway

In October 1832, Julia Ann Dellaway worked an alphabet and flower basket sampler enclosed by an arcaded carnation border (Figure 5-5). The flower basket is flanked by a symmetrical arrangement of small dogs and tall pine trees on which are perched two erect birds. In her inscription, Julia Ann stitched "George-town" as the location of her school.

Her verse is the first stanza of a hymn entitled "Time," the moral of which is to not waste minutes or hours in childish play.[12]

Wave after wave as rivers flow
And to the oceans run
So minutes after minutes go
And are forever gone

There may be an instructional connection between the sampler stitched in 1832 by Julia Ann Dellaway and the 1831 sampler of Ann Lucretia Mayo Scaggs. The alphabets and overall layouts are similar and the focal point of each sampler is a large basket overflowing with various types of flowers. In addition, the placement and wording of the inscriptions are similar, presenting the student's full name, followed by Georgetown, followed by a full date including month, day, and year. Julia Ann did not include her age.

Julia Ann may be a daughter of John Dellaway (ca. 1789-1858) identified in the 1830 federal census as employed in navigation and living in the second ward of Georgetown with a wife and two daughters aged from ten to fourteen and two daughters from fifteen to nineteen. According to the 1834 Georgetown Directory, John Delaway (Dellaway) was a mariner living on Jefferson Street near the waterfront. He captained the brig *Rubicon* that sailed out of New York and made deliveries to the port of Georgetown.[13] At other times he sailed to Saint Thomas and was based in Florida as master of a steamer or in the Gulf of Mexico on a propeller boat, leaving his family for months at a time.[14] By 1853, Dellaway had retired from the sea and

---

11 Her death notice gave her age as younger by two to three years. Susanna Scaggs died in September 1850 in her eighty-eighth year, widow of Richard Scaggs and daughter of Frederick Holtzman of Frederick County, Maryland. She had been a resident of the District for fifty-five years. Washington *National Intelligencer*, September 6, 1850.

12 The first two stanzas read: *Wave after wave, as rivers flow, And to the ocean run, So minutes after minutes go, and are for ever gone. Oh! who would then throw time away, And trifle to his cost? My hours, in idle childish play, Shall never more be lost.* (New York Religious Tract Society, 1823)

13 *U.S. Telegraph*, April 27, 1829.

14 *Daily National Intelligencer*, April 7, 1834. *Register of all Officers and Agents, Civil, Military, and Naval, in the Service of the United States* (Washington: Thomas Allen, printer, 1841), 106, and (Washington: J. & G. F. Gideon, Printers, 1843), 138.

was listed in the city directory for that year as proprietor of a "Segar Store" on Pennsylvania Avenue in Washington City.

Though John Delaway's locations can be documented, details about his wife and children are vague. Two of Julia Ann's sisters, Adeline and Virginia, can be identified through District marriage license records in 1841 and 1850 respectively. Julia Ann may have been the "Julia Ann Deleware" who married Benjamin M. Wall in 1842.[15]

Mary Elizabeth Fearson

Mary Elizabeth Fearson (1824–1858) is the only Georgetown student to record her teacher's name. Using a combination of cross, rice, and four-sided stitches, Mary Elizabeth revealed that her alphabet and verse sampler was "Worked at Miss Bootes's / Seminary Georgetown / Nov 23rd 18—" (Figure 5-6). Although the date has been pulled out, her sampler can be dated to about 1834, the year "Miss Boots Female Academy" was listed on Congress Street in the city directory.[16] For her verse, Mary Elizabeth stitched the first two stanzas of a poem entitled "Industry."

> *Behold fond youth that busy bee*
> *How swift she flies from tree to tree*
> *Extracting flowry sweets*
> *Thus cheerful all the day she'll roam*
> *At evening seek her much lov'd home*
> *To treasure all she meets*
>
> *Full well she knows that winter keen*
> *Must come to blast this painted scene*
> *With famine on its wing*
> *Her prudent labours find repose*
> *Nor winter cold nor want she knows*
> *Till time renews the spring*

Although widely published, the author of this verse is unknown. The poem appeared in almanacs as early as 1789 and in selections of verse for "improvement of the young" in 1819. At some point it was set to music and sung as a hymn in Methodist Sunday schools.[17]

Mary Elizabeth Fearson was the only child of Mary Ann (1805–1867) and Joseph N. Fearson (1796–1867), listed in the 1834 Georgetown directory as a grocer/merchant working with Samuel Fearson at Congress and Water Streets. Joseph later took over the proprietorship of Conrad's Tavern and built up a sizable estate. With her teacher also located on Congress Street, Mary Elizabeth

Figure 5-6. Sampler worked by Mary Elizabeth Fearson. Georgetown, ca. 1834. Inscribed: "Mary Elizabeth Fearson's / sampler / - years / Worked at Miss Bootes's / Seminary Georgetown / Nov 23rd 18 -." Silk on linen. 23 x 18 ¾ in. Daughters of the American Revolution Museum, Friends of the Museum Purchase, 91.291

---

15 My thanks to Ann Donnelly Steuart for sharing her research on this sampler.

16 *Directory for the District of Columbia for the year 1834* (Washington City: E. A. Cohen, 1834). Miss Boot[e]s did not advertise in local newspapers; so her needlework curriculum is not known.

17 Robert K. Dodge, compiler, *A Topical Index of Early U.S. Almanacs, 1776–1800* (Westport, Conn.: Greenwood Press, 1997); E. Hill, ed., *The Poetical Monitor: Consisting of Pieces Select and Original for the Improvement of the Young in Virtue and Piety* (London, 1819).

GEORGETOWN SAMPLERS

Figure 5-7. Sampler worked by Paulina Ould. Georgetown, ca. 1835. Inscribed: "Paulina Ould Aged 11 year's George Tow_n / District of Colubia." Silk on linen. Image courtesy of Horst Auction

had but a short walk to school. She continued to live at home throughout her twenties and early thirties. In January 1858, Mary Elizabeth married Frederick W. Jones, a lawyer, but died in December of the same year at her parents' residence, one day after the death of her infant son, Frederick Fearson Jones. Mary Elizabeth's parents died in 1867 within three months of each other, leaving no direct heirs. Mary Ann Fearson, the second to die, bequeathed much of the family's estate to Catholic charities. Distant relatives questioned her soundness of mind and contested her will in court, providing sensational reading in local newspapers for more than a year.

Paulina Ould

Paulina Ould (1824–1856) stitched her circa 1835 sampler with rows of alphabets separated by cross bands, enclosed in a neat arcaded strawberry border. She used a combination of cross, herringbone, eyelet, and queen stitches in multi-colored silks (Figure 5-7). Eleven-year-old Paulina inscribed her sampler "George Town/ District of Colubia."[18]

Paulina was the third of seven children born to Paulina Gaither (ca. 1795–1876) and Robert Ould (1788–1840), founder and director of the Georgetown Lancasterian School. Although more vibrant than most known Lancasterian samplers (which were usually worked all in black thread)[19] it is possible that Paulina stitched the sampler while attending her father's school. Documents indicate that Robert Ould may have continued as director of the Georgetown school until his death in 1840. A Miss Mary W. Cobb had taken over direction of the female division by 1830, enrolling about seventy girls.[20] Paulina's work may be a rare example of a Lancasterian sampler stitched at the Georgetown school under Miss Cobb's direction.

Paulina married Samuel G. Griffith, a clerk in Baltimore, in 1848. By 1860, Paulina had died and Samuel may have as well. Their six-year-old daughter, Paulina Griffith, was living in Baltimore with her maternal grandmother, Paulina Gaither Ould, and several other members of the Ould family.

Female Seminary of Georgetown

One of Georgetown's most enduring schools was the Female Seminary opened by Lydia English in 1826 at Washington and Gay Streets (now N and 30th Streets, NW). The seminary continued under Miss English's direction until 1852 and finally closed its doors in July 1861, when the building was leased to the U.S. Army for use as a hospital.

---

18 Horst Auctioneers, Ephrata, Pa., October 27, 2007.

19 See Deutsch, "Needlework Patterns and Their Use in America," 373.

20 Jonathan Elliot, *Historical Sketches of the Ten Miles Square* (Washington: J. Elliot, Jr., 1830), 263 and Bernard C. Steiner, *History of Education in Maryland* (Washington, D.C.: Government Printing Office, 1894), 58.

Lydia Scudder English (1802–1866), eldest daughter of David English (1769–1850) and his second wife Sarah Threlkeld (1768–1818), was born March 15, 1802, in Georgetown (Figure 5-8).[21] Her father, a native of Englishtown, Monmouth County, New Jersey, graduated from Princeton College in 1789 where he became a tutor. Later he directed a seminary in Basking Ridge, New Jersey, before moving to Georgetown in the 1790s. With Charles Green he published one of Georgetown's first newspapers.[22]

Lydia and her sister Jane Threlkeld English (1803–1849) attended the Moravian Girls' School in Lititz, Pennsylvania, where Lydia embroidered a silk memorial to her young brother Thomas Beall English.[23] The sisters, students from 1816 to 1818, received instruction in such ornamental subjects as drawing, painting, and fine needlework, as well as a range of academic subjects.[24] Since neither of the two women chose to marry, their well-rounded education prepared them for an eventual career in teaching.

Upon her marriage to David English, Lydia's mother, Sarah Threlkeld, brought to the union two corner lots at the intersection of Washington and Gay Streets, the eventual location of the family home.[25] Lydia and Jane purchased the property from their father around the time he married his third wife in 1819.[26] During the 1820s and 1830s the sisters acquired more lots and in time owned most of the west side of one block in Georgetown.[27] Assisted by her sister, Lydia English opened a female seminary in their residence, a "small two-story building," on the twenty-seventh of

Figure 5-8.
Portrait of Lydia S. English, attributed to John Beale Bordley, II, ca. 1840.
Oil on canvas
33 x 29 in.
Private Collection

---

21 Wesley E. Pippenger, *Oak Hill Cemetery Georgetown, D.C. Monument Inscriptions and Burial Data (Part One)* (privately published for the Oak Hill Cemetery Preservation Foundation, Washington, D.C., 2006), 124. Lydia was named after her father's first wife, Lydia Scudder (born 1767, Princeton, New Jersey, died 1800, Georgetown).

22 Samuel Davies Alexander, *Princeton College During the Eighteenth Century* (University of Michigan, 1872), 245. Green, English & Co. first published *The Centinel of Liberty and George-town Advertiser* in 1796. In later documents David English was referred to as a cashier (the number two position) at the Union Bank of Georgetown. He was also elected as an alderman in Georgetown, was active in the American Colonization Society, and appointed visitor to the Lancasterian School, Georgetown.

23 Patricia T. Herr, *"The Ornamental Branches": Needlework and Arts from Lititz Moravian Girls' School Between 1800 and 1865* (Lancaster, Pa.: Heritage Center Museum of Lancaster County, Pennsylvania, 1996), 25, Plate IX.

24 "Student Merchandise Account Books," 1815–1820, Linden Hall Archives, Lititz, Pa. Information kindly supplied by Patricia Herr.

25 Sarah Threlkeld purchased the lots in 1798 from Thomas Beall and owned them outright at the time of her 1801 marriage.

26 Early narratives suggest that the sisters, around seventeen and sixteen and unhappy with their father's third marriage, were eager to establish their independence. S. Somervell Mackall, *Early Days of Washington* (Washington, D.C.: Neale Co., 1899), 301.

27 Mary Mitchell, *Divided Town* (Barre, Mass.: Barre Publishers, 1968), 50.

February, 1826.[28] The school started with six day-scholars but by 1831 had expanded to include boarding students. Referring to Miss Lydia English, Georgetown resident Ann Shaaff commented: "I respect her very much, she is succeeding wonderfully has just completed a large schoolroom and has between 80 & 90 scholars."[29]

A letter written to the editor of the *Daily National Intelligencer* in 1831 also praised English's seminary:

> *Around this school no trumpet has been blown to summon public attention . . . it has grown up silently and unostentatiously upon the mere force of its merits. Patronage has sought it, instead of its seeking patronage. . . . those [parents] who wish to see in their daughters a mind stored with valuable instruction, accustomed to discrimination, and capable of decision and energy, a task that is refined without being frivolous, the capacity of affording intellectual entertainment, and of appreciating those high gifts in other[s], will do well in my opinion, to apply to Miss English, and test that course of instruction pursued in her truly admirable institution.*[30]

Although Lydia English never advertised her school, a newspaper article and a catalogue published in 1834–1835 indicate that she had 130 students, thirty of whom were boarders paying a basic fee of $150. The tuition for day students ranged from twenty to forty dollars with extra fees for instruction in several ornamental subjects. Miss English was assisted by thirteen teachers in conducting classes for girls ranging in age from six to about twenty.[31] Students were divided into levels designated A through G, with A being the most advanced. Courses were offered in the following subjects: arithmetic, algebra, geometry, history, sacred history, mythology, geography, intellectual philosophy, natural philosophy, chemistry, astronomy, botany, reading, grammar, orthography, writing, composition, elocution, needlework, drawing, music, French, and Latin.[32] Spanish, Italian, painting in watercolors and oil, and lessons on several musical instruments were added within the year.[33]

By 1843 the student body had grown in size to 192 and was taught by twenty-three instructors, many from states to the north.[34] The three-story school building had been expanded with the addition of wings to include nineteen bedrooms with single and double bedsteads, an extensive library, school rooms, music room, and several parlors. Shaded porches and a spacious yard added to the ambiance, and running hot water on all three floors was a noteworthy convenience.[35] However genteel the seminary's

---

28 *Daily National Intelligencer*, October 29, 1866.

29 Letter from Ann Shaaff to Harriet Addison, Georgetown, July 31. No year given, but since Ann refers to the local cholera outbreak it was probably written in 1832. MS 0230, Collection of the Historical Society of Washington, D.C. [hereinafter HSWDC]

30 Signed "A Candid Observer," *Daily National Intelligencer*, October 17, 1831.

31 *Daily National Intelligencer*, March 2, 1835; "Catalogue of the Members of the Female Seminary, for the Year Commencing September 1, 1834 . . ." (Georgetown, D.C.: W. A. Rind, Senior, 1835).

32 "Catalogue of the Members of the Female Seminary, for the Year Commencing September 1, 1835 . . ." (Washington, D.C.: Duff Green, 1836), 16-17.

33 Mary E. Curry, "The Georgetown Female Seminary and the National Park Seminary" (student research paper, American University, Spring 1970), 19.

34 Diarist Caroline Healey of Boston was recruited by Lydia English and, even though the remuneration was small, she accepted English's offer in August 1842 "to be a teacher and resident in an establishment of high repute." Healey's anti-slavery sympathies and her wish to attend religious services at the Unitarian Church in Washington City put her at odds with Miss English, a staunch Presbyterian, and caused her much unhappiness. She resigned at the end of the summer term. Caroline Wells Healey Dall and Helen R. Deese, eds., *Daughter of Boston: The Extraordinary Diary of a Nineteenth-century Woman* (Boston: Beacon Press, 2006), 55–58.

35 Mitchell, *Divided Town*, 51.

accommodations may have been, a former day student recalled the Georgetown neighborhood as less pleasing. "Walking was almost the only way to get anywhere in those days. . . . The mud was awful. Cows roamed the streets at will, and a great many people felt quite unashamed keeping a pig or so where their grounds allowed it."[36]

English's overall objective was "to afford pupils all the advantages of the most liberal course, in both the solid and ornamental branches of education" in order to prepare young women for the discharge of domestic duties and for the "destinies before them."[37] Under her guidance, her graduates would be "active, diligent, amiable, modest, unassuming, intelligent, and virtuous, happy in themselves, and blessings to their families and friends."[38] There was an underlying assumption that the self-discipline required for intellectual studies would, in the future, provide her students with the ability to put aside their own interests and ambitions in favor of helping others.

In lieu of advertising in newspapers, Lydia English used other means to call attention to her seminary. Her annual comprehensive catalogues included her educational philosophy, school regulations, course listings, fees, and student enrollment and were circulated throughout the Washington, D.C. area. Each May she held a public event fondly recalled by a local resident:

> *Every year, on the first day of May, she would have a grand May festival and coronation of three queens and three kings. Each queen would be preceded by two little crown bearers and twenty-four maids of honor. The whole town would be invited to these celebrations and there would be speeches by prominent men, and a whole band furnished the music. In the evening there would be a grand ball in a room built for that purpose adjoining the school; later in the evening the guests would enjoy a handsome supper.*[39]

In July, at the close of the spring term, Miss English invited the public to three days of student examinations, music recitals, and exhibitions of artistic work.[40]

Beautifully painted certificates of merit were awarded to seminary students for punctuality and attendance at the end of each term.[41] For example, Julia Ann Wilmore Fowler merited "Approbation in the highest degree and ranking in the First Grade for Punctuality" by being present at the calling of the roll 120 times during the fall-winter term of 1847–1848.[42] Her certificate, painted and lettered on

---

36 John B. Larner, "Some Reminiscences of Mrs. John M. Binckley," *Records of the Columbia Historical Society* 30 (1927): 347.

37 Catalogue . . . for the Year 1847, 15, 18.

38 *Daily National Intelligencer*, October 29, 1866.

39 Mackall, *Early Days of Washington*, 302–3.

40 The end of July was a busy time of year in Georgetown as Ann Shaaff recalled. "Last week was truly a work of exhibitions, the first three days at the Nunnery [Visitation], Thursday the college boys at the Catholic Chapel, and Friday Mr. M'Cveans at the Presbyterian Church. Miss Lydia English occupies three days this week." Shaaff, July 31, 18[32], MS 0230, HSWDC.

41 Around 1836, over concern of "fostering ambition" in her students, Miss English discontinued awarding prizes for academic accomplishment. She also discontinued ranking students based on First, Second, etc. and rearranged students into groups designated by letters of the alphabet. Curry, "The Georgetown Female Seminary," 6.

42 English did have a problem, which she frequently addressed to parents, with girls being late to school. Depending on the time of year, the school day commenced at 7:30 A.M. or 8:30 A.M. and all students were required to assemble in the main school room on the first floor to answer the roll. Curry, "The Georgetown Female Seminary," 20. Sarah E. Vedder, *Reminiscences of the District of Columbia; or, Washington City seventy-nine years ago, 1830–1909* . . . (St. Louis: A. R. Fleming Printing Co., ca. 1909), 76.

Figure 5-9. Certificate of merit awarded to Julia Ann Wilmore Fowler. Georgetown, 1848. Inscribed: "Female Seminary Georgetown D. C. / February 11th 1848. / . . . has been present at the Calling / of the Roll, One Hundred and Twen- / ty times, thereby meriting approba / tion in the highest degree and / ranking in the First Grade for / Punctuality. / L. S. English / Principal." Watercolor and ink on cardstock. 7 x 6 in.
Abby Aldrich Rockefeller Folk Art Museum, The Colonial Williamsburg Foundation, gift of Julie Grainger, 2008.305.1

Figure 5-10. Certificate of merit awarded to Julia Ann Wilmore Fowler. Georgetown, 1848. Inscribed: "Female Seminary Georgetown D. C. / July 31st 1848: / . . . has been present at the Calling of / the Roll One Hundred and Ten / times, thereby meriting approbation / in a high degree, and ranking in the / Second Grade for Punctuality. / L. S. English / Principal." Watercolor and ink on cardstock. 7 x 6 in.
Abby Aldrich Rockefeller Folk Art Museum, The Colonial Williamsburg Foundation, gift of Julie Grainger, 2008.305.2

cardstock, features a scroll surrounded by flowers (Figure 5-9).[43] During the next term, Julia Ann's attendance record slipped a bit as she only made the calling of the roll 110 times. She merited "Approbation in a high degree and ranking in the Second Grade for Punctuality" and received a certificate painted with a lyre-shaped vase. Both certificates were signed by "L.S. English, Principal" (Figure 5-10).

The Georgetown Female Seminary attracted students from the Washington, D.C. area, neighboring states, and even as far away as New Hampshire, Florida, and Arkansas. A number of the girls were daughters of Washington's elite families, whose fathers served in the military, Senate, or House of Representatives. Several were the pampered daughters of wealthy southern planters. As one student recalled,

> They were beautiful young ladies, dressing elegantly, but, having left their servants, or maids at home, presented the most ridiculous appearance to the girls who had always waited

---

43 Twelve certificates of merit from the Female Seminary are known to this author. They date between 1842 and 1850 and were awarded in mid-February and late July. Most are embellished with painted floral motifs; two are printed with images of Georgetown or "America." All are signed by Lydia S. English and, to date no two painted examples are exactly alike. The artist, or artists, responsible for the painting is unknown. Since so few artifacts have survived from the Female Seminary, the certificates are highly collectable.

upon themselves; their shoes were untied, their hair uncombed, and they were no further advanced in their studies than children in the primary department. . . . of books they knew nothing, and their language was "negro lingo."[44]

One of the better known, but least enthusiastic, students was Jessie Ann Benton, the bright, rambunctious daughter of Thomas Hart Benton, senator from Missouri. Enrolled in 1838 at age fourteen, Jessie flailed at the rigidity of a "society school" and remained for less than a term. At the time of her departure, Miss English wrote to Senator Benton:

Miss Jessie although extremely intelligent, lacks the docility of a model student, moreover, she has the objectionable manner of seeming to take our orders and assignments under consideration, to be accepted or disregarded by some standard of her own.[45]

More docile students also found ways to challenge the system. In February 1834, Margaret Beall, seventeen-year-old daughter of Upton Beall of Rockville, Maryland, complained in a letter to her sister Elizabeth that even though sick with a cold and bad cough, she had to study "14 pages of Geography, 17 pages of Nat Philosophy besides practicing and Music lessons to take." Falling behind in her schoolwork, Margaret told her sister, "I intend writing Mamma to send for me before the examination, my cough has been so bad that after coughing I was so exhausted I was not able to study and am not prepared for it or she must send word to Miss E [English] to excuse me in some of my lessons." However, Margaret still planned to attend a party that evening at Mrs. Washington's with some of the older students and dress in her "silk," even if it meant wearing something unfashionable around her neck to protect her sore throat.[46]

As Lydia English grew older her health declined and the school contracted in size. In 1850 she had nine assistants, thirty-eight boarding students, and an unknown number of day scholars.[47]

In September 1852, the Female Seminary opened under the "exclusive charge of Rev. W. J. Clark," former director of the Episcopal Institute for Young Ladies.[48] Clark and his wife Annabella continued to direct the seminary, possibly at a different location, through 1855 and perhaps until 1857 when Miss M[argaret] J[ain] Harrover took charge of the Seminary at its original location at Washington and Gay Streets.[49] Lydia English, though not active, was still a presence at the school. Harrover's catalogue for 1859 included a letter to parents from Miss English:

At the request of Miss Harrover, who, for two years past, has satisfactorily conducted the Institution over which I so long presided, and the care of which I relinquished, only because of my health and hearing made imperatively necessary. . . . In renting the Seminary, I retain my own suite of apartments.[50]

---

44 Vedder, *Reminiscences*, 77.

45 Ilene Stone and Suzanna M. Grenz, *Jessie Benton Fremont: Missouri's Trailblazer* (Columbia: University of Missouri Press, 2005), 14. At age seventeen, Jessie Benton married army explorer John Charles Fremont.

46 Margaret Beall, Georgetown, to Elizabeth Beall, Washington, February 7, 1834, Library of the Montgomery County Historical Society, Rockville, Md.

47 Federal census, 1850. Jane English's death the year before at age forty-six may have contributed to Lydia's declining health and contraction of the school. Jane had been involved in planning the seminary from the beginning and continued as co-principal into the 1840s, according to a former student. Vedder, *Reminiscences*, 76.

48 *Daily National Intelligencer*, July 23, 1852.

49 The "Catalogue of the Female Seminary, Georgetown, D.C. for the session 1854–1855…" (Washington, D.C.: R. A. Waters, 1855) gives no indication of the seminary's location.

50 Ecker, *A Portrait of Old Georgetown*, 146.

Figure 5-11. "Washington, D.C. Officers at door of Seminary Hospital (formerly Georgetown Female Seminary), 30th St. at N, Georgetown." April, 1865. Photograph. Library of Congress, Prints & Photographs Division

The seminary, long housed at Washington and Gay Streets, closed on July 1, 1861, when the federal authorities leased the building to use as a hospital for war wounded brought into the District (Figure 5-11).[51] As a southern lady, slave owner, and ardent secessionist, turning her property over to the Union must have been a bitter pill for Lydia English.[52] Later that year, perhaps through the urging of parents seeking some normalcy during wartime, Miss English advertised that she would instruct a limited number of students at her new residence at 2812 N Street.[53] Margaret Harrover also opened a school in Georgetown with a female department in Washington City for those unwilling to use the interurban omnibus to Georgetown.[54]

Lydia English died on February 24, 1866. An article published later that year, when her possessions and school furnishings went to auction, noted:

> *Her hearing failing, she was compelled to lay down her armor some dozen years before her death, and her school may be said to have ended at the same time. Several teachers attempted to carry it forward, but with innumerable failures. Her views of female education were in advance of her time.*[55]

At the time of her death, Lydia English was a woman of considerable means and undoubtedly had been a businesswoman of "great sagacity and executive capabilities."[56] She owned six female slaves, from ages one to forty-eight, several of whom may have been employed at the seminary.[57] Her estate included real-estate holdings in Georgetown, the school building and furnishings—a library with 1,800 volumes, 775 schoolbooks, oil paintings, cabinets of engravings, three pianofortes, a seraphina, a harp, and silver plate.[58] More mundane items sold at public auction reflected life in a large residential school and included feather beds, bolsters, pillows, bed coverings and bedsteads, bureaus,

---

51 The first battle of Bull Run, some twenty-five miles away, took place on July 21, 1861, and the former seminary building was soon filled with 150 patients, primarily officers. Mitchell, *Divided Town*, 51.

52 Miss English's friends and neighbors were diehard Georgetown secessionists. They were greatly disturbed when the Stars and Stripes was raised over the former seminary building on the second of July, 1861. Mitchell, *Divided Town*, 49.

53 Ibid., 55. This is the only indication of Lydia English ever advertising her school.

54 Ibid.

55 *Daily National Intelligencer*, October 29, 1866. This article, along with advertisements published by the Reverend Clark, clearly indicates that Lydia English's association with the Female Seminary, Georgetown, ended in 1852 and not in 1861 when the building was leased to the army or in 1866 when she died. I am grateful to Sheryl De Jong for her research and clarification.

56 *Daily National Intelligencer*, October 29, 1866. Unlike other school mistresses, who frequently found themselves in precarious financial situations when enrollment dropped, Miss English never had to advertise her seminary or seek funding from benefactors.

57 U.S. Census Record for 1860, Slave Schedule.

58 Mitchell, *Divided Town*, 51. Will and testament of L. S. English, dated February 24, 1866. *Daily National Intelligencer*, October 29, 1866.

mirrors, wardrobes, chairs, tables, clocks, crockery and glassware, toilet ware, and other furnishings.[59]

Needlework

All students at the Georgetown Female Seminary (except those in level C) had classes in needlework five days a week.[60] No catalogues were published prior to the 1834–35 school year, when Miss English wrote in her comments on the seminary curriculum, "some of the parents having expressed an opinion that sufficient attention has not been bestowed upon Needle-work; we have now engaged a lady to give special attention to what is indeed an important branch of female education."[61] An article published in the February 13, 1839, edition of the *Daily National Intelligencer* commented on the public examinations, concerts, and exhibitions held at the end of the seminary's winter term and noted "Several Specimens of oil painting, drawing and tapestry indicated genius of excellent promise." Needlework continued to be taught through 1851, the date on the latest known sampler worked by a seminary student, eleven-year-old Martha Duncan Abbot.[62]

While there is no textual evidence for needlework instruction prior to 1834, it seems unlikely that Lydia and Jane English, former students at the Lititz Moravian Girls' School, where ornamental accomplishments were emphasized, would not have included plain and fancy needlework in their very complete curriculum. This conclusion is further supported by the existence of samplers stitched by girls who are known from school records to have attended Miss English's Female Seminary at some point in their educational careers. Regrettably, several annual catalogues with student lists are missing, so not all of the samplers described below can be documented with certainty as having been stitched at the Georgetown Female Seminary.

Elizabeth Rind Nicholls

Nine-year-old Elizabeth Rind Nicholls (1819–1904) worked her alphabet and verse sampler around 1828, most likely while a student of Lydia English's. Although she did not include the name of her school, Elizabeth's full name appears in the seminary's record of students for this period. An early photograph of Elizabeth's sampler shows that she used queen and cross stitches to create four alphabets. A leafy vine partially encloses her name and the same verse found on Sarah Kurtz's sampler (Figure 5-1).[63]

> *When wealth to virtuous hands is given*
> *It blesses like the dews of Heaven*
> *Like Heaven it hears the orphans cry*
> *And wipes the tears from widows eyes*

Elizabeth, a daughter of Isaac Smith Nicholls (1790–1871) and his first wife Sarah Rind (1801–1827), was born in Georgetown on February 8, 1819. Elizabeth, one of her sisters, and three first cousins were among the earliest students at the Female Seminary. The 1826–1831 manuscript list of students includes

---

59 *Daily National Intelligencer*, November 13, 1866. Her school was also known for having "a valuable chemical and philosophical apparatus," but the disposition of this and other scientific equipment is unknown.

60 "Catalogue . . . Commencing September 1, 1835 . . . ," 16–17. Level C had needlework lessons Tuesday, Wednesday, and Thursday.

61 "Catalogue . . . Commencing September 1, 1834 . . . ," 14. A manuscript student list in a private collection covers the years 1826–1831. There is no listing of teachers or subjects taught.

62 "Catalogue . . . Commencing September 1, 1847 . . . ," mentions needlework classes for the younger students in the G level. No later catalogues are known.

63 The location of this sampler is presently unknown. It was last seen at the Antonio Raimo Galleries in Atlanta, about 1999.

Figure 5-12.
Sampler worked by
Mary Ann Scott.
Georgetown, 1831.
Inscribed: "Mary Ann
Scott / George Town.
March. 23. 1831. DC."
Silk on linen.
20 ¾ x 17 ½ in.
Image courtesy of
Stephen and Carol Huber

Elizabeth, her sister Joanna, and cousins Mary, Margaret, and Emily Nicholls.[64] Elizabeth continued as a seminary student at least through the 1834–1835 school year, as did Joanna, Margaret, and Emily. Another cousin, Virginia Nicholls was also a student at that time.[65] Elizabeth Nicholls never married and died in Georgetown at the age of eighty-five.

Mary Ann Scott and Artridge Priscilla Jackson

Two very similar samplers, both naming Georgetown, were stitched by Mary Ann Scott (Figure 5-12) and Artridge Priscilla Jackson (Figure 5-13). Both samplers feature a handsome two-and-one-half-story brick

64 The Nicholls cousins were the daughters of William Smith Nicholls and Margaret Doughty. They had eight daughters, so additional Nicholls girls may have attended the seminary.

The 1826–1831 manuscript list includes a Jane Rine [Rind?], probably another cousin.

65 "Catalogue of the Members of the Female Seminary, for the Year Commencing September 1, 1835," 8.

Figure 5-13.
Sampler worked by Artridge Priscilla Jackson. Georgetown, 1829. Inscribed: "Artridge. Priscilla. Jackson. Sampler / Georgetown July 20 1829." Silk on linen. 18 x 18 in.
Daughters of the American Revolution Museum, Friends of the Museum Purchase, 99.35

house flanked by four spade-shaped pine trees and two black dogs.[66] Additional shared motifs include large stylized baskets of fruit on either side of a floral spray. The general layouts of the two samplers are also similar, as are one of their verses and the strawberry border. Only one of the girls can be found in the list of students attending Miss English's Female Seminary, which makes attribution to the school less certain.

Mary Ann Scott's architectural sampler is marked "George Town" and is dated "March. 23. 1831." Mary Ann used cross, satin, four-sided, chain and other stitches to complete a sampler with a lot of decorative flair. For her verse, she stitched one of the most popular sampler verses of the eighteenth and nineteenth centuries, sometimes attributed to Isaac Watts (1674–1748) and at other times to John Newton (1725–1807), although possibly it was written by neither.

> *Jesus permit thy gracious name to stand,*
> *As the first efforts of an infants hand*
> *And while her fingers o'er this canvass move*
> *Engage her tender heart to seek thy love*
> *With thy dear children let her share a part*
> *And write thy name thyself upon her heart*

For her second verse, Mary Ann included the first six lines of a children's hymn.

---

[66] Spade-shaped pine trees were a common motif on samplers stitched in Washington City near the Navy Yard. The Scott sampler, which has a bird perched at the top of each tree, is especially reminiscent of this sampler group.

In the soft season of thy youth
In nature's smiling bloom
Ere age arrive, and trembling wait
Its summons to the tomb
Remember thy Creator, God,
For him thy hours employ:

Mary Ann Scott may have been the Mary A. Scott named in the list of students who attended the seminary between 1826 and 1831.[67] The 1830 federal census for Georgetown recorded Jesse Scott, a grocer on Water Street, with two daughters between the ages of fifteen and nineteen. Little else is known about the embroiderer, possibly she was the Mary Ann Scott who married George W. Mansfield in the District of Columbia on July 1, 1836.

Artridge Priscilla Jackson used cross, outline, and satin stitches to complete her sampler and dated it "July 20 1829," nearly two years before Mary Ann's sampler. Artridge's name, however, is not in the 1826–1831 list of students, thus casting doubt on the attribution of her sampler (and possibly that stitched by Mary Ann Scott) to Lydia English's seminary. The two girls either worked their samplers at some other, still-to-be-identified, Georgetown school or a needlework teacher at the seminary in 1831 provided instruction to students elsewhere in Georgetown prior to joining the school's faculty.

For her verse, Artridge stitched the first two lines of "Jesus permit thy gracious name to stand," but added two lines from an unknown source.

And may my humble piety for eve- prove
The true effects of my dear Saviours love

For her second verse, she chose the tenth stanza of Alexander Pope's "The Universal Prayer," a quatrain much loved by English and American sampler makers.

Teach me to feel Anothers woe
To hide the fault I see
That mercy I to others show
That mercy show to me

More information is available for Artridge Priscilla Jackson (1820–after 1898), in part due to her unusual name. Artridge was born June 14, 1820, in Georgetown, the third child of Joseph Jackson, a grocer on Bridge Street, and Rachel Plummer (born 1782) of Frederick County, Maryland. She was named for her maternal grandmother Artridge Waters (1748–1823) and her mother's older sister "Precilla" Plummer. In 1844, she married Cyrus Waters (ca. 1815–1853), most likely a cousin, in the District of Columbia. They spent their married life in rural Montgomery County, Maryland, where Cyrus was a physician with thirty acres of land. He died in 1853 after a long illness and left his wife his silver watch and large English Bible as personal remembrances.[68] Sometime later, Artridge and her three children moved back to Georgetown. She continued to live in the District of Columbia until at least 1898, the last year she was listed in city directories.

Mary Margaret Meem and Elizabeth Orme

Two Georgetown samplers share a nearly identical central motif of a large cornucopia filled with flowers and may have been worked at Lydia English's seminary. Using a combination of cross, queen, and straight stitches, fourteen-year-old Mary Margaret Meem (1821–1889) marked her sampler "Georgetown" and dated it 1836 (Figure 5-14). Except for a large pheasant and strawberry border, Mary's sampler relies almost entirely on its impressive cornucopia for visual appeal. Mary is listed as Mary M. Meem in the

---

67 This list also included Ann E. Scott and Ellen Scott, possibly sisters.

68 William Neal Hurley, *Our Maryland Heritage Book 32: The Waters Family* (n.p.: Heritage Books, 2002), 249.

seminary catalogue for 1834–1835, along with her older sister Rebecca Ann Meem.[69]

Mary Margaret Meem was the third child of George A. Meem (1795–1865) and his first wife Rebecca Ann Mudd (died 1831). Mary was born October 17, 1821, in Georgetown where her father owned real estate as well as two enslaved workers. In 1842, Mary became the second wife of Seth Hill Nichols (born ca. 1805), a tailor in Frederick, Maryland, where they raised their seven children. After 1870, the widowed Mary Meem Nichols returned to the District of Columbia, where she died October 27, 1889.

Elizabeth Orme (ca. 1825–1892) embroidered the same impressive cornucopia on her sampler, and the original drawing is still apparent beneath the cornucopia and its flowers. She used cross and herringbone stitches and added a verse entitled "The star of Bethlehem" (Figure 5-15). Elizabeth also stitched "Novr 9th" on her sampler, but neglected to include the year. At a later date, someone wrote on the face of her sampler, in ink, "1833 / Age 9." At this point, no list of seminary students is known for 1833, so it cannot be documented with certainty that Elizabeth was a student of Lydia English's when she worked her sampler.[70] The border on Elizabeth's sampler is distinctive and matches in design and color the border found on Julia Ann Dellaway's sampler (Figure 5-5) stitched a year earlier, suggesting there may be an instructional connection.

Elizabeth's verse is the first stanza of a long poem by American author and geologist James Gates Percival (1795–1856). It was frequently included in works for young readers.

> *Brighter than the rising day,*
> *When the sun of sun of glory shines;*
> *Brighter than the diamond's ray,*
> *Sparkling in Golconda's mines;*

LEFT: Figure 5-14. Sampler worked by Mary Margaret Meem. Georgetown, 1836. Inscribed: "Mary M. Meem / finished this work in the fifteenth year / of her age / George Town D·C / A·D 1836."
Silk on linen, 30 by 28 threads per in.
20 ⅝ x 17 ¼ in.
National Museum of American History, Smithsonian Institution, 2004.0246.01

RIGHT: Figure 5-15. Sampler worked by Elizabeth Orme. Georgetown, 1833. Inscribed: "Elizabeth Orme / Novr 9th" [in ink] "1833 / Age 9."
Silk on linen, 30 by 28 threads per in.
20 ⅞ x 17 ¼ in.
National Museum of American History, Smithsonian Institution, T07319

---

69 "Catalogue . . . for the Year Commencing September 1, 1835 . . . ," 8.

70 The manuscript list of students covers the period 1826–1831, and the printed catalogues cover the years from 1834 forward. Elizabeth's name has not been found in subsequent catalogues.

Figure 5-16. Sampler worked by Martha Duncan Abbot. Georgetown, 1851. Inscribed: "Martha D. Abbott in the 12th year of her age 1851." Silk on linen, 28 by 28 threads per in. 17 ½ x 16 ¼ in. Collection of Miss Lilchy Huffman.

Beaming through the clouds of wo,
Smiles in Mercy's diadem
On the guilty world below,
The Star that rose in Bethlehem.[71]

Elizabeth Orme was the second daughter of Thomas Orme (died before 1850), a veteran of the War of 1812 and a hatter by profession, and Sarah Kurtz (1795–1864) of Georgetown. As a young girl, Elizabeth's mother Sarah had stitched a fanciful sampler design of alphabets, verse, and motifs (Figure 5-1). Elizabeth married James Hizer in 1854 but was a childless widow by 1860. She returned to the Orme family home in Georgetown to live with her mother and a sister. Elizabeth Orme Hizer died from tuberculosis at the age of sixty-six.

Martha Duncan Abbot

The latest known sampler that can be attributed to Lydia English's seminary is dated 1851. Worked by eleven-year-old Martha Duncan Abbot (1840–1914) the embroidery is a marking sampler with six complete alphabets, each worked in a different script and/or stitch (Figure 5-16). A seminary catalogue for 1851 has not been located, but Martha's name is listed in the 1854–55 catalogue, and her older sister Mary Moulder Abbot was a seminary student in 1849 when she received a painted certificate of merit for punctuality (Figure 5-17).[72] The Abbot sisters were the daughters of Mary D. Moulder and George D. Abbot (1807–1874), who worked for the U.S. Department of Treasury. The family lived at 53 Bridge Street in Georgetown, a block away from the seminary. At the time Martha stitched her sampler, needlework lessons were being offered only to younger students. Martha Abbot's sampler was completed just a year before Lydia English gave up direction of the school she had guided for twenty-six years.

---

71 Golkonda or Golconda, misspelled by Elizabeth on her sampler, refers to the kingdom and mines in India where the Hope Diamond is alleged to have been found.

72 Olive Graffam, *"Youth Is the Time for Progress": The Importance of American Schoolgirl Art, 1780–1860* (Washington, D.C.: DAR Museum, 1998), 31.

The epitaph for Lydia Scudder English succinctly summarizes a life devoted to educating the nation's daughters.

LYDIA SCUDDER ENGLISH
She founded and sustained a Seminary for young ladies which gave her a national reputation. Learning, energy zeal and fidelity marked all her actions, Her memory is cherished alike by relatives and friends Her well spent Christian life is her monument the character of those she trained in virtue and knowledge her eulogy.[73]

Figure 5-17.
Certificate of merit awarded to Mary Moulder Abbot. Georgetown, 1849. Inscribed: "Female Seminary / Georgetown, D C. / . . . has been present at / the calling of the Roll One Hundred and / Thirteen times, thereby meriting Approbation / in a high degree and ranking in the / Second Grade for Punctuality. / Feb[y] 9th 1849. / L. S. English / Principal."
Watercolor and ink on cardstock.
7 x 6 in.
Collection of Miss Lilchy Huffman.

---

73 Tombstone inscription, Oak Hill Cemetery, Georgetown, D.C., lot 349.

Figure 6-1.
"The Original Building." Georgetown, prior to 1837.
Lithograph.
Georgetown Visitation Monastery Archives

CHAPTER 6

Young Ladies' Academy, Georgetown

Gloria Seaman Allen and Susi B. Slocum

THE SCHOOL

One of the earliest female schools in Georgetown dates its founding to 1799 and continues in operation today as the Georgetown Visitation Preparatory School. The school is located on its original site at 35th and P Streets, formerly known as Fayette and 3rd Streets, and is the only Catholic girls' school in continuous existence within the original thirteen states (Figure 6-1).

Approximately 10 percent of Maryland's first immigrants were Catholic. Arriving on its southern shores as early as 1634, they settled in Saint Mary's County and migrated to the adjoining Charles County and Prince George's County. Initially, Maryland Catholics experienced fluctuating degrees of tolerance toward their religious beliefs, but they gained greater political and social acceptance after the Revolution, largely because prominent Catholic families supported independence. Many of those families played pivotal roles in the establishment and patronage of Georgetown's most enduring female educational institution—the Young Ladies' Academy. Of the twelve known Young Ladies' Academy embroideries and samplers stitched prior to 1830, seven were the work of girls from families with southern Maryland roots.

During the eighteenth century, the children of wealthy Maryland Catholics often went to France or French Flanders to be educated. Young men studied with Jesuits and frequently became priests; young women attended convent schools, and many remained to become contemplative nuns. The French placed considerable emphasis on the education of young females: educated women were esteemed and respected as intellectual equals. After the establishment of Georgetown College for men in 1789, and in response to the steady influx of Catholics from political and social upheavals in France and Saint Domingue (now Haiti), the local education of young Catholic women became a priority (Figure 6-2).

In 1792, during the French Revolution, three members of the contemplative Order of Saint Clare were expelled from their convent at Tours. Mother Marie de la Marche, Sister

Figure 6-2. "The Potomac, Analostan Island and Georgetown College," painted by Caroline Rebecca Nourse. Georgetown, ca. 1838. Watercolor on paper. 4 ¾ x 6 ½ in. Dumbarton House, The National Society of The Colonial Dames of America, Washington, D.C., DH92.4.2

Celeste le Blond de la Rochefoucault, and Sister Luc Chevalier fled their homeland and first sought sanctuary with American Catholics in Charleston. By 1795 the "Poor Clares," as they were called due to the severity of their monastic life, were in Baltimore and may have taught briefly in a female school offering "all kinds of needle-work, either useful, as common sewing, &c. or agreeable only, as embroidery, &c."[1] Evidently unsuccessful in this endeavor, the three women moved to New Orleans to live with the Ursuline Sisters, and may have taught at the Ursuline Academy.

With the encouragement of the Reverend William Du Bourg (1766–1833), third president of Georgetown College and formerly of Saint Domingue, the three Clares came to Georgetown. An advertisement dated September 15, 1798, stated that they intended to open a "New Academy" in October, offering boarding and day students "sewing, embroidery, writing, arithmetic, geography, and the English and French languages taught grammatically by well qualified professors." Music, drawing, and dancing would also be taught by "eminent professors."[2] A house was rented for the sisters at Fayette and 3rd Streets on the heights of Georgetown near the college.

Even without competition from other Catholic female schools, the Poor Clares'

---

1 Baltimore *Federal Intelligencer*, June 4, 1795. The three Poor Clares are identified only as "Three French Ladies" in the school advertisement, which also stated that the Reverend William Du Bourg would teach French grammar, geography, and history. The sisters and Du Bourg apparently became acquainted at that time. Du Bourg became president of Georgetown College in 1796.

2 *Columbia Mirror and Alexandria Gazette*, November 1, 1798. "Sewing" and "embroidery" were listed first in the school's advertisement. This domestic emphasis reflects the long tradition of needlework in French convents and boarding schools, necessitated by the ritual needs of the Catholic faith.

academy failed to attract students. The sisters' inability to speak and teach English and their austere way of life did not appeal to Georgetown's merchant class or to Maryland's Catholic gentry seeking a religious and academic education for their daughters. The sisters proposed a curriculum similar to that offered by other female schools at the time but evidently were unable to hire "eminent professors" to teach subjects they could not.

Madame de la Marche, the academy's titular head, placed a second newspaper advertisement in March 1799 informing the "inhabitants of Georgetown and its vicinity" that she would be assisted by "a very respectable Lady," who had been educated in London and recommended by the Reverend Leonard Neale. Her responsibilities would include teaching "*ENGLISH* and *EMBROIDERY*, which last branch she can teach to perfection, as may be seen by some of her works at the Academy."[3] This skilled embroidery teacher appears to have been affiliated with the academy for at least a year. An unidentified diarist commenting on "the education of young ladies" in Georgetown wrote on February 14, 1800: "Madame De La Marche a year ago brought a lady into her Academy expressly to teach English grammar and embroidery."[4]

Despite the addition of one or more teachers, Leonard Neale (1746–1817) recognized that the Poor Clares could not support themselves or provide an adequate English education for the young Catholic women of Georgetown and southern Maryland and solicited assistance for his endeavor elsewhere. While living in Philadelphia, Neale had served as spiritual advisor to Alice Lalor, a devout woman who assisted him during the yellow fever outbreak of 1797–1798. After Neale relocated to Georgetown as the new president of the college, he invited Lalor and two others, known in Visitation history as the three "pious ladies," to establish a female school in Georgetown.[5]

The backgrounds of the three pious ladies are elusive, and what information exists is shrouded in legend. All three may have been born in Ireland. Alice Lalor (born 1765–1769, died 1836) was a native of Kilkenny and accompanied her older sister Mrs. Michael (Mary Lalor) Doran on her voyage to Philadelphia around 1795, where their father Denis Lalor had established himself as a grocer and tavern keeper. Maria McDermott (died 1820), a widow, may have come to Philadelphia some years earlier, and Maria Sharpe (died 1804), a widow with a daughter, was already living there when Alice Lalor arrived about 1795.[6]

The three pious ladies arrived separately in Georgetown some time prior to June 1799 and

---

3   *The Centinel of Liberty, and George-Town and Washington Advertiser*, March 8, 1799.

4   David Roffman, ed., *Diary of a Georgetowner* (2008), www.georgetowner.com/archives/11_12_08/diary.

5   Leonard Neale served as pastor of Saint Mary's Catholic Church in Philadelphia before his appointment as the fourth president of Georgetown College in 1799.

6   Alice Lalor probably resided with her father, Denis, and mother, Catharine (died July 8, 1801), at 142 South Water Street or with her sister and brother-in-law, Michael Doran, a merchant, at 143 South Front Street. Philadelphia directories suggest that McDermott and Sharpe were already in Philadelphia when Lalor arrived. A Maria M'Dermott, widow of Martin, is listed in directories from 1794 to 1799 as a grocer at 165 South Front Street. Her husband had died in 1793 of yellow fever. The Philadelphia directory for 1791 lists a Maria Sharp, shopkeeper, at 188 Sassafras Street (also known as Race Street) and not far from Front Street.

This information contradicts early accounts of the founding of the school that Mrs. Sharpe traveled with her daughter from Ireland on the same ship with Lalor and McDermott and that the three women became friends during the voyage. See George Parsons Lathrop and Ruth Hawthorne Lathrop, *A Story of Courage, Annals of the Georgetown Convent of the Visitation of the Blessed Virgin Mary* (Cambridge, Mass.: Riverside Press, 1895), 146–49.

at first co-operated with the Poor Clares in their teaching efforts.[7] It soon became clear, however, that the two groups of women could not successfully collaborate due to differences in language, heritage, economic status, and educational objectives. Madame de la Marche may have continued to conduct her own French school while Maria Sharpe, by then identified as Sister Ignatia, became the first directress and principal teacher of the school later known as the Young Ladies' Academy (Figure 6-3).

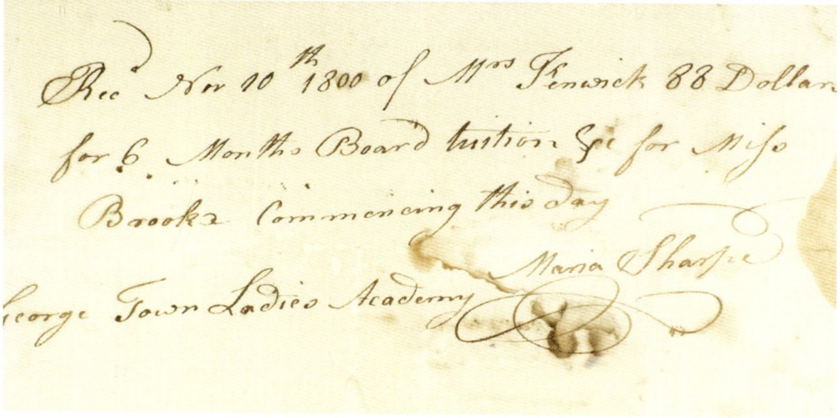
Recd Nov 10th 1800 of Mrs Fenwick 88 Dollars
for 6 Months Board tuition &c for Miss
Brooks Commencing this day
Maria Sharpe
George Town Ladies Academy

Figure 6-3. Receipt. Georgetown, 1800. Inscribed: "Recd Nov 10th 1800 of Mrs Fenwick 88 Dollars / for 6 Months Board tuition &c for Miss / Brooks Commencing this day / George Town Ladies Academy Maria Sharpe." Ink on paper. 5 x 8 in. Georgetown Visitation Monastery Archives

By 1800 the two groups of women were living in separate but adjacent buildings purchased by Madame de la Marche and Leonard Neale and described in contemporary sales promotion literature as:

> *two handsome Dwelling Houses, situated in Georgetown on the Potomac. They contain five rooms with fireplaces, four bed chambers, two closets, and have two handsome piazzas, a kitchen near the house, a beautiful garden ornamented with terraces, well grassed, a large fish pond supplied with a variety of fish and a spring of water, 150 young fruit trees, some beginning to bear, the whole finished and done in the strongest and neatest manner under a handsome and excellent enclosure containing three and a half lots, extending 180 feet on Fayette Street and 192 feet on 3rd Street.*[8]

Early histories of the school take note of the primitive accommodations of the women, especially the Poor Clares, while describing the idyllic nature of their location above the busy port:

> *The crude and simple convent and "Old Academy" now occupied a square of roughly cultivated ground on the heights of Georgetown. Through the middle of the plot ran, from north to south, a creek which emptied into the Potomac far below at the foot of the hill. Its banks were somewhat steep on the western side, but sloped more gradually on the eastern, where lay the convent garden, orchard and meadow. On the west, the land rose in a series of green-sodden terraces bordered with raspberry bushes, lilacs, and other shrubbery. . . . At first, and for a long while, both the nuns and their pupils were obliged to get over the creek as best they could in their constant passing to and fro between convent and academy. . . . Afterwards a rustic bridge was built to span the stream. A spring and fishpond, overhung by forest and fruit trees, made this a charming spot in summer.*[9]

These descriptive passages come to life in the silk embroidered pictures created between 1800 and early 1804 by three of the academy's first students (see Figures 6-12, 13, & 14).

Similar silk embroideries are unknown in the school's later history suggesting use of this design may have ceased with the death of Maria Sharpe in August 1804.[10] Her passing was lamented in a brief obituary.

7 June 24, 1799, is given as the official date for the foundation of the school known today as Georgetown Visitation Preparatory School.

8 *Sentinel of Georgetown*, June 25, 1799. Cited by Eleanore C. Sullivan, *Georgetown Visitation Since 1799*, second edition revised and expanded by Susan Hannan (Washington, D.C.: Georgetown Visitation Monastery, 2004), 51.

9 Lathrop and Lathrop, *A Story of Courage*, 153.

10 See Appendix III for documentary evidence from school ledgers for later embroidery instruction.

> *Departed this transitory life on Wednesday last, after a lingering illness, MARIA SHARP, a teacher in the Young Ladies Academy: in her death, female youth have to bewail the loss of an able, attentive, and tender teacher; the community at large, that of a very useful member—she was recommendable for her unfeigned piety, suavity of manners, and integrity of conduct.*[11]

An early school history notes, "The loss of this, their best teacher caused the school to decline. . . . Only the commonest branches could be taught, now—reading, writing, geography, and arithmetic—with no music or special studies."[12] In all likelihood, embroidery was one of these "special studies."

The young Georgetown school struggled on, either as a united academy or as two separate schools competing for students. In spite of the competition, the teaching of needlework—especially sampler work—appears to have continued. The Poor Clares and the pious ladies both placed advertisements in local newspapers. In July 1803, the pious ladies advertised that their "Young Ladies Academy . . . is provided with tutors of every description necessary for completing a polite, elegant and useful education . . . fine and plain works of all kinds suitable for ladies." In March 1804 their prospectus specified "Sewing, Embroidery, Tambourwork."[13] Within days, Mesdames de la Marche and de la Rochefoucault advertised the opening of a separate young ladies' school "for the French" at their Fayette Street dwelling where they proposed to offer French, music, and dancing.[14]

With the death of Madame de la Marche in 1804, the remaining Poor Clares returned to France, and Leonard Neale, who had been slowly acquiring nearby lots, purchased their Georgetown property. By 1805 the Georgetown academy became the sole responsibility of Alice Lalor (known then as Sister Teresa and later as Mother Teresa Lalor), Sister Mary Frances McDermott, and three additional sisters who had joined the pious ladies. Around 1807, however, Archbishop John Carroll expressed his concern over the sisters' need for assistance in teaching the "elegant accomplishments," considered essential to the education of young Catholic women.[15] His intervention may have resulted in the addition to the school of someone who could teach needlework, because two nearly identical samplers are known to have been worked around this time.

In 1816, Pius VII raised the religious community of Mother Teresa Lalor and the sisters to the rank of monastery, and the members took their solemn vows as sisters of the French Order of the Visitation.[16] At that time the female academy had between twelve and fourteen students, including several who had been there since age five.[17] The direction of the school changed soon thereafter with the death of spiritual leader and school director Leonard Neale, and the arrival of Jerusha Barber (later Sister Mary Augustine), a New England–educated teacher who was

---

11 The date of Maria Sharpe's death is problematic. Visitation records give her date of death as July 31, 1802. This date is put into question by a prospectus for an academy "under the direction of a company of united ladies," published March 1, 1804, that directs letters of inquiry to "Mrs. Maria Sharpe." *Washington Federalist*, March 1, 1804. A recently located obituary appears to confirm the later date. *Washington Federalist*, August 8, 1804. Wesley E. Pippenger, *Georgetown District of Columbia Marriage and Death Notices 1801–1838* (Bowie, Md.: Willow Bend Books, 2004), 10.

12 Lathrop and Lathrop, *A Story of Courage*, 155.

13 *Washington Federalist*, July 6, 1803 and March 1, 1804.

14 Ibid., March 12, 1804.

15 Mada-anne Gell, VHM, "Georgetown Visitation: The Myth of the Finishing School," *Salesian Living Heritage*, 1 (1986): 33.

16 The Visitandine order was founded by Saint Francis de Sales and Saint Jane de Chantal at Annecy in 1610. By the eighteenth century it was a popular order in France and French Flanders, where many Maryland Catholics had been educated.

17 Sullivan and Hannan, *Georgetown Visitation*, 56, 68.

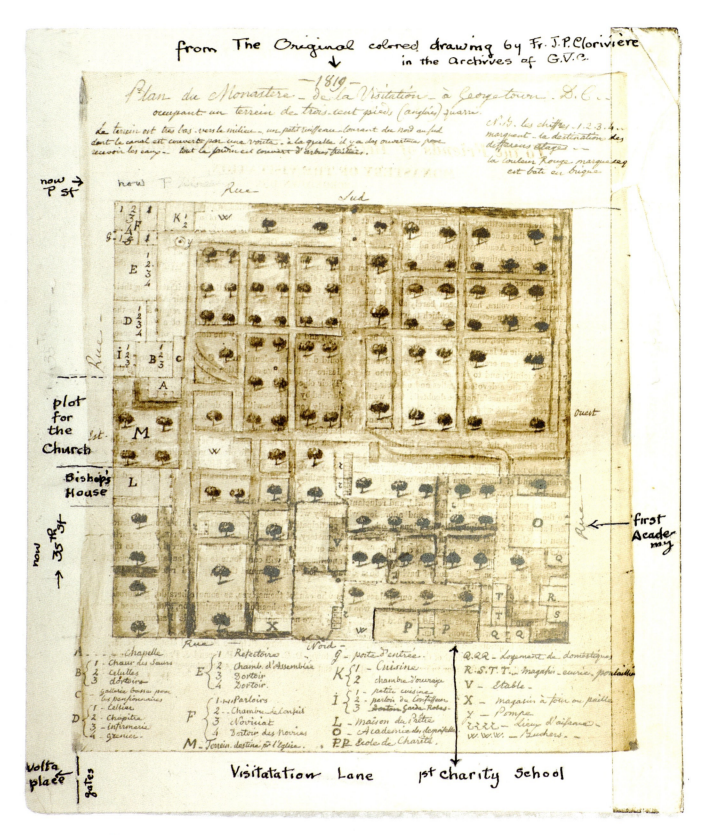

Figure 6-4.
Plan of the Monastery grounds drawn by Father Clorivière. Georgetown, 1819.
Inscribed: "Plan du Monastere de la Visitation à Georgetown. D.C." with twentieth-century inscriptions.
Ink and watercolor on paper.
Georgetown Visitation Monastery Archives

Figure 6-5. View of Georgetown Visitation from 1822 school prospectus. Inscribed: "GEORGETOWN CONVENT of... VISITATION DIS^T of COLUMBIA." Engraving on paper. Georgetown Visitation Monastery Archives

experienced in training young women to teach.[18] Samplers with devout verses date from 1816 to 1818 and may reflect the sisters' renewed association with French Catholic orders.

In January 1819, Father Joseph-Pierre Picot de Limoëlan de Clorivière (1768–1826), an educated French nobleman and priest, and a gifted artist, arrived from Charleston to become spiritual director of the Visitation Monastery. He revised and strengthened the academy curriculum and initiated public oral examinations and distribution of awards in the manner of French schools. He also designed or supervised the construction of new buildings that expanded the monastery and academy (Figures 6-4, 6-5).[19] During Clorivière's seven-year tenure, enrollment grew from sixteen paying students to forty-eight.[20] A prospectus published around 1822 described the academy's curriculum: "The common branches of Education taught in this institution, are Reading, Writing, Arithmetic, English Grammar and Composition, Geography, with the use of Maps and Globes, Elements of History, plain and ornamental Needle Work."

The fee for tuition and board in 1822, which also included washing, mending, books, stationary, and medical services, was $150 per annum with additional quarterly fees for French, drawing, and music.[21] Day scholars

---

18 Jerusha was the wife of the Reverend Virgilius Barber, parents of four daughters and one son. They converted to Catholicism and desired to enter monastic life. To join the religious communities, separation of the husband and wife was required, and Archbishop Neale conducted the ceremony in June 1817. Virgilius Barber became a Jesuit novice and Jerusha Barber received the veil of a Visitation postulant. The Visitation Entrance Book shows their three eldest daughters entered the school at that time with a notation that the Archbishop permitted them to pay when they could. The youngest child was kept in a private home and their son accompanied his father. In February 1820, the Barbers took their vows. The five children later entered the religious life as Visitandine and Ursuline nuns and as a Jesuit.

19 Clorivière oversaw the timely completion of a building to house the Benevolent School in 1819, the year of a financial panic that forced many people into poverty. Non-paying students and orphans had most likely been housed, clothed, and educated by the sisters in less spacious quarters before that time.

20 Mada-anne Gell, "Georgetown Visitation," 38.

21 One hundred fifty dollars was the official rate for tuition and board in 1822, but school documents suggest some students were charged lower fees based on their ability to pay.

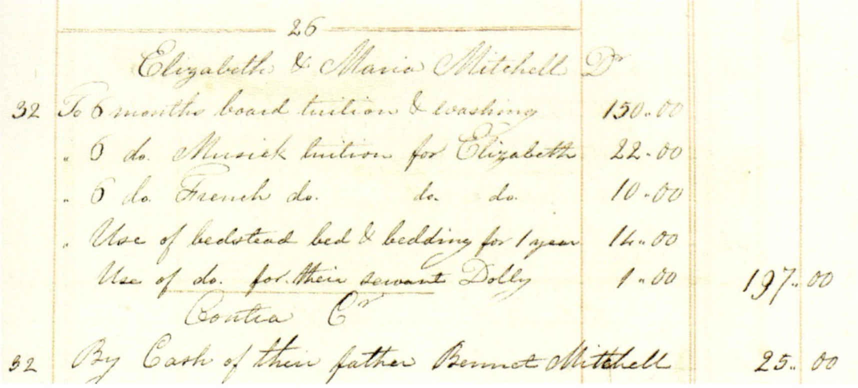
26
Elizabeth & Maria Mitchell Dr
32 To 6 months board tuition & washing 150.00
" 6 do. Musick tuition for Elizabeth 22.00
" 6 do. French do. do. do. 10.00
" Use of bedstead bed & bedding for 1 year 14.00
Use of do. for their servant Dolly 1.00 197.00
Contra Cr
32 By Cash of their father Bennet Mitchell 25.00

Figure 6-6. Account of Elizabeth and Maria Mitchell. September 25, 1825. Georgetown Visitation Monastery Archives

paid five to eight dollars per quarter. A student's parents provided her bed and bedding, knives, forks, spoons, and tumbler or paid fees for the use of those items.[22] School records note that the father of Elizabeth and Maria Mitchell from Baltimore was charged one dollar per year for the bedding of their servant Dolly (Figure 6-6).[23]

School ledgers recording fees charged and payments received exist from 1816 on and provide valuable information about needlework studies.[24] School accounts identify girls who stitched embroideries on silk but very few who stitched samplers. The earliest available charge for sampler materials may have been the notation in the account of Matilda Flanigan in May 1818 for "Canvass & Silks $4.75," which also included a pair of scissors for "50 cents." In 1819 two charges for "Silk(s) for sampler $3.00" were recorded in the school's Letter Book (Figure 6-7 and Appendix III). While there were no fees for teaching sampler work or embroidery, per se, there were various extra charges for sampler and embroidery materials: satin or lutestring, linen for backing, India cotton, tape, shenelle [*sic*], and silks or floss. Fees were also charged for "drawing a piece of embroidery" and rental of an embroidery frame and stand.[25] By 1824 a shift in fashion became apparent in charges for velvet and tapestry work, and materials for card racks and music stool covers.

A more detailed analysis of ledger entries reveals that Visitation students stitched their embroideries through layers of silk and linen, using nearly a half-yard of each. Cotton tape attached the piece to the embroidery frame, which rested on a stand. Embroideries varied in their complexity and density of stitching. One embroidery could require anywhere from twelve to thirty skeins of spool floss at about ten cents apiece and six to twenty-seven

Figure 6-7. Account of Matilda Flanigan. May 1819. Georgetown Visitation Monastery Archives

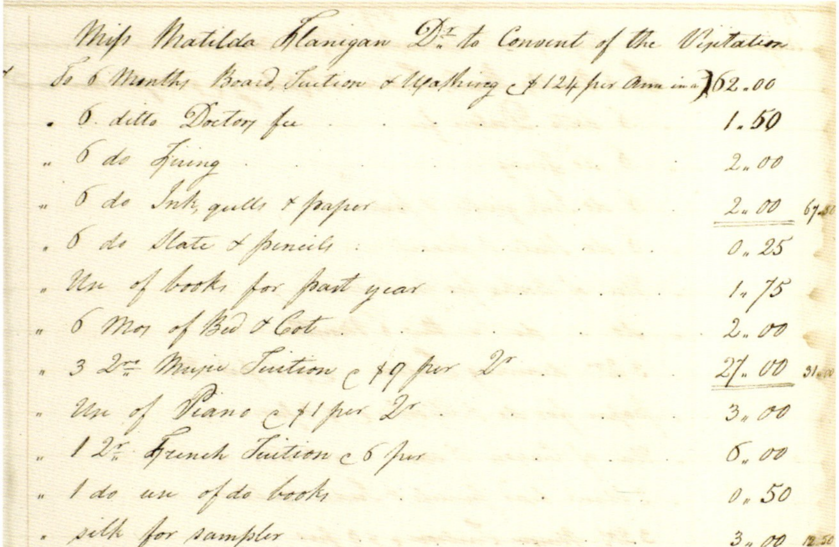
Miss Matilda Flanigan Dr to Convent of the Visitation
To 6 Months Board Tuition & Washing @ $124 per Ann[um] 62.00
6 ditto Doctors fee 1.50
" 6 do Firing 2.00
" 6 do Ink, quills & paper 2.00 67.50
6 do Slate & pencils 0.25
" Use of books for past year 1.75
" 6 Mos of Bed & Cot 2.00
" 3 Qrs Music Tuition @ $9 per Qr 27.00 31.00
" Use of Piano @ $1 per Qr 3.00
" 1 Qr French Tuition @ 6 per 6.00
" 1 do use of do books 0.50
silk for sampler 3.00 12.50
" 50 Skeins spool floss silk @ cts 10 per 5.00
" 42 do card do do @ 6 per 2.52
" 4 pieces shenille @ $1 per 4.00
" Balance on former account 129.48½ 141..
Amount 252..

22 Prospectus reproduced in Lathrop and Lathrop, *A Story of Courage*, 140. School fees were paid by various people—parents, grandparents, aunts, siblings, guardians, members of the clergy. Boarding students frequently had a local contact responsible for their finances.

23 Georgetown Visitation Monastery Archives, Journal, September 25, 1825.

24 Georgetown Visitation Monastery Archives, Letter Book, Entrance Book, and Ledgers.

25 There are several charges from 1818 in the ledgers for a "drawing master's bill." He was probably an artist hired by the sisters to teach a subject they could not. Ledgers, July 2, 8, 11, 1818, Georgetown Visitation Monastery Archives. A February 10, 1819, entry in the account of Rebecca Boarman for "2 Months teaching the art of drawing" may reflect the 1819 arrival of Clorivière, an artist who would have been capable of teaching drawing as well as drawing and painting embroidery designs. A number of Clorivière's miniature paintings are known. See Stephen C. Worsley, "Joseph-Pierre Picot de Limoëlan de Clorivière: A Portrait Miniaturist Revisited," *Journal of Early Southern Decorative Arts*, 28 (2002): 6–9.

skeins of card floss at six cents apiece. Compositions that included expensive chenille required from two to four pieces at one dollar each. Generally, the cost of materials, rental fee, and drawing the design added up to about eleven dollars per embroidery. Students also purchased their own sewing tools, such as scissors, thimbles, needles, and pins. And at least one student had the academy arrange for the framing of her embroidery. The account of a Miss Edwards was charged $14.50 in 1833 for "frames for painting & embroidery" (Appendix III).[26]

The April 5, 1820 ledger entry for sisters Henrietta and Eleanor Waring provides an example: 1 yard of satin for $1.50, 1 yard of fine linen for $1.00, 3 yards of india cotton for $.75, 2 pieces of tape for $.12½, drawing 2 pieces for embroidery for $4.00, use of stands and frames for embroidery for $2.00, 6 pieces of "shenille" for $6.00, 50 skeins of card floss for $5.00, and 29 skeins of spool floss for $2.41¼, totaling $22.78¾ for two embroideries (Figure 6-8). It is interesting to note the order of the charges whereby the ground fabrics were set up, the patterns drawn, and chenille and floss were employed to create the embroideries. The quantity of ground materials and the fee to draw the embroidery were relatively consistent across all student records from 1819 and 1820. Beginning in 1821 and through 1824, a flat fee ranging between $7, $8, or $10 was charged for a "piece of embroidery" (Appendix III).

As reasonable as the rates may have seemed, academy tuition, board, and additional fees were beyond the means of many families who wished a solid education for their daughters. The depression that followed the crash of 1819 continued for several years, causing Archbishop Ambrose Maréchal to write in 1823:

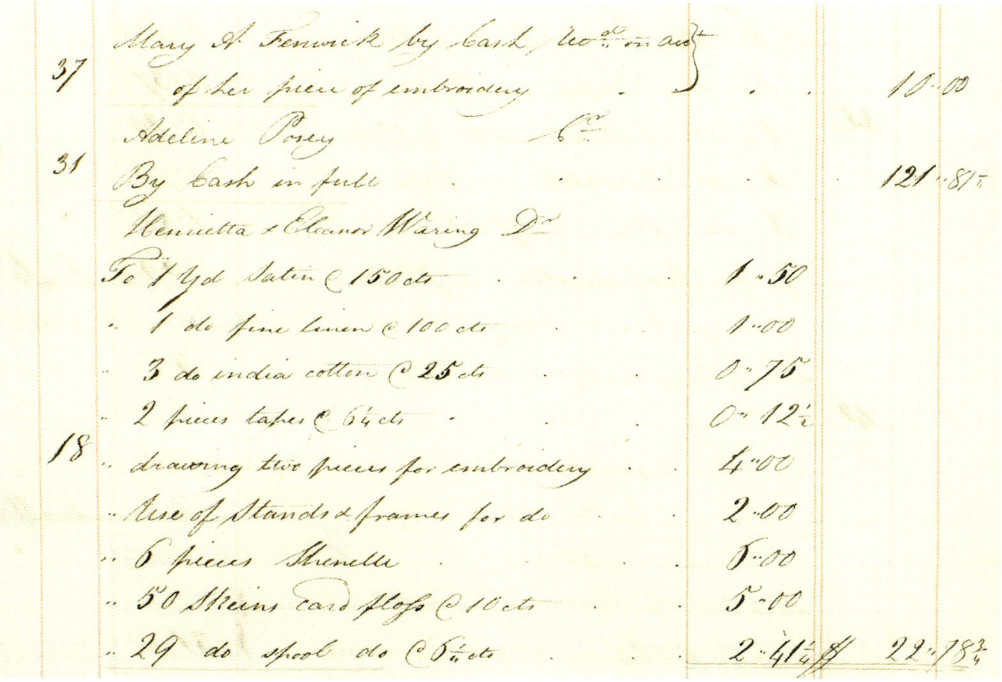
37 Mary A. Fenwick by Cash, rec'd on acct of her piece of embroidery . . 10.00
Adeline Posey Cr.
31 By Cash in full . . 121.81¼
Henrietta & Eleanor Waring Dr.
To 1 yd Satin @ 150 cts . . 1.50
" 1 do fine linen @ 100 cts . 1.00
" 3 do india cotton @ 25 cts . 0.75
" 2 pieces tapes @ 6¼ cts . 0.12½
18 " drawing two pieces for embroidery . 4.00
" Use of Stands & frames for do . 2.00
" 6 pieces Shenelle . 6.00
" 50 Skeins card floss @ 10 cts . 5.00
" 29 do spool do @ 8⅓ cts . 2.41¼ 22.78¾

Figure 6-8. Account of Henrietta & Eleanor Waring. April 5, 1820. Georgetown Visitation Monastery Archives

> *The wealthiest families are suffering to a degree I would not have believed possible. My dear Visitation nuns feel the effects keenly. They get no more sewing to do. Because of lack of means, parents have been gradually forced to withdraw their children.*[27]

School ledgers confirm late payments and money problems at the monastery. Eleanora Neale's account was overdue in 1823, when Sister Mary de Sales Neale wrote to her father:

> *Sir, Your Daughter's account being again due . . . we have taken the liberty of forwarding it to you, requesting you will at least send us a part of it as soon as possible if you cannot raise the whole; you know the times are hard & that money is in great demand, be sure we experience both & are glad to receive ever so small a sum.*[28]

Other parents were less affected by the economic crisis. John Baptist LaSalle, a wealthy New Yorker, paid four hundred dollars for two years of tuition and board in advance,

26 Letter Book, November 4, 1833, Georgetown Visitation Monastery Archives.

27 Sullivan and Hannan, *Georgetown Visitation*, 72.

28 Letter Book, September, 1823, Georgetown Visitation Monastery Archives.

upon the enrollment of his daughters Charlotte and Virginia.²⁹ This 1824 payment helped the school avert a dire financial shortfall.

Over the years, the sisters of Georgetown Visitation supplemented their needs in various ways. They raised cows, chickens, and geese and smoked their own meat. From their woods they gathered fuel, from their orchards fruit, and from their stream fish. A Protestant baker supplied their daily bread at no charge.³⁰ Parents also exchanged goods and services for tuition. The father of Mary Laurence supplied "60 lbs wool at sundry times" and was credited for $21.50 against tuition and other expenses (Figure 6-30).³¹ Mrs. Stanford gave the school her piano in exchange for two years' board, tuition, and "extra branches" for her daughter Helen.³²

In 1824, Anne Royall visited Washington and Georgetown in the District of Columbia. Curious about Roman Catholics, she made a point of going to Georgetown College and the Visitation Monastery.³³

> *How much have I heard said about these Roman Catholics! I have heard them stigmatized by every harsh name, and accounted little better than heretics. But I must confess, I never was amongst people more liberal, more affable, condescending, or courteous, than the citizens of Georgetown. I could have spent my days with this endearing people.*

> *Besides the college, they have . . . a seminary for young ladies, which is also under the dominion of Roman Catholics; and wholly under the direction of the convent; the pupils being taught by the nuns. All denominations send their children to this seminary, which is much celebrated for its salutary regulations.*³⁴

Royall, probably unaware of the sisters' financial situation, went on to describe the school at the "Convent of the Visitation."

> *The seminary is very large, enclosed (together with the convent and a large piece of ground,) with a high wall, the front of the convent answering for part of the wall. The ground within the inclosure [sic] is cultivated as a garden, and adorned with trees, walks, and summer-houses. Here the nuns walk about and amuse themselves, when they choose. They have to cross this garden in going to the seminary, which forms another part of the wall. This seminary embraces every branch of female education, and the strictest attention is paid to the morals of the pupils. By an article of the institution, the pupils must conform to a uniform dress, which is a brown frock and black apron in school, and a white dress on Sunday.*³⁵

The educational direction of Visitation Academy changed once again in 1826 with the death of Father Clorivière. His replacement, Father Michael Wheeler, a Sulpician priest, brought to the academy curriculum his

---

29 Entrance Book, April, 1824, Georgetown Visitation Monastery Archives.

30 Mary Mitchell, *Divided Town* (Barre, Mass.: Barre Publishers, 1968), 93.

31 Ledgers, May 3, 1825, Georgetown Visitation Monastery Archives. Most likely, the wool was spun and woven by the sisters to use for clothing for the Benevolent School. Sullivan also notes evidence from 1817 that the sisters spun, dyed, and wove coarse cloth for their habits. Sullivan and Hannan, *Georgetown Visitation*, 67.

32 Note pasted on inside front cover of Entrance Book, October, 1839.

33 Anne Royall was sufficiently impressed that she selected a drawing of the school buildings as the frontispiece for the publication of her travels, *Sketches of History, Life, and Manners in the United States* (New Haven, 1826).

34 Royall, *Sketches*, 182. Not all thought so highly of a Catholic education. Letitia Tyler, a devout Episcopalian and wife of Senator (and future president) John Tyler, "refused to permit Tyler to place their [four] daughters in the fashionable Georgetown Academy for Girls in Washington because it was a Catholic institution." www.firstladies.org/biographies/firstladies.aspx?biography=10. However, after Letitia died, Tyler married a former Visitation student who had converted to Catholicism.

35 Royall, *Sketches*, 181.

interests in music, mathematics, and science. Within the next two years a "Philosophical and Chemical Apparatus" was acquired at considerable cost, and used for the teaching of fourteen branches of modern science.[36]

The academy prospectus from 1827 mentioned the new "Mantua Room" created in response to parents who had requested a more practical application of needlework studies. "Mantua-work, to compose dress in its various forms, . . . will be provided if required."[37] Basic dressmaking must have been taught earlier. Shortly after Eleanora Neale entered school in March 1820, her account was charged $4.54 for quantities of cambric, ribbon, diaper, India muslin, domestic, and book muslin. Her sewing continued in September 1820 when she was charged a total of $3.96 for yards of bombazette, calico, and flannel as well as balls of cotton, a skein of silk, a piece of tape, and needles and pins. Other students paid for these same fabrics, implying they sewed their own uniforms of "a brown stuff frock and black apron."[38] By 1827, under a new director, "The winter uniform of the young ladies consisted of a crimson bombazette dress and pelerine, with a black apron."[39]

By the late 1820s, the Young Ladies' Academy was recognized for its academic excellence, and the number of pupils increased.[40] Girls, regardless of religion, were accepted at any time during the school year if they were older than seven but younger than fifteen. Most stayed for one to three years.[41] These were privileged young women, whose parents recognized the value of educating their daughters and could afford to pay for it. The children were not needed to help at home or contribute to family income.[42] When the federal census was compiled in 1840, the Academy of the Visitation included 114 scholars.[43] Boarding students, who made up about two-thirds of the enrollment, came from southern and western regions of the United States as well as from Mexico, Cuba, the West Indies, and other exotic locations.[44]

The annual oral examinations, exhibitions of student work, and presentation of prizes held in mid-summer attracted much attention in the local community. In 1828, for example, President John Quincy Adams distributed the prizes, and other presidents continued this practice. Adams wrote in his diary:

> *At the close of the ceremony I addressed a few words to the young ladies, assuring them that I felt as much honored in distributing the rewards as they had been in receiving them—with the difference, however, that on me the honor was gratuitously conferred but theirs was the reward of merit.*[45]

---

36 Sister Mada-anne Gell notes that most secondary schools in the United States had no scientific laboratory equipment until the late 1870s, and those that did used it for demonstration purposes only. At the Visitation Academy, under the direction of Father Wheeler, students were allowed to conduct their own scientific experiments from as early as 1828. Gell, "Georgetown Visitation," 39–40. There was a small charge for "3 Months Use of Apparatus." Letter Book, July 22, 1836, Georgetown Visitation Monastery Archives.

37 Sullivan and Hannan, *Georgetown Visitation*, 87.

38 Ibid., 79.

39 Ibid., 88.

40 The federal census for 1830 listed for the Convent of the Visitation in Georgetown sixty-three residents, probably boarding students, over age five and under age sixteen.

41 Mada-anne Gell, "A History of the Development of Curriculum, Georgetown Visitation Preparatory School 1865–1965" (Ph.D. diss., Catholic University, 1983), 28, 33.

42 Ibid., 24.

43 In a separate column for "Schools &c." the 1840 census reported "114" under "No. of Scholars," and a total of 152 females in different age groups ranging from "10 & under 15" to "50 & under 60." There were additional entries for two free colored females and two female slaves. Over time the monastery owned slaves that were brought by candidates in payment of their dowries. They were employed as servants, carpenters, and farm hands. Sullivan and Hannan, *Georgetown Visitation*, 110.

44 Sullivan and Hannan, *Georgetown Visitation*, 118.

45 Ibid., 90. In 1828, John Quincy Adams had signed into law an act incorporating the Sisters of the Visitation at Georgetown.

Figure 6-9. Reward of merit in the form of a hand screen awarded to Nancy Clark. Georgetown, 1830. Inscribed: "1st Class of Lace-work / Miss Nancy Clark / Ladies Academy of the Visitation G. T. D. C. / July 28th 1830." Color lithograph, paint and gold metallic paper on embossed cardboard. 7 x 8 ¾ in. with ivory handle, 7 ¾ in. Georgetown Visitation Monastery Archives

Others recorded their impressions of the awards ceremony. Ann Shaaff, a Georgetown resident, wrote to a friend around 1832:

I attended two days at the Nunnery . . . and it was very new and somewhat interesting . . . to see the different experiments in Chemistry and Natural Philosophy made by the girls. . . . The third day it was much crowded . . . the premiums were distributed and there was [an] abundance of music both vocal and instrumental . . . the ceremonies concluded with the crowning of three Queens . . . they all had maids of honor, who likewise had bunches of flowers instead of wreaths on their heads.[46]

Another observer, writing about the same time, also commented on the appealing ceremony.

Two young ladies, one from the senior and one from the junior circle, elegantly attired were crowned with splendid wreaths, the testimony of superior merit; and the queens of the day, were each attended with maids of honor decorated in like manner.[47]

Elaborate rewards of merit painted on cards or paper hand screens with applied gilded embellishments were presented for excellence in different subjects during the 1820s and 1830s. Nancy (Ann) Clark, who entered the academy with her sister Eleanor (Ellen) in 1826, was awarded a hand screen with an image of "The Market Place at St. Neots" for excellence in lace work in 1830 (Figure 6-9).[48] Ann Williamson, a boarding student from Baltimore between 1825 and 1829, received an embellished card for music and another for French in 1828, perhaps from the hand of President Adams (Figures 6-10, 6-11).[49] Later students received medals or printed "Tickets of Merit."

The various branches of needlework continued to be offered at the academy at least until the late 1880s. Plain and ornamental needlework, tapestry, and lace work were included in the academy tuition, and several late examples of Berlin wool work are known.[50] The 1852 Distribution of Premiums awarded excellence in "Painting, Drawing, Tapestry, Ornamental and Mantua Work, and Plain Sewing." By the 1870s, the term "Embroidery" had been substituted for "Tapestry" in the listing of premiums, and

---

46 Ann Shaaff to Harriet Addison, undated letter, ca. 1832, MS 0230, Historical Society of Washington, D.C.

47 Sullivan and Hannan, *Georgetown Visitation*, 91.

48 Nancy (1815–1890) and Eleanor (1812–1835) were the daughters of Eleanor Digges Clagett and Benjamin Hall Clark of Mellwood, Prince George's County, Maryland. They were boarding students and the entire cost of their four-year education came to $1,060.75.

49 Ann was a daughter of Maria Tiernan and David Williamson Jr., president of the Baltimore Fire Insurance Company. Her father paid extra fees of $10 for French tuition and $12 for music in 1827.

50 Three examples of Berlin wool work with religious themes are in the collection of the monastery. Two are by unidentified stitchers. It is unclear whether patterns were provided to students at no charge. An ambiguous Letter Book entry for December 9, 1836, showed a credit to the account of Matilda Murphey "for tapestry patterns $7.00." Perhaps her father supplied the school with needlework patterns.

Figure 6-10. Reward of merit awarded to Ann T. Williamson. Georgetown, 1828. Inscribed: "3ᵈ Class 2ᵈ in Music / Ladies' Academy of the Visitation. Georgetown. District of Columbia. July 30ᵗʰ 1828 // At the Exhi / bition passed at / the Ladies' / Academy of the / Visitation on the / 30ᵗʰ of July 1828 / the Academic / Crown in the / Junʳ Circle was / Awarded to / Miss A. T. Williamson / of Baltimore / Md." Watercolor and ink on paper with applied gold metallic paper. 4 ⅝ x 7 in. Georgetown Visitation Monastery Archives

by 1888 needlework premiums were simply described as "Plain and Fancy Needle Work."⁵¹

Early Embroideries

Much of what we know today about students who attended the Young Ladies' Academy during the early decades of the nineteenth century is represented by tangible objects that illustrate their achievements in ornamental education. Three very similar silk embroideries were worked at the academy between 1800 and 1804.⁵² They were stitched by Catharine F. Queen (Figure 6-12), Eliza Jameson (Figure 6-13), and Maria Teresa Lalor (Figure 6-14). The first two embroideries are owned by the Georgetown Visitation Monastery Archives, and were included in Betty Ring's compendium of American schoolgirl needlework.⁵³

Subsequent to Ring's publication, Maria Teresa Lalor's embroidered picture was discovered, owned by a descendant of the maker. Maria Teresa was the niece of Alice Lalor, one of the three pious ladies from Philadelphia and a founder of the Visitation convent. Maria Lalor's embroidery is immediately recognizable as related to the two owned by Georgetown Visitation Monastery.

All three embroideries depict a pastoral scene bisected by a stream with a two-story red brick building on one side and a small blue thatched cottage on the other side. The

Figure 6-11. Detail. Reward of merit awarded to Ann T. Williamson. Georgetown, 1828. Inscribed: "4ᵗʰ Class 2ᵈ. in French Miss Ann T. Williamson. / Ladies' Academy of the Visitation. Georgetown. District of Columbia July 30ᵗʰ 1828." Watercolor and ink on paper with applied paper. 4 ⅝ x 7 in. Georgetown Visitation Monastery Archives

---

51 Extant programs, "Distribution of Premiums at the Academy of the Visitation, Georgetown. July 21st. 1852"; "Academy of the Visitation, Georgetown, District of Columbia. Annual Distribution of Premiums" [ca. 1870]; "Annual Distribution of Premiums, Georgetown Academy of the Visitation. Wednesday, June 20, 1888."

52 An anonymous silk embroidery of a similar pastoral landscape, although using a different color palette and slight variation of building styles, may also be a product of the Young Ladies' Academy. Information courtesy of Van Tassel-Baumann American Antiques.

53 See Ring, *Girlhood Embroidery*, 522–27.

compositions vary, and the different interpretations of the buildings suggest that more than one person drew the designs.[54] The principal elements remain the same and probably represent the buildings and grounds of the Young Ladies' Academy. The school annals describe the scene: "a creek ran through the middle of the grounds in the heights of Georgetown . . . where there were also the convent garden, orchards, meadow, spring and fish pond."[55] The tall, narrow brick building is typical of Georgetown Federal-style architecture and was probably the "Old Academy," home of the three pious women and also the location of the school's classrooms. In contrast, the rustic blue cottage probably served as the residence and convent of the Poor Clares.

These three silk embroideries are unlike any others known from the District of Columbia. They do, however, resemble needlework pictures worked at about the same time from Elizabeth Folwell's embroidery school in Philadelphia. Often drawn and finished with painted details by her husband, Samuel Folwell (1764–1813), the Philadelphia embroideries are more sophisticated and overtly neoclassical than those from Georgetown. Samuel Folwell indicated in Philadelphia newspaper advertisements and city directories that he was a hair worker, engraver, and a painter of miniatures. In 1793, he opened a Drawing School for Young Ladies to teach painting on paper, ivory, or satin. This apparently fueled his artistic talent, whereby his repertory expanded to pattern drawing for decorative silk embroideries taught by his wife, whose school began in the late 1790s.

Folwell's designs for needlework pictures encompassed biblical, literary, allegorical, mythical, historical, and memorial subjects, often in a pastoral setting. While some were original compositions, the sources were often prints from London publishers. Attributes of Folwell's embroidery patterns that specifically characterize his work include crossed trees, feathery willows, striated hillocks, and a pond. In his pastoral scenes, several examples include a thatched cottage with a long sloping roof as well as standing and resting sheep. Folwell's patterns were numerous, and he independently offered them for sale to other teachers.

Because of the many similarities in their design elements, the depiction of the Georgetown convent and school grounds in these embroideries may have been inspired by Folwell's designs. For many years, his Philadelphia address was Laetitia Court (directly behind Front Street) and later Moravian Alley (also known as Sassafras Street). According to city directory addresses, Maria Sharpe, Maria McDermott, and Alice Lalor resided in the same vicinity. Maria Sharpe was probably aware of the artist Folwell and his drawing school and later his wife's embroidery school. Quite possibly she was influenced by Folwell's artistry when drawing her composition of the convent and school property in Georgetown. Since there are no similar embroideries from a later time in the school's history, this particular form of ornamental needlework was apparently only taught by Maria Sharpe and not continued after her death in 1804. Following are the three pictorial embroideries stitched at the Young Ladies' Academy in Georgetown.

Catharine F. Queen

Catharine F. Queen (ca. 1788–1872) was the eldest of six children born to Joseph Queen (1753–1802) and Ann Edwardina Jerningham (1761–1814). They were married in Charles County, Maryland, by a Jesuit priest on December 2, 1787. It is unknown exactly when Catharine (or Kitty, as she was known to her family) Queen attended the Young Ladies' Academy. Her painted and silk embroidered

---

54 Usually the needlework teacher or drawing instructor, not the student, laid out the design for an embroidery or supplied a pattern or engraving for the student to follow. Paper patterns have been found attached to two later samplers.

55 Lathrop and Lathrop, *A Story of Courage*, 153.

picture of the Academy landscape includes a later ink inscription indicating it was completed at the "Academy of the Visitation" in 1799 (Figure 6-12). The stitches she used include satin, stem, long and short, complemented by watercolor trees and a resting sheep. Although there are no other records documenting Catharine's tenure at the Academy, it is known that Catharine's niece, Edwardina Queen, and another relative, Rosana Queen, were day scholars at the Academy in 1825, suggesting a strong family tie to the school —a tie that lasted more than twenty years.

The Queen family can trace its American roots to Samuel Queen (1630–1711), whose 1657 "Queensborough" land grant from Lord Baltimore comprised some of the territory that became the District of Columbia. The 1688 "Inclosure" land grant to Ninian Beall came to the Queen family through sale, marriage, and inheritance. It was on this property that Richard Queen (born before 1732–1794) built his manor house, in what is now the Langdon neighborhood of northeast Washington, D.C.[56]

The birth of Joseph Queen, Richard's son, was recorded in Prince George's County, Maryland. Records from 1784 show Joseph Queen acquired over one thousand acres of the Inclosure tract on the north side of the Eastern Branch of the Potomac River. He later purchased another part of the tract that lay in Washington City. After his death, Ann E. Queen and her children were listed in the 1810 federal census as living in the Rock Creek and Eastern Branch Hundreds of western Prince George's County.[57]

On April 14, 1817, a District of Columbia marriage license was issued to Catharine F. Queen and Robert Boone (1791–1861). They made their home in Frederick County, Maryland.[58] From the census, it appears they

Figure 6-12.
Embroidered picture worked by Catharine F. Queen. Georgetown, 1800–1804.
Inscribed: [in ink by later hand] "Worked by Catharine F. Queen Academy of the Visitation, Georgetown, D.C. 1799."
Silk, watercolor, and ink on silk ground.
14 x 15 ¾ in.
Georgetown Visitation Monastery Archives

---

56 Under Maryland penal laws, between 1654 and 1784 Catholics suffered religious and political intolerance, but practitioners of the faith were allowed to do so privately in their homes. When the wing in Queen's home for the offering of Mass and Sacraments became inadequate, a small chapel was established on the property that accommodated other Catholic families in the surrounding area. These small congregations were ministered to by visiting Jesuit priests. Richard Queen's 1793 will gave and bequeathed to his friend, the Right Reverend John Carroll, Bishop of Baltimore, "two acres of land where the Roman Catholick Chapel now stands being part of a tract of land called Inclosure." This was Queen's Chapel (from which a nearby road in Prince George's County takes its name), and its site today is occupied by the Saint Francis de Sales Church on Rhode Island Avenue in Washington's northeast quadrant near the District of Columbia and Maryland boundary line.

57 It was previously assumed this Queen family resided at Upper Marlboro on the eastern side of the county.

58 In 1837 the governor of Maryland appointed Robert Boone as Judge of the orphans' court. He was elected as a director of the Mutual Insurance Company of Frederick County in 1852 and 1854. Boone went on to be elected a Common Councilman of Frederick City in 1856.

Figure 6-13. Embroidered picture worked by Eliza Jameson. Georgetown, 1800–1804. Silk, watercolor, and ink on silk ground. 13 x 18 in. Georgetown Visitation Monastery Archives

had at least three children. Their son, Jerningham, became a physician. Catharine Queen Boone was living with this widowed son's family near Adamstown, south of Frederick Town, when she died on January 17, 1872. She and her husband are buried in Saint John's Catholic Cemetery at 3rd and East Streets in Frederick.

Eliza Jameson

Eliza Jameson (1785–1853) was a daughter of Walter Jameson (1760–1814) and Teresa Edelen (1767–1812) of Charles County, Maryland. The exact dates of Eliza's time at the Young Ladies' Academy are unknown. A notation on the backboard of her silk embroidery reads: "This is a picture of Georgetown Convent about the year of 1800 made by Eliza Jaimeson [sic] of Charles County Md." Eliza used a combination of satin, stem, long and short, herringbone stitches, and French knots (Figure 6-13). Because she used needlework instead of paint for her trees and sheep, Eliza's picture exhibits far more embroidery than that of Catharine Queen.

Eliza's mother Teresa was a daughter of Joseph Edelen and Catharine Queen (ca. 1731–1776), both of whom died when she was a young girl (her father in 1775, followed by her mother in 1776). Benjamin Jameson became the executor of both estates and the guardian of Teresa and her three siblings.[59] An August 1783 disbursement from the estate of Teresa's older brother, Henry, was made to her upon arriving at the stipulated age of sixteen. That record shows that Teresa was already married to Walter Jameson, the son of her legal guardian. It is possible that these funds contributed to Walter Jameson's purchase the following year of 478 acres on Cornwallis Neck, in upper northwest Charles County, bound by the Potomac River and Mattawoman Creek.[60]

This is where Eliza Jameson spent her childhood before attending the Young Ladies' Academy in Georgetown. As an adult Eliza continued to live in Middletown, Charles County, where she resided as of the 1850 census. Eliza Jameson, who never married, died on July 25, 1853, and was buried beside her father and brother in the graveyard of Saint Charles Catholic Church at Indian Head.

---

59 The fate of the Edelen's four minor children was settled in late 1778 when the fourteen-year-old son, Joseph, appeared in court and chose Benjamin Jameson as his guardian. His three younger sisters, including Teresa, were placed under the same guardianship.

60 Walter Jameson was among five citizens who petitioned the Maryland General Assembly concerning the necessity for a public road from Deep Point, at the tip of Cornwallis Neck, to intersect with the public road at New House on the head of Mattawoman Creek. Their request was enacted in late 1796, and the petitioners were appointed commissioners to survey, lay out, and open such a road at their expense. Using old and new maps, it appears Strauss Avenue is that road. Most of Cornwallis Neck is now under the purview of the Naval Ordnance Station at Indian Head.

Figure 6-14. Embroidered picture worked by Maria Teresa Lalor. Georgetown, 1800–1804. Inscribed: [on églomisé mat] "Maria T. Lalor." Silk, watercolor, ink, and pencil on silk ground. 15 1/8 x 19 7/8 in. Private collection

Maria Teresa Lalor

Maria Teresa Lalor (ca. 1793–1816) was the daughter of John Lalor and Catharine Moroney (widow of Thomas Moroney) whose marriage on October 11, 1792, was conducted by the Reverend F. A. Fleming at Philadelphia's Saint Joseph's Catholic Church.[61] John Lalor kept a tavern on South Water Street in Philadelphia from 1794 until his death in 1818. His sister was Alice Lalor, who left Philadelphia in 1799 in response to Leonard Neale's request for assistance in establishing a Catholic school for young ladies in Georgetown. Thus, when Maria Teresa Lalor arrived in Georgetown to attend the Young Ladies' Academy, she entered the school founded by her aunt. Although it is unknown exactly when Maria attended the academy, she stitched her silk embroidery under the tutelage of Maria Sharpe some time between 1800 and early 1804, making her between seven and eleven years old.

Maria's embroidery (Figure 6-14) depicts the same two buildings, stream, and resting sheep found on the landscapes stitched by Catharine Queen and Eliza Jameson. Unique to this group is her inclusion of a shepherdess. Maria's silk and watercolor picture shows some pencil, and possibly ink, guidelines on a satin-weave silk ground. Although not available to examine, the stitches are probably the usual satin, stem, and long and short. Like the Jameson piece, the leafy trees are embroidered rather than painted, implying a distinct shift in medium after the earlier Queen piece.

Maria made her First Communion on December 16, 1804, and noted this fact on her copy of a religious pamphlet, "The Key of Paradise Opening the Gate to Eternal Salvation." Maria was probably eleven years

---

61 National Society Daughters of the American Revolution Library, GRC PA S1 V153, 11. The records indicate whether the man or woman is Catholic or Protestant. John and Catharine were noted as Catholic.

Figure 6-15
Embroidered picture worked by Maria Teresa Lalor. Philadelphia, ca. 1808. Wool, chenille, silk and watercolor on linen ground. 27 3/8 x 35 1/4 in. Abby Aldrich Rockefeller Folk Art Museum, The Colonial Williamsburg Foundation, gift of Alice Lalor Molten Earle and John B. Earle, 1993.601.1

old when she first received the Sacrament of Holy Eucharist. Although it is unknown whether this significant event occurred at Trinity Church in Georgetown or one of two Catholic churches in Philadelphia, it does suggest she may have left the Young Ladies' Academy by this time and returned to live with her family. This is further supported by evidence that Maria continued her education in Philadelphia.

While attending a school in Philadelphia, Maria stitched a larger and more sophisticated silk needlework picture depicting a maiden in a pastoral setting. The young woman is playing a lyre and has a gold cross in her hair (Figure 6-15).[62] Considering its large size, the silk embroidered picture may have been a product of the Folwell school.[63] A comparison with a number of known Folwell examples, however, indicates the composition is not distinctively the work of Samuel Folwell so Maria may have attended another Philadelphia school. There were numerous women offering an ornamental education for the young girls of Philadelphia, as well as artists willing to draw patterns for schoolgirl embroideries.

Watercolor painting was considered another polite accomplishment for young women, and instruction in painting was often an important part of a girl's later education. In addition to her two known needlework pictures, Maria Lalor painted two well-executed watercolor landscapes on paper

---

62 Although the image source is unidentified, at least one other embroidery with a variation of the lyre-playing woman by a garland-draped flaming urn is extant (advertised by Fred J. Johnston Antiques of Kingston, New York in *Antiques and The Arts Weekly*, June 24, 1994). Both pieces were worked with wool, chenille, and silk embroidery threads.

63 Both embroideries by Maria Teresa Lalor remained together and descended in her female line to the current owner. The piece attributed to the Folwell school is now in the collection of the Abby Aldrich Rockefeller Folk Art Museum, Colonial Williamsburg. I am very grateful to Barbara Luck for providing me with information on the two Lalor pieces, and to Lalor Earle for guiding me through the Lalor family genealogy.

between 1808 and 1810 (Figures 6-16, 6-17).⁶⁴ Both were most likely painted at a Philadelphia drawing and painting school, one that relied on published prints as design sources.

One possible instructor was James Cox (1751–1834), an English drawing master who had been a colorist for the famous London print seller John Boydell and was a competitor of Samuel Folwell. Cox first advertised his Philadelphia "Drawing and Painting Academy" in 1789, when he informed the public of his previous experience in Albany, New York, where he taught upwards of forty young ladies.⁶⁵ Cox was always located either on or in the vicinity of Walnut Street near the harbor, in the same neighborhood as the Lalors and Folwells. His notices usually specified drawing and painting techniques, media, and subjects. He also publicized his hundreds of fine and common prints for sale, probably acquired through his connection to Boydell. As of 1804 he offered to teach watercolor painting. An 1807 advertisement stated, "Where the various branches will be taught as heretofore, including Landscapes, Figures, Fruits, Flowers, and Fancy Work, &c. upon canvas, Sattin, Glass, Paper, &c. either with oil or water colours."⁶⁶ Earlier notices mentioned painting upon muslin, silk, and tiffany. That he made his talents available outside of his academy was announced in 1800 when he noted, "Public Seminaries attended."⁶⁷ Cox's academy continued to operate until at least 1817.

The records of Saint Joseph's Church in Philadelphia show that on November 17, 1811, Mary T. Laller and Barnt D. Laller were married.⁶⁸ Barnt De Klyn Lalor (ca. 1791–1856) of Trenton, New Jersey, was Maria's cousin several times removed. Their common ancestors were Jeremiah Lalor (1703–1778) and his wife, Susan Lacroix (1719–1778). Barnt was the son of Jeremiah Lalor (ca. 1766–1807)⁶⁹ and Catharine (Kitty) De Klyn (1773–1861). Catharine's father, Barnt De Klyn, was descended from wealthy French Huguenots.⁷⁰ In 1784, De Klyn purchased the estate of

LEFT: Figure 6-16. Painting of waterfall by Maria Teresa Lalor. Philadelphia, ca. 1809. Inscribed: [on églomisé mat] "Maria T. Lalor." Watercolor on paper. 11 x 14 in. Private collection

RIGHT: Figure 6-17. Painting of castle by Maria Teresa Lalor. Philadelphia, ca. 1809. Inscribed: [on églomisé mat] "Maria T. Lalor." Watercolor on paper. 10 ½ x 13 ¼ in. Private collection

---

64 The pair of watercolors descended through the family of Maria's grandson, Anderson Brearley (1840–1892), until they were sent to auction in 2009.

65 *Federal Gazette and Philadelphia Evening Post*, September 29, 1789.

66 Philadelphia *Poulson's American Daily Advertiser*, September 1, 1807.

67 *Philadelphia Gazette*, September 22, 1800.

68 Church records misspelled both her first and last name. Hence Maria Lalor became Mary Laller. Her husband's name should have been listed as Barnt D. Lalor.

69 Francis Bazley Lee, *Genealogical and personal memorial of Mercer County, New Jersey*, Volume 1 (1907): 194.

70 He created his own fortune by operating woolen mills in New York (his father was an early settler of Brooklyn) and New Jersey, supplying the cloth for uniforms during the American Revolution.

Figure 6-18. Sampler worked by Mary Ann Carroll. Georgetown, 1801. Inscribed: "Mary Carroll her work / done at the New Ac / ademy George Town / in the 7th year of her / age Anno Domini / 1801." Silk on linen. 16 ¼ x 10 in. Maryland Historical Society, 1987.97.2

Major William Trent and named it Bow Hill after its geographical features at the southern end of Trenton.[71] Bow Hill became the Lalor estate when a grandson of Jeremiah and Kitty Lalor inherited it from Barnt De Klyn at his death in 1824.

The only known child of Maria and Barnt D. Lalor was Catharine Mary Lalor, born in 1814.[72] Sadly, Catharine never knew her mother beyond infancy because Maria Teresa died on December 1, 1816.[73] Her daughter Catharine wed Joseph Gillingham Brearley (1808–1874) in 1839, and they raised a son and daughter in Trenton. Catharine Lalor Brearley lived to the age of eighty-one, and her mother's two silk embroideries descended through her daughter, Alice (1860–1928). After Maria's death, Barnt D. Lalor married Patience Tilton of Burlington County, New Jersey, on April 12, 1820. Barnt Lalor died October 21, 1856, in his sixty-sixth year, and he and the Brearleys are buried in Trenton's Riverview Cemetery.

Samplers

In the first quarter of the nineteenth century, students at the Young Ladies' Academy also worked samplers. Consistent across the known samplers from the school is the strawberry motif. Most of the strawberries on the samplers from the Young Ladies' Academy are stylized representations, but three girls embroidered the fruit with seeds and detailed leaves, imbuing the motif with symbolic meaning.

---

71 Barnt De Klyn and his wife, Mary Van Zant, were wealthy Presbyterians, and they were distraught when their only child, Catharine, eloped with the less fortunate Irish Catholic Jeremiah Lalor after De Klyn had denied them permission to marry. Naming their first son Barnt De Klyn Lalor appeased the family estrangement, and Jeremiah Lalor eventually managed the De Klyn woolen mills in New Jersey.

72 Tombstone Inscriptions of Persons Born Before 1820 and Buried in the Western Half of Riverview Cemetery Trenton, New Jersey, National Society Daughters of the American Revolution Library, GRC NJ S1 V67, 1997, 5.

73 "Mrs. Maria Lalor, daughter of John Lalor," from *Poulson's American Daily Advertiser*, Philadelphia, December 2, 1816. *Collections of the Genealogical Society of Pennsylvania*, vol. 61 (Philadelphia, 1901), 340.

Mary Ann Carroll

A sampler worked by six-year-old Mary (Ann) Carroll (1794–1860) at the "New Academy" in Georgetown in 1801 may be the earliest example of a sampler stitched at the school (Figure 6-18). When the Poor Clares advertised their school in 1798, their notice referred to the "*New Academy* for Young Ladies" (emphasis added).[74] Mary's sampler is relatively simple, possibly reflecting her young age. The sampler includes alphabets and numbers worked in cross and eyelet stitches, separated by decorative bands in satin and cross stitches and surrounded by a strawberry border. In format and content Mary's needlework resembles samplers from the English, not the French, tradition. It is likely that her teacher was the woman from London hired by the Poor Clares to teach English and embroidery,[75] which may explain why the sampler lacks the religious text and symbolism associated with later samplers from the Young Ladies' Academy. It is unfortunate that no early enrollment records or references in the archives help to identify the embroidery teacher responsible for needlework instruction at this time.

Mary Ann Carroll's identity is established through family descent of her sampler, along with a thimble and a hair-worked ladies' pin.[76] Mary Ann was the daughter of Henry Hill Carroll (1768–1804) and Sarah Rogers (ca. 1770–1833).[77] The Carrolls were one of the leading Catholic families in Maryland. Upon their marriage in 1789, Henry and Sarah established their eastern Baltimore County "Sweet Air" residence in an existing two-story, full cellar, brick house with adjoining brick office, two-story piazza, plus separate kitchen and storehouse.[78] It is here that their children Henry and Mary Ann were raised.

Mary Ann was sent to the New Academy girls' school at Georgetown, where her 1801 marking sampler documents her attendance. Probably due to the unsuitability of the Poor Clares' school, Mary Ann switched to the Young Ladies' Academy, a move that is documented by a letter sent to her there by her father in October 1802. Two years later, on October 26, Mary Ann's father died "after a tedious indisposition" at his Sweet Air residence, leaving her fatherless at the age of ten.[79]

A notice in the Baltimore *Federal Gazette* announced that Charles Carroll, Esq. of Washington and Mary Ann Carroll, daughter of Henry H. Carroll of Baltimore County, were wed at Sweet Air by the Reverend Eden on February 4, 1812.[80] They were first cousins. Charles Carroll was the son of Daniel Carroll of Duddington (1764–1849), who had inherited from his father tracts of land that became part of the new federal city, in particular the area that became Capitol Hill.[81] Charles Carroll died in 1819, making Mary Ann a young widow. Children from this marriage are not known. Mary Ann Carroll lived until January 11, 1860, when she died at "Litter Louna," a Carroll

---

74 This advertisement appears on the front endpaper of Ring's *Girlhood Embroidery*, vol. 2, and she partially transcribed it on page 524.

75 *The Centinel of Liberty, and George-Town and Washington Advertiser*, March 8, 1799.

76 Collection of the Maryland Historical Society (1980.41.1, Lady's pin and 1980.41.2, Thimble).

77 The line of descent from Charles Carroll (1660–1720), the Maryland settler from Ireland, was Daniel Carroll (1707–1734) of Duddington, Charles Carroll (1729–1773) of Duddington II and Carrollsburg (cousin of Charles Carroll of Carrollton, one the Maryland signers of the Declaration of Independence), and Henry Hill Carroll.

78 The Georgian home, built before 1772 by a previous owner, is a Maryland Historic Site.

79 Robert Barnes, *Marriages and Deaths from Baltimore Newspapers 1796–1816* (Baltimore: Genealogical Publishing Co., Inc., 1978), 52.

80 Ibid. Joseph Eden was a Catholic clergyman in Harford and Baltimore counties.

81 Daniel Carroll generously supported all of the early Catholic churches in Washington City, even donating one square of land, on which Saint Peter's Church stands, to accommodate Catholics who lived in the eastern and southern areas of the city. Among the prominent contributors to this project was Daniel's brother, Henry Hill Carroll.

Figure 6-19. Sampler worked by Emily Mary Jackson. Georgetown, 1808. Inscribed: "Emily M. Jackson's / work done at the young Ladies' Academy Georgetown in the year / of our Lord. 1808 / CEDAR GROVE." Silk on linen, 28 by 32 threads per in. 16 ½ x 14 ½ in. Georgetown Visitation Monastery Archives

family home at Pikesville, in western Baltimore County named for the Irish ancestral home of Daniel Carroll, Charles's father.

Religious Samplers

A group of five samplers stitched between 1808 and 1818 at the Young Ladies' Academy share a common format and a number of motifs, some of which are clearly tied to Catholicism. All five are vertical rectangles, visually divided into three registers, and bordered on all four sides by strawberries on a vine. The top register contains a centrally located religious symbol, flanked by one or more pious verses. The middle register contains one or more alphabets, and sometimes the inscription. The bottom register is used for additional motifs, including spade-shaped evergreen trees, birds, or a bowl of strawberries. The inscriptions on all five samplers contain the girl's full name, the year in which the sampler was stitched, and the words "Young Ladies Academy Georgetown." Chronologically and thematically they can be divided into two groups, with the earlier group stitched between 1808 and 1810 and the later group between 1816 and 1818.

1808–1810 Sampler Group

Emily Mary Jackson

The earliest sampler to name the Young Ladies' Academy was stitched in 1808 by Emily M. Jackson (1798–1844). It was discovered after a devastating fire that swept the main school building of Georgetown Visitation in 1993, and although it suffered some damage, it is essentially intact (Figure 6-19). Emily used a variety of stitches, including cross, rice, straight, satin, four-sided, eyelet, and queen. The top alphabet was entirely executed in the elaborate queen stitch.

Emily Mary Jackson was born September 25, 1798, to Elijah Jackson (died 1805) and Mary McWilliams (1769–1841), who were married on January 7, 1796, in Saint Mary's County, Maryland. Elijah Jackson belonged to a Philadelphia family of eminent physicians. In 1802, Doctor Jackson purchased five tracts of land totaling two hundred acres in the area of Leonardtown, the county seat. A notice in the *Baltimore Federal Gazette* reported his death on August 25, 1805, resulting from an accidental fall from his horse while calling on a patient, "leaving a wife and infant daughter." By 1808, Emily was a student at the "young Ladies Academy Georgetown," as inscribed on her marking sampler of four alphabets, supplemented by prayers and declarations.

On February 2, 1819, Brigadier General James Forrest (1781–1826) obtained a license to wed Emily Jackson.[82] Two sons are known from this union, which ended when General Forrest died at his Forrest Hall home on September 22, 1826. After her husband's death, orphans' court records show Emily Forrest sought permission to sell some of the property and transport a few of the household slaves to Georgetown where she and her mother lived while her two sons attended Georgetown College. The family later returned to Forrest Hall, where, after a long illness and gradual decline in health, Emily died on February 18, 1844.[83] She is buried in what is now the Saint Francis Xavier Cemetery at Newtown, west of Leonardtown, where her gravestone can still be seen. Next to it is the broken stone of her mother, Mary Jackson. James Forrest is buried in the Saint Andrews Episcopal Church Cemetery at California, east of Leonardtown.

Emily's sampler is similar to a sampler in the collection of the Philadelphia Museum of Art worked by Eleanor Durkee in 1810 (Figure 6-20).[84] The most significant feature of the Jackson and Durkee samplers is the motif of a cross, mounted on three steps—the Cross of Calvary. Although religious symbols are not common on American samplers or embroidered pictures, a Calvary cross is frequently found on French samplers, where it is often the dominant motif. On Eleanor Durkee's sampler, the cross is surrounded by a distinctive border that also encloses the declaration, "love to HIM and you." In the lower third of Eleanor's sampler is another enclosed cross, coupled with the letters IHS, the first three letters of "Ihsus," the Greek form of the name Jesus.

Of their many similarities, both samplers include the same motif along the bottom, a row of evergreens interspersed with letters spelling out, "C E D A R G R O V E."

Figure 6-20. Sampler worked by Eleanor Durkee. Georgetown, 1810. Inscribed: "Elenor Durkee her work done at the / Young Ladies Academy Georg / Town A D 1810 in the 10th / Year of her age / CEDAR GROVE." Silk on linen. 21 x 15 ¾ in. Whitman Sampler Collection, gift of Pet, Incorporated, Philadelphia Museum of Art, 1969-288-216

---

82 During the War of 1812, James Forrest was a captain in the 4th Regimental Cavalry District, representing Charles and Saint Mary's counties. Later, he attained the rank of brigadier general. As of 1806 and until his death, he held the office of Saint Mary's County Register of Wills. James Forrest (1781–1826) was the son of Zachariah and Ann Edwards Forrest. His father was a captain in the Continental Army during the American Revolution, served as the sheriff of Saint Mary's County, and inherited the family property of Forrest Hall at Loveville near Leonardtown. At his death in 1817, Forrest Hall passed to his son, James.

83 From her obituary: "For the last 12 months her health had been gradually declining, under the irritative influence of general rheumatism. Since Sept she had been confined almost entirely to her bed, unable to change her position without assistance. Her children & friends will long mourn the loss of her society & example." Joan M. Dixon, *National Intelligencer Newspaper Abstracts 1844* (Westminster, Md.: Heritage Books, 2005), 103.

84 See Ring, *Girlhood Embroidery*, fig. 586.

Extensive research has not yet identified Cedar Grove as a local place name or as a biblical reference, although various symbolic and emblematic meanings of the cedar are used in scripture.[85] "The Cedars" or "Cedar Grove" are designations shared by numerous locations across America where this conifer flourishes. Its appearance on these two samplers may suggest the presence of a cedar grove on the heights of Georgetown. Supporting this theory is that the 1820s home of Mayor John Cox, called "The Cedars," was built on a part of John Threlkeld's land, which also encompassed the Visitation Convent and school.

Both samplers also include two verses, stitched in the top right and left corners. The same prayer appears in the upper left corner of each sampler, couplets referring to the cross as a reminder that one is always in the presence of God. In the upper right corners, the girls have stitched different prayers asking for guidance and protection, with the Jackson sampler directed to the "Mother of Mercy," and the Durkee sampler directed to the "Angel of God." Emily Jackson and Eleanor Durkee stitched religious declarations below their inscriptions. For example, Emily chose "Lord teach me to know thee"; "Lord teach me to know my self"; and "Jesus Mary and Joseph give me a blessing."

Eleanor Durkee

The birth of twins Eleanor and John Durkee on November 12, 1800, to Mary Hankey and Pearl Durkee was recorded in the registers of Saint Peter's Catholic Church. Jesuit Fathers established this Baltimore church in 1770 for Irish immigrants and French Acadian refugees.

Pearl Durkee, born in 1769, was the son of Phineas and Phebe Pearl Durkee. His arrival in Maryland is undocumented, but it may have been related to his occupation as a mariner. Pearl Durkee married first Joanna Gailes in 1794, then Mary Hankey in 1797, within Saint Paul's Parish of lower Baltimore County. Subsequent records indicate that he was a member of Baltimore's Second Presbyterian Church.

The Baltimore city directories between 1800 and 1808 show Captain Pearl Durkee was a ship master. The family lived at various addresses near the harbor. He did not reappear in the city directory until 1816, as a sea captain. This gap may be due to the 1809 death of the Durkees' newborn daughter, Marie, on January 29, followed by the passing of Mary herself at age thirty-five on February 5. Mary's funeral was conducted from their residence on George Street in Old Town, and mother and child are buried in Baltimore's Catholic cemetery. Pearl Durkee's whereabouts cannot be determined again until 1813 and 1814, when his service in the War of 1812 was recorded. In November 1814, he married Charlotte Rose, his third wife.

After her mother's death, Eleanor Durkee was enrolled in the Young Ladies' Academy in Georgetown. Although school entrance records are unavailable for this period, Eleanor's 1810 sampler, marked "Elenor," was embroidered before her tenth birthday and is evidence of her attendance.[86] As previously noted, her sampler differs from that of Emily Jackson by the inclusion of a second enclosed Christian motif, a combination cross and "IHS" near her inscription. The stitches she employed were cross, satin, eyelet, and double running.

On September 19, 1820, Eleanor Durkee and Henry Green were married at the First Methodist Episcopal Church in Baltimore. Census records indicate that two sons were born to the Green family in Maryland prior

---

85 "The cedar tree, particularly the cedar of Lebanon, is a symbol of Christ: 'his countenance is as Lebanon, excellent as the cedars' (Song of Solomon 5:15)." George Ferguson, *Signs and Symbols in Christian Art* (New York: Oxford University Press, 1958), 14.

86 What happened to her twin brother, John (1800–1866), is unknown, but it is likely he accompanied his father on voyages. A Captain John A. Durkee was noted as a widower in an 1834 obituary of the Baltimore *American and Commercial Daily Advertiser*.

to 1826, after which they relocated to New Orleans. Eleanor Green last appeared on the census in 1870, and Henry Green, who was a printer, died after 1880. Because Durkee relatives still lived in Baltimore, the *Sun* published a death notice for E. Green on October 16, 1875, indicating that she had died at the age of seventy-six years (actually Eleanor was less than one month shy of her seventy-sixth birthday).

1816–1818
SAMPLER GROUP

The remaining three religious samplers were stitched by Celestia Mary Combs in 1816 (Figure 6-21), Mary Rebecca J. Brooke in 1817 (Figure 6-22), and Mary Rose Boarman in 1818 (Figure 6-23). The 1817 sampler is unfinished, but it was clearly intended to follow the model of the embroideries before and after it. As a group the samplers display an increased use of Catholic symbolism, which may reflect the fact that in 1816 the Vatican decreed an Indult granting permission to admit the Georgetown monastery to the Order of the Visitation.

In a manner similar to the earlier religious samplers, an undulating strawberry border encloses three registers:

> The upper section includes a religious verse. In the center of this section is a flower-draped monument surmounted by a golden monstrance from which light radiates and in which is an inscription which reads: VENI LUMEN CORDIUM (Come light of my heart). Suspended within the monstrance is a dove symbolizing the Holy Spirit, from which three streams of light radiate down toward

> two red hearts. The heart on the left is encircled by a crown of thorns and surmounted by a cross. The heart on the right is pierced by a sword and encircled by a ring of flowers. It is surmounted by three flowers on long stems, the number three being a reference to the Trinity. These hearts represent the Sacred Heart [of Jesus] and the Immaculate Heart of Mary, important symbols for the Visitation Order.[87]

---

87 Ann Bigley Robertson, *An Enduring Legacy: The Painting Collection of Georgetown Visitation* (Washington, D.C.: Georgetown Visitation Monastery, 2000), 74. Also see Ring, *Girlhood Embroidery*, figs. 587 and 587a.

Figure 6-21. Sampler worked by Celestia Mary Combs. Georgetown, 1816. Inscribed: "Celestia Mary Combs's work done / at the Young Ladies Academy / Georgetown A.D. 1816 in the 13th / year of her age." Silk on linen. 21 x 16 in. Daughters of the American Revolution Museum, Friends of the Museum Purchase, 98.80

YOUNG LADIES' ACADEMY, GEORGETOWN 125

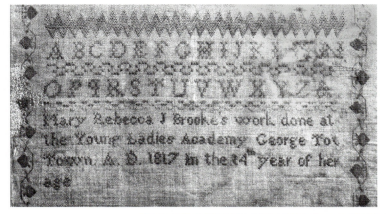

ABOVE: Figure 6-22. Detail of an unfinished sampler worked by Mary Rebecca J. Brooke. Georgetown, 1817. Inscribed: "Mary Rebecca J. Brooke's work done at / the Young Ladies Academy George To / Town. A.D. 1817 in the 14th year of her / age." Silk on linen. Destroyed in fire, formerly, Georgetown Visitation Monastery Archives

Figure 6-23. Sampler worked by Mary Rose Boarman. Georgetown, 1818. Inscribed: "Mary Rose Boarmans' work done / at the Young Ladies Academy George / Town A. D. 1818. in the 14th year of her / age." Silk on linen, 30 by 30 threads per in. 21 ⅝ x 16 ½ in. Georgetown Visitation Monastery Archives, gift of Miss Mary Lee Goddard

The elaborate and finely stitched monstrance described above was embroidered by Mary Rose Boarman in 1818 (Figure 6-23a). This symbol was frequently found on liturgical embroideries stitched by members of the Ursuline Order and could well have become a sampler motif for the students of the Ursuline nuns. The Ursuline convent

126 COLUMBIA'S DAUGHTERS

school in New Orleans was the first in what became the United States, and the Young Ladies' Academy in Georgetown, the second. The sisters of the Young Ladies' Academy were also in contact with the Visitation order in France. Textile experts agree these Georgetown samplers reflect French, and by extension Catholic, influence. The monstrance is otherwise unknown on American samplers, with the exception of a sampler stitched by Eliza Hauman in 1816 (and probably other students) at the Ursuline Convent in New Orleans.[88]

The 1816 Celestia Mary Combs sampler depicts the combined cross and IHS motif from the 1810 sampler stitched by Eleanor Durkee and added two red hearts symbolizing the Sacred Heart of Jesus and the Immaculate Heart of Mary. It is unknown what religious symbol would have been stitched by Mary Rebecca J. Brooke as the upper register on her 1817 sampler was not finished.

The middle register of all three samplers is composed of one uppercase alphabet and the student's inscription giving her full name following the European Catholic naming order: spiritual name, secular name, and surname. This is followed by the school name and location "Young Ladies Academy, George Town," the date, and the girl's age. Above and below this inscription is a dramatic zigzag border of Irish stitch.

The lower section is dominated by a decorated bowl of freshly picked strawberries. The strawberry is an old symbol imbued with the religious significance of perfect righteousness represented by a fruit without pits or thorns, and having pure white flowers with trefoil leaves that signify the Holy Trinity (Figure 6-23b). Flanking the bowl are the same spade-shaped evergreen trees symbolizing eternal life that appear in abundance on the earlier "Cedar Grove" samplers.

---

88 The Hauman sampler was auctioned by the Morton M. Goldberg Auction Galleries, New Orleans, in 1988.

Celestia Mary Combs

Celestia Mary Combs (ca. 1804–1835) embroidered her 1816 sampler in cross and satin stitches when she was nearly thirteen (Figure 6-21). Although her name does not appear in the available ledgers of the school archives, she was evidently a boarding student at the academy. Celestia Mary was a daughter of Enoch Combs (1763–1825) and Ann Roach

Figure 6-23a. Detail of sampler worked by Mary Rose Boarman. Georgetown, 1818.

Figure 6-23b. Detail of sampler worked by Mary Rose Boarman. Georgetown, 1818.

(1765–1825), who were married January 22, 1787, in Saint Mary's County, Maryland. Enoch was the namesake and fifth-generation descendant of Enoch Combs, who arrived in Maryland with his family in 1664. The home place of three hundred acres, now known as Glen Mary, was named Park Hall Freehold and located on the east side of the Saint Mary's River. Today, the name of the Park Hall post office is recognition of this landmark manor.

Enoch Combs established his own home at the time of his marriage to Ann Roach, choosing not to reside at Park Hall. The 1820 census shows Combs and his family were living in the Chaptico area of northern Saint Mary's County. This is across the Wicomico River from Cobb Neck in Charles County, where the family was previously believed to have resided. Enoch Combs's 1825 will acknowledged five daughters, all of whom married.

On November 4, 1828, Celestia Mary Combs wed Edward N. Roach (ca. 1800–1861). Four years earlier her sister, Catherine Caroline Combs, had married James W. Roach, Edward's brother. Both were the sons of Anne Neale and Dr. William Henry Roach (1765–1816), brother to Ann Roach Combs, Celestia's and Catherine's mother. Edward and Celestia Roach resided in Washington City. Her death notice in the *National Intelligencer* stated she died on August 8, 1835, at the residence of Dr. James Roach in Saint Mary's County, "where she had gone a few weeks before, for the preservation of the health of her two little daughters."[89] In April 1836, Edward was appointed register of wills for the District of Columbia, a position he held until his death in 1861. In 1839 he married Catherine A. Manning, and they had seven children. At least two of their daughters attended the Young Ladies' Academy in 1859.

Mary Rebecca J. Brooke

Mary Rebecca J. Brooke (1804–1817) was the third daughter of Elizabeth Millard (1766–1807 or 1809) and Dr. Walter Baker Brooke (died 1815). The family lived at Woodbury Manor, Leonardtown, also in Saint Mary's County.[90] Both of Mary Rebecca's parents had died by 1815 and were buried in Leonardtown's Saint Aloysius Chapel graveyard. Their premature deaths may explain Mary Rebecca's enrollment at the Young Ladies' Academy. Unfortunately, she died while attending the school:

> *Mary Rebecca Brooke 3rd dau—of Walter Brooke and Elizabeth, his wife, departed this life on Friday, 15th of August, 1817, at the monastery in Georgetown, where she was then at school, and was buried the following day in the graveyard of the Roman Catholic Church in Georgetown; aged 13 years, 6 months and 22 days.*[91]

This obituary was kept in a small paper-bound book that had belonged to Mary Rebecca's father. Both were retained by a descendant

---

89 Joan M. Dixon, *National Intelligencer Newspaper Abstracts, 1834–1835* (Bowie, Md.: Heritage Books Inc., 2000), 408.

90 Mary Rebecca J. Brooke had an impressive lineage. She was a direct descendant of the second Lord Baltimore's brother, Leonard Calvert, the first colonial governor of Maryland. In 1664 his daughter, Anne, married Baker Brooke (1628–1679) of De La Brooke Manor on the south side of the Patuxent River in Saint Mary's County. He was the son of the English immigrant and Calvert friend, Robert Brooke, Esquire (1602–1655), and his wife, Mary Baker. Lord Baltimore (Cecilius Calvert), first proprietor of Maryland, commissioned Robert Brooke Commander of the County upon his arrival in 1650, when he also received a manorial patent of two thousand acres for De La Brooke. His land holdings amounted to eight thousand acres by the time of his death in 1679.

91 In 1787, the Reverend Doctor John Carroll acquired the deed for Georgetown Lot 72 whereupon Trinity Church was built, the first Catholic Church within the ten-mile-square area that would become the District of Columbia. Alice Norris Parran, *Series II of "Register of Maryland's Heraldic Families"* (Baltimore: The Southern Maryland Society of Colonial Dames, 1938), 170.

along with other family artifacts, including "an old Brooke 'sampler' made by the little Mary Rebecca in the very year of her death, 1817, while at the convent."[92] Mary Rebecca's unfinished sampler was fully inscribed with her name and date, revealing that, contrary to the usual assumption, an embroidered date and age do not always indicate when a sampler was completed (Figure 6-22).

Mary Rose Boarman

The inscription on Mary Rose Boarman's (ca. 1805–1836) 1818 sampler indicates she was in her fourteenth year (Figure 6-23). This means that she was actually thirteen years old and therefore born about 1805.[93] Mary Rose's exquisite needlework is composed of nine different stitches—cross, Smyrna cross, satin, stem, straight, herringbone, single chain, queen, and Irish. Remarkably, the entire inscription was wrought in the painstaking queen stitch. Although the earliest available ledgers for the Young Ladies' Academy have some entries for 1816, Mary Rose Boarman's name is not to be found. The 1819 ledgers, however, do include her cousin Rebecca's account of embroidery expenses (Figure 6-24).

Mary Rose Boarman was the daughter of Raphael W. Boarman and Mary Smith of Charles County, Maryland.[94] Her father's name appears in District of Columbia probate records concerning the wills of Boarman relatives and others in Georgetown between 1811 and 1819. The 1813 will of John B. Boarman transferred his half of two Charles County tracts of land to his friend and cousin, Raphael W. Boarman of George Town, and stated they had a partnership in the wood business. The Boarman family became residents of Georgetown, so Mary Rose was probably a day scholar.

On February 3, 1825, Mary Rose Boarman became the second wife of Horatio Dyer (ca. 1789–1866). Horatio was the son of Giles Green Dyer and Susanna Smith of Stone Hill in Prince George's County. In 1819 he had married Eliza Simpson as his first wife at the Catholic church in Bryantown. Eliza died in 1821, leaving a young daughter. Mary Rose and Horatio Dyer had been married for eleven years and were the parents of four

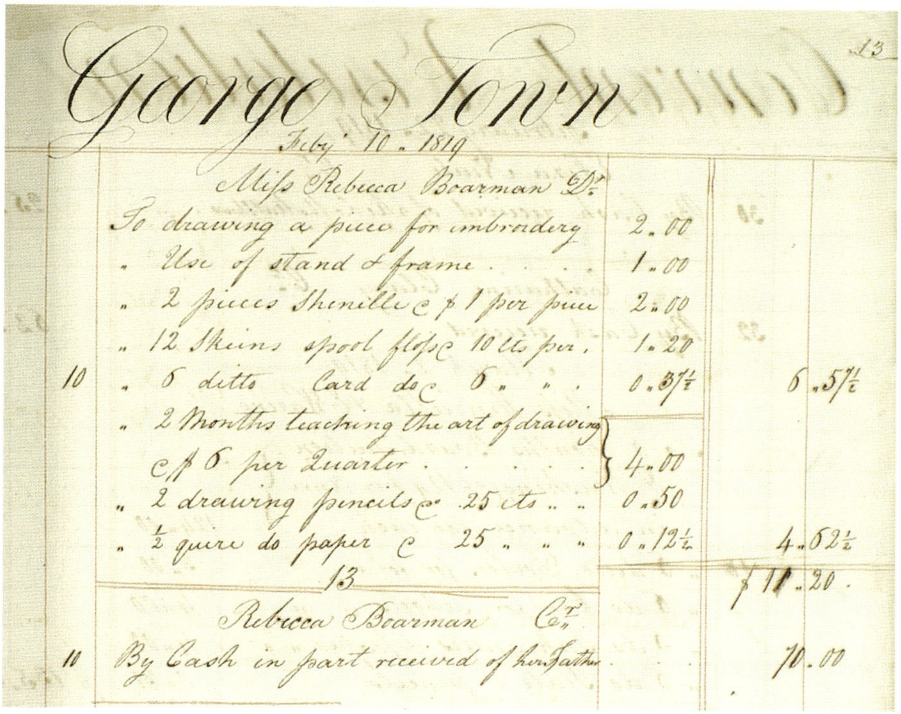
George Town 13
Feby 10. 1819
Miss Rebecca Boarman Dr.
To drawing a piece for embroidery 2.00
" Use of stand & frame 1.00
" 2 pieces Shenille @ $1 per piece 2.00
" 12 Skeins spool floss @ 10 cts per. 1.20
10 " 6 ditto Card do @ 6 " " 0.37½ 6.57½
" 2 Months teaching the art of drawing @ $6 per Quarter 4.00
" 2 drawing pencils @ 25 cts 0.50
" ½ quire do paper @ 25 0.12½ 4.62½
13 $11.20
Rebecca Boarman Cr.
11 By Cash in part received of her Father 10.00

Figure 6-24. Account of Rebecca Boarman. February 10, 1819.
Georgetown Visitation Monastery Archives

92 Ibid.

93 Mary Rose's sampler suffered water damage in the 1993 fire. It was treated by a textile conservator soon afterward.

94 The progenitor of the Boarman family in America was William Boarman (1630–ca. 1709), a Roman Catholic of English heritage who was in the province of Maryland by 1650. His proprietor patent of one thousand acres was granted by Cecilius Lord Baltimore in 1674 and later expanded to 3,333 acres. This plantation, Boarman's Rest, was known as Boarman's Manor. Near his dwelling he built a twenty-by-thirty-foot chapel, which was the forerunner of Saint Mary's Parish Church located at Bryantown in Saint Mary's County, later Charles County. His twelve children by three wives were the ancestors of generations of Boarmans who continuously resided on the extensive property of Boarman's Rest. William Boarman was a gentleman, Indian trader, negotiator and interpreter, Justice of the Peace, high sheriff, officer of the provincial militia, assemblyman, and magistrate in Saint Mary's County local courts.

children when she died on August 30, 1836. Mary Rose Boarman Dyer is buried in the cemetery of Saint Mary's Parish Church at Bryantown, where her great-great-grandfather William Boarman established his private chapel. Horatio subsequently married Elizabeth Blanford in 1839.[95]

Parrot Samplers

Not all students at the Young Ladies' Academy of Georgetown worked overtly religious samplers. Between 1819 and 1829, Eleanor Waring (Figure 6-25), Eleanora Neale (Figure 6-26), and Mary Elizabeth Laurence (Figure 6-27) stitched very similar samplers, each following the same general format. The upper register includes an elaborate basket of flowers, flanked by multiple alphabets or secular verses that emphasize virtue and morality. Below a cross border of leafy grapevine or band of Irish stitch are the inscriptions, each including the girl's full name, year, and "Young Ladies Academy George Town." Dominating the lower register is a colorful parrot. Its entire paper pattern remains on the back of the unfinished Neale sampler, and the Laurence piece also retains remnants of patterns.

The parrot is not an uncommon sampler motif, but this one is unusually large and stitched in careful detail. It is unknown whether there is any religious significance to the inclusion of such a large parrot.[96] In Renaissance and Baroque art, however, the parrot occasionally appears as an attribute of the infant Jesus because of its ability to say "Ave Maria." Interestingly, the convent annals contain an anecdote regarding a parrot owned by the Poor Clares. Evidently they became so impoverished that they were obliged to sell their parrot to save themselves from starvation.[97]

Two of the samplers are bordered on three sides with leafy vines and natural looking fruit (one with grapes and one with strawberries), complemented by a flowering vine on the remaining top or bottom border. The third sampler is enclosed by a simple, more stylized arcaded strawberry border similar to the earlier samplers from this school. Like the strawberry, the grapevine is imbued with religious significance: the grape represents the Blood of Christ, and the vine expresses the relationship between God and man through Him. "The vine sometimes also represents the vineyard as the protected place where the children of God (the vines) flourish under the tender care of God (the Keeper of the Vineyard)."[98]

Eleanor Waring

Georgetown Visitation entrance and ledger books show that the sisters Henrietta and Eleanor Waring (1808–1834) entered the Young Ladies' Academy in September 1817 as boarding students. On April 5, 1820, a group of embroidery charges were recorded in their account (Figure 6-8). Of the sisters' needlework, however, only Eleanor's 1819 sampler, embroidered at the age of eleven years, is currently known (Figure 6-25). In addition to the motifs described above, Eleanor transcribed in tiny cross stitches a variation of the first stanza and first three lines of the fourth stanza from "The Rose," a children's song by English hymnist Isaac Watts. Eleanor omitted the morbid last line,

---

95 They are buried in Saint Mary's Catholic Churchyard at Clinton in Piscataway Parish, Prince George's County, Maryland.

96 George Ferguson wrote on page 2 in *Signs and Symbols in Christian Art* that birds were often used as symbols of the "winged soul." "Long before any attempt was made by the artist to identify birds according to species, the bird form was employed to suggest the spiritual, as opposed to the material. The representation of the soul by a bird goes back to the art of ancient Egypt. This symbolism may be implied in the pictures of the Christ Child holding a bird in His hand or holding one tied to a string. Saint Francis of Assisi is often represented preaching to the birds."

97 Lathrop and Lathrop, *A Story of Courage*, 150.

98 Ferguson, *Signs and Symbols in Christian Art*, 16, 21.

"This will scent like a Rose when I'm dead."[99]

In the school's Entrance Book, the girls' father was recorded as Henry Waring, Esq. of Middle Brook Mills in Montgomery County, [Maryland], residing on the east side of the Great Seneca Creek by the Frederick Road bridge. This central part of the county was a thriving area for various types of mills. Henry Waring (1762–1835) was born in Prince George's County, probably in the area now known as Largo, where his father Basil Waring Sr. resided on property called Heart's Delight (also the site of a Waring family cemetery). At the age of twenty, Henry moved to Georgetown and by 1793 had married Henrietta Hall (ca. 1773–1795) and relocated to property at Middlebrook, named Norway. Henrietta and her infant died while visiting a family home, Mount Pleasant. They were buried there in the Clagett Waring family cemetery in Upper Marlborough, Prince George's County.

In 1805, Henry Waring wed Millicent Brooke (died 1847) at the home of Mrs. Fenwick on Capitol Hill in the District of Columbia. Eleven children are known from this marriage, with the first two being Henrietta Maria Susannah born in 1806, and Eleanor Mary born June 2, 1808. Henry Waring was listed in the 1810 federal census of Montgomery County, and presumably this is where most of the children were born. The Henry Waring family was associated with Saint John's Church at Rock Creek (the area is now known as Forest Glen) in southern Montgomery County. Baptismal records exist for one child and several grandchildren of Henry and Millicent.[100]

The school records for Henrietta and Eleanor (Ellen) show that by September 1819 Henry Waring was a resident of Georgetown again, which is substantiated by the 1820 census. Between 1822 and 1837 six more daughters of Henry and Millicent Waring enrolled in the academy as day scholars or

Figure 6-25. Sampler worked by Eleanor Waring. Georgetown, 1819. Inscribed: "Eleanor Waring Ladies / Academy George Town / A D 1819 Aged 11 years." Silk on linen. Image courtesy of Sotheby's

---

99 Isaac Watts, D.D., *Divine Songs, Attempted in Easy Language for the Use of Children* (Baltimore: Printed by Warner & Hanna, 1801).

100 This was the first Catholic church established in Montgomery County, and where Father John Carroll (1735–1815) began his American ministry in 1774 at the home of his mother (Elizabeth Darnell Carroll). A room in her manor house became a chapel. Within ten years a separate chapel was built on the property to accommodate the increasing size of the Rock Creek congregation. By 1813 there were four other areas of Catholic concentration spread north and westward in the county. One was the Seneca congregation that worshipped in a small brick building on the Waring estate. In the Saint John's records, it is noted as Seneca, Mr. Waring's neighborhood, or Middlebrook. Missionary Jesuits took over care of these four missions after John Carroll became Archbishop in 1808.

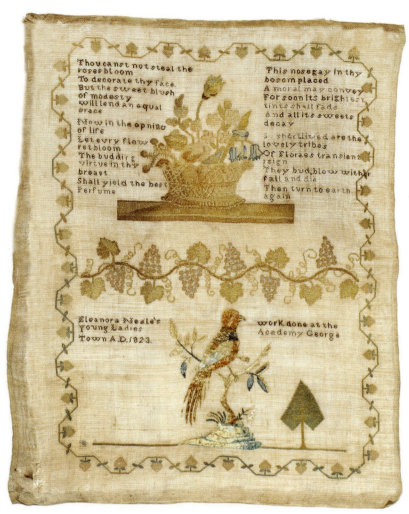

Figure 6-26. Sampler worked by Eleanora Neale. Georgetown, 1823. Inscribed: "Eleanora Neale's / work done at the / Young Ladies / Academy George / Town A.D. 1823." Silk on linen. 20 ½ x 15 ⅜. Georgetown Visitation Monastery Archives

boarding students. An extra fee was paid for two of them to take music lessons in 1824 and 1825. In addition, daughter Josephine's account was charged for tapestry in 1834 and 1835, while Matilda's account incurred a tapestry charge of $1.50 in 1837. Daughters Elizabeth Anne and Josephine Jane became Visitation nuns, making their vows in 1841.

In 1831, Eleanor became the second wife of James Brent.[101] The *Columbian Gazette* announced the wedding of James R. Brent, Esq. of Charles County, Maryland, and Miss Eleanor Waring, daughter of Henry Waring, Esq., by the Reverend Mr. Young on May 12, 1831, in Georgetown.[102] The Waring estate, Norway, at Middlebrook apparently operated successfully while Henry Waring resided in Georgetown, where he was a director of the Farmers' & Mechanics' Bank. Henry died at Georgetown in 1835, and his Maryland property evidently passed to his eldest son, Henry B. Waring (1810–1873), who was farming there by 1840 and onward. It was at Norway that Eleanor Waring Brent died on September 4, 1834, at the age of twenty-six. Only one child is known from her marriage to James Brent: Henry W. Brent (born ca. 1832). He attended Georgetown College and became a physician. James R. Brent married twice more, in 1836 and 1851.

Eleanora Neale

Eleanora Neale (1808–1845) entered the Young Ladies' Academy as a boarder in March 1820, under the account of her father, Henry Neale (died 1844) of Charles County, Maryland. Entries in school records show Eleanora attended until September 1823, the year inscribed on her sampler (Figure 6-26),[103] which is very similar in appearance to that of Eleanor Waring. Eleanora's cross, satin, short and long stitches were employed in surface embroidery for the parrot motif and mostly worked over one linen thread for the rest of the large sampler.[104] The poem in the upper register of her sampler records in cross stitches the first, fourth, fifth, and sixth quatrains from "To a Young Lady with a Nosegay," a popular work by an unidentified author.[105] Although it is unknown why Eleanora or her teacher chose to include these specific quatrains and omit others, those included

---

101 In 1827, James R. Brent (ca. 1802–1858) married Susannah Brooke, who apparently died early in the marriage. Susannah Brooke and Eleanor Waring were cousins.

102 Pippenger, *Georgetown District of Columbia Marriage and Death Notices 1801–1838*, 186.

103 Ring, *Girlhood Embroidery*, vol. 2 endpaper.

104 Eleanora's needlework was water damaged in the 1993 fire that swept through the academy building of Georgetown Visitation.

105 This poem was included in such publications as *Selection of Poems* (London, printed for Longman, Hurst, Rees, and Orme, 1808), 5, and in various juvenile magazines dating from the late eighteenth century.

speak to virtue and modesty versus vanity and pride, common moral themes in nineteenth-century education.

Eleanora's sampler remains unfinished. Evidently she was unable to complete her stitching before the spring/summer school term ended in August. It appears the ongoing economic depression caused her to be withdrawn, probably after Sister Mary de Sales Neale pleaded with Henry Neale for payment on her past due account. Eleanora's three and one-half years of tuition and board cost $653, with extra fees paid for music and drawing. Neale is a prominent Maryland Catholic surname, and girls of other Neale families in the area also attended the Young Ladies' Academy, founded by the Reverend Leonard Neale.

In 1827, Eleanora became the second wife of James Henry Neale (1802–1872). Their familial relationship, however, has not been determined.[106] Various Charles County federal census records indicate Eleanor and James had at least five daughters and one son. Two of the daughters were Jane Neale and Mary Eleanora Neale. Neither married, and both became school teachers in Port Tobacco in central Charles County. They and their parents are buried in the Saint Ignatius Catholic Church Cemetery at Port Tobacco. Eleanor(a) Neale's death notice in *The [Baltimore] Sun* stated her husband was James H. and that she died on May 31, 1845.[107]

Mary Elizabeth Laurence

The third sampler of the parrot group was stitched by Mary Elizabeth Laurence (1812–1905) and dated 1829 (Figure 6-27). As discussed below, Mary Elizabeth attended the Young Ladies' Academy from 1824 to 1827, so her sampler date is two years after she left school. Close examination reveals the "9" is stitched in a thread of a different color, and the reverse side shows that no thread was dragged from the number "2" to the "9" as found elsewhere on the sampler. The most common reason for changing the date was a desire by the stitcher, usually at some later time, to appear younger than she was. Given that Mary Elizabeth was twelve when she entered the school, it is more likely that she stitched the sampler in 1824 or 1825. This conclusion is supported by a change in the school's curriculum in 1826 (following the arrival of Father Wheeler) which emphasized math and science over plain and ornamental needlework. Mary Elizabeth's stitches span the range of tent, cross, satin, Holbein, straight, outline, split, and Irish. Professional conservation of this family piece revealed that paper patterns were used for both the parrot and floral basket.

Mary Elizabeth was a daughter of John Laurence (1786–1852) from Baltimore, and Elisabeth Earp (1791–1861) of Virginia, who were married in Georgetown in 1809. John and Elisabeth were the parents of one son and three daughters. Their daughter Mary and her younger sister, Catherine A. T. Laurence (1816–1908), attended the Young Ladies' Academy between 1824 and 1831. John Laurence resided at 1314 35th Street in Georgetown, which backed the Trinity Catholic Church on 36th Street.

---

106 The Neale family of Charles County was not only one of the leading aristocratic families of colonial Maryland but also comprised the Catholic elite. Lord Baltimore granted a patent of two thousand acres with full manorial rights to Captain James Neale (1615–1683), Gentleman, in 1642. Neale named the manor "Wollaston" after the family home of the same name in England's Northamptonshire. The land lay on Cobb Neck, between the Wicomico and Potomac Rivers. The building of the Wollaston Manor house was contracted in 1661, and it stood at Swan Point on the Potomac River until at least 1900. James Neale was appointed to various positions in the provincial government. Archbishop Leonard Neale (1746–1817), discussed earlier, was a descendant.

107 Hollowak, *Index to Marriages and Deaths in The [Baltimore] Sun, 1837–1850*, 435.

Figure 6-27. Sampler worked by Mary Elizabeth Laurence. Georgetown, 1829. Inscribed: "Mary Elizabeth Laurences Work done at the Young Ladies / Academy George Town in the Year of our Lord 1829." Silk on linen, 32 by 30 threads per in. 17 ¾ x 16 in. Private collection

Mary and her sister Elisabeth (1815–1834) were devout Catholics who supported Trinity Church by dipping candles for the altar, embroidering altar cloths, and decorating the church with flowers from their garden. In 1823, Mary received a French holy card from Archbishop Maréchal recognizing not only her First Communion but also rewarding her for good behavior (Figure 6-29).[108] The obliterated writing has not been deciphered, but it probably pertains to a religion class. Another holy card for Mary, from Trinity Church in 1824, was inscribed as a premium for her proficiency and good conduct in Christian Doctrine.

In the spring of 1824, Mary Laurence became a day scholar at the Young Ladies' Academy, less than two blocks from her home. She attended until the spring of 1827 when her sister, Catherine, entered the academy and remained a student until the fall term of 1831. Both girls were enrolled for the usual one- to three-year period. The total cost of their education was $249.77. This included two, one-dollar charges to Mary in 1826 for the use of books, maps, and globes, reflecting Father Clorivière's elevation of the curriculum. The school account books show at least fourteen entries whereby the Laurence girls' tuition was paid "by wool at sundry times." John Laurence and his son, Joseph, operated a "morocco" tannery that produced leather from hides.[109] His source of wool to render payment for tuition may have been either goat hair, which is used in woolen blends, or sheep's wool (Figure 6-30).

Mary and Catherine's sister, Elisabeth, was just nineteen years old when she died in 1834. Elisabeth's sisters probably painted the holy card and wrote the inscription dedicating it in

---

108 The Sulpician Ambrose Maréchal, a native of France, was the third Archbishop of Baltimore. He dedicated the Cathedral of the Assumption of the Blessed Virgin Mary (Baltimore Basilica) in 1821.

109 It is unclear whether the Laurences were producing a fine pebble-grained Morocco leather from goatskin or French Morocco, an imitation made from sheepskin.

LEFT: Figure 6-28. Holy card painted by Mary or Catherine Laurence on the death of a sister. Georgetown, 1834. Inscribed: "To the memory of / Elisabeth S. Laurence, who departed / this life the 26th day of June A. D. 1834." Watercolor on paper. 7 ¾ x 6 in. Private collection

her memory (Figure 6-28). The emblem on the card almost replicates that on Mary Rose Boarman's sampler (Figure 6-23a) and symbolizes love in a Catholic representation of devotion to the Sacred Heart of Jesus and the Immaculate Heart of Mary.

The Georgetown *Columbian Gazette* announced the marriage of Mary Elizabeth, eldest daughter of John Lawrence (common alternative spelling), and William G. Love on April 19, 1831, by the Reverend Van Lommel of Trinity Church.[110] William Gunnell Love (1808–1839) had come from Fairfax County, Virginia, to work at the U.S. Department of Treasury. The couple lived with Mary's parents on 35th Street. Prior to William's premature death in 1839, they became the parents of one daughter and three sons. The last born, Richard Henry, died at seven months, a month after his father.[111] Mary and the three surviving children continued to live with her parents (Figure 6-31).[112]

Figure 6-29.
French First Communion Holy Card presented to Mary Laurence. Georgetown, 1823.
Inscribed: "A reward for good behavior from the most / Revd Abp Marechal. To Miss Mary Laurence of the . . . / Mary Lawrence a fait sa 1ère Communion / dans l'Eglise de la Trinité __ du mois de / Mai, de l Année 1823." Engraving. 6 ⅝ x 4 ¾ in. Private collection

---

110 Pippenger, *Georgetown District of Columbia Marriage and Death Notices 1801–1838*, 184.

111 Father and son were buried in the Upper Graveyard of Trinity Church, which became known as Holy Rood Cemetery, now the property of Georgetown University. Her sister, Elisabeth, is also buried there.

112 Catherine Laurence married John Lansdale Kidwell, who established an apothecary in Georgetown and occupied the Federal-period Stoddert House at 3400 Prospect Street, overlooking the Potomac River. Mary Love's two sons worked in the Kidwell apothecary, with one studying at Georgetown College, becoming a druggist, and working at the Kidwell and successor's drug store for his entire career. Her other son became a lawyer, and later an officer of the Virginia Gold Mining Company.

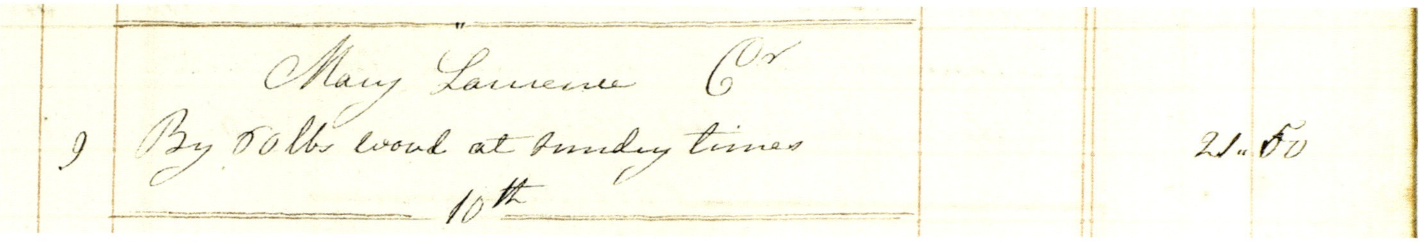

Figure 6-30. Ledger entry for Mary Laurence. "Mary Laurence Cr / By 60 lbs wool at sundry times / 21.50." May 3, 1825. Georgetown Visitation Monastery Archives

The *Washington Post* published notification of Mary E. Love's death on January 27, 1905, at almost ninety-three years of age.[113] Her funeral was held at the church then known as Holy Trinity, and she was interred at Oak Hill Cemetery in Georgetown, near other members of the Laurence, Love, and Kidwell families.[114]

Figure 6-31. Photograph of Mary Elizabeth Laurence Love. Georgetown, ca. 1860. 5 x 4 in. Private collection.

Wool Work Pictures

Needlework instruction continued at the academy until the late 1880s and several mid-nineteenth-century examples of Berlin wool work are known. Three such pieces are in the collection of the Georgetown Visitation Monastery, two by girls who have not yet been identified.

Catherine Ann Lavinia Clemens

Catherine Ann Lavinia Clemens (1840–1860) was the eldest daughter of John Clemens (Clements) (1799–1887) and Catherine Shipley (1803–1889). Known as Lavinia, she attended the "Academy of the Visitation" in 1857, where she received one of the annual premiums awarded by the school for meritorious work. It is unknown if this premium included embroidery. Lavinia Clemens's needlework picture of King Solomon, rendered in wool using tent stitch and French knots, was enhanced by lustrous silk-stitched highlights and beads for the eyes, hair, and crown (Figure 6-32).

In 1859, Lavinia became the second wife of William Raymond Collins (1829–1891), whom she married at Georgetown. In 1860 she gave birth to their only child, a daughter named Ada Genevieve. Later the same year she suffered for eleven weeks with a painful illness before her demise in Georgetown on November 3, 1860.[115] The obituary of Catherine Ann Lavinia Clemens Collins stated:

> On the occasion of the annual distribution of premiums at the Academy of the Visitation, in Georgetown, in the year 1857, five of the amiable and accomplished young ladies who obtained the highest honors of the institute were bound together by the strongest ties of friendship. Of the five but one now survives.

After Lavinia's death, Ada Genevieve was raised by her father and his third wife. The family of Ada's daughter, Catherine Lavinia Gaskins Cook (1898–1988), donated the wool work portraying King Solomon to Georgetown University. The university subsequently gave the piece as a gift to Georgetown Visitation Monastery, where it joined other pieces of religious canvas work.[116]

---

113 *Washington Post*, January 29, 1905; ProQuest Historical Newspapers: The Washington Post (1877–1992), 3.

114 The 1965 family history by Ellen Lane Love, granddaughter of Mary Elizabeth Laurence Love, and Frank Earl Cooley Jr. is gratefully acknowledged.

115 Washington *Evening Star*, November 5, 1860.

Figure 6-32. Embroidered picture attributed to Catherine Ann Lavinia Clemens. Georgetown, ca. 1857. Silk, wool, and glass beads on canvas, 24 by 24 threads per in. 19 x 17 in.
Georgetown Visitation Monastery Archives

Summary

The different genres of known needlework from the Young Ladies' Academy chronicle the evolution of this long-standing Georgetown girls' school directed by the Order of the Visitation. The first group, completed between 1800 and 1804, portrayed the landscape of the campus and are the only known silk embroideries associated with the school. The 1808 and 1810 samplers are noteworthy for the first use of the Calvary Cross, religious inscriptions, and naming the "Young Ladies Academy Georgetown" as well as the puzzling "Cedar Grove." Possibly significant, it was in 1808 that Bishop Leonard Neale formalized the status of the pious ladies as Sisters of the Visitation and transferred by deed all of the property he had acquired for them.

After an intervening gap, the 1816 to 1818 group shows an increased emphasis on

---

116 For more on wool work religious pictures stitched in Maryland Catholic schools, see Allen, *A Maryland Sampling*, 182 and 251–53.

specific Catholic and Visitation symbolism. This may correlate in time with the long awaited admission of the monastery to the Order of the Visitation in 1816. The last sampler group to emerge was that of the perched parrot, stitched from 1819 to 1829 with secular verses praising morality and virtue. This new design may reflect the more academic curriculum supported by secular priest Father Clorivière, who arrived at Georgetown in 1819. Decades later, some students were engaged in stitching biblical stories, using religious patterns designed for pictorial wool work.

The body of known embroidery from the Young Ladies' Academy under the purview of the Visitation Order is uncommon within the realm of American needlework for its frequent inclusion of Christian elements, many aligned specifically with the Catholic faith. In a school under the province of the Catholic Church, needlework with pious symbolism would have been expected (Figure 6-33). Teachers at the Young Ladies' Academy adapted to educational and societal trends so the overt Christian symbols of religious objects, such as the cross and monstrance, eventually disappeared.

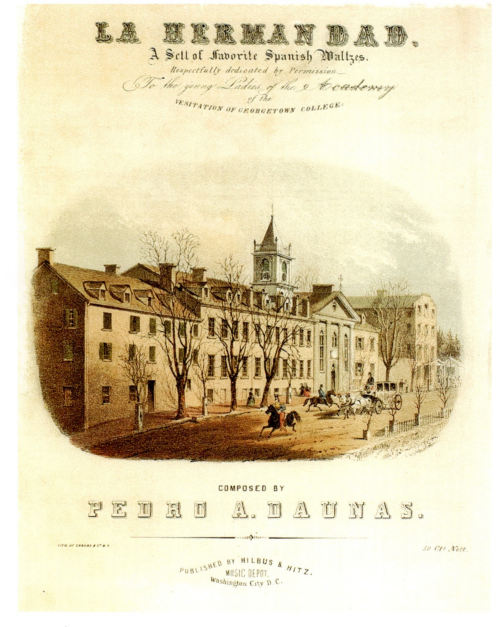

Figure 6-33. Detail from the cover of sheet music, ca. 1843. Inscribed: "La Hermandad. / A Sett of Favorite Spanish Waltzes. / Respectfully dedicated by Permission / To the young Ladies of the Academy / of the / Vesitation of Georgetown College / Composed by / Pedro A. Daunas." Color lithograph by Sarony & Co.
Georgetown Visitation Monastery Archives

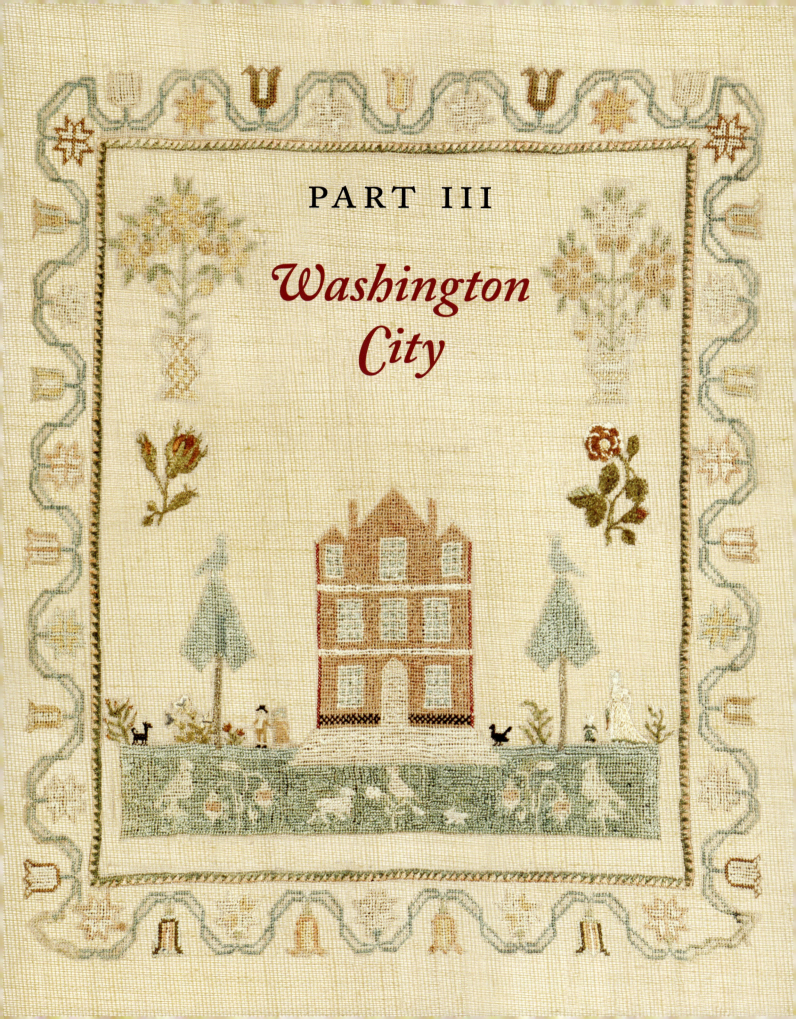

PART III
Washington City

Figure 7-1. "George Town and Federal City or City of Washington," 1801.
Color aquatint by T. Cartwright after George Beck.
Published by Atkins & Nightingale, London and Philadelphia.
17 ¾ x 20 ¾ in.
Library of Congress, Prints & Photographs Division

CHAPTER 7

Introduction to Washington City and Its Schools

IN 1790, the First Federal Congress created a ten-mile-square federal district at a site designated by George Washington along the Potomac River.¹ As a compromise to satisfy northern and southern states, Washington selected an area at the geographic center of the young republic, one with access to the Ohio River Valley. The following year Pierre (Peter) Charles L'Enfant conceived his plan to lay out a new city on this undeveloped land, which had been conveyed by local owners to the federal government. L'Enfant overlaid a grid pattern of streets on major avenues radiating from two hubs, the Capitol and the President's House, in the process creating multiple squares and public spaces. Washington City was approximately three miles from north to south and about two miles wide. Long established port towns of Georgetown and Alexandria and recently formed Washington and Alexandria counties composed the rest of the District of Columbia. "Washington City," with or without the further identification of "D.C.," can be found on a number of samplers from the District of Columbia region.²

By 1800, when Congress relocated from Philadelphia to the District, the plan for Washington City was taking shape and major federal buildings were under construction, but by one count only 107 brick houses and 261 wood buildings had been completed (Figure 7-1).³ A visitor to the new city that year recorded his impressions in a letter home:

> *The situation is the finest imaginable, whether considered in relation to its commercial advantages, or its variety and grandeur of its prospects; from the Capitol, we behold*

---

1 Known as the Residence Act, it created the federal district and authorized George Washington to select a site, to purchase land for use of the United States, and to provide suitable accommodations for the government. The act further stipulated that Congress would first meet in Philadelphia for ten years.

2 With the annexation of Georgetown in 1878, the name Washington City became coterminous with the District of Columbia.

3 Count as of May 15, 1800. Ruth Ann Overbeck and Lucinda P. Janke, "William Prout: Capitol Hill's Community Builder," *Washington History* 12 (Spring/Summer 2000): 131.

141

Figure 7-2 "The Capitol, Washington, D.C. West Front from the City Hall." ca. 1832. Drawn by T. Doughty. Published by Childs & Inman's Lith[ographic] Press, Philadelphia.
Library of Congress, Prints & Photographs Division

both branches of the Potowmac, we mark their junction, and the eye embracing the whole of that noble river, follows its majestic course as far as vision can extend—it may be then cast with a single glance over the flourishing towns of Alexandria, and Georgetown and a wide range of the surrounding country. The city is laid out fancifully enough, and if buildings already erected had been concentrated, it would wear a rich and splendid appearance, but they are widely separated, the intervening spaces are filled with a confused mixture of stumps, trees, huts, lime-kilns and brick yards.[4]

Some twenty-four years later, visitor Anne Royall's first impression was of lack of progress, and that the "mighty city" was "nothing more than distinct groups of houses, scattered over a vast surface . . . more the appearance of so many villages, than a city."[5] As she explored the area and visited the Capitol, the President's House, and other federal buildings, Royall revised her initial opinion and described Washington City in a more favorable light (Figure 7-2).

These edifices, the elevated site of the city; its undulating surface, partially covered with very handsome buildings; the majestic Potomac, with its ponderous bridge and gliding sails; the eastern branch with its lordly ships; swelling hills which surround the city; the spacious squares and streets, and avenues adorned with rows of flourishing trees, and all this visible at once; it is not in the power of imagination to conceive a scene so replete with every species of beauty.[6]

As was her custom with most places Royall visited during her travels in the early republic, she recorded her impressions of the inhabitants as well as of the physical structures and geographic features. Regarding the manners and appearance of the residents, Royall found "no body of people . . . equal in number, in which there is less similarity . . . [due to] a flood of emigration to the metropolis from all parts, both of Europe and the United States." She added that "the population of Washington may be said to consist of four distinct classes of people, whose pursuits, interests and manners, differ as widely as though they lived on opposite sides of the globe . . . those who keep congress boarders and their mutual friends . . . the laboring class . . . the better sort; and fourthly, the free negros." Royall judged the ladies to be quite handsome. "They have delicate features, and much expression of countenance, and excel in beauty and symmetry of their persons; but (excepting the higher class, who are females of education) are, withal, most detestably proud."[7]

Royall was less sanguine about the quality of education available to the young ladies of Washington City.

---

4 "Letter from Washington, D.C.," first published. December 15, 1800, in the *Albany [NY] Gazette*, quoted in Kenneth R. Bowling, "A Foreboding Shadow: Newspaper Celebration of the Federal Government's Arrival," *Washington History* 12 (Spring/Summer 2000): 6.

5 Anne Royall, *Sketches of History, Life, and Manners, in the United States* (New Haven, 1826), 130.

6 Royall, *Sketches*, 131.

7 Ibid., 155, 156. Royall qualified her comment on beauty to "only be said of the natives, as the foreigners are very coarse and ill shaped."

From the limited opportunity afforded me, I am unable to affirm any thing positively, respecting the encouragement given to learning. From all accounts, education is in its infancy. There are no academies, no grammar schools, and but two free schools, for the exclusive benefit of the poor: these are supported by the corporation. A number of other schools are kept by indifferent teachers, where little children are taught to read, write, and "cipher!" I have seen girls of fourteen years, learning to cipher, who did not understand a word of grammar. This gives the best idea of the sort of instruction bestowed on the youth of Washington.[8]

Contrary to Royall's negative impression of the diffusion and quality of female education in the District, the rudiments of education were available to almost everyone, and for those able to pay a fee, there were many opportunities to study the higher and ornamental branches of learning. As another writer noted in 1830: "There are also a great many well conducted schools in Washington, where the usual branches of education are taught. . . . Schools for young ladies are also established in various parts of the city."[9] Between 1797, when Ann Vidler offered instruction in "plain, open, and Tambour Work," and 1860 approximately 135 individual teachers or schools included plain sewing, embroidery, or other forms of needlework as part of their curricula.[10]

FREE AND PUBLIC SCHOOLS IN WASHINGTON CITY

Public, or free, education was available by 1806 when two schools, known as the Washington Academies, opened. Both were funded by local taxes and provided instruction in reading, writing, mathematics, Latin, and geography. Some of the students attended free of charge; others paid tuition. Although needlework was not specifically noted, evidence suggests the option for needlework instruction may have been offered to girls who attended the Washington Academies. In 1806, Mrs. Richard White advertised instruction in "various useful and ornamental kinds of work." Her husband was principal teacher of the Western Academy on Pennsylvania Avenue west of the President's House from January 1806 through September 1807, so she may have taught needlework to the girls who attended the school, either during school hours or afterward.[11]

In 1812, a reduction in funding may have resulted in replacing the academies with a single co-educational school run on the Lancasterian system which, like similar schools in Georgetown and Alexandria, was less expensive to operate (see Chapter 1).[12] Needlework, a core component of the female Lancasterian system, would have certainly been included in the curriculum. In 1818 a national lottery was proposed to fund two public schoolhouses, a penitentiary, and a town hall. Unfortunately, the money did not become available until 1826.[13]

By 1830 a local writer described public education in Washington City in the following manner: "There are two public free schools, within the City, one in the Eastern, and another in the Western section. . . . About 400 children are annually admitted and educated, without charge to their parents or guardians."[14] For the girls, needlework was part of the curriculum. In 1831 and 1832, for example, a Miss Young was engaged to teach

---

8 Ibid., 150.

9 Jonathan Elliot, *Historical Sketches of the Ten Miles Square* (Washington: J. Elliot, Jr., 1830), 256.

10 *Washington Gazette*, April 22, 1797.

11 Washington *National Intelligencer*, December 31, 1806.

12 It should be noted that conflicting historical information makes uncertain whether the Washington City Lancasterian school was implemented or the academies remained the only early institutions of public education in the city.

13 Washington *Daily National Intelligencer*, August 2, 1818.

14 Elliot, *Historical Sketches*, 256.

Figure 7-3.
Sampler worked by
Ella Hancock.
Washington City, 1853.
Inscribed:
"Ella Hancock
Aged 9 years. 1853."
Wool on linen ground.
18 ¼ x 17 in.
Collection of
William Seippel

"Needlework" at the Western Academy.[15] Needlework remained in the curriculum into the 1850s, as confirmed by Ella Hancock's sampler, known to have been stitched in the Washington City public school system.

Ella Hancock

In 1853, nine-year-old Ella Hancock stitched a colorful alphabet sampler in wool on linen using cross, eyelet, satin, and Irish stitches (Figure 7-3). Descended with the sampler is a certificate that states: "Ella J. Hancock / For Plain and Fancy Needle Work / Awarded by the Trustees of the Public Schools / of the / City of Washington, D.C." (Figure 7-4).[16]

Ella (born ca. 1844) was a daughter of Drucilla E. Smith (1818–1886) and Andrew Hancock (1804–1881), the second of their five children. Andrew was the keeper of a curiosity shop and tavern on Pennsylvania Avenue that was frequented by "Benton, Calhoun, Webster, Clay, Cass and other great men."[17] However successful Hancock's tavern was, he may have disgraced his daughter in the eyes of some observers by sending her to public school. Sarah Vedder, reminiscing about her life in Washington between 1830 and 1850 commented, "No greater stigma could be attached to a boy or girl than to have said of them: 'They go to the free school.'"[18] The 1850 census recorded Ella Hancock as living with her parents and four siblings. Sadly, Ella died a few years later at the age of twelve.

Girls orphaned or otherwise destitute after the War of 1812 appear to have benefited from a number of charitable groups in Washington City. The Orphan Asylum, lauded by Anne Royall as "the glory of Washington," was established in 1815 by a group of public-spirited ladies with Dolley Madison as first directress and volunteer seamstress. The Orphan Asylum was managed by a board of women whose object was to protect, educate,

---

15 Washington *Daily National Intelligencer*, September 30, 1831.

16 The collection of the DAR Museum includes medals awarded by the Washington public school system. See Olive Blair Graffam, *"Youth Is the Time for Progress": The Importance of American Schoolgirl Art, 1780–1860* (Washington, D.C.: DAR Museum, 1998), 59.

17 *Washington Post*, March 12, 1881. Andrew Hancock's obituary stated that "in early life Mr. Hancock had developed a fondness for what was queer and curious in art." Hancock's Tavern, located in the same building as his "Old Curiosity Shop," was a Washington institution that continued in operation from 1840 to 1914.

18 Sarah E. Vedder, *Reminiscences of the District of Columbia* (St. Louis: A.R. Fleming Printing Co., 1909), 26.

and reform the children of poverty and vice, and to prepare them for useful and respectable stations in life. In the flamboyant language of Anne Royall, the goal was "to cherish and protect their infant state; to sweeten their cup of sorrow; to sow the seeds of virtue, and to draw out the hidden beauties of the mind, which gain our admiration, and fit them for the various duties of life." Visiting in 1824, Royall observed "fifteen female children in the asylum, from five to twelve years of age. . . . they were neat, and well clad, and had a healthy appearance. . . . They are taught reading, writing, and needle-work. . . . When they arrive at an age sufficient to procure a livelihood, they are discharged."[19]

Other charitable groups established free schools for girls during the 1830s. The Female Charity School was dedicated to "the instruction of poor white children in the rudiments of a common English education, in sewing, knitting, and other useful employments," and the Central Female Free School offered necessary instruction to prepare its students to become seamstresses.[20]

Children of color had fewer educational opportunities than children in white families. Teaching enslaved children to read and write was illegal prior to the Civil War, although some may have attended church Sunday schools where they could acquire reading skills while studying the Bible. Andrew Hunter, the white principal of a female academy on Capitol Hill, defied the law when he openly advertised in 1816 that he would teach "colored children, whether bond or free," every Sunday afternoon in his schoolroom.[21]

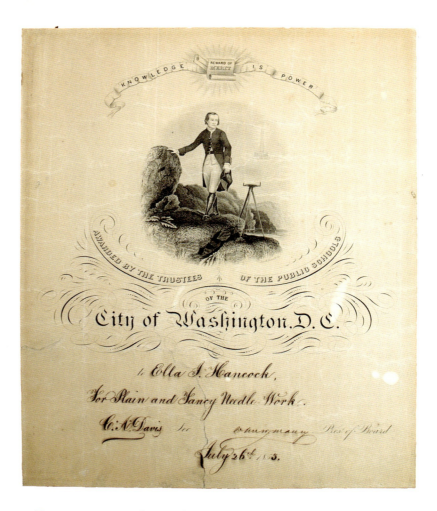

Between 1800 and 1820 the number of free blacks in Washington City increased from 120 to 1,700, and by 1830 free blacks outnumbered those held in bondage.[22] In 1807, when there were fewer than five hundred free blacks in the area, three former slaves erected the Bell School House near the Navy Yard. The school continued for only a few years but was revived in 1818 as the Resolute Beneficial Society with the aim of improving the intellect and morals of black children through the instruction of reading, writing, arithmetic, and English grammar.[23] A school conducted by white teachers at the Navy Yard also taught enslaved

Figure 7-4. Certificate for Plain and Fancy Needlework Inscribed: "Awarded by the Trustees of the Public Schools / of the / City of Washington, D. C. / Ella J. Hancock / For Plain and Fancy Needle Work . . . / July 26th 1853."
Ink on paper.
13 ¾ x 10 ¾ in.
Collection of William Seippel

---

19 Royall, *Sketches*, 144.

20 Washington *Daily National Intelligencer*, June 4, 1834 and October 10, 1835.

21 Ibid., May 17, 1816. Public school for African American children was not an option until after 1862, when an act of Congress required that a primary level public school education be provided for all black and white, male and female children. Each ward had responsibility for its schools and supported them through property taxes.

22 Mary Beth Corrigan, "Making the Most of an Opportunity: Slaves and the Catholic Church in Early Washington," *Washington History* 12 (Spring/Summer 2000): 95–96.

23 Emmett D. Preston Jr., "The Development of Negro Education in the District of Columbia," *Journal of Negro Education* 9 (1940): 595.

and free children of color, many of whose fathers were employed in shipbuilding and maintenance trades at the Yard. Margaret Dove, wife of sailing master Marmaduke Dove, was one of the teachers. It is unknown if she provided any of the female students with instruction in sewing or other useful needle applications.[24]

In 1851, Arabella Jones (born 1835), a woman of color and educated by the Oblate Sisters of Providence in Baltimore, established Saint Agnes' Academy for tuition and free students. The 1852 Prospectus of Saint Agnes' Academy stated, "here the poor are educated gratuitously, the orphans clothed, educated, and a good trade given them."[25] Miss Jones was described as someone who "had a good English education, wrote and spoke with ease and propriety the French tongue, was proficient in music and in all useful and ornamental needlework branches."[26] It is highly likely that Miss Jones taught needlework in her academy, as she left teaching after several years to pursue a more lucrative career using her skill with the needle.[27]

Firm evidence of sewing instruction for women of color in Washington City comes from the 1860s, when "Industrial Schools" came into being as a means of providing the poor with practical instruction in various trades.

Miss [Susan] Walker had under training, six hours a day, about 70 scholars, mostly women, who were taught various kinds of plain sewing, she preparing the work for them, cutting the garments, etc., in the evening. As these women could not afford to take the time even for instruction, unless receiving some remuneration, Miss Walker adopted the plan of paying them proportionately from the articles of clothing made.[28]

CATHOLIC SCHOOLS IN WASHINGTON CITY

Catholic orders served the poor regardless of race or gender. Saint Ann's Infant Asylum, managed by the Sisters of Charity, took in abandoned children under the age of six, whether male or female, black or white. Saint Vincent's Female Orphan Asylum, an orphanage and free school founded in 1825 by Father William Matthews of Saint Patrick's Roman Catholic Church (also run by the Sisters of Charity), looked after girls from age six to fourteen[29] and instructed them in plain and fancy needlework and "tapestry," in addition to basic academic subjects.[30] Funding came from parishioners but also from the charitable impulses of the elite regardless of their religion. In 1857 a bequest from Father Matthews helped Saint Vincent's build a larger school on G Street. At that time there

---

24 John Sharp, "Extracts from the Diary of Michael Shiner, 1805–1880, Slave, Freeman and Entrepreneur." http://genealogytrails.com/washdc/shinerdiary.html. Teachers of African American children, who rarely advertised, are known from written sources such as Michael Shiner's diary and the commissioner of education's report.

25 Tuition students paid eighteen dollars per quarter and additional fees for French and music.

26 Moses Goodwin, Reconstruction-era federal official, quoted by Diane Batts Morrow in *Persons of Color and Religious at the Same Time: The Oblate Sisters of Providence, 1828–1860* (Chapel Hill: University of North Carolina Press, 2002), 243.

27 Henry Barnard, *Special Report of the Commissioner of Education . . .* (Washington, D.C.: Government Printing Office, 1871), 242–43.

28 Ibid.

29 Not until 1868 did people recognize that girls as young as fourteen should not be turned out into the community. At that time, Saint Rose's Industrial School for Girls, under the direction of the Sisters of Charity, was founded as an extension of Saint Vincent's. It continued the care, education, and training of white girls aged fourteen to twenty-one in housekeeping, sewing, and dressmaking. The institution earned, by the work of its students and the sisters, a portion of its maintenance costs. Other funding came from donations.

30 Washington *Daily National Intelligencer*, July 3, 1827.

Julia Lacey

In 1848, eight-year-old Julia Winona Lacey (1840–1874) stitched a simple alphabet sampler using just cross stitch (Figure 7-6). Although some of the letters are missing, it clearly references her school, Saint Vincent. Julia Lacey may have been orphaned, for in the 1850 census, at age eleven, she was living in the household of Henry Walker, a shoemaker, along with three adult women of his family: Emily, Ann, and Florence. On July 20, 1857, Julia married Almanzer W. Layton (born 1837) a lumber measurer from Montgomery County. The couple apparently first settled in Maryland, but then returned to live in Washington City where they raised four daughters: Etta, Fanny, Florence, and Catherine Winona. In the 1870 census, Almanzer Layton was head of a multi-family household that included a member of the Walker family, twelve-year-old Emily Walker. The relationship between the Lacey/Layton family and the Walker family is not clear. Julia died in December 1874 at the age of thirty-four. Almanzer remarried in 1880 and then again in 1887.

Figure 7-5. Sampler worked by Catharine Vonderlehr. Washington City, 1837. Inscribed: "Catharine Vonderlehr / St VINCENT SCHOOL JUNE 12th / 1837." Silk on linen. 14 x 14.5 in. Photograph courtesy of JD Schlipf

Figure 7-6. Sampler worked by Julia Winona Lacey. Washington City, ca. 1848. Inscribed: "Julia Lacey St Vince—.Sch—." Wool on blue-line cotton canvas, 23 by 26 threads per in. 7 ¼ x 7 ¼ in. National Museum of American History, Smithsonian Institution, T08869

were 115 orphans and 300 day students, some of whom probably paid tuition. Saint Vincent's played a significant role in the education of both Catholic and non-Catholic girls in nineteenth-century Washington. Three pieces of needlework are known from this school.

Catharine Vonderlehr

In 1837, Catharine Vonderlehr (born ca. 1824) stitched a naturalistic floral basket sampler using cross, satin, and stem stitches.³¹ Her central motif is partially enclosed by a flowering vine and on four sides by a deeply arcaded border (Figure 7-5). Catharine inscribed her work with her name and "St VINCENT SCHOOL JUNE 12th / 1837." She was a daughter of Catharine (1796-1856) and George Vonderlehr (born ca. 1801), a stonemason. The family had emigrated from Germany in 1832, initially arriving in Baltimore. They may have resided in Washington near Saint Patrick's Church, which was founded in 1794 to minister to stonemasons working on the Capitol.

---

31 This sampler was sold on eBay in 2011. Its current whereabouts are unknown.

INTRODUCTION TO WASHINGTON CITY AND ITS SCHOOLS

Figure 7-7. Sampler worked by Mary Ridgway. Washington City, ca. 1850. Inscribed: "Worked at the School of S!: Vincent by Mary Ridgway." Wool on fine linen ground. 17 ¼ x 18 in. Collection of Natalie D. Grossman.

Mary Ridgway

An undated cross-stitch mourning picture was worked by Mary Ridgway "at the School of St Vincent" around 1850 (Figure 7-7). On a lawn of variegated green grass, Mary stitched a large funerary urn draped with a garland, flanked by a bush with large flowers and an arching tree. Mary is probably the Mary Anna Columbia Ridgway (1839–1901) born to Mary Ann Howe (1812–1850) and Enoch William Ridgway (1809–1888), a slater (roof tile layer) in Washington City. It is likely that Mary stitched her mourning sampler in 1850 after the death of her mother, who died in April of that year of "inflamed bowels." Mary (also known as Columbia) married John Wesley Hayes (1831–1907), a paperhanger from Baltimore on March 3, 1855. They made their home on O Street, NW, in Washington City and together had thirteen children.

In the 1900 census Mary, age sixty-two, was listed as the head of household in her Washington City home and living with her were two adult children, thirty-four-year-old Lillie, a government clerk, and twenty-three-year-old Rutherford B., a dry goods salesman. Mary's husband John seems to have been plagued by health problems in his later years. The 1880 census listed him as disabled with rheumatism and in 1896 he was admitted to the Home Hospital for Volunteer Soldiers in Hampton, Virginia (housed in the buildings and grounds of what had originally been the Chesapeake Female College), where he spent the rest of his days. Mary died in November 1901 and was interred in the Hayes family plot in Washington's Congressional Cemetery, joining the five children who had predeceased her. Her husband died in October 1907 and was buried next to her.

Catholic orders also conducted schools for which parents paid tuition. The Sisters of Charity established Saint Paul's Female Academy on Capitol Hill in 1831 and included plain and fancy needlework as well as lace-making in their extensive curriculum. In 1847 the Sisters of Charity opened Saint Joseph's School for Young Ladies on E Street. Saint

Joseph's offered instruction in the higher and ornamental branches, including "Cotton Embroidery, Plain and Ornamental Needlework; *Cheneille* and Silk Embroidery."[32] One sampler is known from this school.

Caroline R. Masi

One of the first students at Saint Joseph's School for Young Ladies was Caroline Rosella Masi (1837–1867), who worked her alphabet sampler in cross and eyelet stitches in November 1847 (Figure 7-8). The 1850 federal census for Washington's Fourth Ward recorded Caroline as being twelve years old and the fourth of Catherine Ann Bradford (1805–1884) and Seraphim Masi's (1797–1884) eight children. Seraphim Masi an émigré from Frascati, Italy, was a noted silversmith who became a major retailer of silver and jewelry. Although his silver work is eagerly sought by collectors, Masi is also known for the die he created for the United States Treaty Seal of 1825. Catherine Bradford Masi opened a boarding house in 1841, four years after Caroline's birth.[33] The 1850 census lists nine members of the Masi family and thirteen boarders, including other members of the Bradford family.

By 1860, Caroline had become a schoolteacher living at home with her family and twenty-five boarders. In 1862 she married Charles de Frondat (1830–1886), a French professor and inventor from Nantes, who had emigrated to the United States. The couple settled in Washington where their first daughter, Marie Louise Octavia (1863–1944), was born. They later moved to Boston and had two more daughters: Elise Josephine (1865–1950) and Rene Caroline (1866–1866), the younger dying within a month of her birth. Caroline herself died the following year at the age of thirty. Charles de Frondat

remarried in 1871 and died in France in 1886.

Caroline's two surviving daughters first lived with their maternal grandparents in Washington and then were adopted by Caroline's older sister, Frances Virginia Masi (1835–1915) who in 1855 had married Alexander James Dallas III, an officer in the U.S. military. Upon adoption, both girls took the last name Dallas and were raised amid social and economic privilege.

A number of additional samplers were stitched at private and non-denominational schools in Washington City. Unlike the samplers of Catholic schoolgirls, these examples do not identify the girls' school or teacher. A diverse selection of samplers, almost all naming "Washington City," follows in Chapter 8. In Chapter 9, a group of architectural samplers is discussed, all stitched by girls whose families lived in the vicinity of the Navy Yard.

Figure 7-8. Sampler worked by Caroline R. Masi. Washington City, 1847. Inscribed: "Caroline R. Masi * / November 18th 1847 * St Joseph's School E. Street / Washington D. C." Wool on linen ground, 30 by 30 threads per in. 15 x 11 ½ in. Georgetown Visitation Monastery Archivs

---

32 Washington *Daily National Intelligencer*, May 14, 1831 and January 9, 1847. Saint Joseph's was transferred to the Sisters of the Visitation in 1850. It was separate from the poor school, of the same name, run by the Sisters of the Visitation in Georgetown.

33 A newspaper notice advised, "Mrs. S. Masi has taken the house recently occupied by Miss Corcoran, corner of 4 ½ street and Pennsylvania avenue. House is furnished entirely new and prepared to accommodate boarders." Washington *Daily National Intelligencer*, May 22, 1841.

Figure 8-1.
"View of F Street, Washington." 1817.
Inscribed: "Le coin de F. Street Washington vis-à-vis nôtre maison été de 1817."
Watercolor on paper by Anne Marguerite Henrietta Hyde de Neuville.
7 5/16 x 11 5/16 in.
I. N. Phelps Stokes Collection, Miriam and Ira D. Wallach Division of Art, Prints and Photographs,
The New York Public Library, Astor, Lenox and Tilden Foundations

Baroness Hyde de Neuville (died 1849), wife of Jean-Guillaume, baron Hyde de Neuville, French ambassador to the United States, 1816–1822, was a noted watercolorist who captured numerous scenes of everyday life. Her view of F Street, as seen from her house, reveals early Washington as a city of contrasts—substantial brick buildings back up to rolling farm land, horses and carriages share the road with roaming cows, and ladies and gentlemen greet each other while laborers and servants go about their work.

CHAPTER 8

Washington City Samplers

Iconic among the District of Columbia girlhood embroideries are the architectural samplers worked by girls living in the vicinity of the Washington Navy Yard (discussed in Chapter 9). No other major stylistic groups have been identified for Washington City, and many of the samplers discovered thus far feature a series of alphabets with a scattering of motifs rather than a complex design. There is no doubt, though, that early nineteenth-century teachers in Washington City offered instruction in many advanced forms of needlework such as tambour-work, flowering, filigree, open-work, print-work, and embroidery.

A Mrs. Howard, for example, was probably one of the more knowledgeable teachers when it came to the latest needlework fashions. She described herself as having "for years been an approved Instructress of youth in the most enlightened and polished societies of Europe and America" and offered in her seminary instruction in "Plain, embossed and open Cotton work, Netting and Tetting [*sic*], Landscape, Flower and Fancy Crewel Works, Embroidery in Gold, Silver, Silk and Worsted, Tambour . . . with other useful and ornamental accomplishments."[1] Unfortunately, no known examples of schoolgirl embroidery can be attributed to her instruction. The following, in approximate chronological order, are samplers stitched by girls who attended school in Washington City.

Susan and Mary Ann Borrows

The earliest dated sampler identified with Washington City was stitched by Susan Borrows in 1803 (Figure 8-2). Worked in cross, rice, satin, eyelet, four-sided, and chain stitches, it features four alphabets, two baskets of flowers, and an arcaded strawberry border. Susan's inscription appears in a rectangular cartouche set off by a leafy vine and includes full name, "Washington City," and complete date, "June 3ᵈ 1803."

Susan (Susannah) Borrows (ca. 1788–1854) was born in Pennsylvania, the oldest daughter of the ten children born to Sarah Jeffers (1764–1819) and Joseph Borrows (1767–1837). Susan's family came to Washington City in 1800 when Congress moved from Philadelphia to the new federal district. Joseph found employment as a messenger for the general post office.[2] During

---

1 Washington *Daily National Intelligencer*, May 13 and July 14, 1815.

Figure 8-2.
Sampler worked by Susan Borrows. Washington City, 1803.
Inscribed: "Susan Borrows / Washington City / June 3ᵈ 1803."
Silk on linen ground, 28 by 28 threads per in.
16 ⅝ x 17 ⅝ in.
Collection of David and Mary Bell

Susan's school years, the family lived near the Navy Yard, where her parents were active in founding the Second or Navy Yard Baptist Church in 1810.³ In 1812, Joseph Borrows built a house on E Street between 9th and 10th Streets in the northwest section of the city that remained in the family for seventy-five years. Susan's sampler does not anticipate any of the motifs found on Navy Yard samplers stitched in 1810 and later.

Susan's younger sister, Mary Ann (1802–1826), was born in Washington City. In 1811 she worked a sampler that she marked, "Mary Ann Borrows / Aged 9 years July 21 / 1811, wrought this / Sampler at Mrs. Gray's / School in the city of / Washington."⁴ In all likelihood she attended the school conducted by Mr. and Mrs. Gray on G Street where they taught "Reading, Writing, Geography, Grammar, Arithmetic, and all kinds of Needle work."⁵

---

2 Joseph's father, John, also came to Washington City in 1800 when he received an appointment with the comptroller's office. Captain John Borrows, as well as several sons, had carried mail between New York City and Philadelphia for a number of years.

3 Three of the five founding members of the Navy Yard Baptist Church were Joseph and Sarah Borrows and Clement Boswell, father of Navy Yard sampler maker Maria Boswell, discussed in Chapter 9. Wilhelmus Bogart Bryan, *A History of the National Capital: From Its Foundations Through the Period of the Adoption of the Organic Act* (New York: Macmillan, 1916), 604.

4 Unfortunately, this sampler is known only from a family memoir.

5 The Grays' school was not in the Navy Yard Hill settlement but closer to the War Office and other federal buildings near Pennsylvania Avenue, the location of a number of other early schools. *National Intelligencer & Washington Advertiser*, October 6, 1809.

On April 20, 1824, Mary Ann married Andrew Rothwell (1801–1883) in the Navy Yard Baptist Church. Less than three years later Mary Ann died, leaving an infant daughter, Laura Elizabeth Rothwell (1825–1893), who at age eight would work an alphabet sampler that is still in the possession of family members. Susan Borrows, who never married, took over the care and education of her young niece. When Susan died in 1854, a local newspaper noted:

> The deceased came with her father, the late Joseph Borrows, on removal of the offices of the National Government from Philadelphia, to this city. . . . She lived to see what was a mere wilderness converted into a large city. She was for many years a professor of religion. . . . She died in the midst of her family, for whom she had lived and sacrificed with noble generosity the prime of her life.[6]

Ann Carlon

Ann Carlon's 1812 sampler is one of the most decorative and accomplished of the early Washington City samplers. It features a basket full of strawberries and a poem entitled "On Virtue" (Figure 8-3). The verse, written by an unknown author, reads:

> *Of virtue who can estimate the worth?*
> *her obligation time can ne'er unhinge;*
> *nor creature will, nor fancy gave her birth*
> *reality incapable of change.*
> *Wit, learning, beauty, each ennobling art*
> *shall like a dream, or airy Phantom, fly;*
> *but virtue, twisted round the human heart,*
> *soars with the soul to immortality.*

Ann demonstrated her skill with a needle when she used both silk and chenille thread in a combination of chain, cable chain, coral knot, tent, outline, couched, queen, and satin stitches. She enclosed her composition with a serpentine border of a naturalistic vine with queen-stitched strawberries. It is possible that Ann attended the school conducted by Miss Margaret Sinnott, who taught "plain and ornamental needle work of every description" from 1808 to the 1840s. In 1808, Sinnott opened her school on "North G Street near the Treasury Office" and before 1810 relocated to 14th near F Street.

Figure 8-3
Sampler worked by Ann Carlon. Washington City, 1812. Inscribed: "Ann Carlon Her Work / Washington City May 9th / 1812." Silk and silk chenille on linen ground, 29 by 34 threads per in. 16 ⅜ x 12 ¼ in.
The Colonial Williamsburg Foundation, Museum Purchase, 1996-228,A

---

6 Washington *Daily National Intelligencer*, May 17, 1854.

7 *National Intelligencer & Washington Advertiser*, May 20, 1808 and April 18, 1810; Washington *National Intelligencer*, April 21, 1812.

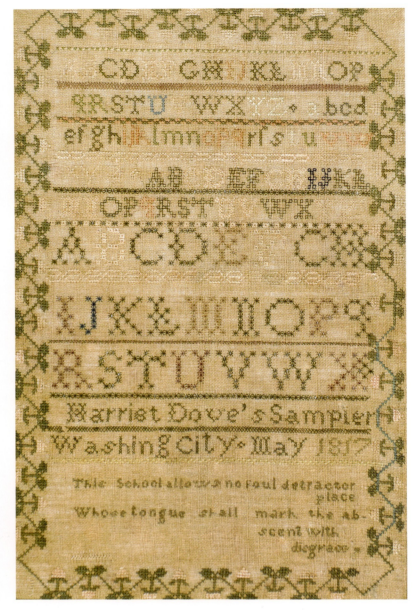

Figure 8-4. Sampler worked by Harriet Dove. Washington City, 1817. Inscribed: "Harriet Dove's Sampler / Washing City * May 1817." Silk on linen ground, 26 by 26 threads per inch. 17 ¼ x 11 in. Private collection

Harriet Dove and Elizabeth S. Dove

Samplers stitched by Harriet and Elizabeth S. Dove in 1817 and 1820, respectively, feature four alphabets with letters worked in the same style and formed from the same selection of stitches—cross, four-sided, and eyelet. Both samplers also have a neatly arcaded border of strawberries and leaves on a vine. Harriet added her name, date, "Washing City," and a short verse: *This school allows no Foul detractor / place / Whose tongue shall mark the ab-/scent with / disgrace* (Figure 8-4). Elizabeth stitched a more complex composition with a seven-bay brick building flanked by evergreens and paired motifs of hearts, diamonds, and baskets of flowers. In addition to her name, age, and date, it is inscribed "Washington City" (Figure 8-5). Elizabeth's verse is the second stanza from the hymn, "The Child's Request," published in 1817 in a collection of hymns compiled for use in the Baptist Church.[8]

> *May my fond genius as I rise*
> *Seek the fair fount where knowledge lies*
> *On wings sublime trace Heaven's abode*
> *And learn my duty to my God*

Elizabeth may have stitched a seven-bay structure known as "Seven Buildings" on Pennsylvania Avenue where several teachers had classrooms.[9]

Elizabeth S. Dove (1807–1885) was a daughter of Elizabeth Hopkins (1770–1857) and Thomas Dove (1773–1849), a messenger for the Treasury Department. At the time that Elizabeth worked her sampler, the Dove family lived either in the vicinity of Washington Circle, a relatively dense area of settlement considered "to be the best residence section of the city" or on Vermont

Ann Carlon's parents have not been identified. Possibly she was a daughter of James and Margaret Carlon or of William Carlon and his unidentified wife. According to the 1800 federal census for Washington City, both households included one or more girls under the age of ten. Unfortunately, the 1810 federal census for Washington City has not survived, so neither Carlon family can be documented as living in Washington City at a time closer to the year that Ann stitched her 1812 sampler.

---

8 William Parkinson, compiler, *A Selection of Hymns and Spiritual Songs in Two Parts: . . . As an Appendix to Dr. Watts's Psalms and Hymns* (New York: printed for John Tiebout, 1817).

9 Alternatively, Elizabeth's design may depict a large building at Eighth and M Streets, SE, still standing across from the Navy Yard. Information courtesy of Paul Turczynski.

COLUMBIA'S DAUGHTERS

Avenue between H and I (Eye) Streets, North.[10] In 1827, Elizabeth married Samuel Harkness Jr. (1803–1866), a house carpenter in Washington City, and by 1830 she and her husband resided next door to her parents in Ward Three. After Elizabeth's father died in 1849, her mother and a brother joined the Harkness household. Elizabeth and Samuel never had children and she died in 1885 at the residence of her brother Robert Dove after "a long illness of paralysis."[11]

Harriet Dove (ca. 1805-1838) is less well documented. She may have been another daughter of Thomas and Elizabeth Dove. According to the 1820 federal census for the District of Columbia, the Thomas Dove household contained three boys under the age of ten, two girls age ten to fifteen, and one girl age sixteen to twenty-five. Elizabeth was one of the Dove girls in the ten to fifteen age group and Harriet may have been the other.[12] A Harriet Dove married Edmund M. Preston Jr., a victualler and butcher at the Centre Market, on June 1, 1837. She died less than a year later on May 22, 1838, at the age of thirty-two.[13] If this is the same Harriet Dove, she would have been eleven years old when she stitched her sampler in 1817. Edmund remarried in 1846 and returned to his native Baltimore.

Ann Ward and Sarah Eliza Ann Trunnel

Ann Ward stitched a colorful sampler with "A garland of flowers so gay" and a verse lauding Washington as "Columbia's palladium," or protector. The sampler is worked all in cross stitch and features an open wreath of roses, tulips, carnations, and star flowers (Figure 8-6). The signature line reads, "Ann Ward . . . Washington City / 1826." A sampler with an almost identical arrangement and selection of stylized flowers was stitched in cross and

Figure 8-5
Sampler worked by Elizabeth S. Dove. Washington City, 1820. Inscribed: "Elizabeth S. Dove aged 13. Washington City Septem- / -ber 6th 1820." Silk and wool on linen ground, 28 by 34 threads per in. 16 ¼ x 16 in. Collection of Paul Turczynski

---

10 Quoted from the obituary of Elizabeth's brother, Richard G. Dove, "born in the Vicinity of Washington Circle, on the 26th day of January 1814." Washington *Evening Star*, December 11, 1891. The 1822 city directory and later directories give a Vermont Avenue location for Thomas Dove.

11 *Interments in the Historic Congressional Cemetery* http://www.congressionalcemetery.org/interment-index-o.

12 Assuming Harriet was born around 1805–1806, as indicated by the death notice cited below, several other Dove families in Washington City can be eliminated by the ages of female household members given in the 1820 federal census.

13 The records of Washington's Rock Creek Cemetery state, "Preston, Harriet (Mrs. Edmund M.) d. 22 May 1838, age 32, removed in 1881 from Holmead's Burying Ground to Rock Creek Cemetery, Sect. K48," and her gravestone in Rock Creek Cemetery validates this information. Wesley Pippenger, *Dead People on the Move!* (Westminster, Md.: Willow Bend Books, 2004), viii, 330.

Figure 8-6.
Sampler worked by
Ann Ward.
Washington City,
1826.
Inscribed: "Ann Ward
Washington City /
1826."
Silk on linen ground,
39 by 36 threads
per in.
20 ¼ x 16 in.
The Colonial Williamsburg
Foundation, Museum
Purchase, 1998-16

eyelet stitches by eleven-year-old Sarah Eliza Ann Trunnel (known as Eliza), probably about 1825 (Figure 8-7).[14] The wreath encloses a melancholy poem entitled "To Despondency."[15] Although Ann did not tell us her age and Eliza did not record her location, these samplers may have been worked under the direction of the same teacher. Possibilities include Mrs. Cottringer, who taught plain and ornamental needlework from 1822 until at least 1825, and

---

14 A related floral wreath sampler with similar roses, tulips, carnations, and star flowers was worked in cross stitches by Elizabeth Smith at the Germantown Boarding School in 1835. One by Martha Ann Rogers of Loudoun County, Virginia, features a similar wreath enclosing an alphabet. Her October 16, 1827, sampler was worked in cross and eyelet stitches. Most likely all four samplers were based on a printed pattern in circulation during the 1820s and 1830s. Margaret B. Schiffer, *Historical Needlework of Pennsylvania* (New York: Charles Scribner's Sons, 1968), 85, and Betty W. Flemming, *Threads of History: A Sampler of Girlhood Embroidery, 1792–1860, Loudoun County Area* (Leesburg, Va.: The Loudoun Museum, 1995), 10.

15 The poem "To Despondency" was published in Baltimore in 1821 by a local printer, R. J. Matchett and attributed to twelve-year-old Edgar Allan Poe on the basis of the signature, "Edgar." John Wooster Robertson, *Edgar A. Poe: A Study* (San Francisco: Bruce Brough, 1921), 415–16.

Mrs. Bonfils, who offered instruction in the ornamental branches between 1825 and 1827. It is also possible, given Ann's Catholic upbringing, that she and Eliza attended the newly established Saint Vincent's Free School as paying students.[16]

Ann Ward was a daughter of Irish immigrants Mary Delany[17] and William Ward (1775–1851), who operated a dry goods store on the north side of Pennsylvania Avenue. In 1820 his household included three females under the age of ten, one of whom was probably Ann. In 1834, Ann married Massachusetts-born Joseph Little Peabody (1806–1857), also employed in the dry goods business in Washington City. Ann and Joseph had one daughter, Mary Delany Peabody, born in 1836. Ann Ward Peabody appears to have died between the recording of the 1840 and 1850 federal censuses.

William Ward left a sizable legacy to his granddaughter and specified that "she be educated at either the Academy of the Visitation at Georgetown, or the Catholic Female School in Frederick City, Md., or St. Joseph's Female Institution near Emmitsburg, Md." His will further provided that if his granddaughter should die before reaching twenty-one, her stocks and money should go to four Catholic educational institutions, including the "Sisters of the Convent of the Visitation, near Georgetown, for support of poor women who may be there candidates for admission to the Religious Sisterhood."[18]

Sarah Eliza Ann Trunnel (Trunnell) (1813–1884) was a daughter of Catherine Boose (born ca. 1790) and Horatio Trunnell (born before 1790), a livery stable owner and coach maker with a business on Washington Street in Georgetown.[19] To attend school in Washington City, Eliza may have taken the stage that traveled along Pennsylvania Avenue and connected Georgetown to the Capitol.[20] Eliza Trunnel married Daniel Ragan (1810–1846) in 1833 and, according to family

Figure 8-7. Sampler worked by Sarah Eliza Ann Trunnel. Probably Washington City, ca. 1825. Inscribed: "Sarah Eliza Ann Trunnel Aged 11." Silk on linen ground. 21 1/8 x 17 1/8 in. Daughters of the American Revolution Museum, gift of Miriam Talbot Chapin, 87.72.3

---

16 William Ward's 1846 will provided a generous legacy to Saint Vincent's: "in lieu of funeral, Exr. to give to the trustees of St. Vincent's Orphan Asylum, of City of Washington, new Catholic books in my possession at the original cost amounting to $100; to trustees 10 shares in stock of Rockville and Washington Turnpike Road Company, 5 shares in Chesapeake and Ohio Canal Company, and 1 share of Washington & Baltimore Steamboat or Steam Packet Company stock." District of Columbia Probate Records, book 5, 430–35.

17 Ann's mother's name is a presumption based on Ann's naming of her only child Mary Delany.

18 District of Columbia Probate Records, book 5, 430–35.

19 Washington Street, now known as M Street, intersects Pennsylvania Avenue before it crosses Rock Creek into Washington City.

20 Connecticut congressman John Cotton Smith noted that southern congressmen tended to lodge in Georgetown and used hackney coaches to get to the Capitol. Suzanne Berry Sherwood, "Foggy Bottom 1800–1975: A Study in the Uses of an Urban Neighborhood," *GW Washington Studies*, no.7 (December 1974): 2.

Figure 8-8. Sampler worked by Margaret C. Simmons. Washington City, 1827. Inscribed: "[Margaret] C. Simmons Work Washington City Oct.th 2d / 1827." Silk on linen ground, 29 by 29 threads per in. 16 ½ x 12 ⅜ in. National Museum of American History, Smithsonian Institution, 2000.0143.01

Figure 8-9 Margaret Simmons Dowling. Washington City, 1845–1850. Private collection.

tradition, left her sampler with her mother for safekeeping when her husband's military career sent the family west.[21] Eliza and Daniel had two children, Horatio and Catherine, both born in Missouri. After her husband's death, Eliza returned to live in the District where she kept house for her children and her widowed mother.

Margaret C. Simmons and Maria Brightwell

Margaret C. Simmons finished two samplers in quick succession, one dated October 2, 1827 (Figure 8-8) and the other January 7, 1828 (Figure 9-15).[22] Margaret's 1827 sampler is unusual for Washington City samplers with its bold basket of strawberries and downward

---

21 Eliza also declared that her sampler never be sold. It remained in her family until it was given to the DAR Museum in 1987. Graffam, "Youth is the Time for Progress," 59.

22 Margaret's earlier sampler is identified only as "—C. Simmons Work Washington City Oct th 2d / 1827." The discovery of Margaret's later sampler in a private collection led to Sheryl De Jong's identification of the maker of the Smithsonian's sampler.

Figure 8-10.
Sampler worked by Maria Brightwell. Washington City, 1827. Inscribed: "Maria Brightwell's Work Washington City Oct. 16th 1827." 17 x 17 in. Location unknown.

hanging leaves, flanked by large urns of flowers, and enclosed in a geometric border. It is worked in a combination of cross, satin, Algerian eye, rice, herringbone, and stem stitches.

A similar sampler, worked by Maria Brightwell and dated October 16, 1827, shares enough stylistic characteristics to indicate that Maria and Margaret studied needlework with the same teacher, probably in the vicinity of the Navy Yard. Maria, daughter of James Brightwell, a Navy Yard rigger, stitched a smaller but nearly identical strawberry basket with downward hanging leaves (Figure 8-10). Maria also stitched alphabets divided by decorative bands and composed a similar signature line. She enclosed her composition in an arcaded floral border much like borders found on the more elaborate architectural samplers associated with the Navy Yard (see Chapter 9).[23]

Eight-year-old Margaret Simmons (1819–1847/50) was a daughter of Mary M. Barclay and James Simmons (born 1794), a cooper. In 1822 the family was residing at 11th Street, East, between L and M Streets, South, in the populous Navy Yard Hill area.[24] Like James Brightwell, James Simmons was probably employed at the Yard. In 1839, Margaret married Irish-born Patrick Dowling (ca. 1816–1864), a stonecutter. Margaret died sometime after the birth of her second son in 1847 and before 1850 (Figure 8-9). She does not appear in the 1850 census, which records her husband Patrick living with the Simmons family, along with their two sons William Daniel (born 1840) and Julius (born 1847). Patrick married for a second time in 1852, and the stepmother raised Margaret's sons.

---

23 Such a border is found on Margaret's architectural sampler (see Figure 9-15), dated only three months later. Consequently, it seems unlikely that she switched teachers between working her first and second sampler.

24 James Simmons lived a long life. The 1880 federal census located him in Utah, a widower, working as a farmhand at age eighty-six.

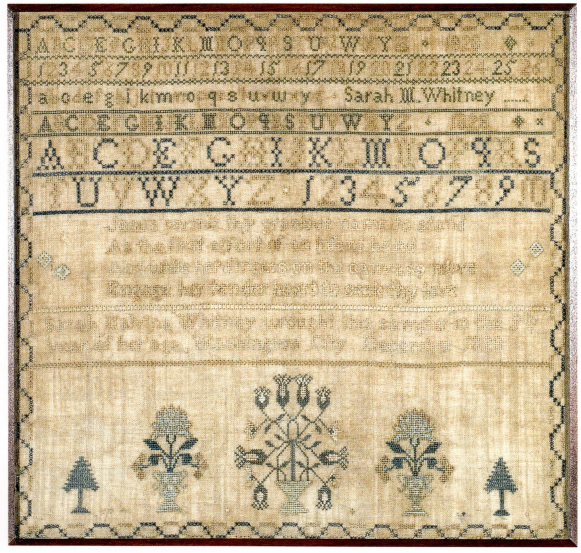

Figure 8-11. Sampler worked by Sarah Malvina Whitney. Washington City, 1828. Inscribed: "Sarah Malvina Whitney wrought this sampler in the 9th / year of her age, Washington City December 1828." Silk on linen ground, 30 by 28 threads per in. 17 x 17 ½ in. Collection of Virginia D. Dickie

Sarah Malvina Whitney

Eight-year-old Sarah Malvina Whitney worked a sampler in 1828 that features four alphabets in cross, four-sided, queen, and eyelet stitches. She also included the popular sampler verse beginning with, "Jesus permit thy gracious name to stand." Below is her signature, which reads "Sarah Malvina Whitney wrought this sampler in the 9th year of her age, Washington City December 1828." This is followed by a row of symmetrical motifs including matching urns with stylized flowers flanking a central container of thistles (Figure 8-11). Sarah filled empty spaces at the end of her alphabets with her name (using only a middle initial), and the year.

Sarah (1819–1873) was born in Clinton, New Jersey, the eldest child of William Whitney (1800–ca. 1878) and his first wife Permelia Cogswell (1796–1839). William Whitney moved back and forth between New Jersey and the District of Columbia while carrying on the business of boot and shoe manufacturer. Sarah's sampler with its designation of "Washington City" confirms the Whitney family location in the District as of 1828. It is possible that Sarah studied with Miss J. Herbert, who conducted a school in her house on 8th Street, near Pennsylvania Avenue, a block or two distant from the Whitney residence near 9th and Pennsylvania.[25] Between 1826 and 1829, Miss Herbert offered instruction in "Lace and Ornamental Needle Work and Plain Sewing" in addition to the traditional English curriculum.[26] In 1850, Sarah, unmarried, was living with her father and his second wife, who was her mother's sister. They resided in Clinton, New Jersey, where Sarah died in 1873.

---

25 Location listed for William Whitney in the 1834 publication, *A Full Directory, For Washington City*.

26 Washington *Daily National Intelligencer*, September 1, 1826, April 4, 1827, and Washington *Daily National Journal*, August 31, 1829.

COLUMBIA'S DAUGHTERS

Julianna Lawrence

Between 1829 and 1832, at least twenty-one women in Washington City advertised for the first time in local newspapers that they would be teaching plain and fancy needlework, lacework, and other ornamental branches (see Appendix II). Most teachers were well located in the more populous northwest quadrant of the city, near Capitol Hill, the President's Square, and along Pennsylvania Avenue. With the exception of Catholic and public school samplers, only a few samplers marked "Washington City" are known from the 1830s and later.

One of these is a sophisticated architectural sampler with an incomplete signature stitched in 1830, signed "—lianna –awrenc— Work Washington City July 1830" (Figure 8-12). The sampler has been attributed to a Julianna Lawrence, born in the District around 1820. Dominating the sampler is an elaborately stitched brick building with central bell tower labeled Saint Patrick's Church, a well-known Baltimore edifice. The image on Julianna's sampler is almost identical to one of Saint Patrick's Church stitched on a sampler by Elizabeth Harley of Baltimore in 1824.[27] Both girls also stitched the same two lines of scripture, engraved in stone on tablets above the church windows: "In this place I will give / Peace saith the Lord of hosts" and "Blessed are they that / Dwell in thy house / O Lord."[28] The oversize serrated leaves and berries that decorate Julianna's church lawn, however, are unique to the Washington City sampler.

It is unclear how Julianna happened to stitch such a prominent example of Baltimore architecture on her sampler. A variety of possibilities can be envisioned, but answers are elusive. It is possible that Julianna's teacher formerly taught in Baltimore and brought a pattern for the impressive building with her to Washington City. It is also possible that Julianna's teacher was inspired by one of the engravings of Saint Patrick's that was in circulation at the time.[29]

Another explanation might be that Julianna attended Saint Vincent's Female Orphan Asylum and Free School operated by the Sisters of Charity and affiliated with Saint Patrick's Church in Washington. Although Saint Vincent's began as a free school for orphans and destitute children, it soon became a popular girls' school for the entire parish, including the wealthy.[30] Samplers known from that school were worked in diverse designs. Given that her father's will specified he be buried according to the "Holy Rites of the Roman Catholic and Apostolic Church,"[31] it is likely her parents chose a Catholic school for Julianna to attend.

Juliannna Lawrence was born about 1820 to Margaret James (born ca. 1794) from England and Baltimore-born James Lawrence (1793–1852), a tobacconist on

---

27 See Allen, *A Maryland Sampling*, figure 12-23. Washington City's Saint Patrick's Catholic Church, constructed as a brick Gothic Revival meeting hall, was later enlarged to a T-shape by flanking wings. It did not have a bell tower.

28 Haggai 2:9 and Psalms 84:4.

29 For example, L. H. Poppleton's *Plan of the City of Baltimore*, published in 1823. See Kimberly Smith Ivey, *In the Neatest Manner: The Making of the Virginia Sampler Tradition* (Austin, Tex.: Curious Works Press, 1997), figure 63.

30 Although this was an orphanage and free school, the operation was financed by private contributions and expanded with its move in 1828 to a new building at 10th and G Streets. "Contrary to expectations, however, St. Patrick's, which had assumed responsibility to nurture the orphan, soon found itself with a popular girls' school on its hands. From the beginning, the day students greatly outnumbered the orphans." Morris J. MacGregor, *A Parish for the Federal City: St. Patrick's in Washington, 1794–1994* (Washington: Catholic University of America Press, 1994), 75.

31 Wesley E. Pippenger, *District of Columbia Probate Records, Will Books 1 through 6, 1801–1852 and Estate Files 1801–1852* (Westminster, Md.: Family Line Publications, 1996), 365.

Figure 8-12. Sampler attributed to Julianna Lawrence. Washington City, 1830. Inscribed: "—lianna —awrenc – Work Washington City July 1830." Silk on linen ground, 29 by 32 threads per in. 16 x 16 in. The Colonial Williamsburg Foundation, Museum Purchase, 1996-229

Pennsylvania Avenue near 4th Street, West.[32] Julianna married Thomas H. Parsons (born ca. 1818), an agent for the Baltimore and Ohio Railroad, on November 25, 1845. When the 1850 federal census was recorded, the couple was still living with her parents, along with two young sons. In two years they would welcome a daughter, Julia. The 1852 probate records reveal that at the time of her father's death, Julianna received considerable real estate and shares in the Central Building Association.[33] This inheritance may have helped finance the building of the family's three-story mansion on Delaware Avenue, valued at $30,000.[34] Thomas later worked as a clerk for the War Department, and their son John, who continued to live at home, became a

---

32 James Lawrence is listed as a tobacconist at "n side Pen av btw 3 and 4 ½ w" in Washington directories for 1827 and 1830, and in 1834 at "n side C n, btw 18 and 19 w."

33 Pippenger, *District of Columbia Probate Records*, 365.

34 In 1848, Parsons speculated in land on Delaware Avenue and by 1860 the family was living in the three-story mansion he had erected on that property. James Croggon, Washington *Evening Star*, September 27, 1913. In 1865, both Thomas and Julia[nna] were assessed excise taxes on their incomes, watches, and Julia's piano, evidence of their inherited and acquired wealth.

physician and surgeon. John married Mary Thomas from Ohio in 1884, and by 1900 they were living in Chicago with their fourteen-year-old daughter Julia.

Helen M. Carbery

Helen Mary Carbery (Carberry) (ca. 1822–1863) stitched an alphabet sampler adorned with a simple image of a brick church and inscribed, "Helen M Carbery/ August 25th 1832/ D C" (Figure 8-13). Her sampler omits the words "Washington City" but is among the earliest to refer to the District of Columbia.[35]

Helen was a daughter of Emza (Emma) Cloud and James Carbery (1792–1851), a naval architect in charge of timber supplies for shipbuilding at the Navy Yard and brother of Thomas Carbery (1791–1863), sixth mayor of Washington City.[36] The James Carbery family resided on Virginia Avenue between 3rd and 4th Streets, East, and James was one of the original members of Saint Peter's Roman Catholic Church, established in 1820 to serve the Capitol Hill and Navy Yard communities. It is possible that Helen initially attended Saint Paul's Female Academy, located near Saint Peter's Church.

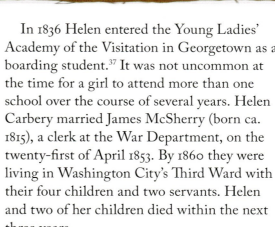

In 1836 Helen entered the Young Ladies' Academy of the Visitation in Georgetown as a boarding student.[37] It was not uncommon at the time for a girl to attend more than one school over the course of several years. Helen Carbery married James McSherry (born ca. 1815), a clerk at the War Department, on the twenty-first of April 1853. By 1860 they were living in Washington City's Third Ward with their four children and two servants. Helen and two of her children died within the next three years.

Figure 8-13. Sampler worked by Helen Mary Carbery. Washington City, 1832. Inscribed: "Helen M Carbery / August 25th 1832 / D C." Silk on linen ground. 17 x 18 in. Historical Society of Carroll County, Maryland

---

35 The earliest known Washington City sampler to include the initials "D.C." was worked by Eliza Thompson, a resident of the Navy Yard Hill community in 1823 (Figure 9-13). However, the words "District of Columbia" first appear on a pictorial Alexandria sampler worked by Rebecca Suter in 1819 (Figure 2-19).

36 Thomas and James Carbery's sister, Ann Carbery Mattingly, was diagnosed with a breast tumor and was critically ill in 1824. With the simultaneous prayers of Father Matthews from Saint Patrick's Church and those of a prince-priest in Bavaria, who was famous for miraculous cures, Mrs. Mattingly made an astonishing recovery. Grateful for her return to health, Thomas Carbery made a significant contribution to Saint Patrick's Church, which helped to expand its female school. The Catholic Church considered this much-publicized incident to be one of the first miracles documented in the United States. William M. Warner, *At Peace with All Their Neighbors: Catholics and Catholicism in the National Capital, 1787–1860* (Washington, D.C.: Georgetown University Press, 1994), 194–95.

37 Entrance Book, October 24, 1836, Georgetown Visitation Monastery Archives.

Figure 8-14. Sampler worked by Sarah Ann Carter. Washington City, 1834. Inscribed: "Sarah Ann Carter Washington City January th 2nd 1834." Silk on linen ground. 17 x 17 in. Image courtesy of M. Finkel & Daughter

Sarah Ann Carter

An 1834 architectural sampler marked "Washington City January th 2nd" does not fit neatly into a defined stylistic group, and its embroiderer, Sarah Ann Carter, is elusive (Figure 8-14). This sampler is interesting because it incorporates motifs that recall Virginia samplers. The Georgian three-bay, brick house stitched below "The Universal Prayer" suggests the architecture of the Tidewater region, while the flanking cropped diamond-shaped evergreen trees worked in two shades of silk are found on an 1832 sampler attributed to Alexandria and an almost identical example attributed to Henrico County (Richmond), Virginia.[38] The paired bird in wreath motif is also typical of Alexandria samplers (see Chapter 2) and of Quaker samplers from many regions. Fashionably dressed ladies and gentlemen strolling on the lawn, accompanied by dogs, sheep, and other animals, are found on Washington City samplers, especially those stitched in the vicinity of the Navy Yard. In this example, the inclusion of an African American man holding a basket on his head (far left) is notable.

Sarah Ann Carter eludes positive identification. Carter is a common name in the District of Columbia, in Maryland, and even more so in Virginia, where Carters were major landholders in the eighteenth and nineteenth centuries. An analysis of District of Columbia directories and federal census records from 1820 to 1840 locates at least twelve Carters in various sections of Washington City. In 1847, a Sarah A. Carter (1822–1880), born in Washington City, married Englishman David Taylor Shaw in Baltimore County. By 1850 their Baltimore household included their two-year-old daughter Mary, and Sarah's mother, sixty-five-year-old Leah Carter. If this is the correct Sarah Ann Carter, she would have been about twelve when she stitched her sampler in 1834. Until more evidence is available one can only speculate that Sarah Ann Carter or her teacher may have had a Virginia connection, perhaps

---

38 Both Virginia samplers feature a three-bay brick building with hip roof and contrasting belt course that is very similar to the house on the Carter sampler. Mary Filana F. Gonsolve worked her sampler with identical trees in 1832. Research by the private collector located her in Alexandria, the daughter of Mary Byrne and Captain Samuel Gonsolve, originally of Providence, Rhode Island. Unexplained is a very similar sampler with identical trees, brick building, and populated landscape attributed to Henrico County, Virginia. It is inscribed, "Mary Jane Glenn Wrought in A D 1831" and was published in *Samplings* XIV, 29. No marriage record has been found for Mary Gonsolve [and spelling variations], but District of Columbia and Richmond, Virginia, marriage records have been found for several young women named Mary Jane Glenn married between 1841 and 1844.

Mrs. Eliza B. Mills, who noted she came from "the South" before taking over a school on E Street in 1832.

Alletha F. F. Ourand

Twelve-year-old Alletha Frances Findley Ourand (1827–1879) used silk floss in a skillful combination of cross, double cross, rice, four-sided, satin, Smyrna cross, and Algerian eye stitches to work her sampler in 1839 (Figure 8-15). Her colorful rows of alphabets and numbers are followed by a somber verse, the first lines of an Anglican funeral hymn composed by Bishop Reginald Heber (1783–1826).[39]

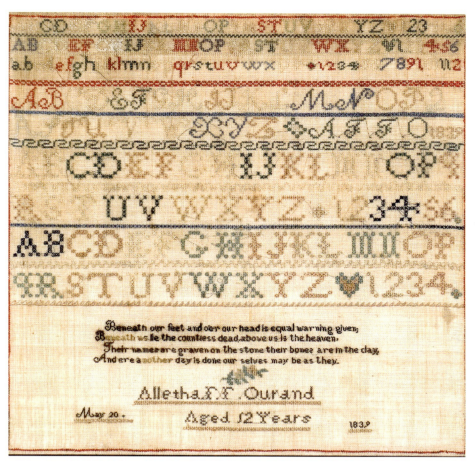

*Beneath our feet and o'er our head,
is equal warning given;
Beneath us lie the countless dead
above us is the heaven.
Their names are graven on the stone
their bones are in the clay,
And er'e another day is done
our selves may be as they.*

Reminiscent of the sampler stitched in 1828 by Sarah M. Whitney, Alletha used spaces at the end of her alphabet to tuck in an extra date and also her full initials: AFFO, 1839.

Although Alletha did not stitch a place name, she can be located in Washington City. She was the third of thirteen children born to Catherine Prickett (1805–1888) and Elijah Ourand (1801–1877), who married at the Foundry Methodist Episcopal Church on 14th Street in 1823.[40] Alletha's father Elijah held positions as superintendent of chimney sweeps for the First Ward and messenger for the Treasury Department. In 1834 the family resided on H Street, North, between 21st and 22nd Streets, West.

On January 3, 1848 Alletha married Thomas Livingston Potter (1819–1863) in a double wedding with her sister Sophia, who married John M. Riggs. The Potters had as many as seven children, at least three of whom died young. In 1863, Alletha lost both her two-year-old son Henry and her forty-four-year-old husband. As a widow with underage children, marriage was a necessary means of support for Alletha. Subsequently, the 1870 federal census for the Fourth Ward recorded "Alethia" as the wife of George W. Martin, a clerk at the Treasury Department. Their household included their one-year-old daughter Georgeanna and four surviving Potter children. Orphaned by 1880, young "Georgie" was raised by a half-sister.

Figure 8-15. Sampler worked by Alletha Frances Findley Ourand. Washington City, 1839. Inscribed: "Alletha. F. F. Ourand / Aged 12 Years / May 20./ 1839." Silk on linen ground, 28 by 30 threads per in. 17 ⅛ x 17 ½ in. Collection of Susi B. Slocum.

---

39 Heber's hymn appeared in several publications around 1828 and in many thereafter. The first eight lines were frequently carved as an epitaph.

40 Different branches of the Ourand family, originally from Prussia, spelled their surname Aurandt [Pennsylvania], Ourant [Ohio], and Ourand [D.C.]. Other variations include Aurand and Orand. Alletha is referred to as Alethia or by her middle name, Frances, in local documents.

Figure 9-1.
"City of Washington from beyond the Navy Yard," ca. 1834.
Painted by G. Cooke, engraved by W. J. Bennett.
Published by Lewis P. Clover, New York.
Aquatint on paper.
Library of Congress, Prints & Photographs Division

CHAPTER 9

Navy Yard Architectural Samplers

SAMPLERS AND EMBROIDERED PICTURES produced at schools in Washington City over nearly a century vary widely in design, reflecting the diversity of the city's population that Anne Royall observed in 1824. One group of architectural samplers, however, shows a consistency in style and selection of motifs over a period of more than thirty years, from 1810 to 1842. All but one can be assigned with confidence to students who lived in the vicinity of the Navy Yard in the southeastern section of Washington City.[1]

BACKGROUND

The Washington Navy Yard was officially established on October 2, 1799, by President John Adams. Land was acquired along 9th and M Streets, Southeast, "occupying a high plateau extending down to the waters of the Anacostia River . . . the superior of many parts of the city."[2] Building commenced in 1800, and by 1803 the Marine Barracks were included under the command of the Navy Yard.[3] Workers, newly hired by the Yard, quickly settled this part of the Federal City. Most of the initial two hundred or so

---

1 This group of samplers was first identified by Elisabeth Donaghy Garrett as worked by girls living near the Washington Navy Yard. "American Samplers and Needlework Pictures in the DAR Museum, Part II: 1806–1840," *The Magazine Antiques*, 107, no. 4 (April 1975): 694–98. Betty Ring expanded on her research and published several examples in *Girlhood Embroidery*, 528–31. Kimberly Smith Ivey and Olive Blair Graffam furthered the discussion: Ivey, *In the Neatest Manner: The Making of the Virginia Sampler Tradition* (Austin, Tex.: Curious Works Press, 1997) and Graffam, *"Youth Is the Time for Progress": The Importance of American Schoolgirl Art, 1780–1860* (Washington, D.C.: DAR Museum, 1998).

2 Madison Davis, "The Navy Yard Section during the Life of the Rev. William Ryland," *Records of the Columbia Historical Society*, 4 (1901): 200. The Anacostia River was known as the Eastern Branch of the Potomac River at the time the Navy Yard was established.

3 When the federal government moved from Philadelphia to Washington in 1800, the Marine Corps came to protect federal buildings. In 1801, President Jefferson located the site for the Marine Barracks near the Navy Yard, easy marching distance to the President's House and the Capitol.

employees, many of whom were immigrants, were engaged in the trades and crafts associated with shipbuilding and refurbishing—carpenters, shipwrights, joiners, mast makers, blacksmiths, sail makers, rope makers, and caulkers. By 1810 the Navy Yard had become the largest commercial enterprise in the city, with 380 civilian employees and sixty-seven officers and enlisted men engaged in the building and repair of ships.[4]

At the bottom of the pay scale were the laborers who earned seventy cents or less a day. Carpenters, on the other hand, earned upwards of two dollars a day and, along with shipwrights, were better educated and considered the trade elite. For the most part, the Yard provided steady, though seasonal, employment and subsistence for a large number of the District's inhabitants.[5] Lacking public transportation and even paved roads, most employees lived near the Yard, within the District's Sixth Ward. The settlement, known as Navy Yard Hill, had the appearance of an English village with its neatly laid out squares, public market and village green, churches, private schools, benevolent associations, and roads bordered by fields of grass or grain and lined with fruit and shade trees. Cows and chickens roamed at will.[6]

August 24, 1814, changed this bucolic scene as the War of 1812 closed in on Washington. With the advancement of British troops on the city, Commandant Thomas Tingey ordered the burning of the Navy Yard's buildings and ship stores to keep them out of enemy hands. Burning and pillaging by locals continued from August 25th through the 27th, and damages eventually amounted to more than half a million dollars.[7] The shipyard, consisting of barracks, workshops, and storage buildings, was slowly rebuilt and by 1816 was again in full operation, albeit on a smaller scale (Figure 9-1).[8] The community surrounding the Navy Yard, mostly untouched by the conflagration of 1814, continued to expand. David Bailie Warden described Navy Yard Hill in his 1816 publication:

> *This part of the city contains about a third of the whole population: Most of the houses consist of but one story, and are about forty feet square. The number of inhabitants does not exceed three thousand, and nevertheless there are four churches, viz. Episcopalian, Baptist, Catholic, and Methodist.*[9]

Needlework Teachers

The thirteen Navy Yard samplers known to date fall within three ranges of time, 1810–1813, 1814–1826, 1823–1842, each displaying distinct styles. Six samplers are known from the first period, representing the instruction of at least two teachers. Three samplers in the second group were taught by one teacher. The remaining four samplers represent the instruction of at least three teachers.

---

4 John G. Sharp, *History of the Early Washington Navy Yard, 1799–1860* (Washington, D.C.: Naval District Washington, 2005), 6. The Yard encompassed approximately thirty-seven acres between 6th and 9th Streets, East, and from M Street, South, to the river.

5 As Sharp has pointed out, carpenters and shipwrights had to be able to read enough to follow specifications and measurements. Ibid., 6–7 and personal communication, October 14, 2010.

6 Ibid., 9.

7 D. B. Warden, *A chorographical and statistical description of the District of Columbia: the seat of the general government of the United States* (Paris: Smith, 1816), 58. Damages estimated in 1816 currency valuation.

8 Shipbuilding gradually gave way to weapons production as the Eastern Branch, or Anacostia River, was too shallow and remote from open water for building large vessels.

9 Warden, *A chorographical and statistical description*, 64–65.

Unfortunately, it has not been possible to identify the instructor or instructors responsible for any of the Navy Yard samplers, including those whose distinctive characteristics helped to establish the Navy Yard style.

There are references to the existence of schools in the Navy Yard Hill community, but relatively little mention of female education in general or teachers of needlework specifically.[10] Few teachers from this populous area advertised in the local newspapers or were listed in city directories as teachers from 1810 through the 1840s, the period when girls living in the vicinity stitched their samplers. Yet needlework instruction, offered by more than one talented teacher, was clearly available. Although adopting several different designs, the samplers share certain characteristics, some of which reflect a Philadelphia heritage and suggest that what emerged as a Navy Yard sampler style and format may have originated with a teacher who came from that city.

One of the earliest teachers known to have a school near the Navy Yard was John McLeod, who became director of the Washington Academy East in 1808. The school had been established in 1805 by the Washington City Council, primarily for students from poor families, but it also accepted up to fifty paying students whose families were charged five dollars tuition per quarter. McLeod greatly expanded enrollment at the school and within a few years required a larger building. He invested $6,000 of his own money to construct near the Navy Yard what was later judged to be the "the only decent schoolroom in Washington."[11] By 1812 the faculty at "Mr. McLeod's School" had expanded to eight teachers, with four in the Female Department.[12]

As British forces approached Washington in August 1814, McLeod was forced to dismiss all 172 students at the academy out of fear for their safety. In 1816, McLeod moved classes to his new Central Academy in another part of the city, allowing other teachers to rent his Navy Yard Hill building. Although there is no documentation that needlework was a part of the curriculum during the years McLeod directed the Washington Academy East (1808–1815), it is known that he advertised instruction in plain and ornamental needlework at other Washington City schools during his more than forty-year career as an educator (see page 205).[13]

In 1814 a Miss Evans, located in the vicinity of the Navy Yard, announced on October 5, 1814, that she would commence teaching "Needle Work in its various branches" at her location on 8th Street, East, opposite the Marine Barracks.[14] Miss Evans' notice was only six weeks after the August burning of the Navy Yard. It is possible that she had been teaching in the neighborhood before the destruction of the Yard, and she wanted to advise patrons that her school was back in business. Since Miss Evans's whereabouts prior to her advertisement cannot be confirmed, considering her the needlework teacher responsible for the 1810–1813 group of Navy Yard samplers is

---

10 Davis, "The Navy Yard Section during the Life of the Rev. William Ryland," 221; James Croggon, "History of Southeast," Washington *Evening Star*, June 9, 1907, 11.

11 Harvey W. Crew, William B. Webb, and John Wooldridge, *Centennial History of the City of Washington D.C.* (Dayton, Ohio: United Brethren Publishing House, 1892).

12 The four teachers named in the Female Department were Verlinda Burch, Juliana Anders, Evelina McClain, and Jane Sandford. Dixon, *National Intelligencer & Washington Advertiser Newspaper Abstracts 1811–1813*, 161.

13 Washington *Daily National Intelligencer*, August, 8, 1821.

14 *Daily National Intelligencer*, October 13, 1814.

uncertain. She relocated her school in 1818 to an area near the Capitol.[15]

In 1819, Mrs. D. McCurdy advertised that she would teach "needlework" as part of an "English education" in a school on "Ny Hill." She was probably Mary S. Mudd, who married educator and textbook publisher Dennis McCurdy in the District on the seventeenth of April 1817. Mary McCurdy may have shared instructional facilities with her husband, who "taught the common branches of an English education" at his residence near the Navy Yard in 1819.[16] According to the federal census for 1820, however, the McCurdys had relocated to the First Ward. Given McCurdy's short stay near the Yard and the absence of any samplers dated 1819 or 1820, it is unlikely that she was responsible for any of the early Navy Yard samplers. No other newspaper advertisements placed by teachers in this part of Washington are known.

Two additional women were listed as "school mistress" in the 1822 Washington City directory (the first year it was published) and again in 1827. Their place of business at 7th Street, East, between L and M Streets, South, was in a rapidly growing area adjacent to the Navy Yard.[17] Rebecca Russ (ca. 1776–1852) and Ann Nesmith (ca. 1785–1868) had emigrated from England some years earlier. Ann Nesmith, mother of two children and possibly the wife of Ebenezer Nesmith, may have come to the area as early as 1803.[18] Rebecca Russ had been in the United States for fifty-eight years [since 1794] and the "greater part of that time a resident of this city." Her obituary stated this fact when she died in 1852 at age seventy-six.[19] Rebecca may have been the wife of Samuel Russ, who resided near the Navy Yard as early as 1805.[20]

Both Samuel Russ and Ebenezer Nesmith had financial problems by 1810, which may have encouraged their wives to open a school to sustain their families. It is not known how long Russ and Nesmith had been teaching together on Navy Yard Hill, but one can speculate that one or both were teaching before the 1822 directory listing.[21] Since neither woman advertised in local newspapers—it was hardly necessary in a small close-knit community where word-of-mouth would have sufficed—nothing is known of the subjects they offered or if they were responsible for any of the known samplers believed to have been stitched in the Navy Yard Hill area. Nonetheless, Russ and Nesmith seem to have had the longest presence among teachers in the area.[22]

---

15 Washington *Daily National Intelligencer*, October 5, 1814, January 18 and June 11, 1818. Miss Evans's first name and parentage have not been discovered. The 1822 Directory lists Jesse Sr. and Jr., Phillip, and Walter Evans, all with Navy Yard addresses.

16 *Daily National Intelligencer*, August 14, 1819; Crew, et al., *Centennial History*, 475.

17 James Croggon, "Near Navy Yard Gate," *Evening Star*, June 22, 1907.

18 Ebenezer Nesmith placed an advertisement for a servant stolen near the Navy Yard. *National Intelligencer*, March 25, 1803. Several years later Ebenezer was insolvent. After his death in 1820, his possessions were sold for the benefit of his heirs. *Daily National Intelligencer*, April 4, 1820.

19 *Daily National Intelligencer*, May 13, 1852. Her funeral took place at the residence of her widowed daughter, Ann Ober, 10th and K Streets, Navy Yard.

20 In 1805, Samuel Russ advertised a two-story brick house for sale near the Navy Yard. By 1810 he was insolvent. See *National Intelligencer*, March 5, 1805 and August 29, 1810. A presumed relation, Francis Russ, was a spar maker at the Navy Yard and listed in the 1827 city directory.

21 Historian James Croggon, writing about the Navy Yard community as it was populated circa 1820, mentioned Russ and Nesmith's school. He also noted that A. Nesmith's property was valued at three hundred dollars. Croggon, "History of Southeast," *Evening Star*, June 9 and 22, 1907.

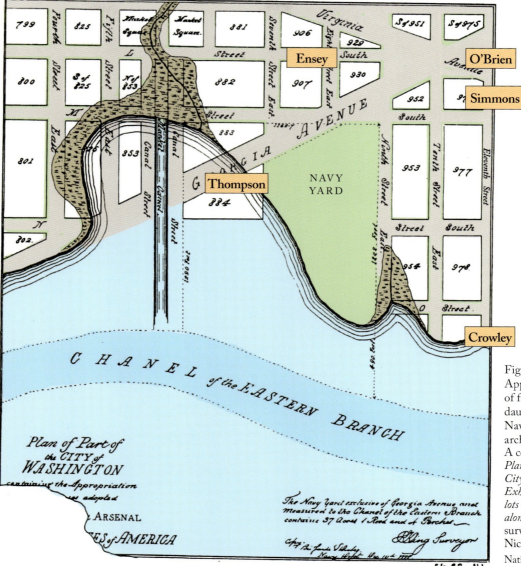

Figure 9-2. Approximate locations of families whose daughters stitched Navy Yard architectural samplers. A copy of Sheet 9 of *Plan of Part of the City of Washington Exhibiting the Water-lots and Water Street along...*, surveyed by Nicholas King, 1797. National Archives.

Early Navy Yard Samplers

Six Navy Yard samplers stitched between 1810 and 1813 appear to fall into two stylistic subgroups, each united by a common overall format, common border patterns, and a small selection of nearly identical motifs. What distinguishes the two subgroups is the central architectural motif. Three of the samplers include a large brick building with triple-peaked roofline, and three include a brick building with a bell tower. All of the girls who stitched samplers between 1810 and 1813, as well as those in the later time periods, can be identified as daughters of families living by or near the Navy Yard (Figure 9-2).

---

22 Since both Rebecca Russ and Ann Nesmith had surnames that were unusual in the Washington area, the mention of others with those surnames suggests relationships and provides evidence—before the existence of city directories—of their presence in the Navy Yard Hill area.

Figure 9-3. Sampler worked by Julia Ann Crowley. Washington City, 1810. Inscribed: "Julia Ann Crowley. / Aged 10 years. th' 14th / of Dec' 1809. / Washington Navy Yard February th' 10th 1810." Silk and silk chenille on linen ground, 30 by 27 threads per in. 21 ⅜ x 17 ¾ in. The Colonial Williamsburg Foundation, Museum Purchase, 1991-25

Julia Ann Crowley

In 1810, ten-year-old Julia Ann Crowley (1799–ca. 1832) stitched the first and only known sampler to identify the school's location as the Washington Navy Yard (Figure 9-3). Stitched at the bottom of the sampler, her inscription reads: "Washington Navy Yard. February th' 10th 1810." Julia Ann used chenille and silk threads in cross, satin, outline, hem, buttonhole, and Roumanian stitches. Her verse, the third stanza from "The Spacious Firmament," was paraphrased from Psalms 19:1–6 by English poet Joseph Addison (1672–1719) in 1712, and set to music by Franz Joseph Haydn (1732–1809) in 1798.

What tho' in solemn silence all.
Move round this dark terrestrial ball.
What tho' nor real voice nor sound.
Amid their radiant orbs be found.
In Reason's ear they all rejoice.
And utter forth a glorious voice.
For ever singing as they shine.
The hand that made us is Divine.

Just below her eight-line verse, Julia Ann stitched her full name, age, and the day and month of her birth, enclosed in an oval-shaped cartouche—letting us know that she was ten years old on "th' 14th of Dec'r 1809."

Julia's sampler employs a layout that appears more or less consistently in all thirteen of the samplers associated with the Navy Yard stylistic group. This layout includes: (a) a centrally aligned verse at the top; (b) a pair of matched motifs flanking the verse; (c) a dividing line and/or signature reserve, separating the verse from other parts of the sampler; (d) another pair of matched motifs floating to the right and left, approximately in the middle of the sampler; (e) a centrally positioned brick structure with steps leading down to a grassy lawn; (f) a yard populated with flowers, people, animals, and birds; (g) two or more tall trees with straight trunks and green foliage flanking the building; (h) an inscription with location and full date below (or sometimes on) the grassy yard; and (i) a four-sided double border with a simple interior enclosure around verse, building, and motifs, surrounded by a more elaborate floral (or sometimes berry) serpentine or arcaded border.

The teacher who designed this sampler format to showcase her students' work is unknown, but it is possible that she came from Philadelphia, based on similarities between some of the early Navy Yard samplers and those stitched in Philadelphia as early as the 1790s.[23] In the case of Julia Ann Crowley's 1810 sampler, these similarities include an imposing brick building with triple-peaked roofline, contrasting belt courses of white brick, and a checkerboard foundation set in a yard with people, animals, and plants. Her building recalls, for example, the structure stitched by Catharine Hay in Philadelphia circa 1802 and was most likely copied from a print (Figure 9-4).[24] Also recalling Philadelphia samplers are the flanking two-handled vases of flowers, spade-shaped trees, and her border of tulips and starflowers connected by an interlacing vine.

Julia Ann Crowley was born in Alexandria, Virginia, where her father, Timothy Crowley, worked in the local shipyard as a carpenter. Prior to 1810 he moved to Washington City, where he carried on his profession as one of about fifty ship carpenters then employed at the Navy Yard.[25] Crowley was not a member

Figure 9-4.
Sampler worked by Catharine Hay. Philadelphia, ca. 1802. Inscribed: "Catharine Hay's / Work Wrought / In Her Eleventh / Year."
Silk on linen ground.
21 ¾ x 17 ⅜ in.
Image courtesy of Stephen and Carol Huber

---

23 Ring, "Philadelphia in the Federal Period," *Girlhood Embroidery*, 361–69.

24 Stephen and Carol Huber, *The Sampler Engagement Calendar*, 1992 (Old Saybrook: Conn.: 1992), 22, and Ring, *Girlhood Embroidery*, 366–67.

25 Surviving lists of Navy Yard employees indicate that in 1811 Crowley earned $1.81 per diem as a ship carpenter. During 1818–1819 he was employed as gun carriage maker with a reduction in daily wages to $1.58. Sharp, personal correspondence, October 15, 2010. http://www.genealogytrails.com/washdc/wny1811.html, and http://genealogytrails.com/washdc/wny_payroll1819–1820.html.

"almost a saint, a good Catholic and everything that was good."²⁸

Julia O'Brien

Julia O'Brien's 1812 sampler, worked on a dyed linen ground, is nearly identical to Julia Ann Crowley's 1810 sampler. Julia O'Brien (1800–1866) stitched her striking sampler using the same general layout of verse, motifs, and multi-story brick building with triple-peaked roofline, flanked by spade-shaped trees and enclosed by an arcaded floral border (Figure 9-5). Both girls also stitched versions of a vase with three stylized flowers flanking their verse and more natural looking sprays of flowers floating below. Julia dated her sampler "June the 4th 1812,"²⁹ and stitched the words from "Grace," a hymn by Isaac Watts.

Figure 9-5. Sampler worked by Julia O Brien. Washington City, 1812. Inscribed: "Julia O Brien / Washington City. June the 4th 1812." Silk on dyed linen ground. 20 x 20 in. Image courtesy of Skinner, Inc.

of the wealthy elite, but he was among the elite of the shipbuilding craftsmen and able to afford to send his daughter to private school.²⁶ The Crowleys lived close to the Navy Yard on 11th Street, East, in a growing settlement near a newly constructed bridge over the Eastern Branch (Anacostia) of the Potomac River.²⁷ In 1820, Julia Ann married English-born Thomas Fitten (born 1799), also a ship carpenter at the Yard. She died around the age of thirty-three in Norfolk, Virginia, and was remembered as

Grace! 'tis a sweet, a charming theme.
My thoughts rejoice at Jesus' name!
Ye angels dwell upon the sound!
Ye heav'ns reflect it to the ground!
O may I live to reach the place
Where he unveils his lovely face!
Where all his beauties you behold
And sing his name to harps of gold!

Julia O'Brien was a daughter of Michael O'Brien, employed as a turner or block maker

---

26 Henry B. Hibben, *Navy Yard, Washington: History from Organization, 1799 to Present Date* (Washington: Government Printing Office, 1890), 37.
    Miss Evans, the only Navy Yard teacher to publish her fees, charged five dollars per quarter for reading, writing, spelling, grammar, arithmetic, and needlework, four dollars if grammar and arithmetic were not included. *Daily National Intelligencer*, October 5, 1814.

27 Croggon described the neighborhoods within Navy Yard Hill and noted that "the bridge at 11th street attracted a settlement of considerable size" and listed Timothy Crowley among its first settlers. Croggon, "History of Southeast," July 9, 1907.

28 Quoted by Elisabeth Donaghy Garrett from a 1925 letter in the DAR Museum object file. Garrett, "American Samplers," 694, 695, 697.

29 Listed by Bolton and Coe in 1921 as "O'Brien, Julia. 1812. Washington City. 20" x 20." Cross-stitch. Border of conventionalized tulips and roses. At bottom, large brick house with garden, trees, woman, duck, etc. Verse 435. A. Piatt Andrew." Bolton and Coe, *American Samplers*, 202.

at the Navy Yard.[30] The O'Briens lived near the Yard and about three blocks from the Crowleys at the corner of L Street, South, and 11th Street, East. On March 27, 1820, Julia O'Brien married Antonio Catalano (ca. 1797–1854) from Palermo Sicily, and employed at the Navy Yard as a carpenter and joiner. He was the son of Salvatore Catalano, sailing master.[31] Their Irish-Italian marriage reflected the ethnic diversity of the community and its workforce.

There is no record of any children born to Julia and Antonio Catalano, who at the time of the 1850 federal census were still living in Washington City. Antonio's last will and testament, signed February 10, 1854, bequeathed "unto my affectionate and beloved wife Julia Catalano, all of my personal property, and real estate, to have and hold for her sole use, benefit and behoove forever, to hold and dispose of as she may deem proper or consider best for her."[32] Antonio Catalano died May 14, 1854. Julia died September 19, 1866, at age sixty-six and is interred at Congressional Cemetery.

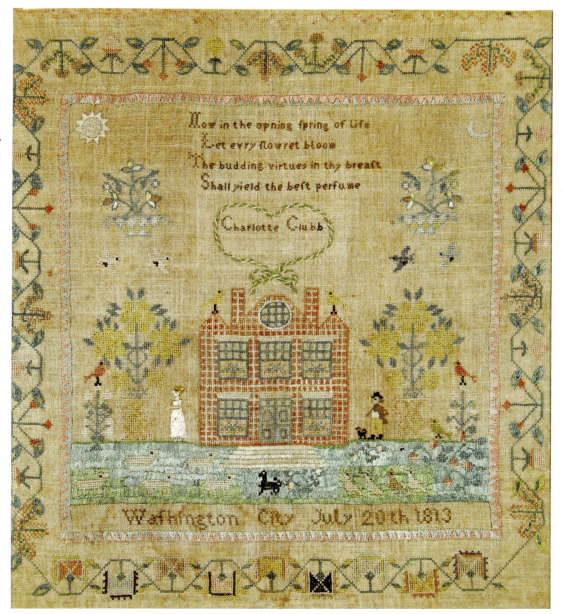

Charlotte Clubb

Third in this subgroup is Charlotte Clubb's 1813 sampler. It is attributed to the Navy Yard group based on the location of the embroiderer, yet it has enough stylistic differences to suggest that it was worked under the direction of a different teacher. Charlotte used a combination of cross, satin, and knot stitches in silk and silk chenille and

Figure 9-6. Sampler worked by Charlotte Clubb. Washington City, 1813. Inscribed: "Charlotte Clubb / Washington City July 20th 1813." Silk and silk chenille on linen ground, 34 by 35 threads per in. 20 x 17 ½ in. American Museum in Britain

---

30 O'Brien, in a less skillful craft than Crowley or Boswell, earned $1.36 per day in 1819. http://genealogytrails.com/washdc/wny_payroll1819–1820.html.

31 Salvatore Catalano, a native of Palermo, Sicily, was appointed sailing master of the United States Navy in 1811, after earlier distinguishing himself in the Battle of Tripoli Harbor, February, 1804.

32 Last Will and Testament of Antonio Catalano, District of Columbia Archives filed as: Catalano, Antonio 1854, Box 23.

Figure 9-7. Sampler worked by Maria Boswell. Washington City, 1812. Inscribed: "Maria Boswell / Aged 12 years th' / 4th of April /1812 / Washington City. Augst th' 18th 1812." Silk and silk chenille on dyed linen ground. 18 × 18 in. Location unknown

completed her sampler on "July 20th 1813" (Figure 9-6). Charlotte's short verse comprises four lines from "Verses Accompanying a Nosegay," a popular selection for young readers.

*Now in the opning spring of life
Let every flowret bloom
The budding virtues in thy breast
Shall yield the best perfume*

Like Crowley and O'Brien, Charlotte stitched a multi-story brick house with triple-peaked roof surrounded by strolling people, birds, and animals. Her large brick building differs sufficiently from those of Crowley and O'Brien to indicate another pattern or design source. Charlotte embellished her house with a four-paneled door with transom, five open windows with pots of flowers, and a circular window in the central gable. An identical house can be found on an undated sampler made by eight-year-old Nancy Cooper of Camden, New Jersey.[33] These two samplers also share the motifs of a flock of grazing sheep, a man in a top hat with a black dog, and a blazing sun.

Although Clubb's sampler adopts the same general layout as the samplers stitched by Crowley and O'Brien, there are noticeable differences: the top motifs flanking the verse (a sun and moon) are not a matched pair, and there are no spade shaped trees flanking the house. Instead, large vases with a tripartite arrangement of flowers, similar to those found floating on Crowley's and O'Brien's samplers, have been positioned firmly on the satin stitched lawn in place of trees. Although all three samplers include a full date with day, month, and year, Charlotte's deviates somewhat by not including "the" in between the month and day.

Charlotte Clubb (1801–1846) was a daughter of Elizabeth and John Clubb, formerly of Portsmouth, Virginia, and a sister of (John) Lewis Clubb, who later became a fife major in the Marine Band. The Clubbs evidently relocated between 1810 and 1813 from the shipbuilding port of Portsmouth to the Navy Yard community in Washington City. John Clubb's occupation is unknown, but it seems likely he was employed in one of the ship trades at the Yard. By 1820, Elizabeth Clubb was a widow residing with a daughter and son between the ages of sixteen and twenty-five in the Fifth Ward, just a few doors away from the family of sampler maker Maria Boswell.[34] When forty-five-year-old Charlotte died unmarried in 1846, her brother

---

33 Collection of the Philadelphia Museum of Art, 1969-288-86. Camden is located across the Delaware River from Philadelphia, so Nancy Cooper may have attended school in Philadelphia.

34 A John Clubb was located in Portsmouth in 1810, and his household included two females under age ten. He was not listed in the 1820 census for Virginia or the District, but his widow "Eliz Clubb" was recorded that year in Washington City.

Lewis Clubb made the arrangements for her interment at the Congressional Cemetery.[35]

Maria Boswell

A second subgroup of three samplers was stitched in 1812 and 1813. All three, using silk and silk chenille thread, followed the Navy Yard layout but adopted a different architectural structure as the dominant motif. Instead of a brick house, the girls stitched a large two-story brick school or church, with rows of multi-paned windows, a bell tower, and an offset door.[36] Flanking the building are six spade-shaped trees, three on each side.

Twelve-year-old Maria Boswell's 1812 sampler, worked on a dyed linen ground, is the earliest known sampler to depict this building (Figure 9-7).[37] Although its identity and purpose are unknown, the many windows, bell tower, and lack of any religious symbols suggests it probably represents a school, possibly a specific school in the Navy Yard community. The year 1812 is about the time that John McLeod's large new building for the Washington Academy East was constructed near the Navy Yard, so it is possible that Maria's sampler provides an image of this new and impressive building. If so, then it is also likely that she attended this academy, a conclusion further supported by the fact that her father was one of 177 subscribers when the school was established by the Washington City Council in 1805.

Maria stitched the popular sampler verse beginning "Jesus permit thy gracious name to stand" (see page 95). On either side of the verse are matching vases with the same three stylized flowers found on Crowley's 1810 and O'Brien's 1812 samplers. In between her verse and the brick building is Maria's signature in a heart-shaped enclosure in which she included her full name and shared that she turned twelve years old on "th' 4th of April 1812." Floating delicately on either side are sprays of naturalistic flowers, similar to those on the Crowley and O'Brien samplers. Maria's inscription sits below the unpopulated school yard, documenting her location in Washington City and completion date of "Augst th' 18th 1812."

Maria Boswell (1800–1868) was one of three daughters of Eleanor Collard (1778–1842) and Clement Boswell (1775–1835), originally from Prince George's County, Maryland. The Boswell family lived on O Street, South, between 1st and ½ Streets East.[38] This would have placed Clement Boswell in the Fifth Ward and several blocks west of Navy Yard Hill.[39] In 1811 he was listed on Navy Yard rolls as a joiner earning $1.36 per day.[40] The previous year he had been one of five constituting members of the Navy Yard Baptist Church.

Maria Boswell had a child out of wedlock; her daughter, Mary Ann Boswell was born in 1822. Mary Ann married

---

35 Congressional Cemetery is the burial ground for Christ Church, Navy Yard. The parish was established in 1794 by an act of the Maryland General Assembly, and Christ Church, erected in 1808, was the earliest structure in Washington City built to serve an ecclesiastical purpose.

36 It has been suggested that this building is a representation of Christ Church. The first structure had two stories but did not have a bell tower. The bell tower was added in 1849 when the church was "modernized" with a Gothic Revival façade.

37 Private collection. See Ring, *Girlhood Embroidery*, vol. 2, frontispiece. The image has also been posted online with the Bradbury Morris Family Tree, http://trees.ancestry.com/tree/31462573/person/18052415152?ssrc=.

38 "In 1801 [Clement Boswell] lived at First and O streets, s.e.," from "Interments in the Historic Congressional Cemetery."

39 The 1820 federal census located the Clement Boswell family in the Fifth Ward, next door to the Collards, Maria's mother's family. In 1834, James Boswell, probably Maria's brother, was listed in the city directory as a shoemaker with a residence/business on Seventh, East, "near NY."

40 Sharp, http://www.genealogytrails.com/washdc/wny1811.html.

Figure 9-8. Sampler worked by Julia Ann Crowley. Washington City, 1813. Inscribed: "Julia Ann Crowley / Washington City. the 14th of April. 1813." Silk and silk chenille on dyed linen ground. 20 ¼ x 18 ⅛ in. Daughters of the American Revolution Museum, gift of Mrs. W. W. Brothers, 63.11

William Grinder, a brick maker, in 1842. The 1850 federal census located Maria Boswell in the Fifth Ward in the household of her daughter, where she may have helped look after her seven grandchildren. By 1860, Maria's status in the household had curiously changed to that of "servant."[41]

Julia Ann Crowley

Three years after completing her first sampler, Julia Ann Crowley completed a second one, dated "the 14th of April 1813" (Figure 9-8). For this work, she used chenille and silk thread on a dyed linen ground and stitched the same brick building with bell tower that appears on the 1812 sampler of Maria Boswell. Julia Ann added a verse by an unidentified poet:

---

41 Although Clement Boswell's will has not been located, he evidently left a sizeable estate. In 1892, Mary Ann Boswell Grinder's children sued their uncle over use of the land Mary Ann had inherited from her grandfather in 1835. The question of Mary Ann's illegitimacy was an issue in her legal right to her inheritance. The lawsuit has been posted at http://trees.ancestry.com/tree/31462573/person/18052415152?ssrc=.

178 COLUMBIA'S DAUGHTERS

Oh virtue! thou daughter of grace.
Come dwell in my bosom for guest.
And banish foul vice from that place.
In which thou intendest to rest.
Oh come thou delight of my heart.
Deny not thy visit to me.
I'll supplicate GOD on my part.
To increase my attention to thee.

Floating beside the verse is the same pair of vases with three stylized flowers that appear on her earlier sampler (as well as those of O'Brien, Boswell and Ensey). Julia Ann's full name is stitched within a heart-shaped cartouche. She does not include a date and age, choosing instead to decorate the enclosure with two facing doves each holding what may be an olive branch. Totally new in this sampler are the leafy tree branches that appear on either side, framing the scene. Julia Ann's composition is enclosed by an arcaded border of tulips, carnations, poppies, roses, and daisies, created by a combination of French knots, cross, satin, stem, and chain stitches.

Martha Ensey

Ten-year-old Martha Ensey (born 1803) used similar stitches on her 1813 natural linen sampler that features the same brick building and six spade-shaped trees found on the Boswell and Crowley dyed linen samplers (Figure 9-9).[42] Martha and Julia Ann apparently worked their samplers simultaneously, both stitching the same verse and finishing two days apart, Martha on April 12 and Julia Ann on April 14. In addition to stitching the same multi-flowered border on a serpentine vine, both girls also included waving tree branches emerging into the scene from left and right.

Martha placed her name, age, and February birthday (now partially missing) in a heart-shaped cartouche tied with a bow and included the same pair of doves holding small branches.

Martha Ensey was the daughter of William Ensey (1769–1832), a tailor who worked and probably lived on the north side of L Street, South, between 7th and 8th Streets, East, on Navy Yard Hill. The 1820 federal census for Washington City recorded "William Ensey," "S Catalano," and "Nich^s Cassady" on the same page, all names associated with girls who stitched Navy Yard architectural samplers.[43]

Figure 9-9. Sampler worked by Martha Ensey. Washington City, 1813. Inscribed: "Martha Ensey / Ag– 10 / —f Feb / —13 / Washington City / Ap-il the 12th 1813." Silk and silk chenille on linen ground. 22 x 17 ½ in. Image courtesy of Sotheby's

---

42 Formerly in the collection of Betty Ring. See Sotheby's January 22, 2012, catalogue lot 666. See also Garrett, "American Samplers and Needlework Pictures . . . ," 694–698..

43 The Ensey household in 1820 included William, his wife, a son and daughter at least sixteen years old, and two enslaved males, who may have been learning the trade of tailoring.

One of Ensey's next door neighbors in 1820 was John Jenkins (born 1786), identified in city directories as a grocer with a business on "Pen av near Eastern Branch upper bridge." On February 22, 1821, Martha Ensey and John Jenkins were married in Christ Protestant Episcopal Church near the Navy Yard. Little is known about their married life or whether they had children. By 1827, Jenkins seems to have run into economic trouble that led to a lawsuit with Matthew Jarboe, probably his landlord. The following two announcements were published in the local newspaper.[44]

> *SAT AUG 11, 1827 Pblc sale of a parcel of hsehold furn at the Mkt Hse, today; seized as the prop of John Jenkins, & will be sold to satisfy rent due to Matthew Jarboe.*
> —*Richd H Harrington, Baliff*
> *MON AUG 20, 1827 Notice: I forewarn all persons from buying of John Jenkins or Thos Jones, a negro girl & one sorrel mare, as I have a writ of injunction on the property.*
> —*Mathew Jarboe*

SAMPLERS WITH STEPPED TERRACES

Over a period of at least twelve years (1814 to 1826), a second group of samplers emerged, also stitched by girls living in the Navy Yard community. A comparison of the similarities and differences of these samplers with those of the previous two subgroups suggests they were created under the direction of a third unidentified teacher—but one who was intimately familiar with the Navy Yard stylistic conventions. The distinguishing feature of this second group is the positioning of the main architectural structure, a large brick building, on a stepped terrace flanked by eight triangular pine trees, four to a side. Well-dressed couples appear to be enjoying the shade of each tree, and sheep graze on the ground in front of the building, leaving open space or a reserve for the embroiderer's name, location ("Washington City"), and date. The building, with three distinct towers surmounted by crosses, differs from the triple-peaked buildings on the Crowley, O'Brien, and Clubb samplers and recalls the Pennsylvania interpretation of the three-tower castle found on eighteenth-century German-influenced samplers.[45]

Catherine Cassady

The first of these samplers was stitched by Catherine Cassady (ca. 1804–1827) in 1814 at the age of ten (Figure 9-10). Catherine's sampler is the only one of this group that overlaps in time with the previously discussed early Navy Yard sampler subgroups, and its similarities in layout, building, and border are noteworthy. For example, Catherine stitched a centrally located verse at the top of the sampler, flanked by two sets of vases with flowers, one of which matches the two-handled vases of the earlier samplers. The design is enclosed by a floral border and serpentine vine similar to previously discussed examples but displaying larger leaves and smaller flowers.

In a departure from other known samplers of the period, the central architectural feature on Catherine's sampler is a large brick building with crosses on each of three towers, sitting on a stepped terrace populated with sheep. The stepped terrace lined with triangular pine trees is characteristic of

---

44 Joan M. Dixon, *National Intelligencer Abstracts 1827–1829* (Bowie Md.: Heritage Books, Inc., 2000), 103, 105.

45 Ring attributes this style to Mary Zeller, who was active in Philadelphia from about 1793 until her death in 1818. Ring, *Girlhood Embroidery*, 361–69. See especially Ann Heyl's 1789 sampler and Catharine Goodman's 1803 sampler, both with a three-tower building with crosses, Ring, figures 384 and 385. Jennifer Core has kindly brought to my attention a three-tower building with crosses on a Tennessee sampler worked by Minerva Ann Elam, Harpeth Female Academy, Murfreesboro, Tennessee, 1831.

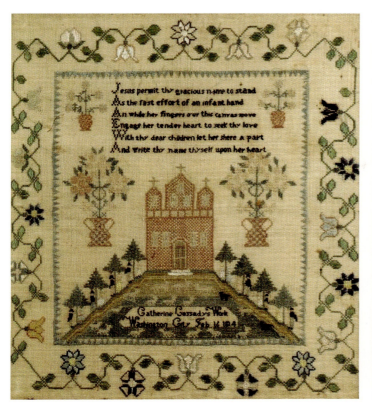 

architectural samplers stitched in Philadelphia, the Delaware Valley, central Maryland, and westward but not seen on other samplers from the District of Columbia. Catherine stitched the same verse as Maria Boswell, making an additional connection to the earlier group. Ten-year-old Catherine Cassady completed her sampler "Feb 14 1814," six months before Washington was attacked by the British and the Navy Yard set on fire.

Catherine Cassady was a daughter of Irish immigrants Margaret (1778–1846) and Nicholas Cassady (died 1832). Nicholas was a shoemaker with business sufficiently large to support several apprentices.[46] The Cassadys lived on 8th Street, East, near I (Eye) Street, South, opposite the Marine Barracks. Catherine was their eldest daughter. She never married and died in her twenty-fourth year on February 19, 1827.[47]

Margaret A. Cassedy

Margaret A. Cassedy[48] stitched a nearly identical sampler twelve years later dating it "Oct. 3 1826" (Figure 9-11). In addition, Margaret stitched a few new motifs: flower sprays, hearts, and multiple birds—two large parrots and smaller birds perched on the trees. Margaret's verse, labeled "The source of happiness" comprises two couplets from Alexander Pope's "An Essay on Man" (1733–1734):

Reason's whole pleasure, all the joys of sense
Lie in three words, health, peace and competence:
But health consists with temperance alone:
But peace, O virtue: peace is all thy own

The exact relationship between Catherine Cassady and Margaret Cassedy has puzzled researchers and collectors over the years. The

LEFT: Figure 9-10. Sampler worked by Catherine Cassady. Washington City, 1814. Inscribed: "Catherine Cassadys Work / Washington City Feb 14 1814." Silk on linen ground. 16 ½ x 15 ½ in. Metropolitan Museum of Art Image courtesy of Sotheby's

RIGHT: Figure 9-11. Sampler worked by Margaret A. Cassedy. Washington City, 1826. Inscribed: "Margaret A Cassedys / Work Washington Oct 3 1826." Silk on linen ground. 16 ½ x 15 ½ in. Metropolitan Museum of Art Image courtesy of Sotheby's

---

46 Apprentice records place Nicholas Cassady in the Navy Yard Hill area by 1810.

47 The widowed Margaret Cassady lived on 8th Street until her death in 1846. Catherine's death announcement from the *National Intelligencer*, February 21, 1827, reads, "Cath. Cassedy, died in her 24th year, eldest daughter of Nicholas Cassedy, funeral at father's residence opposite the Marine Garrison today."

48 Different sources spell the name Cassady, Cassedy, Cassidy, Cassaday.

Figure 9-12. Sampler attributed to Amelia James. Washington City, ca. 1826. Inscribed: "Am— J— / — Was—C—." Silk on linen ground. 17 ½ x 17 in. Collection of Jeffrey and Donna Litwin. Photography by Alina Bliach

may have been a younger daughter of Margaret and Nicholas Cassady, born about 1815 and named after her mother. Other children of Nicholas and Margaret Cassady include Nicholas Jr. (died 1824), Andrew (1800–1825), Catherine (ca. 1804–1827), Michael (died 1836), Eleanor (1810–after 1860), and possibly John and Peter.[50] Marriage records also provide inconclusive evidence. In 1833 a Margaret Ann Cassedy married John B. Davis of Portsmouth, Virginia, and another Margaret Cassady married a John Tennant. Margaret apparently died prior to 1846, when her mother's will listed only one beneficiary, her widowed daughter Eleanor Cassedy O'Donnell.[51]

Amelia James (attributed)

A girl who may have been named Amelia James stitched a sampler that is a variation of the one stitched by Margaret A. Cassedy in 1826 (Figure 9-12). The differences are the central building, the verse, and a few minor motifs. Like Margaret, Amelia included two small birds on the trees nearest the building, two larger parrot-like birds, and flower sprays. The first lines of her verse read "The path of

fact that the two samplers descended together in the same family strongly suggests that the girls were related.[49] Considering the interval of a dozen years between these sisters' rare southern embroideries, their similarities yield an exceptional family pair.

Although no birth or death record has been found for Margaret A. Cassedy, she

---

49 The two samplers have remained together but have changed owners several times. They sold at Sotheby's on January 29, 1994, and soon thereafter as separate lots at the Skinner's June 12, 1994, sale. They sold as one lot at the Sotheby's January 20, 2007, auction (Susan and Mark Laracy Sale) to Amy Finkel representing the Metropolitan Museum of Art. In cataloging for the 2007 sale, Sotheby's restated the 1994 provenance: "From the collection of W. [Winthrop] Murray and Josephine Boardman Crane, descended to Louise Crane. The family's firm, Crane and Co. has been a leader in the paper industry for seven generations. W. Murray Crane was Governor of Massachusetts and a U.S. Senator. These needleworks were found in a shoebox in the Crane home along with several other needleworks and 18th century blankets and linens."

50 Two men listed in the Washington City Directory for 1834 may have been Nicholas' sons John and

Peter. Their surname is spelled incorrectly as "Cassada," but John was located at the same address as the elder Margaret Cassady, and Peter was one block away. The large number of Cassady children fills in the gap for years between the births of Catherine and Margaret.

51 Two District of Columbia marriage records for a Margaret Cassady/Cassedy in 1833 add to the difficulty in making a positive identification. Margaret Cassaday married John Tennant on February 15, 1833, and Margaret Ann Cassedy married John B. Davis on May 14, 1833. Until other evidence is found, I prefer the second option since it uses the sampler surname spelling and provides a middle name that fits the initial that Margaret stitched. Margaret A. Davis, with husband John, has not been found in the 1850 federal census. However, Margaret Tenant, wife of John Tennant, born ca. 1815, was located in the District's First Ward in that census.

sorrow, and that path alone / Leads to a land where sorrow is unknown" by English poet William Cowper (1731–1800).[52] This sampler, with its noticeable similarity to Margaret's work, probably also dates to around 1826. Unfortunately, the stitches in the area where she embroidered her name, place, and date have badly disintegrated, while the rest of the sampler remains relatively intact. Based on an analysis of the remaining stitches in her inscription, the sampler is tentatively identified as the work of Amelia James, who married Henry Murris in the District of Columbia in 1846.[53]

Later Variations

From 1823 to 1842, additional architectural samplers appeared in Washington City that evoke the styles of the earlier Navy Yard groups. Four samplers have been identified to date, all of which can be documented as stitched by girls living in the area of Navy Yard Hill. Consistent in all four is a prominent, centrally located house with shuttered windows flanked by evergreen trees. All four also include a four-line verse at the top, with matching motifs in symmetrical fashion down the left and right sides. On three of the samplers the house sits on a lawn or stepped terrace populated with people, animals, or birds. Differences in the style of the house and differences in motifs demarcate these from earlier samplers stitched in the same geographical area.

Eliza Thompson

In 1823, Mary Ann Eliza Thompson created two embroideries, an alphabet sampler and one that contained many of the same stylistic features of earlier Navy Yard architectural samplers (Figure 9-13). Known as "Eliza," she stitched a central brick building with a triple-peaked roofline, two contrasting courses of white brick, and a checkered foundation on raised steps, similar to houses on Crowley's 1810 sampler and O'Brien's 1812 sampler. Eliza's imposing house with closed shutters is flanked by a pair of pine trees, while people and animals

Figure 9-13. Sampler worked by Mary Ann Eliza Thompson. Washington City, 1823. Inscribed: "Eliza/ Thompson / aged 14 th 3d of / Dr. 1823 / Washington City D.C. September 22th 1823." Silk on linen ground. 17 x 14 ½ in. Private collection

---

52 The stitched verse is from Cowper's epistle, "To an Afflicted Protestant Lady in France," and is often quoted.

53 Writing on the back of the sampler attributed it to Lydia James, 1791, Chester Co., Pennsylvania, but so far this person cannot be documented. The sampler was sold by Pook & Pook, September 21, 2002, as a Washington, D.C. sampler.

Figure 9-14. Sampler worked by Mary Maury Tait. Washington City, 1825. Inscribed: "Mary Tait / Aged 10 years / Aug 3d 1825 / WASHINGTON CITY D. C. JUNE 11th 1825." Silk on linen ground, 28 by 28 threads per inch. 19 ½ x 16 ¼ in. Collection of Anna Marie Witmer

stroll on the grass. Recalling Crowley's 1810 sampler, Eliza stitched birds perched on top of the trees and strawberry plants growing in the grassy yard. Variations of her verse appear on many samplers, "Eliza Thompson is my name / And with my needle I work the same / That all of you may plainly see / The care my parents took of me."

In a central octagonal cartouche below her verse Eliza stitched her name, age, and birth date: "Eliza / Thompson / aged 14th 3d of / Dr. 1823" using the same format found on the Crowley (1810), Boswell, Ensey, Tait, and Simmons samplers. Below the grassy lawn Eliza stitched her location and a second date "Washington City D.C. September 22th 1823." Comparing the two dates reveals that Eliza was thirteen at the time of completing her sampler, not fourteen as suggested by her signature. Eliza's sampler is the earliest of the Navy Yard stylistic group to include the abbreviation "D.C." for the District of

Columbia. Although Eliza's brick house remains unfinished, she added an architectural structure not seen on other Navy Yard samplers—a pair of garden gazebos or pergolas on either side of the house.

Mary Ann Eliza Thompson (born 1809) was a daughter of James Thompson, a naval block maker who lived on Georgia Avenue, South, near the Navy Yard.[54] In 1826, three years after completing her two samplers, Eliza married Charles B. Brown in Washington City. Their daughter Ann Eliza (1831–1916) stitched a sampler in 1842 on which she noted, "My age is half a score / My native place is Washington / My parents kind though Poor / Washington City D.C. January 14th /1842."[55]

Mary Tait

In 1825, Mary Tait also stitched a sampler that can be attributed to a teacher familiar with earlier samplers in the Navy Yard style (Figure 9-14). The overall layout with a central architectural feature, matching floating motifs in symmetrical fashion, and paired vases with three stylized flowers echoes many of the samplers in the earlier groups. The central building, however, is a modest two-story, three-bay brick house with shuttered windows, marking an important variation from the more imposing buildings seen previously. Although Mary's house is flanked by familiar Navy Yard spade-shaped trees topped with birds, it is not perched on a grassy lawn or stepped terrace.

Further variations include two motifs not seen in the earlier groups—fruit baskets and eight-pointed stars. Mary used a combination of cross, satin, outline, rice, and stem stitches to create her sampler. Her short verse, the same stitched by Elizabeth S. Dove (Figure 8-5), is the second stanza from the hymn, "The Child's Request." The selection appeared on American samplers as early as 1803.[56]

Below her verse Mary enclosed her name, age, and birth date in an octagonal cartouche similar to that of Eliza Thompson. Mary Tait's completion date (June 11, 1825) also predates her birthday (August 3), indicating she was in fact nine years of age when she embroidered her sampler.

Mary Maury Tait was born August 3, 1815, in Scotland to Jane (1787–1874) and Alexander Tait (1780–1848). By 1822 if not earlier, Alexander Tait was employed as a stone cutter with a residence or business south of Capitol Hill and north of the Navy Yard. Mary married Donald Stewart in 1841 and they had at least five children before his death on March 9, 1855. As a widow, Mary supported herself, her mother, and her children by keeping a "fancy store." Her fourth child, Alexander Tait Stewart (Stuart), became a prominent District of Columbia educator and held the position of superintendent of public schools during the early 1900s.

Margaret C. Simmons

Margaret C. Simmons stitched two known samplers: an alphabet and motif sampler in 1827 (Figure 8-8) and an architectural sampler completed on her birthday "January 7th 1828" (Figure 9-15).[57] Margaret's 1828 sampler repeats several

---

54 James Thompson earned $1.36 per day as a block maker at the Yard in 1819–1820, the latest year for which early payroll information is available. http://genealogytrails.com/washdc/wny_payroll1819-1820.html.

55 The two Thompson samplers and the Ann Eliza Brown sampler are in the same private collection.

56 Bolton and Coe, *American Samplers*, 305. The sampler was stitched by Eliza Harden of Portland, Maine, and dated October 12, 1803 (page 168).

57 Margaret's earlier sampler is identified only as "—C. Simmons Work Washington City Oct th 2d / 1827."

Figure 9-15. Sampler worked by Margaret C. Simmons. Washington City, 1828. Inscribed: "Margaret C Simmons Aged 9 years Jan. 7th 1828 / WASHINGTON CITY D. C. Jan. 7th 1828." Silk on linen ground. 16 x 16 in. Private collection

motifs from Julia Ann Crowley's 1810 sampler: strawberry plants and a bird in a densely worked lawn with a pair of spade-shaped pine trees, enclosed in an arcaded tulip border. Margaret's building, however, is a three-story federal-style house with shuttered windows and off-set door. Similarities in motifs (spade-shaped trees, stylized fruit baskets, eight-pointed stars) and inscriptions suggest that Margaret Simmons and Mary Tait may have received received instruction from the same teacher when working their Navy Yard architectural samplers. Margaret's lines on friendship by Irish poet and novelist Oliver Goldsmith (1728–1774) read:

> And what is Friendship but a name,
> A charm that lulls to sleep
> A shade that Follows wealth or Fame,
> But leaves the wretch to weep

Margaret was a daughter of Mary M. Barclay and James Simmons, a cooper residing at 11th Street, East, between L and M Streets, South, near the Yard. For more details on her life, see Chapter 8, page 159.

Mary Christeen Bohlayer

The latest known sampler with features echoing the Navy Yard style was worked in 1842 by thirteen-year-old Mary Christeen Bohlayer, who also lived in the vicinity of the Navy Yard (Figure 9-16). Mary Christeen used wool and silk cross and satin stitches to create her design. Her three-story brick house is situated on a stepped terrace lined with triangular pine trees that clearly recall the three samplers by Catherine Cassady in 1814, Margaret A. Cassedy in 1826, and Amelia James, ca. 1826. Sheep, birds, and flowers fill in the lawn leaving a reserve for her place name and date, "Washington City D C 1842." A pair of fat parrots, identical to those on Margaret A. Cassedy's 1826 sampler, further connect her work to the Navy Yard samplers of an earlier period. Floating vases of flowers flank the building, and a cartouche above repeats the date. Similar to the other later variations in the Navy Yard style, her building is a house with closed shutters. Mary Christeen's verse begins with the lines, "Jesus permit thy gracious Name to stand / As the first efforts of an Infant's Hand," evidently a favorite with Navy Yard sampler makers.

Mary Christeen (Christine) Bohlayer (1828–1867) was a daughter of Ann Underwood (1793–1871) and John Bohlayer (1794–1850), a native of Württemberg, Germany. John was a butcher who lived near the Yard at the corner of I (Eye) Street, South, and 9th Street, East. He was once described as "an old citizen of the Navy Yard section undistinguished by education, wealth, or public spirit, . . . noted as having been one of the Imperial Guard of Napoleon. . . . He came to this country immediately after the downfall of Napoleon, and carried on the business of a butcher in this city."[58] Mary Christeen Bohlayer continued to live at home with her mother until June 1852, when she became the second wife of Theodore Joseph Sniffin (1811–1900), a merchant. They had six children before Mary's death in 1867.

---

58 Davis, "The Navy Yard Section during the Life of the Rev. William Ryland," 219.

Figure 9-16.
Sampler worked by Mary Christeen Bohlayer. Washington City, 1842. Inscribed: "Mary Christeen Bohlayer age 13 years / 1842 / Washington City D C 1842." Wool and silk on linen ground, 31 by 28 threads per in. 15 ½ x 16 ½ in. Collection of Rear Admiral and Mrs. Daniel W. McKinnon, Jr.

Summary

Thirteen samplers (one attributed) are known to have been stitched by girls living near the Washington Navy Yard over a period of at least thirty-two years, 1810 to 1842. Most of the girls' fathers either worked at the Navy Yard or in trades that supported Navy Yard activity and the surrounding community.

Visually and technically, the samplers represent four groups, and at least six different teachers, over three time ranges: 1810–1813, 1814–1826, and 1823–1842. Remarkably, all thirteen samplers are stylistically similar and also distinct from samplers stitched in neighboring localities, suggesting a community identity that was captured in its samplers. Common to ten of the thirteen Navy Yard samplers is the cachet motif of a variegated vase with a tripartite array of flowers. However, the other three samplers are strongly associated through other dominant motifs or borders of the genre.

The first six samplers date from 1810 to 1813. They fall into two subgroups, based on the predominant architectural structure, and together they set the initial parameters for the Navy Yard architectural style. Many features are shared across the two subgroups, including the overall layout and inscriptions, as well as motifs such as vases with stylized flowers, delicate floral sprays, and spade-shaped trees. In addition, five of the six samplers share an identical border of tulips, carnations, poppies, roses, and daisies on a serpentine vine.

Five of these first six samplers were most likely stitched under the instruction of the same teacher, or at least the same school. If the brick building with bell tower stitched on three of these early samplers is the Washington Academy East, directed by John McLeod from 1808 to 1815, then it is possible that a teacher at the academy is responsible for launching the Navy Yard architectural style.[59] More research is needed to confirm or disprove this possibility.

The teacher for the sixth early sampler, Clubb (Figure 9-6), adopted the same layout, teaching a sampler that is similar enough to be

---

[59] Dixon, *National Intelligencer & Washington Advertiser Newspaper Abstracts 1811–1813*, 161.

Figure 9-17. Sampler worked by Eliza Jane Herbert. Portsmouth, Virginia, 1834. Inscribed: "Eliza Jane Herbert Portsmouth VA 1834." Silk on linen ground, 28 by 30 threads per in. 16 ⅝ x 17 ¼ in. Collection of Anna Marie Witmer

recognizable as belonging to the group but distinctive in identifiable ways. This suggests that the teacher or school responsible for the original design was well known and respected. To be competitive, the second teacher may have felt it prudent to adopt a sampler style that was already associated with the Navy Yard community and successful at attracting students. Unfortunately, the teacher or teachers who taught these distinctive early samplers seems to have discontinued instruction in needlework in the Navy Yard area after 1813.

The Stepped Terraces samplers form a second group, one that spanned twelve years (1814 to 1826) with relatively little change. The central architectural motif and landscape reflect a Philadelphia heritage, but there is no known teacher in the Navy Yard with a background in that city. A tribute to the longevity and popularity of this style is the appearance of a similar sampler stitched in 1842 (Figure 9-16), modified to accommodate new patterns and needlework techniques.

The last group, Later Variations, is a more diverse lot and illustrates the various adaptations that occur when an accepted style is taken up by multiple teachers. All of these later samplers feature elements from earlier examples of the Navy Yard stylistic group and conform to the same general layout. None, however, are closely matched to each other, with the possible exception of Mary Tait, 1825, and Margaret C. Simmons, 1828. This is further testimony to the enduring qualities of a community style, adopted and adapted over time.

Washington needlework teachers were an itinerant group and as they traveled so did the styles of the samplers they taught. It may be this migration within a city and between cities that accounts for later samplers in the Navy Yard architectural style appearing elsewhere in Washington City and even in distant towns. In 1834, for example, Sarah Ann Carter from Washington City's First Ward stitched a sampler following the Navy Yard format, but with motifs that recall Alexandria and other Virginia traditions (Figure 8-14). Although not teaching in 1834 (and therefore not responsible for the stylistic similarities on Sarah Ann's sampler), Mary McCurdy was a needlework teacher from the Navy Yard community who moved to the First Ward in 1819 and resumed teaching. There may have been others at a later time.

A similar story of migration might explain the appearance of architectural samplers in Portsmouth, Virginia, that are stylistically similar to those stitched in the environs of Washington's Navy Yard. Two nearly identical samplers were stitched in 1834 by Portsmouth cousins Sarah B. Herbert and Eliza Jane Herbert (Figure 9-17), both recalling the brick house with triple-peaked roofline and stepped terrace samplers stitched by Navy Yard girls. Washington City and Portsmouth both had large shipyards, and workers moved between the two cities in pursuit of employment opportunities. It is possible that wives, widows, or teachers followed the same path, electing to teach needlework in their new locations and adapting the Navy Yard style to fit local traditions and tastes.

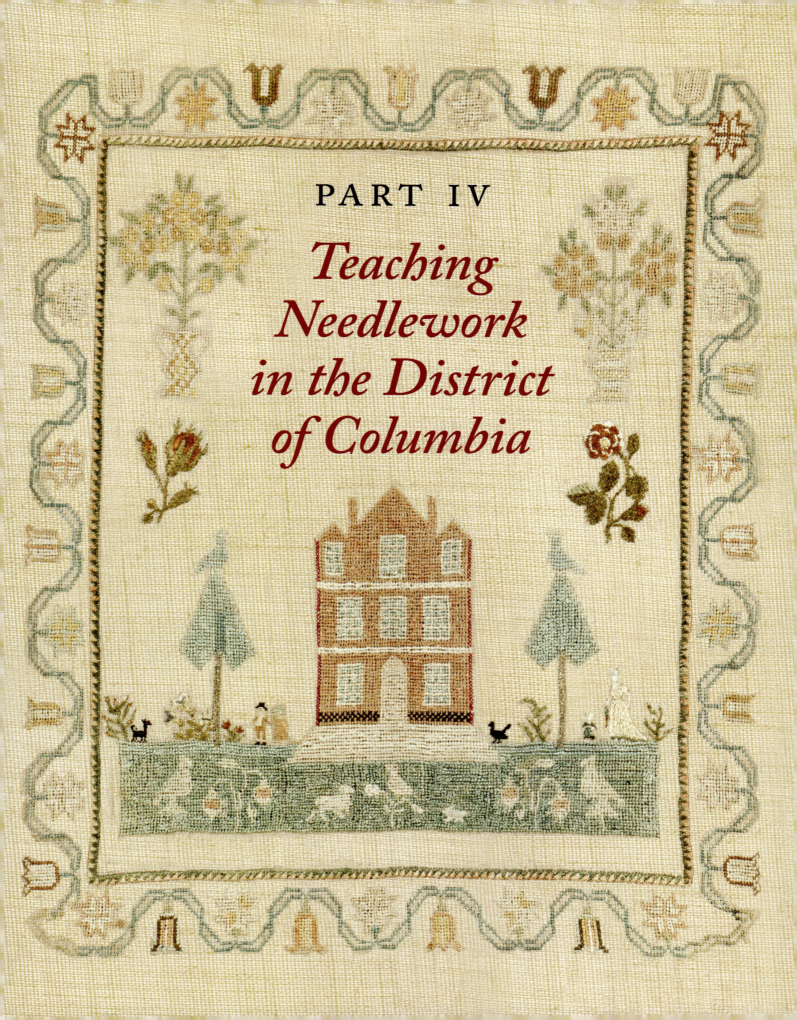

PART IV
Teaching Needlework in the District of Columbia

Figure 10-1.
View of Washington City by Augustus Kollner, 1839.
Inscribed: "Near Pennsylv. Ave. and 7th St. at Washington City."
Ink wash over graphite on paper.
Library of Congress, Prints & Photographs Division

CHAPTER 10

The Teachers and Schools

Sheryl De Jong

WITH ITS TWO ESTABLISHED TOWNS and fledgling federal city, the District of Columbia attracted a large number of educators, including talented teachers of needlework. Upon arrival in the young nation's capital, these teachers had to adjust to its climate, terrain, location, and a transient population. Although many have now been forgotten, more than a few are known today through examples of their students' needlework and their published efforts to recruit students.

Appendix II is a database of all known teachers and schools in Alexandria, Georgetown, and Washington City from 1780 to 1870, with dates of their teaching, location, and the branches of needlework taught. At the time of publication this number totaled 246 (See www.dcneedlework.com for updated information). Many of the teachers and schools were identified from newspaper advertisements, an important source of information about the early education of young ladies in the District of Columbia.

There were about 14,000 residents in the urban and rural areas of the newly formed District of Columbia in 1800, but by 1820 that number had grown to about 24,000 (Figure 10-1). As the population increased so did the opportunities for needlework teachers, who came from many states and foreign countries and thus reflected the diverse backgrounds of the residents. Jobs in the government attracted people from all over the country—Members of Congress came from sixteen different states in 1800 and twenty-three states in 1820. In addition, the number of foriegn ambassadors steadily increased.

TEACHER ITINERANCY

Analysis of the data (Appendix II) indicates that teachers came to the District from such faraway places as England, France, and Moscow.[1] Mrs. E.

---

1 In descending order of frequency, needlework teachers who advertised their place of origin or previous teaching location came from Baltimore (10), France (4), Philadelphia (4), New York (4), England (3), Boston (2), Charleston (2), Bermuda (1), Moscow (1), Scotland (1) and Virginia (1).

Philips, Charlotte Taylor, and Mrs. Maria Stone all came from England. Miss Hauel came from France with John Quincy Adams, who as secretary of state under President James Monroe, had been on a diplomatic visit. Madame Du Cherray, a lady of French descent, arrived from Moscow, "where she has for several years been at the head of the most respectable academies in that city."[2]

Some of the teachers came from places closer to the District, especially Baltimore, Philadelphia, and Boston. In 1805, Miss Ann Smith, formerly preceptress of the Old Gum Academy, came from Baltimore to teach in Georgetown. In 1808 she moved on to Lexington, Virginia, and founded the Ann Smith Academy.[3] Also from Baltimore, Mary Hardester went to Alexandria to teach "Reading and Needle-Work."[4] The Misses Wright relocated from New England to teach in Georgetown. For several years they had "conducted a large and respectable school in Boston."[5]

Miss Heaney also came to the District from the Boston area, where she had been the principal of the Derby Academy in Hingham, and in 1831 opened an academy in Washington City. In 1834 she returned to the Boston area to teach, but she was in Washington City again by December 1844 and continued to advertise in local newspapers there through 1852. Mrs. Fales had taught in Philadelphia and Marietta, Pennsylvania, prior to coming to Washington City to open a boarding school for young ladies. In her Washington City advertisement she included an announcement from the local Pennsylvania paper that had deplored her departure because "Her residence here has endeared her to all the inhabitants; and the rapid improvement of the young ladies under her care."[6]

Teachers frequently moved between Georgetown, Alexandria, and Washington City. Mrs. Isabella Smith moved from Georgetown to Washington City "in consequence of the injury sustained by Mr. Smith in one of his limbs."[7] Mr. and Mrs. Waugh moved from Alexandria to Georgetown "at the instance of several ladies and gentlemen of Georgetown."[8] Elizabeth Smith in 1843 commenced a school for African American children on "the island" in Washington City but in 1860 was an assistant to the Reverend William H. Hunter who operated a large school in Zion Wesley Church in Georgetown.[9]

Marital Status

A number of married couples opened schools in the District of Columbia. Mr. and Mrs. Maurice P. Hore advertised that Mr. Hore would "instruct in the elementary branches of education," and Mrs. Hore would "assist in superintending the Female Department and will give instruction in plain and ornamental needle work" (Figure 10-2).[10] Mr. and Mrs. Sketchly advertised that they had "two separate school rooms, one for young ladies, and the other for young gentlemen."[11] Mr. and Mrs. Webber and their daughter moved to Georgetown to teach. While Mr. Webber taught the young gentlemen, "Mrs. and Miss Webber, in a

---

2 *National Intelligencer & Washington Advertiser,* November 28, 1807: *Daily National Intelligencer,* December 2, 1818.

3 Herbert Adams, *Thomas Jefferson and The University of Virginia* (Washington: Government Printing Office, 1888), 304.

4 *Alexandria Advertiser,* December 13, 1805.

5 Washington *National Messenger,* November 4, 1818.

6 Washington *Daily National Intelligencer,* November 11, 1820 and May 19, 1831. See Ring, *Girlhood Embroidery,* 152–57.

7 Washington *Daily National Intelligencer,* July 26, 1830.

8 Washington *Globe,* March 5, 1832.

9 A canal built in 1815 formed a barrier between most of Washington's southwest quadrant and the rest of the city. This section was called "the island."

10 Washington *Daily National Journal,* Sept 8, 1828.

11 *Alexandria Daily Gazette,* April 27, 1811.

> **SELECT SCHOOL,**
> *12th Street West, next to F Street.*
>
> MAURICE P. HORP, Professor of French, &c. most respectfully announces to the Parents and Guardians of children, that he has, at the recommendation of his friends, removed his school to a most spacious and airy house in 12th Street; where he will, in addition to his Day School (which he proposes to limit to twenty-five pupils) commence a Night school on the evening of Monday, 9th instant, for such persons as may find it more convenient to attend. He will teach the elementary branches of education, comprising English (grammatically) Writing, Arithmetic, Book-keeping, by single and double entry; Geography, History, and French.
>
> Mrs. Hore will assist in superintending the female department, and will give instruction in plain and ornamental needle work.
>
> For terms, please apply to the Principal at the Academy.
> Nov. 9—tf

Figure 10-2. Advertisement in the Washington *Daily National Journal*, November 28, 1829.

separate apartment will teach young ladies every branch of useful and ornamental needlework."[12]

Many of the teachers in the database were single or widowed at the time they taught needlework in the District. Because teaching was one of very few respectable occupations for women of the antebellum period, it was a frequent choice for new widows. Four months after her husband died, Mrs. Emmeline Pope came to Georgetown "for the purpose of teaching a boarding school . . . her school room will be convenient to persons in the city, as well as to those in Georgetown."[13] Some of the widowed women were assisted by relatives. Mrs. Ann Mark opened a school in Alexandria and advertised "she will be assisted by her daughters (now in Philadelphia qualifying themselves) when she will be enabled to receive more scholars."[14] Mrs. Mary Ann Evans of Washington City was assisted by her mother Mrs. Mary Brush, "in the care and discipline of the children."[15]

Sisters also taught together. Miss Mary Johnston and her sister opened a school in Alexandria. Their course of instruction was "the usual branches of a plain and ornamental education."[16] The Misses Doyle opened a school in Georgetown and advertised that they "hope by their attentions to merit the patronage of the public."[17] The better-known Mary A. Tyson and her five sisters had a school first in Baltimore and then in Washington City (See pages 206-8).

Advertisements

Eighty-three percent of the teachers in the database (Appendix II) used local newspapers to advertise their schools. Some advertised only once, others at the beginning of each school quarter or school year. Mrs. Isabella Smith placed at least 354 advertisements between August 14, 1829, and December 1832, and Mr. and Miss Gray ran 288 advertisements in the *Daily National Intelligencer* between March 9, 1831, and November 6, 1832. The Grays' advertisement was the same every time while Mrs. Smith varied hers. With few exceptions, there is little evidence that African American teachers advertised in early newspapers.[18]

To help establish that their schools were credible, some teachers included the names of references in their advertisements. Mrs. Isabella Smith listed seven gentlemen from Washington and seven from Georgetown, including several who were ministers or lawyers. Clever Mrs. L. Henry Cutts from Washington City sent the prospectus of her boarding school to President Andrew Jackson and printed his reply in her advertisement: "It appears to be well adapted to the system of instruction which improves the affections at the same time that it cultivates the intellect of the female mind."[19] For her school in

---

12 Washington *Daily National Intelligencer*, January 2, 1819.
13 Ibid., May 21, 1823.
14 *Phenix Gazette*, March 20, 1827.
15 Washington *Daily National Intelligencer*, October 10, 1821.
16 *Alexandria Daily Gazette*, August 25, 1840.
17 *The Messenger*, July 17, 1816.
18 One exception is the Resolute Beneficial Society. Washington *Daily National Intelligencer*, August 29, 1818.
19 Washington *Daily National Intelligencer*, August 28, 1835.

Figure 10-3. "The Highlands," painted by Caroline Rebecca Nourse Dulany. Georgetown, ca. 1850. Watercolor on paper. 8 ½ x 10 ¾ in. Dumbarton House, The National Society of The Colonial Dames of America, Washington, D.C., L2010.009.0001

Alexandria, Mrs. Hagerty included three testimonials from recognized male teachers in Washington City: John McLeod, Philip Smith, and James Caden.

Other advertisements included the name of a previous teacher or school at the same location with the hope of luring former students. In 1831, Miss Heany advertised that she was using the former home of Mr. and Mrs. Bonfils for her academy. The Misses Sawkins in 1834 advertised that they were opening a school in the house recently occupied by Miss Heany, who by then had returned to the Boston area to teach. Miss Hawley used the house once occupied by Mrs. Howard and later Mr. John McLeod on Tenth Street. Mrs. Tastet was the next teacher to use that same house; it may have been a convenient location or well-known site.

Location

The most frequently advertised location for a school was in a home. Women taught either in their own homes or in a room rented in a more centrally located house. In Georgetown, Miss Rosa M. Nourse opened her school at the "Highlands, the late residence of her father (Figure 10-3). The position is remarkably healthy, convenient, and easy of access, and the house large and commodious" (See Figure 4-3).[20] Mr. and Mrs. Larkin used their residence on

---

20 Washington *Daily National Intelligencer*, August 27, 1845. Rosa Morris Nourse was the daughter of Rebecca Morris and Charles Nourse. She was born on October 10, 1823, in the District of Columbia and died in 1903.

Fairfax Street in Alexandria for their school and promised "unremitting attention to the improvement of the pupils, to merit the confidence of those parents whose children may be entrusted to their care."[21] Miss S. Evans had her school in the house "belonging to Mr. Daniel Carroll, fourth door north of Dr. Thomas Ewell's and opposite the Capitol."[22] Obviously, these were place names that everyone would recognize and could locate.

Many teachers stayed for only a short time or kept a small school, so that a large building was not needed. Exceptions to this practice were Mary A. Tyson and her sisters, John McLeod, and Lydia English. Each had enough students to warrant a large building. Miss Margaret Sinnott taught from 1808 to 1842 but moved frequently, never having a permanent location (See pages 204-6).

Pierre (Peter) L'Enfant's original plan for the federal city was to widen the Tiber Creek so it could be used for commercial purposes. However, that did not happen and it became an open sewer, malodorous and fetid, and the probable cause of much disease and death in the city. John Melish commented in 1806,

> *Capitol Hill is elevated above the river upwards of 70 feet. Between this and the river there is a low meadow, about a mile broad, abounding with swamps and shrubbery. In the autumn these swamps send out an effluvia, which often affects the health of those who live on the hill.*[23]

In response to these distasteful conditions, several teachers felt compelled to comment on their school's healthy environment (Figure 10-4).

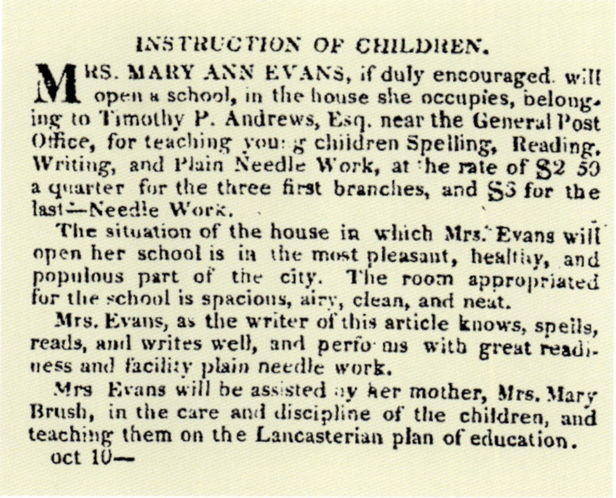

INSTRUCTION OF CHILDREN.

MRS. MARY ANN EVANS, if duly encouraged, will open a school, in the house she occupies, belonging to Timothy P. Andrews, Esq. near the General Post Office, for teaching young children Spelling, Reading, Writing, and Plain Needle Work, at the rate of $2 50 a quarter for the three first branches, and $3 for the last—Needle Work.

The situation of the house in which Mrs. Evans will open her school is in the most pleasant, healthy, and populous part of the city. The room appropriated for the school is spacious, airy, clean, and neat.

Mrs. Evans, as the writer of this article knows, spells, reads, and writes well, and performs with great readiness and facility plain needle work.

Mrs Evans will be assisted by her mother, Mrs. Mary Brush, in the care and discipline of the children, and teaching them on the Lancasterian plan of education.

oct 10—

Figure 10-4. Advertisement in the Washington *Daily National Intelligencer*, October 10, 1821.

> *The situation of the house in which Mrs. Evans will open her school is in the most pleasant, healthy, and populous part of the city. The room appropriated for the school is spacious, airy, clean, and neat.*[24]

Mr. and Miss Gray stated that their school was "in a healthy situation where the streets are well paved, and the water good."[25] Across Rock Creek in Georgetown, Mr. and Mrs. Waugh noted they were in "one of the most advantageous situations in town, in reference to good water, health, and other comforts."[26]

The Curriculum

Early teachers frequently offered only reading and writing in addition to needlework instruction. Mastering the basic stitches of sewing was an important skill for most young ladies, and embroidery was an elite accomplishment. "The alphabets that embellished schoolgirl samplers signified both a girl's literacy and her future role as keeper of household textiles, which before industrialization were far more valuable than furniture."[27]

---

21 *Alexandria Daily Gazette,* May 27, 1819.

22 Washington *Daily National Intelligencer,* January 9, 1813.

23 John Melish, *Travels through the United States of America in the years 1806 & 1807, and 1809, 1810, & 1811* (London and Dublin: Melish, Cowie and Cumming, 1818), 149. John Melish was a Scottish textile manufacturer who settled in Philadelphia in 1811. He wrote to promote British emigration to the United States.

24 Washington *Daily National Intelligencer,* October 10, 1821.

25 Ibid., March 9, 1831.

26 Washington *Globe*, March 5, 1832.

27 Laurel Thatcher Ulrich, "A Bed Sheet in Beinecke," *Common-Place*, vol. 2, no. 1 (October 2001): 1. www.common-place.org.

Figure 10-5. Matilda Cecilia Dowdall Shedden (1781–1855), 1847. Oil on canvas, by James C. Bogle. 30 x 24 ¾ in. Maryland Historical Society, 1949-90-7

The words "plain and ornamental needlework" were frequently used by teachers in their advertisements. Other teachers used such terms as "fancy work," "embroidery," or "marking." "Marking" included just the basic cross stitch that would be used to put initials and numbers on linens. "Fancy work" and "embroidery" might include more decorative stitches or advanced techniques. In 1797, Ann Vidler in Washington City and Mrs. Tannent in Alexandria were the first to offer "tambouring." Tambouring is a continuous worked chain stitch created with a tambour hook, which forms a loop similar to a crochet chain.

In 1806, Mrs. Reagan enumerated all the branches of needlework she would teach. She included "Tamboring, embroidery, open work, queenswork, marking, all kinds of plain sewing."[28] In "open work" or "Dresden" the threads of the fabric are pulled to create holes that resemble lace. "Queenswork" involves the use of the queen stitch, a relatively difficult diamond-shaped stitch worked on samplers and pocketbooks by advanced needle workers. Mrs. O'Reilly of Alexandria in 1805, Sarah Edmonds of Alexandria in 1810, and Miss S. Evans of Washington City in 1813 were the only teachers to include "print work" in their advertisements. "Print work" attempted to reproduce the look of an etching by using many tiny straight stitches in black silk. Teachers who included the words "silk" and "chenille" in their advertisements were usually teaching their students pictorial embroidery on a silk ground. Their subjects might be a memorial to a departed loved one, a pastoral scene, or a depiction of a classical theme.

Teachers frequently offered young women instruction in French, considered to be the language of diplomacy and a sign of gentility.[29] Mrs. Shedden, at her seminary in Georgetown, charged ten dollars per quarter for French (at a time when Fancy work was only five dollars per quarter).[30] She advertised in both French and English (Figure 10-5).[31] As early as 1797, Mrs. Lee in Alexandria included French instruction as part of her curriculum. In Washington City, Madame Dorman advertised that she devoted "the afternoon conferences and conversation in French, for the improvement

---

28 Washington *National Intelligencer*, July 18, 1806.

29 French was the language used for international commerce until it was replaced with English after World War I.

30 Matilda Cecilia Dowdall was born April 1781 in Ireland to Walter and Ann Johnston Dowdall. She married Thomas Shedden in 1806 in New Jersey. Thomas Shedden died in 1816 and left his wife Cecilia practically penniless. She first was a governess and then opened her seminary in a house on Cox's Row in Georgetown in 1823 and later on Pennsylvania Avenue in Washington City. She died June 19, 1855. Information from Andreas F. von Recum and http://www.royalblood.co.uk

31 Washington *Daily National Intelligencer*, September 3, 1825.

of young ladies, who have already acquired some knowledge of the language."[32] Mesdames Chevalier, De La Marche, and LeBlond de la Rochefoucault spoke only French when they opened their academy in Georgetown in 1798 and hired other teachers to provide instruction in English grammar.

Over time, instruction in the sciences was added to the curriculum. In 1823, Miss Searle, a teacher in Georgetown, may have been the first to offer a course in Chemistry. Her course offerings were diverse and approached that of a high school today. Miss Searle also stated, however, that "Needle work, if desired, will receive its due share of attention" (Figure 10-6).[33] In 1828 the Young Ladies' Academy of the Convent of the Visitation at Georgetown offered fourteen branches of modern science while continuing to provide needlework instruction. The school ordered almost $2,500 of philosophical and chemical apparatus to demonstrate the theories of many useful branches of natural philosophy.[34]

Although a number of teachers taught "Fancy Work" at this time, many had ceased to include it in the curriculum. Alfred Armstrong's advertisement in 1827 reflected the changing emphasis in female education.

> *His plan contemplates chiefly the instruction of young ladies in the HIGHER BRANCHES of Female education; the inferior branches, however, will also be taught so as to meet the minds of all who may be disposed to patronize his school.*[35]

An advertisement for Capitol Hill Seminary in 1833 indicated a similar sentiment: "particular attention is given to the more solid

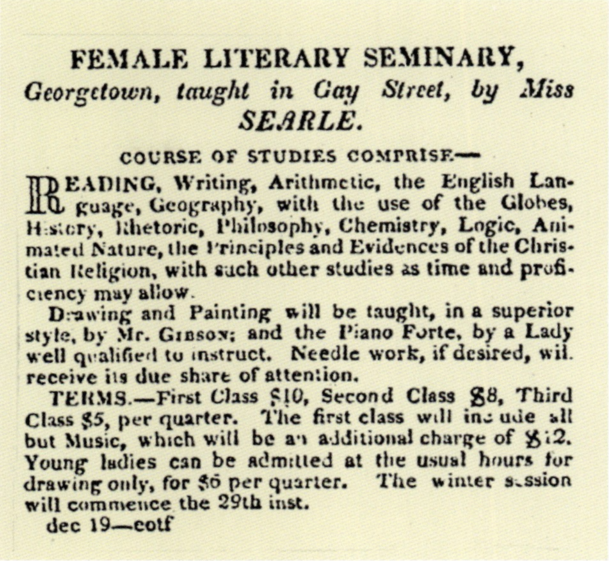

FEMALE LITERARY SEMINARY,
Georgetown, taught in Gay Street, by Miss SEARLE.

COURSE OF STUDIES COMPRISE—

READING, Writing, Arithmetic, the English Language, Geography, with the use of the Globes, History, Rhetoric, Philosophy, Chemistry, Logic, Animated Nature, the Principles and Evidences of the Christian Religion, with such other studies as time and proficiency may allow.

Drawing and Painting will be taught, in a superior style, by Mr. GIBSON; and the Piano Forte, by a Lady well qualified to instruct. Needle work, if desired, will receive its due share of attention.

TERMS.—First Class $10, Second Class $8, Third Class $5, per quarter. The first class will include all but Music, which will be an additional charge of $12. Young ladies can be admitted at the usual hours for drawing only, for $5 per quarter. The winter session will commence the 29th inst.

dec 19—eotf

Figure 10-6. Advertisement in the Washington *Daily National Intelligencer,* December 24, 1823.

branches of education. The ornamental branches form a separate charge."[36]

If space and patronage permitted, the teacher would employ masters with expertise in various academic or "ornamental" subjects. Most often they secured the services of a French or music teacher. Mr. William Peerce taught for Mrs. Du Cherray, Mrs. Greentree, and Mrs. Gaither before starting his own school. Mrs. Hebb advertised that she would be "assisted by the best instructors in the various departments of knowledge proposed to be taught."[37] Miss Sinnott, of a slightly different mind, made a point of advertising in 1827 that she was "teaching independent of any male."[38]

District of Columbia teachers often conducted public examinations and held demonstrations and exhibitions of student work. Mr. and Mrs. Waugh, in Alexandria, intended "to afford, in a few weeks, an opportunity of proving the success of their Institution by a public examination."[39] Mrs. Isabella Smith advertised that "A Review of the young Ladies' studies is held once a fortnight, when the school will be open for

32 Ibid., August 31, 1840.

33 Washington *Daily National Intelligencer,* Dec 24, 1823.

34 Eleanore C. Sullivan, *Georgetown Visitation Since 1799,* second edition revised and expanded by Susan Hannan (Washington D.C.: Georgetown Visitation Monastery, 2004), 86.

35 Alexandria *Phenix Gazette,* August 18, 1827.

36 Washington *Daily National Intelligencer,* October 22, 1833.

37 Ibid., August 13, 1830.

38 Ibid., March 7, 1827.

39 Alexandria *Phenix Gazette,* March 25, 1830.

parents and guardians."[40] In addition to public examinations, Mrs. Porter in Alexandria advertised that "parents are particularly requested to visit the school-rooms during the hours of recitation, and examine the mode of instruction, discipline and progress of the pupils."[41] Mary Ann Tyson and her sisters sent out quarterly statements of the "progress of the pupils, exhibiting a correct and faithful account of their conduct and advancement."[42]

Some District of Columbia teachers published information about their pedagogical approach and instructional goals. Because the primary objective for Mrs. Cutts's seminary was to "form intelligent and efficient managers," she indicated that "every thing will be subservient and taught with reference to domestic economy."[43] Mrs. Evans, with the assistance of her mother Mrs. Mary Brush, planned to use the "Lancasterian plan of education."[44] And Mrs. and Miss Webber proposed to teach in a method that was "not merely a repetition, but in an interrogatory and explanatory system."[45]

The dates on which school terms began and ended varied considerably, with little evidence of the standard academic year as we know it today. For many teachers, the school year began when they arrived in the city. Madame Du Cherray, newly arrived in Georgetown, announced that she would begin teaching "after the Easter Holidays."[46] Maria Dunlap opened her school in Alexandria on October 8, and Mrs. Bage opened her Washington City school on "the 2nd of April."[47] Mrs. Cutts, also of Washington City, and Mrs. Porter in Alexandria each had a school year of forty-eight weeks.[48] In contrast, Miss Hogan offered "two sessions of 20 weeks each" in her Washington City school, beginning in September. To accommodate area families, however, Miss Hogan indicated she would receive pupils at any time and they would be charged from the "date of their entrance."[49]

Only one teacher, Mrs. Fales, thought it was important to advertise what time school would start each day. Her hours of instruction were from nine to twelve in the morning and from two to five in the afternoon.

Congress was usually in session from December through March or May of the following year, and teachers were apparently willing to accommodate those members of Congress who brought their families to the nation's capital. Aca Nada Seminary appealed to "Members of Congress, strangers, or naval and army officers who are frequently called to the seat of government" by stating that they "would find it an agreeable home for their daughters or wards."[50] Miss Charlotte Taylor also encouraged parents or guardians to send "their children and wards either during the session of Congress, or for a longer period, to commence or progress in their Academical pursuits."[51]

Manners and Morals

In his farewell address in 1796, George Washington emphasized the importance of morals and religion.

And let us with caution indulge the supposition that morality can be maintained without religion. Whatever may be conceded to the

---

40 Washington *Daily National Intelligencer,* May 7, 1831.

41 *Richmond Enquirer,* August 24, 1832.

42 Washington *Daily National Intelligencer,* August 23, 1847.

43 Ibid., August 28, 1835.

44 Ibid., October 10, 1821.

45 Georgetown *National Messenger,* December 30, 1818.

46 *Washington Federalist,* February 17, 1808.

47 *Alexandria Daily Gazette,* October 6, 1810; *City of Washington Gazette,* March 9, 1821.

48 Washington *Daily National Intelligencer,* August 28, 1835; *Richmond Enquirer,* August 24, 1832.

49 Washington *Daily National Intelligencer,* September 7, 1855.

50 Ibid., June 16, 1851.

51 Ibid., July 30, 1818.

influence of refined education on minds of peculiar structure, reason and experience both forbid us to expect that national morality can prevail in exclusion of religious principle.[52]

On September 12, 1815, a person writing as "Cornelia," placed a communication in the *Daily National Intelligencer* on this theme.

> *In every society which is desirous of having its foundations in good morals, public instruction is a primary object; and, if one particular department of public instruction be of more importance than another, it must be that which concerns the education of young ladies. Whatever may be our politics, it is the well-instructed women that chiefly decide the character of our morality and determine our inclinations to religion.*

Teachers' advertisements reflected the prevailing concern with religion and morals. Mrs. Henderson offered "religious instruction in common with her children."[53] Jane Herbert noted she would not "lose sight of the improvement of the heart, but regard with assiduous attention the moral deportment of her pupils,"[54] while in Washington City Miss Heaney "offered religious instruction simply to cultivate the purest moral feelings." Miss Heaney's students also participated in a charity project. They held a fair and "by their noble exertions" raised $234.57 for the Washington City Orphan Asylum.[55]

Since teachers who accepted boarders wanted to assure the girls' parents that their daughters would be well cared for, their advertisements emphasized the things that concerned parents: morals, manners, health, deportment, discipline, and religion. Mrs. Bell advertised that "every effort will be used to make the Institution a happy home for all its inmates," and Mrs. Simson wished "to cultivate their young minds as well as to form their manners, and shall spare no pains to effect it." Miss O'Brien promised that "The children committed to her care shall be treated with maternal tenderness."[56]

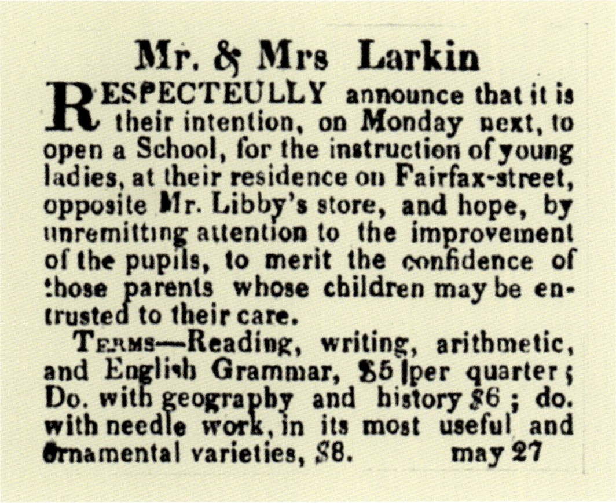
Mr. & Mrs Larkin
RESPECTFULLY announce that it is their intention, on Monday next, to open a School, for the instruction of young ladies, at their residence on Fairfax-street, opposite Mr. Libby's store, and hope, by unremitting attention to the improvement of the pupils, to merit the confidence of those parents whose children may be entrusted to their care.
TERMS—Reading, writing, arithmetic, and English Grammar, $5 per quarter; Do. with geography and history $6; do. with needle work, in its most useful and ornamental varieties, $8. may 27

Figure 10-7. Advertisement in the *Alexandria Gazette*, May 27, 1819.

FINANCES

Teachers generally charged by the quarter or year, with extra fees for specific subjects, such as music, French, drawing, etc. Mrs. Bell's terms per quarter were "from $3 to $9. Drawing, Painting and Needle-work, extra charges."[57] John Lathrop charged "forty dollars per annum, five dollars in advance, to be deducted from the amount of the first quarter bill; ink and quills, fifty cents per quarter."[58] Mr. and Mrs. Larkin advertised the following terms: "Reading, writing, arithmetic, and English grammar, $5 per quarter; Do. [ditto] with geography and history $6; do. [ditto] needle work in its most useful and ornamental varieties, $8" (Figure 10-7).[59]

52 Philadelphia *Daily American Advertiser*, September 19, 1796.

53 Washington *Daily National Intelligencer*, July 26, 1831.

54 Georgetown *National Messenger*, July 2, 1819.

55 Washington *Daily National Intelligencer*, September 10, 1831 and May 11, 1832.

56 Ibid., January 7, 1837 and September 5, 1859; *Colonial Mirror and Alexandria Gazette*, July 24, 1793.

57 Washington *Daily National Intelligencer*, October 12, 1850.

58 Ibid., May 23, 1815.

59 *Alexandria Gazette*, May 27, 1819.

Teachers with boarding students typically advertised an amount for the full year. In 1797, Mrs. Lee's terms included "French, English, Writing, Grammar, Arithmetic, and Fancy Work, ten pounds per annum and three dollars entrance — Without French, six pounds, per annum, and two dollars entrance — Geography, Drawing, Dancing, and Music a separate charge."[60] Mrs. Stone in 1820 advertised "for English tuition 6, 8, or 10 dollars per quarter, according to the branches taught. Board, washing, English, French, Music and Drawing at $300 per annum: or, without Music and Drawing, $200 per annum—one quarter in advance."[61] At Mrs. Smith's and Mrs. Wily's boarding school in Georgetown, the terms for day scholars also included half a cord of wood for the winter.[62]

In 1819 the nation experienced a financial panic and depression brought on by "speculation in land and the issuance of paper money by the unregulated banks of the period."[63] Mrs. Cottringer responded by advertising that "in consideration of the peculiar distress of the times, she had reduced the charges of her school, which in the future will be as follows: Board and English tuition, (per ann.) D[ollar]160, Including Washing, 180. . . . Stationary and the use of school library supplied at a reduction of 20 per cent."[64]

Rachel Painter[65] was fortunate to be hired in 1815 at the rate of $500 per year as a teacher for a new female school started by the Religious Society of Friends in Alexandria. In 1820, "when the school committee proposed a reduction in her pay of $100 a year," she responded by "taking the School upon her own footing" and paying the Society of Friends rent of six dollars per month for the school room. She also reduced the price of tuition and managed to support herself and keep the school going for another ten years. In 1830 she resigned but named Mary Anna Talbott as her successor, so the school could continue.[66]

Several teachers supplemented their income from a business that made use of their needlework skills. Mrs. Phillips offered to teach Mantua making and Millinery, Ann Godfrey said she would "take in work both of gentlemen and ladies," and Mrs. J. A. Davis "mends and joins lace, [and] makes socks" (Figure 10-8).[67]

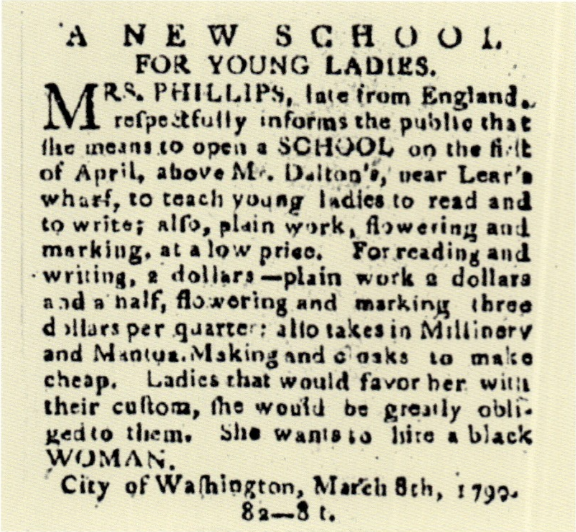

Figure 10-8. Advertisement in the *Centinel of Liberty & Georgetown Washington Advertiser*, March 8, 1799.

> A NEW SCHOOL
> FOR YOUNG LADIES.
> MRS. PHILLIPS, late from England, respectfully informs the public that she means to open a SCHOOL on the first of April, above Mr. Dalton's, near Lear's wharf, to teach young ladies to read and to write; also, plain work, flowering and marking, at a low price. For reading and writing, 2 dollars — plain work 2 dollars and a half, flowering and marking three dollars per quarter: also takes in Millinery and Mantua Making and cloaks to make cheap. Ladies that would favor her with their custom, she would be greatly obliged to them. She wants to hire a black WOMAN.
> City of Washington, March 8th, 1799.
> 82—3 t.

---

60 *Alexandria Advertiser*, September 29, 1797.

61 Washington *Daily National Intelligencer*, August 29, 1820.

62 Georgetown *Centinel of Liberty*, November 4, 1800.

63 John W. Reps, *Washington on View: The Nation's Capital Since 1790* (Chapel Hill: University of North Carolina Press, 1991), 54.

64 *Alexandria Gazette*, October 28, 1819.

65 Rachel Painter was born in 1792 in East Bradford, Chester County, Pennsylvania. She was a student at Westtown Boarding School in 1812 and left in 1815 after being offered and refusing a job as a teacher at Westtown. She married John James on May 14, 1834, in Chester County as his second wife, and they had one son, Jesse B. James. Rachel Painter James died on November 8, 1863, in West Chester, Pennsylvania. http://www.rootsweb.ancestry.com/. Joan M. Jensen, "Not Only Ours but Others: The Quaker Teaching Daughters of the Mid-Atlantic, 1790–1850," *History of Education Quarterly* 24 (Spring 1984): 14.

66 Abstract of Quaker Records by Lora Anderberg, Norfolk, Va., 1988; Joan M. Jensen, "Not Only Ours but Others: The Quaker Teaching Daughters of the Mid-Atlantic, 1790–1850," 14–15; Alexandria *Phenix Gazette*, March 3, 1830.

67 *Centinel of Liberty & Georgetown & Washington Advertiser*, March 8, 1799 and February 21, 1800; Washington *Daily National Intelligencer*, August 26, 1848.

Figure 10-9. A view of the growing Washington community from the west front of the Capitol in 1813.
Image courtesy of the Historical Society of Washington, DC

Madame De La Marche of Georgetown found another way to secure income. She informed "the public that she has EXCELLENT WATERS for the cure of almost all kind of SORE EYES. She has also Salves for the cure of different sorts of Sores, hurts, wounds, &c." She added that "It is more the good of humanity, than her own interest that induces her to advertise the above mentioned things."[68]

Taking in boarders was also a way for teachers to supplement their income, or as Mrs. Rowen advertised "to accommodate those who live at a distance, she will take a few young ladies to board and educate."[69] Teachers were very explicit in what they expected their boarding students to provide. The advertisement of Mr. & Mrs. Bonfils stipulated that boarding students should "bring Bed, Bedding, Towels, Knife, Fork, a Silver Goblet and Table and Tea Spoon. It is requested that the clothes of the Young Ladies should be marked in full in Durable Ink; also the names in full, to be engraved in the Goblet, Fork, Spoon, &c. &c."[70] Mrs. Cottringer advertised that "Bed and Bedding [was] a separate charge, if not furnished by parents. Each young lady to supply her own towels, tumbler, and spoon."[71] In addition to the above, Mrs. Porter required her students to dress alike. The winter uniform, "consisting of a blue worsted dress and black apron; a plain muslin handkerchief, leather shoes, and colored hose. . . . Summer Dress of blue gingham during the week and on Sunday a white dress, blue belt, and the same bonnet as in winter, with blue ribbon."[72]

Appendix II provides a foundation for understanding the personal and professional demographics of teachers who chose to provide academic and needlework instruction to girls and young women in the District of Columbia. It also reveals the breadth of education in the District and some of the things teachers had to contend with as they pursued their chosen or necessary occupation. Although a single newspaper advertisement is limited in the information it can provide, looking at a large number of them allows interesting information to emerge and makes possible conclusions about the teaching population as a whole.

---

68 *Centinel of Liberty & Georgetown & Washington Advertiser*, March 8, 1799.

69 *Alexandria Daily Gazette*, March 14, 1811.

70 Washington *Daily National Intelligencer*, May 11, 1825.

71 Ibid., April 27, 1824.

72 *Richmond Enquirer*, September 24, 1832.

Figure 11-1
View of Washington City by Augustus Kollner, 1839.
Inscribed: "Capitol at Washington D.C. / West view."
Watercolor on paper.
Library of Congress, Prints & Photographs Division

CHAPTER 11

The Teaching and Learning Enterprise

THREE VIGNETTES

Sheryl De Jong

By the nineteenth century, there was general agreement on the need to provide education and training to the district's male youth. Whether girls and young women should be educated beyond grammar school was still open to question. In 1819 a forum, consisting only of men, was held in Washington City to discuss the following: *"Would it be for the benefit of society that women should have the same education as men?"* The first gentleman asked, "Of what use, would the *exact sciences* be in cutting a gown or making a pudding? What use would a lady make of Algebra or geometry in her household affairs?" Another countered: "For if women continue to study only *amusements* instead of *knowledge*, she becomes a voluntary slave of man, for *ignorance* is another word for *slavery* and *knowledge* for *independence*"[1]

In spite of the ongoing debate, most parents of girls and young women in the District of Columbia were able to piece together some form of education or training for their daughters. The venues for this education varied, as did the goals, but instruction in needlework was a consistent theme.

At one end of the education continuum was apprenticeship and indenture for a specified period of years. As described in Chapter 2, 1803 records for apprenticeship indentures in Alexandria reveal that Elizabeth Reardon was apprenticed to Jacob Leap's household at the age of six "to learn the mystery of house keeper and seamstress."[2]

---

[1] *City of Washington Gazette,* June 15, 1819.

[2] T. Michael Miller, *Portrait of a Town, Alexandria, District of Columbia 1820–1830* (Bowie, Md.: Heritage Books, 1995), 409.

In 1811, David Ollphin apprenticed his almost nine-year-old daughter, Anna, to Thomas Richardson until the age of sixteen "to learn common housework and needlework."[3]

Another option was for girls to receive instruction at home from their mothers or from a private governess. This was the venue chosen by Mary Hazelhurst and Benjamin Henry Latrobe, architect for the Capitol, who elected to educate their daughter Julia at home.[4] Not all mothers welcomed this responsibility. Margaret Bayard Smith, who lived in Washington from 1800 to 1840, related some of the problems she encountered while trying to teach her daughters:

> *As for the poor girls, [her daughters] the regular lessons I planned to give them are out of the question, for as I said before Bayard [infant son] and company break through all regularity, and they have had but one or two lessons; if Mr. S. [Smith] would let me I should immediately send them to school, for under present circumstances joined to the prospect before me, I do not see how I can possibly teach them.*[5]

These difficulties may help to explain the huge popularity of more formal schooling opportunities for girls and young women in the District, both public and private. Although needlework was an integral part of the curriculum until almost the middle of the century, teachers adapted to meet whatever trends developed in this increasingly cosmopolitan and diverse society. Course offerings were especially broad in schools where the teachers had themselves received a well-rounded education, or in schools that were sufficiently successful that they could hire masters with training in the higher branches of learning.

Figure 11-2. Advertisement in the Washington *National Intelligencer*, May 23, 1808.

Most teachers in the District of Columbia left little in the way of evidence to document their existence. However, it is sometimes possible to lift the veil on the teaching and learning enterprise by reading between the lines of teachers' advertisements or uncovering the memoires of a former student. Following are three vignettes that help to illuminate early female education in the District.

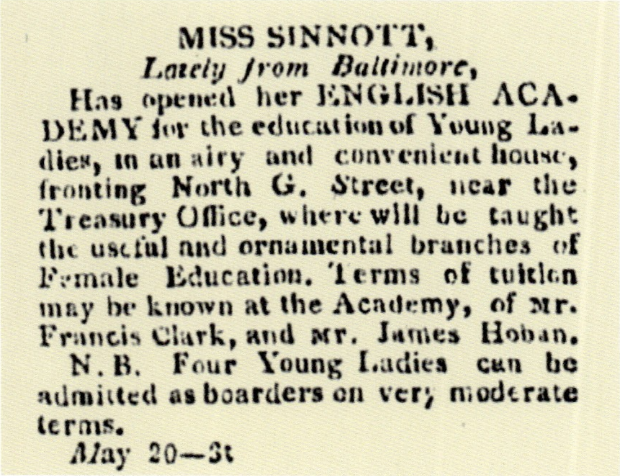

> MISS SINNOTT, Lately from Baltimore, Has opened her ENGLISH ACADEMY for the education of Young Ladies, in an airy and convenient house, fronting North G. Street, near the Treasury Office, where will be taught the useful and ornamental branches of Female Education. Terms of tuition may be known at the Academy, of Mr. Francis Clark, and Mr. James Hoban.
> N. B. Four Young Ladies can be admitted as boarders on very moderate terms.
> May 20—3t

MISS MARGARET SINNOTT: AN ENDURING TEACHER

One District needlework teacher's long career can be traced through the many advertisements she placed in local newspapers over a period of thirty-four years. In 1808 (her first known advertisement), a Miss Sinnott informed the residents of Washington City that she was from Baltimore and prepared to teach "the useful and ornamental branches of Female Education" (Figure 11-2). Her "ENGLISH ACADEMY" was located "in an airy and convenient house, fronting North G Street, near the Treasury Office," with room for four boarders. In 1809, Miss Sinnott requested that parents and guardians "cause the Young Ladies to be punctual to meet in their respective classes." In 1810 she added writing, arithmetic, English grammar, and

---

3 Dorothy S. Provine, *District of Columbia Indentures of Apprenticeship 1801–1893* (Lovettsville, Va.: Willow Bend Books, 1998), 48.

4 Talbot Hamlin, *Benjamin Henry Latrobe* (New York: Oxford University Press, 1955), 459.

5 Margaret Bayard Smith, *The First Forty Years of Washington Society in the Family Letters of Margaret Bayard Smith*, Gaillard Hunt, ed. (New York: Frederick Ungar Publishing Co. 1906), 84.

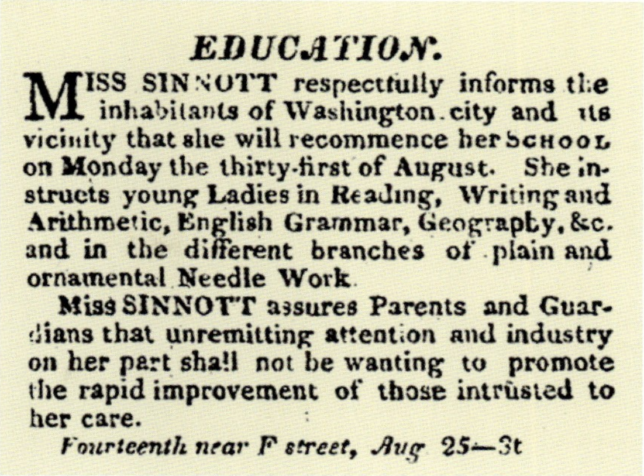

EDUCATION.

MISS SINNOTT respectfully informs the inhabitants of Washington city and its vicinity that she will recommence her SCHOOL on Monday the thirty-first of August. She instructs young Ladies in Reading, Writing and Arithmetic, English Grammar, Geography, &c. and in the different branches of plain and ornamental Needle Work.

Miss SINNOTT assures Parents and Guardians that unremitting attention and industry on her part shall not be wanting to promote the rapid improvement of those intrusted to her care.

Fourteenth near F street, Aug 25—3t

Figure 11-3. Advertisement in the *National Intelligencer*, August 25, 1812.

geography to the curriculum of plain and ornamental needlework, and she announced a new location for her school on 14th Street near F Street (Figure 11-3).[6]

Miss Sinnot did not list her first name in her advertisements until 1827, at which point she referred to herself as "Miss Margaret Sinnott."[7] Being a single woman in nineteenth-century America was a socially undesirable position. Possibly Miss Sinnott chose to use only her last name in early advertisements in order to draw attention to her family name, a name that may have carried status.[8] It is also possible that after nineteen years of teaching she finally felt comfortable relying on her own reputation as a teacher.

Government imposed embargoes on foreign trade leading up to the War of 1812 resulted in economic hardship for the residents of the District of Columbia, as elsewhere.[9] To supplement her teaching income in 1812, Miss Sinnott offered "Fancy-Dress Ornaments" for sale. These included gold and silver trimmings for dresses and ornaments for the head. She also had room in her house to take in six boarders. To remain competitive, Miss Sinnott expanded her curriculum by offering French and reading. Evidently this move was not as successful as hoped, for in October 1814 she returned to Baltimore to open an academy in her brother's house.[10] She may have remained there for several years, offering the same subjects she had taught in Washington City. It is unknown whether the failing economy, instructional competition, or even homesickness caused her to return to Baltimore, but her brother was a doctor who provided free or inexpensive space for her school in the center of the city.[11]

Margaret Sinnott's Washington City advertisements resumed in 1821, and she advertised her school periodically through 1842. She changed locations frequently but was always well situated and close to the population centers of the President's House and Capitol Hill. In 1822 she moved to "11th street nearly opposite Mr. J. M'Leod's new building."[12] This may have not been an auspicious choice. John McLeod was a well-known teacher in Washington City, and he offered "Plain and ornamental Needle Work . . . cheaper than ever taught before in this district."[13] The next year she moved once again to D Street, Varnum's Row.[14] This was near

---

6 *National Intelligencer and Washington Advertiser*, May 20, 1808, August 18, 1809, and November 5, 1810. Her departure from Baltimore in 1808 corresponds in time to her father James's second marriage, to Ann Doyle.

7 Washington *Daily National Intelligencer*, March 7, 1827.

8 http://www.term-papers.us/ts/aa/aky82.shtml.

9 *Embargo Act* of 1807, and *Non-Intercourse Act* of 1809.

10 *National Intelligencer*, April 21, 1812. Dr. Jonah D Sinnott left Baltimore and moved to Washington City in 1825. See ibid., December 13, 1825.

11 Margaret Sinnott may have spent some of the intervening years on the Eastern Shore of Maryland, where the family had roots. The federal census for 1820 located a "Margt Sennott," next door to a Solomon Sennott in Queen Anne's County. Also in 1820, Miss Sinnott had a letter waiting for her in the Baltimore post office, suggesting she was elsewhere at that time.

12 McLeod's 1846 obituary states, "He was a native of Ireland, but for more than 40 years past was a citizen of Washington, during all of which time he was successfully engaged in the education of youth & the embellishment of the city having built 4 handsome seminaries & done more by his system of education than any other man who ever resided among us." Dixon, *National Intelligencer Newspaper Abstracts*, 576.

13 Washington *Daily National Intelligencer*, August, 8, 1821.

14 Ibid., October 14, 1823.

the intersection of 10th Street, D Street, and Pennsylvania Avenue, halfway between the President's House and the Capitol.

No samplers have been identified from Miss Sinnott's school, but because of an intriguing advertisement published in 1823, one can conclude that sampler making was part of her needlework curriculum.

> LOST, on Tuesday forenoon last, the 18th inst. by one of Miss Sinnott's pupils, on her way to school . . . a partly finished SAMPLER; it was folded up in a spotted blue and white handkerchief marked T.K. and enclosed in a black bombazette bag. There were a half dozen different kinds of sewing silk also in the bag.[15]

In 1810, early in her teaching career, Miss Sinnott informed her patrons and the public that "she has employed a gentleman of respectability to attend daily to her academy."[16] Teachers often listed men in their advertisements as references to add propriety or support an expanded curriculum. By 1827 times had changed, and Miss Sinnott no longer felt she needed the respectability or assistance of a male teacher. She boasted that she was teaching "by herself, independent of any male Teacher."[17]

Over the years other subjects were added to the curriculum, including orthography (spelling), the use of maps in geography, French, and Latin. Her last advertisement appeared in September 1842. At this late date Miss Sinnott still offered the "ornamental branches," even though most other teachers had discontinued them in favor of a more rigorous academic education. She modestly stated that she "does not wish to boast of her ability; she simply refers to the numerous families whose children she has taught for many years."[18]

Margaret Sinnott's long teaching career in Washington City testifies to her talent and her love of teaching. By frequently changing locations, yet maintaining patronage, she managed the financial aspects of teaching and consequently supported herself as a single woman for thirty-four years.

THE TYSON SISTERS: A FAMILY AFFAIR

One of the few occupations open to females was teaching school. Mary A. Tyson, and eventually all five of her sisters, chose teaching as their career and means for economic independence. Instead of teaching in different schools, though, they teamed up to teach together. The Tyson sisters began teaching in Baltimore, then moved to Washington City, and finally settled in Prince George's County, Maryland.

Mary A. Tyson (1811–1906) and her sisters Elizabeth E. (1813–1898), Frances E. (1815–1898), Jane S. (1817–1878), Martha A. (1822–1898), and Letitia E. (1825–1907), were all born in Baltimore to Elizabeth Ellicott (1785–1834) and William Tyson (1782–1863), who were married on October 26, 1803, at the Friends Meeting in Elk Ridge, Maryland. William's father, Elisha Tyson, was a prominent Quaker abolitionist and owned a prosperous flour mill that he left to William and his brothers. Elizabeth Tyson died in 1834, leaving thirteen children. It was probably economic necessity that prompted the Tyson sisters, with Mary as their leader, to open a "Seminary for Young Ladies" in Baltimore shortly after their mother's death. After teaching in Baltimore for several years, they moved to Washington City in

---

15 Ibid., November 21, 1823. Bombazette is a worsted (wool) cloth which could be twill or plain weave and was finished without glaze. See Florence M. Montgomery, *Textiles in America 1650–1870* (New York: W. W. Norton & Company, 1984), 172.

16 Washington *National Intelligencer,* April 25, 1810.

17 Washington *Daily National Intelligencer,* March 7, 1827.

18 Ibid., September 15, 1842. Around that time she had "14 scholars" in what the 1840 federal census referred to as a "primary/common school."

1840. Their new seminary was located on F Street between 12th and 13th Streets, and by 1845 the sisters taught

> *a thorough knowledge of all the solid branches of education, and the French and Latin languages; Music on the Piano and Guitar; Worsted and Ornamental Needlework in all its various branches; also the making of Wax Flowers, with a knowledge of the preparation of the wax.*[19]

In 1845 the number of pupils was limited to thirty-six day scholars (Figure 11-4). The Tyson sisters advertised in 1847 that they were opening an additional establishment so they could accommodate boarding students. They noted that "the Institution is in the healthiest part of the city; the water is excellent, the air pure, and the play grounds are sufficiently large to permit the pupils to use healthful exercise."[20] The school evidently prospered enough that they could buy the house and adjoining property, just a few blocks from the President's House.

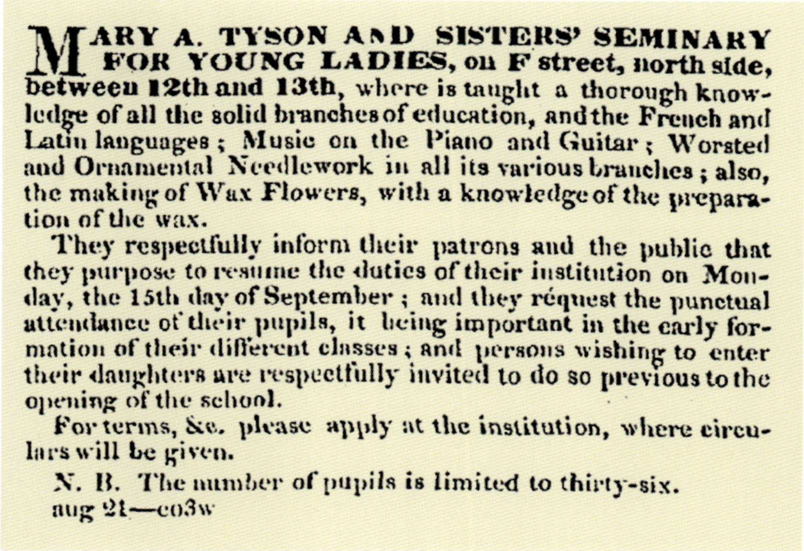

MARY A. TYSON AND SISTERS' SEMINARY FOR YOUNG LADIES, on F street, north side, between 12th and 13th, where is taught a thorough knowledge of all the solid branches of education, and the French and Latin languages; Music on the Piano and Guitar; Worsted and Ornamental Needlework in all its various branches; also, the making of Wax Flowers, with a knowledge of the preparation of the wax.

They respectfully inform their patrons and the public that they purpose to resume the duties of their institution on Monday, the 15th day of September; and they request the punctual attendance of their pupils, it being important in the early formation of their different classes; and persons wishing to enter their daughters are respectfully invited to do so previous to the opening of the school.

For terms, &c. please apply at the institution, where circulars will be given.

N. B. The number of pupils is limited to thirty-six.

aug 21—eo3w

Figure 11-4. Advertisement in the Washington *Daily National Intelligencer*, September 5, 1845.

Like Margaret Sinnott, the Tyson sisters continued to teach ornamental needlework long after other teachers had dropped it from the curricula. One example is known. Mary M. Bryant worked a "Map of Asia" at the "M. A. Tyson & Sisters Seminary / July 11th. 1848." (Figure 11-5).[21]

In 1850 the Tyson sisters expanded again and "erected a large and well ventilated apartment," for which they added a charge of $1.50 for fuel during the winter season.[22] Their father's name appears on all the deeds and loan transactions, but he promptly deeded the property in its entirety to his six daughters, indicating it was the sisters' money that had been used for the purchases.[23] Mrs. Jeannie Tree Rives remembers the Misses Tysons' school as the largest school for girls in Washington when she was a child. "They occupied two houses, so numerous were the pupils."[24]

The Tyson sisters remained steadfast members of the Religious Society of Friends (Quakers). The parents of boarding students were informed that "the pupils will attend public worship at that meeting, unless a different arrangement be desired by their parents or guardians. There will be no interference with their religious principles further than to instruct them in the practice of virtue and truth."[25]

---

19 Washington *Daily National Intelligencer*, September 5, 1845.

20 Ibid., August 23, 1847.

21 Mary was probably a daughter of John Y. and Ann Moulder Bryant and was born in 1836 in Pennsylvania. John Bryant was an attorney and leader of the Northern Liberty Fire Company in Washington City during the 1840s. In 1864, Mary married Joseph Meyers.

22 Washington *Daily National Intelligencer*, September 5, 1850.

23 Probably a necessity of business at the time. Research by Lawrence L. Lacquement, correspondence to Gloria Seaman Allen, May 23, 1995.

24 Mrs. Jennie Tree Rives, "Old-Time Place and People in Washington," *Records of the Columbia Historical Society* (November 7, 1898): 78. Mrs. Rives was the daughter of Lambert and Laura Borrows Tree and was born ca. 1842 in Washington, D.C.

25 Washington *Daily National Intelligencer*, August 23, 1847.

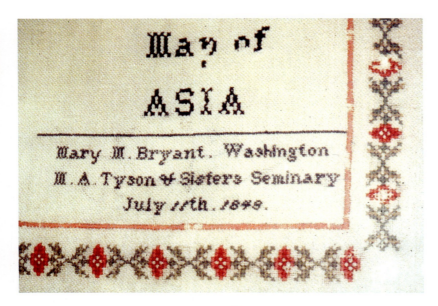

Figure 11-5. Detail of map sampler worked by Mary M. Bryant. Washington City, 1848. Inscribed: "Map of / ASIA / Mary M. Bryant. Washington / M. A. Tyson & Sisters Seminary / July 11th. 1848." Wool and silk on wool ground. Location unknown

In 1855 the Tyson sisters sold their property and moved to the family's country residence near Laurel in Prince George's County, Maryland.[26] The need to care for their ailing father, increasing competition for pupils, and the economy may have been reasons for this move. They again opened a seminary and called it the "Alnwick French and English Female Seminary of M.A. Tyson and Sisters."[27] It was situated "sixteen miles from Washington City, near the Baltimore and Washington Railroad and Turnpike, in a place at once beautiful and healthful." Ornamental needlework remained an option in their curriculum.[28]

The 1860 census indicates that the Tyson sisters were living with their father and siblings. By 1870 they had a few boarding students, and a younger relative named Elizabeth was teaching with them. How long the school continued is unknown, but in the 1880 census Mary, Elizabeth, Martha, and Letitia were still listed as teachers. Mary A. Tyson enjoyed a long life and died on February 6, 1906.

JULIA HIERONYMOUS TEVIS: A STUDENT IN THE DISTRICT OF COLUMBIA

Relatively little is known about the lives of young girls growing up in the early years of the District of Columbia. The many newspaper advertisements for teachers and schools offering needlework instruction along with reading and writing, suggest that most female students in the district were acquiring sewing skills as well as a basic education. Julia Hieronymous (1799–1880) was one of those students, and she wrote about her educational experiences in her book *Sixty Years in a School-Room*. Julia attended at least three different schools while she lived in Georgetown and Washington City.

Julia Hieronymous was born on December 5, 1799, in Clark County, Kentucky, to Pendleton and Mary Bush Hieronymous. Her grandparents were part of the early migration from Virginia to Kentucky in search of land for farming. At the age of four, Julia went with her older brother to the local country school and learned to read. When she was seven, the Hieronymous family moved from Kentucky in the hope of finding better schools. First they settled in Paris, Virginia, where Julia attended the local day school. The subjects covered were reading, writing, cyphering, and spelling, as well as instruction in manners. On Saturdays she attended dancing school.

The family next relocated to Winchester, Virginia, where Julia attended a Female Academy under the superintendence of the Reverend Dr. William Hill, a Presbyterian minister. School hours were from eight to twelve in the morning and from two until four in the afternoon. Hill placed great emphasis on writing compositions. During

---

26 From research conducted by Lawrence L. Lacquement, 1996.

27 Named for the Tyson ancestral home in Wales. See Allen, *A Maryland Sampling*, 119.

28 *Alnwick French and English Female Seminary of M.A. Tyson & Sisters: Circular for the Seventeenth Annual Session* (Washington: Henry Polkinhorn, 1856).

the summer months Julia attended a sewing school from four until six in the afternoon. Her teacher was from Philadelphia and loved to tell the girls stories about the time of the "yellow fever plague." Julia wrote: "No wonder our samplers and various kinds of needlework dropped from our trembling hands, while, panic stricken, we were prompted to run as if the terrible plague was already rushing upon us."[29] Even at a young age, Julia understood it was important to begin learning sewing skills that she would later use to make her own clothing. On Friday afternoons and Saturdays, Julia attended dancing school.

The family moved to Georgetown in November 1813, just in time to celebrate the victory of General William Henry Harrison over the British and Indians at the Battle of the Thames.[30] While in Georgetown, Julia attended a school conducted by Mr. and Mrs. Simpson, where she studied "music, drawing, French and various kinds of embroidery." Julia wrote that "the girls in this school wrought the most elaborate samplers with a variety of stitches and bordered them with pinks, roses, and morning-glories, and sometimes, when the canvas was large enough, with the name and age of every member of the family."[31] Acquiring needlework skills made it possible for Julia and the other students to embroider their own fashionable French-worked collars instead of buying them.[32]

In spite of the external pressures and difficulties caused by the War of 1812, Julia was happy attending school and after the bombardment of Fort McHenry had vivid memories of Mr. Simpson playing the "Star-Spangled Banner" and everyone singing it with great patriotic fervor. However, life was not easy in the District. The war caused shortages of food and wood for fuel. The government had few resources and so limited itself to helping the army. A few days before the British descended on Washington City on August 24, 1814, Julia and her siblings were sent to safety in the country while their parents remained in the city.

In 1815, Julia attended the boarding school taught by English-born Miss Charlotte Taylor and her sister. Although the girls disliked the sister (and often disobeyed her), they loved and adored Miss Charlotte. While at school the students occasionally attended social events "not as young ladies, but schoolgirls, to profit by what we saw and heard." Julia's first and only public ball was the inauguration *fete* for President James Monroe. "The impression made was that of an ostentatious display of wealth and splendor, little in accordance with the republican simplicity which should constitute the dignity of a nation so utterly rejecting high sounding titles and oriental magnificence." Miss Taylor was also responsible for the religious education of the girls and took them to Saint John's Protestant Episcopal Church, near the President's House. The Reverend Mr. Hawley was the pastor, "an evangelical preacher of the deepest piety."[33]

In February 1818, the *Daily National Intelligencer* published an article about Miss Taylor. The anonymous writer said:

> we have long witnessed with regret and mortification the want of an institution amongst us, of the first order, for the education of young ladies. . . . The character of Miss Taylor, . . . leave[s] us no doubt of her patronage and success. . . . [we] feel great confidence in the

---

29 Julia A. Tevis, *Sixty Years in a School-Room* (Cincinnati: Western Methodist Book Concern, 1878), 69.

30 After the British defeat in the Battle of Lake Erie, U.S. troops under Gen. William H. Harrison pursued retreating British soldiers across the Ontario peninsula. A combined force of British and their Indian allies met an American army of of 3,500 at the Thames River, and the resulting U.S. victory ended the Indian alliance with the British and made Harrison a national hero.

31 Tevis, *Sixty Years in a School-Room*, 84.

32 French-work was elaborate embroidery using white thread on white muslin fabric. The stitches were mostly satin and eyelet.

33 Tevis, *Sixty years in a School-Room*, 110, 113.

satisfaction she will give to the parents and friends of her pupils, both as to their personal accomplishments and moral correctness.[34]

Charlotte Taylor's sister married John Anderson, an officer in the U.S. Army, in May 1818, and they settled in Detroit. Miss Charlotte went with them, thus ending her teaching career in Washington City.

Julia stayed home a few months to acquire some household skills and then entered the school of Mrs. Henry Stone in Washington City. Mrs. Stone, "an educated and highly accomplished English woman, of well-deserved reputation as a teacher . . . spent two years in Paris, where she acquired a thorough knowledge of the French language, which she spoke fluently."[35] "The greatest delight of the older girls was to see Mrs. Stone dressed for one of Madame de Neuville's gay parties, and admire her petite figure, covered with rich laces and jewels; then await her return and listen to her descriptions of all she had seen in the gay world" (See Figure 8-1).[36]

Mrs. Stone offered reading, writing, and arithmetic, as well as history, geography, and the usual needlework. Mr. Stone was a lithographic printer who taught drawing and painting to the students and provided patterns for their needlework. Since Mrs. Stone's residence was on Pennsylvania Avenue in the busiest part of the city, Julia's parents decided to have her board there and also sent her three younger sisters. In addition to her own studies, Julia helped her sisters prepare their lessons. When Congress was in session, the older girls "were taken by Mrs. Stone once a week to hear the celebrated speakers, or listen to debates on interesting subjects."[37]

During the winter, dancing lessons were provided once a week, as well as music and drawing three times a week for an hour. French was also taught and the girls had a French governess "who chatted French incessantly."[38] While keeping up with her studies, Julia also made her own clothes as well as clothing for her sisters, giving her plenty of opportunity to use the needlework skills she had learned during her earlier schooling.

Mrs. Stone's "pupils were endeared to her by a thousand little delicate attentions and unexpected favors." However, in comparing Miss Taylor and Mrs. Stone, Julia wrote that the latter was "kind, indulgent, and forgiving, but was no disciplinarian; hence scenes of confusion frequently occurred among the boarding pupils never witnessed under the firm but gentle sway of Miss Taylor, whose dignified presence was alone sufficient to still the troubled waters."[39] When Julia entered her nineteenth year, she left school and returned to live with her family in Georgetown. While at home she continued French and music lessons.

Julia's father had lent a large amount of money to a friend who turned out to be a bad risk. By 1820 this resulted in financial difficulty for the Hieronymous family.[40] Mr. Hieronymous went to Saint Louis to get help from relatives and Julia realized she should find suitable employment. Mrs. Stone wrote a recommendation for her, and in 1820 Julia obtained a teaching position in Abingdon,

---

34 Washington *Daily National Intelligencer*, February 12, 1818.

35 Tevis, *Sixty years in a School-Room*, 117.

36 Baron Hyde de Neuville came to Washington as the French ambassador in 1816. Mrs. Stone had become a friend of the baroness when she attended school in Paris, and even though they now moved in different social circles, their friendship was renewed.

37 Tevis, *Sixty years in a School-Room*, 118.

38 Ibid., 118.

39 Ibid., 117, 125.

40 Seeking to curb speculation in commodities and western lands following the War of 1812, the Second Bank of the United States sharply contracted its extension of credit and in doing so provoked the panic of 1819. The downturn hit the southern and western states hardest, and many banks suspended specie payments or closed their doors.

Virginia. Mrs. Stone also gave her "a number of patterns for drawing and painting and a quantity of white velvet on which to paint in water-colors."[41]

Julia Hieronymous married the Reverend John Tevis on March 19, 1824, and they moved to Shelbyville, Kentucky (Figure 11-6). Once there, they founded the Science Hill Female Academy. Despite the prevailing wisdom that girls only needed reading and writing, Julia also included science, math, history, and rhetoric in the curriculum. Needlework was not neglected and the students stitched samplers with tall brick houses using the "twenty different stitches taught in the olden times."[42] Julia Hieronymous Tevis continued to teach at Science Hill Female Academy until she sold the school in 1879. She died a short time later on April 21, 1880.

Figure 11-6.
Julia Hieronymous Tevis, (1799–1880), 1861.
Oil on canvas, by Charles V. Bond.
35 x 28 in.
The Filson Historical Society, Louisville, Kentucky

---

41 Tevis, *Sixty Years in a School-Room*, 168–69.

42 Ibid., 326.

AFTERWORD

Some Reflections on Samplers from the District of Columbia

THIS SELECTION OF SAMPLERS, albeit from a small geographic area, illustrates the variety of needlework styles that were present in late eighteenth-century Alexandria, and after 1800 in the District of Columbia. The stylistic range reflects the demographics of the District's three distinct urban areas and their varied influences on needlework instruction for girls and young women. Although there was some stylistic fluidity between Georgetown and Washington City, styles popular in Alexandria did not seem to cross the Potomac River.

Samplers stitched in the new federal city of Washington show the influence of Philadelphia, as teachers and students relocated from the former seat of government. Alexandria samplers, on the other hand, frequently reflect a Quaker influence—their teachings, migratory patterns, and the early establishment of meeting houses in northern Virginia and central Maryland. The high style pictorial embroideries on silk with applied paper features and the embroidered replicas of the "Plan of the City of Washington" are unique to Alexandria with its affluent merchant class.

Samplers from the Young Ladies' Academy in Georgetown, unusual in their use of religious motifs and verses, reveal the school's appeal to wealthy Catholics in that town and southern Maryland. Surviving silk embroideries made by students at the academy confirm the school's popularity among the elite.

The early instability of Washington City, whose population and economy were dominated by the federal government, is reflected in the diverse styles of its needlework. One exception is the Washington Navy Yard, a community of its own within the city that provided employment, ancillary trades, and greater stability. Samplers from the daughters of Navy Yard families reveal similar design formats and repeated motifs over a period of more than thirty years, attesting to the relative continuity of their community.

Given the variety of needlework traditions entering the District with a growing number of newcomers, the absence of certain regional needlework forms is striking. Even though Georgetown was established in what was then Maryland, and an additional area of Maryland was ceded to the District, no Baltimore influence has been found. Missing are the monumental building samplers. Stitched images of the President's House and the Capitol are unknown, as are scenes of the city burning during the War of 1812, such as the one believed to depict the Richmond Theatre fire of 1811.[1] Missing, too, are genealogical samplers, even though Julia Hieronymous recalled in her memoirs that large samplers "with the name and age of every member of the family" were stitched by classmates in the Georgetown school of Mr. and Mrs. Simpson.[2]

Samplers with religious imagery distinguish those of the Young Ladies' Academy of Georgetown. However, none are graveside memorials to loved ones, a popular needlework form from a rival female Catholic school, Saint Joseph's Academy in Emmitsburg, Maryland. Also puzzling are the different survival rates for samplers and pictorial embroideries from these two schools of long duration. From the Young Ladies' Academy, founded in 1799 and still in existence today with an active alumnae association, fewer than fifteen examples of needlework are known to exist. Saint Joseph's Academy was established a decade later by the Sisters of Charity and ceased as a preparatory school in 1901, yet the order's archives contain more than thirty-five needlework examples, and more than a dozen other pieces can be found in museum and private collections.

No samplers by African American students have been found from schools operating in the District of Columbia, though many teachers, both black and white, provided needlework instruction to young women of color throughout the nineteenth century. In addition, no samplers can be associated with certainty to a Lancasterian school, despite the fact that these schools established in Georgetown, Alexandria, and Washington City were among the first in the United States. Assuming they followed the British program, a marking sampler would have been a student's final sewing project.

We can hope that some of the missing pieces of this puzzle will someday emerge. As previously unknown samplers and pictorial embroideries make their way to auction, or surface from private and public collections, we anticipate that more examples of schoolgirl needlework will be recognized as being similar to pieces from the District of Columbia. As the body of girlhood embroideries from its three major urban centers increases, scholars will be able to construct an even clearer picture of what Columbia's daughters created in their needlework classes.

---

1 Virginian Sally Clark Washington stitched a sampler in 1812 that commemorates the Richmond Theatre fire of December 26, 1811. Collection of The Valentine Richmond History Center, Richmond, Virginia.

2 Tevis, *Sixty Years in a School-Room*, 84.

Appendices

Figure I-1.
Embroidered picture worked by Jane Whann Balch, 1819.
Moravian Girls' School, Lititz, Pennsylvania.
Silk, chenille, watercolor, and ink on silk ground.
16 ½ in. diameter.
Dumbarton House, The National Society of The Colonial Dames of America, Washington, D.C., 42.2

Jane Whann Balch (1805-1884) was born in Georgetown, D.C. to Elizabeth Beall and the Reverend Stephen Bloomer Balch. She attended the Moravian school in Lititz, Lancaster County, Pennsylvania, where she stitched this embroidery at the age of fourteen. Her subject, the parable of Palemon and Lavinia, was included in the "Autumn" passage of Scottish poet James Thomson's widely circulated poem *The Seasons*. This subject appears frequently on schoolgirl embroideries.
(See Figure 3-4).

APPENDIX I

SAMPLERS AND EMBROIDERED PICTURES FROM THE DISTRICT OF COLUMBIA

Susi B. Slocum

Until 1847, the District of Columbia was an amalgamation of two thriving seaport towns, Alexandria and Georgetown, and the new federal area known as Washington City. The Navy Yard, on the Eastern Branch of the Potomac River, dominated the southeast quadrant of Washington City. Providing various levels and types of education across these localities were churches, church affiliates (such as the Young Ladies' Academy of Georgetown), private enterprises, and public schools.

Because the position of teacher was one of the few acceptable occupations for women, many chose female education as a career, either temporarily or permanently. Embroidery was a mainstay of early female education, and there is ample evidence that numerous teachers provided various types of needlework instruction in the District of Columbia, beginning in the late eighteenth century and continuing through the first half of the nineteenth century. Unfortunately, only a small proportion of the samplers and embroidered pictures that resulted from this instruction have been located.

Appendix I provides information for 128 known examples of needlework documented as being stitched within the geographical boundaries of the District of Columbia. Arranged alphabetically by maker and city (Alexandria, Georgetown, Washington City), the diverse pieces of schoolgirl embroidery date from 1784 to 1860. Only sixteen are silk embroideries, comprising both embroidered pictures and maps. Three of the four maps are the spectacular "Plan of the City of Washington," and feature a portrait of George Washington. The remaining 112 schoolgirl embroideries are samplers.

Information in Appendix I about the maker includes whenever possible the full name, age, date of birth, and home place. Each sampler or embroidered picture is further identified by a brief description. Also listed, if known, is the completion or inscribed date, location where the embroidery was made, and current or last known owner. The list segregates the three governing entities and adds a brief section for District of Columbia girls who wrought known embroidery outside of the locality. Information in brackets indicates missing letters, assumed designation of an initial, or known names not marked on the embroidery. Additional ascribed information, such as a misspelled name or known name, is denoted by parentheses. Based on research or stylistic resemblance, some information is marked as "[attributed]."

A few observations, drawn from the data in Appendix I:

- The known schoolgirl embroideries from the District of Columbia are spread across the three cities as follows: forty-six examples from Alexandria, thirty-three from Georgetown, and forty-nine from Washington City. However, of the examples from Washington City, only one is a silk embroidery.

- Of the 128 known embroideries listed for the District of Columbia, thirty-nine are noted as being known from or attributed to twelve schools, academies, or seminaries:

  For Alexandria's forty-six examples, ten samplers or silk embroideries are from two schools.

  For Georgetown's thirty-three examples, twenty-one samplers or silk embroideries are from four academies or seminaries.

  For Washington City's forty-nine examples, eight samplers are from six schools.

- Just over 59 percent of all of the needlework examples were stitched in the first three decades of the nineteenth century. Work from the eighteenth century is only known from Alexandria and Georgetown. The earliest Washington City sampler in this study is dated 1803.

- A high percentage (69 percent) of the known needlework documented as being from the District of Columbia has an inscribed place name: e.g., Alexandria, Georgetown, and Washington City.

- Dating practices for samplers from Washington City were unusually complete. For 59 percent of the examples, the date included month, day, and year. Adding those with only month and year, the percentage increases to 69 percent. In 47 percent of Washington City samplers, the day in the date is stitched as an ordinal number, e.g., July 20th 1813.

- Of the thirteen samplers stitched in the vicinity of Washington City's Navy Yard between 1810 and 1842, six include a date that refers to the girl's birth date (day and month), in addition to a full date of completion.

KEY TO OWNER ABBREVIATIONS

AM	American Museum in Britain, Bath, UK
B&C	*American Samplers* by Ethel Stanwood Bolton & Eva Johnston Coe
CHS	Cohasset Historical Society, Cohasset, MA
CWF	Colonial Williamsburg Foundation, Williamsburg, VA
DAR	National Society Daughters of the American Revolution, Washington, D. C.
DH-CDA	Dumbarton House, The National Society of The Colonial Dames of America, Washington, D. C.
FAMCC	Fredericksburg Area Museum and Cultural Center, Fredericksburg, VA
GVM	Georgetown Visitation Monastery Archives, Washington, D. C.
HSCC	Historical Society of Carroll County, Westminster, MD
Lyceum	The Lyceum, Alexandria's History Museum, Alexandria, VA
MdHS	Maryland Historical Society, Baltimore, MD
MESDA	Museum of Early Southern Decorative Arts, Winston-Salem, NC
MMA	The Metropolitan Museum of Art, New York, NY
MMS	Manassas Museum System, Manassas, VA
MV	George Washington's Mount Vernon Estate, Museum & Gardens, Mount Vernon, VA
NMAH	National Museum of American History, Smithsonian Institution, Washington, D. C.
PMA	Philadelphia Museum of Art
RH	Ruggles House, Columbia Falls, Maine
SSM	Sandy Spring Museum, Sandy Spring, MD
Winterthur	Henry Francis du Pont Winterthur Museum, Garden & Library, Wilmington, DE
WFCHS	Winchester-Frederick County Historical Society, Winchester, VA
WSHS	Washington State Historical Society, Tacoma, WA

DOCUMENTED DISTRICT OF COLUMBIA SAMPLERS AND EMBROIDERED PICTURES
Italics denote an actual inscription on the needlework.

ALEXANDRIA

Last Name	First Name	Age	Birth Date	Date Made	Type
Atkinson	Sarah E. (Elizabeth)		1 OCT 1843	1850-1855	Sampler, pictorial, mourning verse
Barton	Elizabeth	11	1798	ca. 1809	Sampler, architectural, pictorial, verse
Beal	Mercy			1796	Band sampler
Bontz	Mary Ann	9	22 DEC 1818	JUNE 1828	Sampler, floral, basket, verse "Religion"
Brown	Sarah N. (Neill)	8	1805	ca. 1813	Sampler, marking
[Campbell]	[Anne]		8 JULY 1796	1810-1815	Embroidered picture, Palemon and Lavinia
Carson	Ann	10	4 MAY 1808	JULY 1818	Sampler, architectural, (cornucopia motif)
Copper	Christiana Davis		1774	ca. 1786	Sampler, motifs, verse
Custis	Martha	7	31 DEC 1777	DEC 1784	Sampler, religious, verse
Fifield	Rebecca Ann	7	1816	SEPT 1823	Sampler, marking
Fleming	Margaret	9	26 APR 1801	ca. 1810	Sampler, architectural, verse
[Fleming]	[Margaret]		26 APR 1801	1810-1815	Embroidered picture, classical
Gonsolve	Mary Filana			1832	Sampler, architectural, pictorial, verse
[Graham]	[Elizabeth]		1790	1800-1803	Embroidered map, *Plan of the City of Washington*
Green	Betsy	12	ca. 1786	1798	Sampler, marking, verse
Harrison	Mary	11	1819	JULY 1830	Sampler, architectural, verse
Hooff	Julia Maria		1798	ca. 1815	Embroidered picture, Dido and Aeneas
H. [Horwell]	A. [Ann] [May]		ca. 1780	1798	Sampler, verse "On War"
[Horwell]	[Ann]			ca. 1819	Sampler, floral
Horwell	Sarah M. (May)	8	ca. 1799	1807	Sampler, marking, verse
[Horwell]	[Sarah May]		1799	ca. 1809	Sampler, floral
Janney	Hannah		19 MAY 1774	1785	Sampler, motifs, verse "On Education"
Janney	Rebecah	9	14 AUG 1776	1786	Sampler, motifs, verse
Leadbeater	Anna	9	2 OCT 1842	1852	Sampler, marking
Leadbeater	Anna	10	2 OCT 1842	8 mo 1852	Sampler, marking, Quaker dating
Leadbeater	Lucy		DEC 1838	FEB 1852	Sampler, marking
Leap	Ann		11 MAY 1789	1799	Sampler, marking, motifs, verse
[Leap]	[Ann]		11 MAY 1789	1801	Embroidered picture, *An Emblem of America*
[Lemoine]	[Maria Magdalene]		1792	1800-1804	Embroidered map, *Plan of the City of Washington*

Where Made	Home Place	Owner
Alexandria?	Alexandria and "Rippon Lodge", Prince William Co. VA	Private
Alexandria	Alexandria	Private
	Alexandria or Fairfax Co. VA	Private
Alexandria (Mary Lang Muir school) [attributed]	Alexandria	Private
Alexandria	Alexandria	WFCHS
Alexandria (Sarah Eliza Edmonds school) [attributed]	Alexandria	Private
Alexandria (Mary Lang Muir school) [attributed]	Alexandria	B&C
Alexandria [attributed]	Alexandria	MMS
"Abington", Alexandria	"Abington", Alexandria	MV
Alexandria	Alexandria	Private
Alexandria	Alexandria	Private
Alexandria (Sarah Eliza Edmonds school) [attributed]	Alexandria	Private
	Alexandria?	Private
Alexandria	Alexandria	Winterthur
Alexandria		B&C
Alexandria (Mary Lang Muir school) [attributed]	Alexandria	NMAH
Alexandria (Sarah Eliza Edmonds school)	Alexandria	Private
Alexandria [attributed]	Alexandria	CWF
Alexandria [attributed]	Alexandria	B&C
Alexandria	Alexandria	Private
Alexandria [attributed]	Alexandria	B&C
Alexandria [attributed]	Alexandria or Loudoun Co. VA	B&C
Alexandria [attributed]	Alexandria or Loudoun Co. VA	CWF
Alexandria Va	Alexandria	NMAH
Alexandria	Alexandria	NMAH
Alex. Va	Alexandria	Lyceum
Alexandria	Alexandria	Private
Alexandria	Alexandria	Private
Alexandria	Alexandria	DH-CDA

Last Name	First Name	Age	Birth Date	Date Made	Type
Mankin	Elizabeth		1819	OCT 1832	Sampler, marking
McFarlane	Margreter (Margaret)		ca. 1823	1831	Sampler, flower basket, verse
McFarlane	Elizabeth	6	ca. 1834	1840	Sampler, marking
[McKnight]	[Martha Bryan]		7 MAY 1802	1810-1815	Embroidered picture, The Finding of Moses
Muir	Mary	12	2 NOV 1805	JUNE 1818	Sampler, architectural, verse "Religion", (cornucopia motif)
Plummer	Ann	9	ca. 1791	1800	Sampler, marking, Quaker motifs
Potts	H. [Hannah?]			1799	Sampler, map, The State of Maryland
Resler	Eve		ca. 1786	1800-1804	Embroidered map, Plan of the City of Washington
Robertson	Williamina	9	ca. 1818	SEPT 1827	Sampler, marking, verse
Rudd	Ann Tottington	12	1804	1817	Sampler, marking, verse, "George Washington"
Stabler	Mary P. (Pleasants)	11	30 JAN 1809	ca. 1820	Sampler, marking
Suter	Rebecc[a]	10	1809	APRIL 1819	Sampler, verses, "Religion", (cornucopia motif)
Taylor	Hester Dashiell	10	1790	1800	Sampler, marking, architectural, verse, (cornucopia motif)
Vowell	Mary Stewart	8	19 AUG 1823	1831	Sampler, marking
Wood	Ann Maria	7	1825	ca. 1832	Sampler, flower basket, verse
Wood	Marian	13	1805	MAY 1818	Sampler, architectural, floral
Anonymous				1803	Sampler, memorial, Respectfully Addressed to, Mrs Brown On the death of an Infant.

GEORGETOWN

Last Name	First Name	Age	Birth Date	Date Made	Type
Abbot	Martha D. (Duncan)	11	1840	1851	Sampler, marking
Beall	Harriet	13	ca. 1788	1801	Embroidered map - A chart of the World
Beall	Harriet	9	9 MAR 1811	FEB 1821	Sampler, pictorial, landscape
Boarman	Mary Rose	13	ca. 1805	1818	Sampler, marking, religious, verse
Brooke	Mary Rebecca J.	13	25 JAN 1804	1817	Sampler, marking, [religious, verse, unfinished]
Burton	Hannah E.			JULY 1847	Sampler, marking
Carroll	Mary [Ann]	6	1794	1801	Sampler, marking
[Clemens]	[Catherine Ann Lavinia]	17	1840	1857	Wool work, religious - King Solomon
Combs	Celestia Mary	12	ca. 1804	1816	Sampler, marking, religious, verse
Copley	Mary	12	1817	APRIL 1830	Sampler, architectural

Where Made	Home Place	Owner
Alexandria	Alexandria	Private
Alexandria	Alexandria	Private
Alexandria	Alexandria	Private
Alexandria (Sarah Eliza Edmonds school) [attributed]	Alexandria	Private
Alexandria (Mary Lang Muir school)	Alexandria	Lyceum
Alexandria	Alexandria	WSHS
Alexandria	Alexandria?	MdHS
Alexandria	Alexandria	CWF
Alexandria	Alexandria or Fairfax County	Private
Alexandria	Alexandria	Lyceum
Alexandria	Alexandria	NMAH
Alexandria District of Columbia (Mary Lang Muir school) [attributed]	Alexandria	Private
Alexandria	Alexandria	B&C
Alexandria	Alexandria	CHS
Alexandria	Alexandria	Auction
Alexandria (Mary Lang Muir school) [attributed]	Alexandria	CWF
Alex[a] Alexandria		Lyceum
Georgetown Female Seminary (Lydia English)	Georgetown	Private
Georgetown	Georgetown	B&C
Georgetown	Georgetown	MESDA
Young Ladies Academy George Town	Georgetown	GVM
Young Ladies Academy George Tow Town	"Woodbury Manor," Leonardtown, Saint Mary's Co. MD	GVM
Geo Town		Auction
New Academy George Town	"Sweet Air," Baltimore Co. MD	MdHS
Georgetown, Academy of the Visitation	Georgetown	GVM
Young Ladies Academy Georgetown	Chaptico District, Saint Mary's Co. MD	DAR
Georgetown D. C.	Georgetown	Auction

Last Name	First Name	Age	Birth Date	Date Made	Type
Dellaway	Julia Ann			OCT 1832	Sampler, marking, floral, verse
[Dunlop]	[Elizabeth Peter]		1771	ca. 1790	Embroidered picture, floral
Durkee	Elenor	9	12 NOV 1800	1810	Sampler, marking, religious, verse
Fearson	Mary Elizabeth		1824	NOV 18 - - (ca. 1834)	Sampler, marking, verse
Jackson	Artridge Priscilla	9	14 JUN 1820	JULY 1829	Sampler, architectural, (shuttered windows), motifs, verse
Jackson	Emily M.		25 SEP 1798	1808	Sampler, marking, religious, verse
[Jameson]	[Eliza]		1785	1800-1804	Embroidered picture, pastoral
Kurtz	Sarah	9	1795	1804	Sampler, marking, motif, verse
Laird	Barbara L.		1795	ca. 1807	Sampler, marking, floral, verse
Laird	Margaret		1797	ca. 1809	Sampler, marking, floral, motifs, verse
[Lalor]	[Maria Teresa]		ca. 1793	1800-1804	Embroidered picture, pastoral
Laurence	Mary Elizabeth		16 FEB 1812	1829	Sampler, marking, floral, (parrot motif)
Meem	Mary Margaret	14	17 OCT 1821	1836	Sampler, pictorial, (cornucopia motif)
Neale	Eleanora	15	1808	1823	Sampler, floral, verse, (parrot motif)
Nicholls	E. (Elizabeth)	9	8 FEB 1819	ca. 1828	Sampler, marking, verse
Orme	Elizabeth	9	ca. 1825	NOV 1833	Sampler, pictorial, verse, (cornucopia motif)
Ould	Paulina	11	24 MAR 1824	ca. 1835	Sampler, marking
[Queen]	[Catharine F.]		ca. 1788	1800-1804	Embroidered picture, pastoral
Scaggs	Ann Lucretia Mayo	12	ca. 1819	MAR 1831	Sampler, marking, floral basket, verse
Scott	Mary Ann			MAR 1831	Sampler, marking, architectural, (shuttered windows), motifs, verse
Waring	Eleanor	11	2 JUN 1808	1819	Sampler, floral, verse, (parrot motif)
Anonymous				ca. 1800-1804	Embroidered picture, pastoral
Anonymous				ca 1813	Embroidered picture, Wisdom Directing Innocence to the Temple of Learning

WASHINGTON CITY

Last Name	First Name	Age	Birth Date	Date Made	Type
Adams	Elizabeth George	13	13 SEP 1822	MAR 1836	Sampler, marking
Blair	Sarah Jane	9	1817	1827	Sampler, marking, verse
Bohlayer	Mary Christeen	13	19 JAN 1828	1842	Sampler, architectual, (shuttered windows), verse - Navy Yard area
Borrows	Mary Ann	9	12 FEB 1802	JULY 1811	Sampler
Borrows	Susan (Susannah)		1788	JUNE 1803	Sampler, marking, motifs

Where Made	Home Place	Owner
George-town	Georgetown	Private
Georgetown [attributed]	"Tudor Place", Georgetown	Auction
Young Ladies Academy Georg Town	Baltimore	PMA
Miss Bootes's Seminary Georgetown	Georgetown	DAR
Georgetown Female Seminary (Lydia English) [attributed]	Georgetown	DAR
young Ladies Academy Georgetown	Leonardtown, Saint Mary's Co. MD	GVM
Georgetown, Young Ladies Academy	Cornwallis Neck, Charles Co. MD	GVM
	Georgetown	NMAH
Georgetown [attributed]	Georgetown	B&C
Georgetown [attributed]	Georgetown	B&C
Georgetown, Young Ladies Academy	Philadelphia	Private
Young Ladies Academy George Town	Georgetown	Private
George Town DC Female Seminary (Lydia English)	Georgetown	NMAH
Young Ladies Academy George Town	Charles Co. MD	GVM
Georgetown Female Seminary (Lydia English)	Georgetown	Dealer
Georgetown Female Seminary (Lydia English) [attributed]	Georgetown	NMAH
George Town District of Colubia	Georgetown	Auction
Academy of the Visitation, Georgetown. D.C.	Eastern Branch of Potomac, Prince George's Co. MD	GVM
Georgetown	Georgetown	Private
George Town DC. Female Seminary (Lydia English) [attributed]	Georgetown	Dealer
Ladies Academy George Town	Middle Brook Mills, Montgomery Co. MD and Georgetown	Auction
Georgetown, Young Ladies Academy [attributed]		Dealer
	Georgetown?	DAR
Washington City	Spotsylvania VA	FAMCC
Washington City	Washington City	Private
Washington City DC	Washington City, Navy Yard area	Private
Mrs. Gray's School in the city of Washington	Washington City, Navy Yard area	Private
Washington City	Washington City, Navy Yard area	Private

APPENDIX I 225

Last Name	First Name	Age	Birth Date	Date Made	Type
Boswell	Maria	12	4 APR 1800	AUG 1812	Sampler, architectural, verse - Navy Yard
Brightwell	Maria			OCT 1827	Sampler, marking, motifs
Brown	Ann Eliza	10	AUG 1831	JAN 1842	Sampler, figurative, verse
Bryant	Mary M.		1836	JULY 1848	Embroidered map, *Map of ASIA*
Carbary (Carbery)	Ann Asenath	7		JULY 1828	Sampler, marking
Carbery (Carberry)	Helen M. (Mary)		ca. 1822	AUG 1832	Sampler, marking, architectural
Carlon	Ann			MAY 1812	Sampler, fruit basket, verse "On Virtue"
Carter	Sarah Ann			JAN 1834	Sampler, architectural, (shuttered windows), verse
Cassady	Catherine		ca. 1804	FEB 1814	Sampler, architectural, verse - Navy Yard
Cassedy	Margaret A.		ca. 1815	OCT 1826	Sampler, architectural, verse - Navy Yard
Clubb	Charlotte	12	1801	JULY 1813	Sampler, architectural, verse - Navy Yard
Crowley	Julia Ann	10	14 DEC 1799	FEB 1810	Sampler, architectural, verse - Navy Yard
Crowley	Julia Ann	13	14 DEC 1799	APRIL 1813	Sampler, architectural, verse - Navy Yard
Dove	Elizabeth S.	13	1807	SEPT 1820	Sampler, architectural, verse
Dove	Harriet		ca. 1805	MAY 1817	Sampler, marking, verse
Ensey	Martha	10	FEB 1803	APRIL 1813	Sampler, architectural, verse - Navy Yard
Hancock	Ella	9	ca. 1844	1853	Sampler, marking
Holleran	Kate A.		6 OCT 1848	ca.1860	Embroidered picture, wool work, religious
James [attributed]	Amelia			ca.1826	Sampler, architectural, verse - Navy Yard
Latrobe	Juliana E.	8 or 9	17 JULY 1804	JULY 1813	Sampler, marking, verse
Lacey	Julia [Winona]	8	1840	1848	Sampler, marking
[L]awrenc[e]	[Ju]lianna		ca. 1820	JULY 1830	Sampler, architectural, verse, *St. Patricks Church*
Masi	Caroline R[osella]	10	1837	NOV 1847	Sampler, marking
M. [Massoletti]	J. [Julietta] M. [Marie]		16 JAN 1825	1835-40	Silk embroidery, floral
O'Brien	Julia	12	1800	JUNE 1812	Sampler, architectural, (shuttered windows), verse - Navy Yard
Ourand	Alletha F. (Frances) F. (Findley)	12	26 MAY 1827	MAY 1839	Sampler, marking, verse
Prout	Mary	7	1810	APRIL 1817	Sampler, marking

Where Made	Home Place	Owner
Washington City	Washington City, Navy Yard area	Private
Washington City	Washington City, Navy Yard area	Private
Washington City D.C.	Washington City	Private
Washington M.A. Tyson & Sisters Seminary	Washington, D.C.	Dealer
Washington City	Washington City	HSCC
D C	Washington City	HSCC
Washington City	Washington City	CWF
Washington City	Washington City?	Dealer
Washington City	Washington City, Navy Yard area	MMA
Washington	Washington City, Navy Yard area	MMA
Washington City	Washington City, Navy Yard area	AM
Washington Navy Yard	Washington City, Navy Yard area	CWF
Washington City	Washington City, Navy Yard area	DAR
Washington City	Washington City	Private
Washing City	Washington City	Private
Washington City	Washington City, Navy Yard area	Auction
Public Schools of the City of Washington	Washington, D.C.	Private
Washington DC	Washington, D.C.	Auction
Was - - - - - - - (thread disintegration)	Washington City	Private
	Probably Washington DC [or Baltimore]	MdHS
St Vince---. Sch---. (St. Vincent School), Washington, D.C.	Washington, D.C.	NMAH
Washington City	Washington City	CWF
St Joseph's School E. Street Washington D.C.	Washington, D.C.	GVM
	Washington City	Private
Washington City	Washington City, Navy Yard area	Auction
Washington City	Washington City	Private
Washington City	Washington City, Navy Yard area	Private

APPENDIX I

Last Name	First Name	Age	Birth Date	Date Made	Type
Ridgway	Mary		1839	ca. 1850	Embroidered picture, wool work, mourning
Rothwell	Laura E.	8	4 FEB 1825	1834	Sampler, marking
Simmons	[Margaret] C.	8	7 JAN 1819	OCT 1827	Sampler, marking, motif
Simmons	Margaret C.	9	7 JAN 1819	JAN 1828	Sampler, architectural, (shuttered windows), verse - Navy Yard
Slade	Jane Maria	6	9 SEP 1819	JULY 1826	Sampler, marking
Sutherland	Charlotte			DEC 1809	Sampler, floral, verse
Tait	Mary	9	3 AUG 1815	JUNE 1825	Sampler, architectural, (shuttered windows), verse - Navy Yard
Thomp[s]on	Eliza		3 DEC 1809	1823	Sampler, marking
Thompson	Eliza	13	3 DEC 1809	SEPT 1823	Sampler, architectural, (shuttered windows), verse - Navy Yard
Trunnel	Sarah Eliza Ann	11	1813	ca. 1825	Sampler, floral wreath, verse
Vonderlehr	Catharine		ca. 1824	JUNE 1837	Sampler, floral
Ward	Ann			1826	Sampler, floral wreath, verse
Waring	Eliza M.			1828	Sampler, floral, verse
Wendell	Anna Mary	9	8 SEP 1845	1854	Sampler, marking
Whitney	Sarah Malvina	8	28 DEC 1819	DEC 1828	Sampler, marking, motif, verse
Wilson	Charity			FEB 1835	Sampler, marking, verse
Anonymous				After 1820	Sampler, marking, basket

Samplers and Embroidered Pictures Worked by District of Columbia Girls at Non-Local Schools

Last Name	First Name	Age	Birth Date	Date Made	Type
[Balch]	[Jane Whann]		14 FEB 1805	ca. 1819	Embroidered picture, Palemon and Lavinia
English	Lydia		1802	ca. 1816	Embroidered picture, memorial
I[rwin]	H[annah]	11	22 MAY 1792	1803	Sampler, Quaker motifs
Stabler	Elizabeth	13	1797	1810	Sampler, marking, Quaker motifs, verse

Where Made	Home Place	Owner
School of St Vincent, Washington, D.C.	Washington City	Private
Washington City	Washington City	Private
Washington City	Washington City, Navy Yard area	NMAH
Washington City D.C.	Washington City, Navy Yard area	Private
Washington District of Columbia	Washington City	Auction
Washington	possibly Washington City, D.C.	Auction
Washington City D. C.	Washington City, Navy Yard area	Private
Washington City	Washington City, Navy Yard area	Private
Washington City D.C.	Washington City, Navy Yard area	Private
Washington City?	Georgetown	DAR
St Vincent School	Washington City	Auction
Washington City	Washington City	CWF
Miss Pennell's school Washington DC	Washington City	Private
Washington D.C.	Washington, D.C.	Private
Washington City	Washington City	Private
Washington.DC.NY (Navy Yard)		PMA
Washington DC		B&C
Lititz, PA Moravian Girls' School	Georgetown	DH-CDA
Lititz, PA Moravian Girls' School	Georgetown	Private
Weston, Westtown Boarding School, PA	Alexandria	RH
Sandy Spring, Montgomery Co. MD	Alexandria	SSM

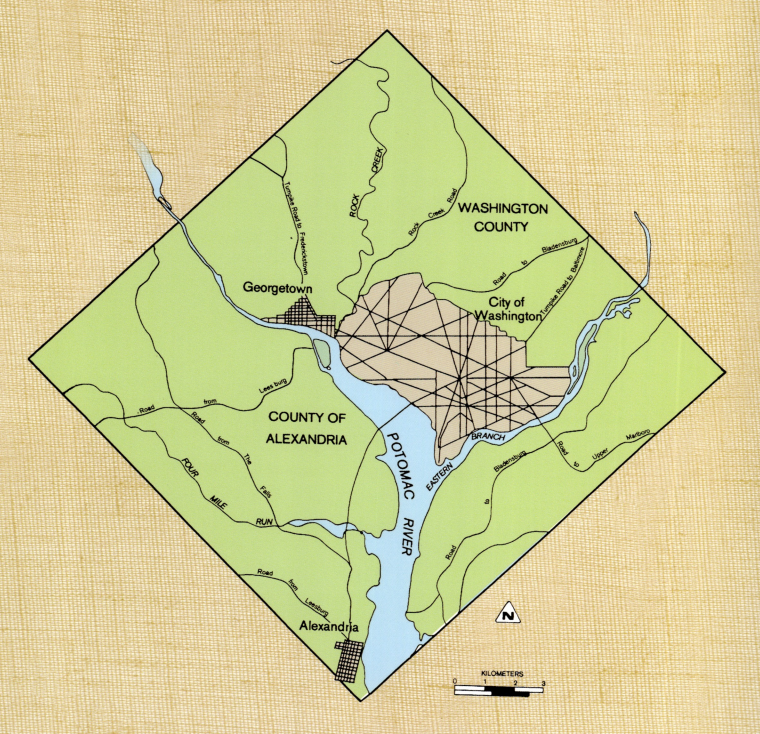

Figure II-1. District of Columbia as originally laid out in 1790.

APPENDIX II

DOCUMENTED NEEDLEWORK TEACHERS AND SCHOOLS IN THE DISTRICT OF COLUMBIA

Compiled by Sheryl De Jong

Young girls learned their needlework skills either at home or in school. In the District of Columbia many teachers advertised to teach needlework along with reading, writing, and other subjects. Public schools were not available to all students until 1862, but numerous private schools operated before that date.

Up until 1847, the District of Columbia consisted of three communities: Alexandria, Georgetown, and Washington City. A list of schools and teachers where needlework is known to have been in the curriculum has been compiled for each of the three communities. Although intended to be as complete as possible at the time of publication, additional sources will continue to reveal new names and details. The Alexandria list ends with the date of 1847, when Alexandria retroceded to the state of Virginia.

Three primary sources were used to compile the entries: 1) the samplers themselves; 2) newspaper advertisements of the period; and 3) the Craftsman Database at the research center of Old Salem/Museum of Early Southern Decorative Arts (MESDA) in Winston-Salem, North Carolina. If an entry ends with an M and a number, it is part of the MESDA database, which includes a full text transcription of the newspaper advertisement.

ALEXANDRIA SCHOOLS AND TEACHERS

Name	Location	Date(s)
Alexandria Free School for Girls/Female Lancastrian School	218 N. Columbus.	1812-61
Armstrong, Alfred		1827
Bell, Mrs.	Fairfax St.	1795
Bradshaw, Mr.	Prince St., between Washington and St. Asaph Sts.	1830
Cameron, Mrs.	Corner Duke and Fairfax.	1809
Cooke, Mrs./**Embroidery School**	Prince and Washington Sts.	1801-03
Cottringer, Mrs.	Oronoko and Washington Sts.	1817-21
Dunlap, Mrs. Maria Anne	Opposite Mr. Plummer's store at the head of King St.	1810
Edmonds, Sarah (Mrs. Edmund)/**Edmonds School**	Prince St., three doors above the late Col. Hooe's.	1810-23
Edmonds, Sarah Eliza		1810-15+
Farnsworth, Mrs.	House adjoining Col. Hooe's garden, in Water St.	1802
Ford, Mrs. Andrew	At her husband's school between Prince and Duke Sts.	1799
Fulton, Mrs.	Washington St.	1821-29
Hagarty, Mrs.		1828-29
Hallowell, Margaret Farquhar (Mrs. Benjamin)	220 North Washington St.	1827-31+
Hannah, Elizabeth	House of Mr. Robert Bryce.	1784-85
Hardester, Mary	Washington St.	1805
Jacks, Ann	300 block of King St.	1806-07
Jamieson, Mrs. P.		1821
Janney, Mrs. Mary and Miss	Same place as ENGLISH SCHOOL, lately kept by William Kenworthy.	1805
Johnston, Miss Mary & sister	King St. opposite the Engine House.	1840
Judge, Miss Margaret		1825-27
Judge, Rachel, later Mrs. Townsend Waugh		1812-15
Larkin, Mrs.	Fairfax St. opposite M. Libby's store.	1819
Lee, Mrs.	Rented house, corner of Water and Duke Sts.	1797-98
Lunt, Betsey	House corner of Fairfax and Queen Sts.	1798
Mark, Ann Smith (Mrs. Samuel) and daughters		1826-30
Mason, Marian (Mrs. John)	House of John Mason next door to the Indian Queen on King St.	1803
May, Ann	Prince St. between Union and Water Sts.	1797
Morris, Sylvia	Near Lancastrian school.	1826-46
Moulton, Miss	On Prince St., corner of Alfred St.	1818-19
Muir, Elizabeth Welman (Mrs. Rev. Dr. James)	Royal St.	ca. 1817-30
Muir, Mary Lang (Mrs. John)	Royal St.	1818-21

Comment

Lancastrian School; Rachel Judge first teacher; *plain needlework, knitting, and mantua making* assumed.

Needle Work taught.

From Charleston and Norfolk; in 1799 in Richmond, VA; *Plain Work, Marking, Open Work and Embroidery.* M2569

Beadwork &c. will claim a proper share of attention.

From Virginia; white teacher; taught a primary school for African American boys and girls; *needlework* assumed.

Taught *embroidery.* M77026

From Philadelphia; in 1822 teaching in Washington City; *needlework* assumed.

Taught *Embroidery, Tambour, Marking, Working Maps, plain work, &c. &c.* M16623

Taught *Embroidery in chenilles, gold, silver and silk. Maps wrought in do.[ditto] Print work in figures, or landscapes. Tambour and Needle work, plain and fanciful. Fringe, and Netting, in all its variety.* M10296

Taught *Embroidery, Fancy Work*; assoc. needlework: **Julia Maria Hooff ca. 1815**, attrib. needlework: **Anne Campbell 1810-1815, Margaret Fleming 1810-1815,** and **Martha Bryan McKnight 1810-1815**.

From Norfolk, VA; taught *sewing in its different branches, Embroidery, &c.* M11196

Taught *various branches of needle work.* M76998

Taught *plain and ornamental Needle Work of every description.*

From Georgetown; *taught useful and ornamental Needle-work.*

School operated by Mr. Hallowell; taught *plain sewing.*

Taught *needle-work.* M15044.

From Baltimore; taught *Needle-Work.* M76997

Taught *plain Sewing, Marking, Netting, Tamboring, Embroidery.* M77015

Taught *needlework.*

Operated school with L. Janney; mother and daughter *will instruct in plain Sewing, Marking, and in all kinds of useful Needle-work.* M77022, M77023

Taught *usual branches of a plain and ornamental education.*

sewing and needlework assumed.

Lancastarian; *plain needlework, knitting, and mantua making* assumed.

Operated school with Mr. Larkin; taught *needle work in its most useful and ornamental varieties.* M77021

Taught *Fancy Work.* M21052

Taught *Plain Needlework, Fancy Work.* M22294

Taught *Cotton and Lace Work.*

Taught *Needle work.* M23120

Taught *different branches of needle-work.* M76999

African American; *sewing* assumed.

Taught *plain and ornamental Needle Work.* M77020

From Bermuda; taught with daughters; *needlework* assumed.

From Scotland; taught *tambouring, needlework*; assoc. samplers: **Ann Carson 1818, Mary Muir 1818, Marian Wood 1818,** and **Rebecca Suter 1819**.

Name	Location	Date(s)
Muir, Misses Jane, Mary, and Elizabeth/ **Misses Muir Boarding and Day School for Young Ladies**	Corner of Prince and Washington Sts.	1830-40+
Muir, Rev. Dr. James		1790
Nichols, Mrs. Celina [Selina]		1810-11
O'Reily, Mrs. Robert		1804-05
Painter, Rachel	Alfred, near King St.	1815-30
Porter, Mrs. Eliza	1828 - Washington St., 1832 - Duke & Washington Sts., 1834 - Alexandria Bank - corner of Fairfax and Cameron.	1827-34
Porter, Mrs. Fitz John	Prince and Washington Sts.	1812-30
Rowen, Mrs.	At the corner of Washington and Prince Sts.	1811
Simson, Mrs.	Queen St.	1793
Sketchley, Mrs.	Spacious house next door to Mr. Weightman's, Prince St., one door from the corner of Fairfax St.	1811
Smith, Christian	Next door to Mr. Joseph Janney's on Fairfax St.	1786
St. Francis Xavier Academy/Academy for Young Ladies	109 N. Fairfax; Duke and Fairfax	1832-39
Tannent (Tennent) Mrs./**Tambouring School**	Prince St., near Mr. Love's.	1797-98
Tutten, Mrs.	Corner of Pitt and Prince.	1809
Washington Free School	Housed in Alexandria Academy.	1786-1812
Waugh, Rachel Judge (Mrs. Townsend)/ **Female boarding School**		1827-30
Wilbar (Wilber) Mary Ann	One door below the house of Thomas Swann, Esq.	1811
Wily, Mrs.	King St., house lately occupied by Dr. Rose.	1798
Winter, Mrs.	Next door to Mrs. Mills'.	1820

GEORGETOWN SCHOOLS AND TEACHERS

Name	Location	Date(s)
Academy of the Visitation, [so named in 1817 - previously known as **New Academy for Young Ladies; Young Ladies' Academy, Georgetown**; aka **Georgetown Visitation** and now as **Georgetown Visitation Preparatory School**]	At the Convent of the Visitation in Georgetown, D.C.	1799 - present time
Barnard, Mrs.	Near the Old Columbia Bank.	1838
Becraft, Maria	Dumbarton St; later across the street from Convent of the Visitation.	1820-31
Benevolent School/ Poor School/ St. Joseph's School	Located next to convent of the Visitation.	<1817-1918
Billing, Mrs. Mary	Dumbarton St. opposite the Methodist Church between Congress and High Sts.	1807-20

Comment

Polite and ornamental education, Needle Work.

…*a person shall be engaged capable to teaching the branches peculiar to the Female Education.*

Taught *different branches of useful and ornamental education.*

From Baltimore: taught *Embroidery in chenilles, gold, silver, silks, &c. comprising figures, historical and ornamental, landscapes, flowers, fruit, birds, &c. maps wrought in silks, chenilles; gold &c. print work in figures or landscapes, cloth work in fruit, birds, flowers, &c. tambor and dresden, cross stitch, tent stitch tapestry, &c.* M27115

From Pennsylvania; Quaker; former student at Westtown; turned school over in 1830 to Mary Anna Talbott; assoc. sampler: **Mary Pleasants Stabler ca. 1820**.

Primary class taught *Plain and Ornamental Sewing in all their varieties.*

Taught at Lancasterian school; later opened her own school; *needlework* assumed.

Taught *various kinds of needle work, Embroidery.* M77019

From New York, Charleston, Philadelphia and Baltimore; *teaching all kind of needlework in silk and worsted, crowning, darning and plain work…tambour and embroidery…she designs the work and executes the drawing.* M35682

From New York; then in Belfield, VA in 1811-12; operated school with Mr. Sketchley; taught *plain and ornamental Needle-work.* M50167

From Charleston; *needle work.* M36071

Catholic; Sisters of Charity; taught *Embroidery, Plain and Fancy Needle-Work.*

From Norfolk; taught *embroidery, tambouring, open and needle work, flowering, sewing, marking.* M39482

From Virginia; white teacher; taught African American children; *needlework* assumed.

Twenty percent female quota, after 1812 girls went to the Lancasterian school; *needlework* assumed.

Operated school with Mr. Waugh; *sewing* assumed.

Taught *Plain & Ornamental Needle Work, Embroidery Netting, &c. &c.* M43776

In 1800 taught in Georgetown; *needlework* assumed.

Operated school with Mr. Winter; taught young misses to *become complete sempstresses.*

Comment

Taught *Embroidery, plain and ornamental Needle-work*; assoc. needlework: **Eliza Jameson ca. 1800, Catharine Queen ca. 1800, Maria Teresa Lalor ca. 1800,** and **Catherine Ann Lavinia Clemens, 1857** - wool work; assoc. samplers: **Mary [Ann] Carroll 1801, Emily M. Jackson 1808, Elenor Durkee 1810, Celestia Mary Combs 1816, Mary Rebecca J. Brooke 1817, Mary Rose Boarman 1818, Eleanor Waring 1819, Eleanora Neale 1823,** and **Mary Elizabeth Laurence 1829**.

School operated with Mr. Barnard; taught *plain and fancy needlework.*

African American; *needlework* assumed.

Free school; Catholic; Sisters of the Visitation; *sewing* assumed.

From England; first taught white and African American children; in 1810 only African American; in 1820 went to Washington City; *sewing* assumed.

Name	Location	Date(s)
Bootes, Miss/**Miss Bootes's Female Academy**	Congress St. east side	1834
Briscoe, Isabella	Montgomery St., near Zion Wesley church.	1850-61
Brown, Mrs.	House formerly occupied by Captain John Mitchell, near the market.	1814
Brown, Mrs. K. [Katharine Wigglesworth]	Bridge St., opposite the Farmers and Mechanics Bank.	1814
Chevalier, Madame [Sister Luc] /**New Academy for Young Ladies**	Fayette and 3rd St.	1798-1804
Cobb, Miss Mary W./**Georgetown Lancasterian School**	Jefferson St.	<1830
De La Marche, Madame [Mother Marie de la Marche] /**New Academy for Young Ladies**	Fayette and 3rd St.	1798-1804
Doyle, Misses	4th St., nearly opposite Mr. Ritchie's store.	1816
Du Cherray, Madame/**Young Ladies Academy**	House now occupied by Mrs. Smith and Mrs. Wiley; 1810 - Mrs. Beck's house on Jefferson St.	1807-16
English, Miss Lydia S./**Female Seminary**	3017 N Street, later a block away on 30th St.	1826-52
Gaither, Mrs.	1809 - Brick house on High St.; 1813 - next door east of General Smith's.	1809-13
Georgetown Lancasterian School/Georgetown School/Mr. Robert Ould, Principal	Jefferson St.	1811-42
Grant, Nancy		1828+
Greentree, Mrs./**Young Ladies Academy**	March 1809 - house lately occupied by Major Beall; May 1809 - Washington St. lately occupied by Capt. Mackall; 1813 - Beall St.	1809-11 1813
Hagarty, Mrs.	Contiguous to the Rev. Mr. McIlvaine's Church.	1824
Hart, Deborah, (Mrs. Levi)	Over Mr. Jewell's shop; opposite the Farmers' and Mechanics' Bank.	1827
Henning, Miss [Eliza]	1/2 West near the Eastern Branch.	1800
Herbert, Jane		1819
Hill, Margaret	Near Miss English's seminary.	1840-60
Howard, Mrs./**Ladies' Seminary**	Bridge St., opposite the Farmer's and Mechanic's Bank; June 1815 moved to Washington City.	1815
Judge, Miss Margaret/**Georgetown Lancasterian School**	Jefferson St.	1814-16
Lalor, Miss Alice [Sister Teresa]/**Young Ladies Academy, Georgetown** - later **Visitation**	Corner of Gay and 4th Sts.	1799-1836
Lathrop, Mrs. John/**Lyceum**	Congress St.	1815
LeBlond de la Rochefocault, Madame [Sister Celeste le Blond]/**New Academy for Young Ladies**	Fayette and 3rd St.	1798-1804
McDermott, Mrs. Maria [Sister Mary Frances]/**Young Ladies Academy, Georgetown** - later **Visitation**	Corner of Gay and 4th Sts.	1799-1820
Nourse, Miss Rosa M.	Highlands, late residence of her father, Major C. J. Nourse.	1845

Comment

Assoc. sampler: **Mary Elizabeth Fearson ca. 1834**.

African American; *sewing* assumed.

Taught *Plain and Ornamental Needle Work.* M4157

From Newburyport, MA where she taught embroidery from 1800-1813; *needlework* assumed.

Catholic; from France; taught with Madame De La Marche and Madame LeBlond de la Rochefocault; *sewing, embroidery.* M6177

Plain needlework, knitting, and mantua making assumed.

Catholic; from France; taught with Madame Chevalier and Madame LeBlond de la Rochefocault; *sewing, embroidery.* M8891

Taught *Embroidery and all kinds of Needle-work.* M77205

From Moscow; *taught Embroidery, and all sorts of Needle-work, which form a part of a Young Lady's education.* M68752

Taught *needlework*; attrib. samplers: **Elizabeth Nicholls ca. 1828, Artridge Priscilla Jackson 1829, Mary Ann Scott 1831, Elizabeth Orme 1833, Mary M. Meem 1836, and Martha D. Abbot 1851**.

Taught *various kinds of Needle Work.* M63785

Plain *needlework, knitting, and mantua making* assumed.

African American; Aunt of Maria Becraft; *sewing* assumed.

In 1811 moved to Washington City and moved back in 1813 to Georgetown; *taught needle work in its various branches.* M68762

Operated school with Mr. Hagarty; taught *useful and ornamental NEEDLE-WORK.*
Will teach a class of young ladies to make their own *LACE.*

Needlework assumed.

Taught *Marking, plain and ornamental Needle Work, Print Work.* M64175

African American; *sewing* assumed.

Taught *NEEDLE WORKS -- VIZ. Plain, embossed and open Cotton-work, Netting and Tetting, Landscape, Flower, and Fancy Crewal works, Embroidery in Gold, Silver, Silk and Worsted, Tambour.* M17293

Taught *useful needle-work...and the manufacture of yarn shawls*; in 1816 went to Woodlawn Boarding School (near Sandy Spring, MD) to teach.

Catholic; from Ireland and Philadelphia; taught with Mrs. Maria Sharpe and Mrs. Maria McDermott; *Sewing, Embroidery, Tambourwork.*

Operated school with Mr. Lathrop; taught *plain or ornamental needle work.* M70791

Catholic; from France; taught with Madame Chevalier and Madame De La Marche; *sewing, embroidery.* M21017

Catholic; from Philadelphia; taught with Mrs. Maria Sharpe and Miss Alice Lalor; *Sewing, Embroidery, Tambourwork.*

Taught *useful and ornamental Needlework.*

Name	Location	Date(s)
Peerce, Mr. William	House next door to Mr. Samuel Turner's on Cherry St.	1810
Pennell, Miss Alice Hart/**Classical School for Young Ladies**	Over Mr. Jewell's shop; opposite the Farmers' and Mechanics' Bank.	1827-28
Philips, Mrs. E.	North side of Bridge St., nearly opposite to the Printing Office.	1800
Pope, Emmeline (Mrs. William)		1823
Searle, Miss/**Female Literary Seminary**	Gay St.	1823-24
Sharpe, Mrs. Maria [Sister Ignatia] /**Young Ladies Academy, Georgetown** - later **Visitation**	Corner of Gay and 4th Sts.	1799-1804
Shedden, Mrs. Thomas (Matilda Cecilia Dowdall)/**Mrs. Shedden's Seminary**	House lately occupied by Captain Mix, in Cox's Row.	1823-40+
Simpson, Mr. and Mrs.		1813-1814
Smith, Ann	Fall St.	1805-06
Smith, Clement/**Classical School for Young Ladies**		1827
Smith, Elizabeth	Zion Wesley Church.	1860
Smith, Mrs.	1800 - George -Town - in the vicinity of the City of Washington; 1802 - moved to the three story brick house nearly opposite to the bank; 1805 - moved from the house on Water St. to a large Brick house, near Francis Lowndes.	1800-08
Smith, Mrs. Isabella and daughters	1829 - former residence of Clement Smith, and more recently Mrs. Lee, 2d street; 1830 - moved to Washington City	1829-30
Smith, Mrs. Middleton	At her own house; hill above the Methodist church.	1810
Waugh, Mrs. Townsend (Rachel Judge)	House in Cox's Row	1830-32
Webber, Mrs. and Miss/**Seminary for young ladies**	Corner of Bridge and Green Sts.	1819
White, Miss	Next door to the Columbia bank.	1806
Wilbar, Sarah	In Mr. Beck's house, Jefferson St.	1819
Wily (Wiley), Mrs.	1800 - George -Town - in the vicinity of the City of Washington; 1802 - moved to the three story brick house nearly opposite to the bank; 1805 - moved from the house on Water St. to a large Brick house, near Francis Lowndes.	1800-08
Wright, Misses	1818 - Bridge St., near the Indian Department; 1823 - corner house of Col. Cox's Row, 1st St.	1818-24

WASHINGTON CITY SCHOOLS AND TEACHERS

Name	Location	Date(s)
Aca Nada Seminary for Young Ladies/Mrs. Molly Bowie, Principal	Two miles from the Capitol.	1851
Annin, Mrs.	Capitol Hill.	1829

Comment

if required, *needlework*.

Taught *all kinds of plain and ornamental needlework*; assoc. sampler: **Eliza M. Waring 1828**.

From England; taught in Washington City in 1799; *Sewing, both plain and ornamental, likewise the making of their own Dresses either in Mantua making, or in Millinery.* M67289

Taught *needle work, as neatly as any that can be produced, plain and embroidery.*

Needle work, if desired will receive its due share of attention.

Catholic; from Philadelphia; taught with Miss Alice Lalor and Mrs. Maria McDermott; *Sewing, Embroidery, Tambourwork.*

From New Jersey; taught *Fancy Work*.

Taught *various kinds of embroidery including worked muslin [genealogy samplers].*

From Baltimore; went to Staunton, VA, Lexington, VA, and Fredericksburg, VA; taught the *ornamental branches*.

Will be assisted by a lady... who will give instruction *in all kinds of useful and ornamental needlework*.

African American; from Washington City; assisted Rev. Wm. H. Hunter; *sewing* assumed.

Taught with Mrs. Wily (Wiley); *Plain Work, Marking, Embroidery in Lambs Wool, Silks, and Chenille, with a variety of other kinds of Needle Work.* M51289

From New York; taught *all the branches of useful and ornamental education.*

Taught *needle work*. M63823

From Alexandria; operated school with Mr. Waugh; *taught the ornamental branches*.

School operated with Mr. Webber; taught *Every branch of useful and ornamental needlework*. M64020, 64021

From England; taught *plain work, Fancy Work* if required.

Taught *plain and ornamental Needle-work, in all its varieties.* M64023

Taught with Mrs. Smith; *Plain Work, Marking, Embroidery in Lambs Wool, Silks, and Chenille, with a variety of other kinds of Needle Work.* M51290

From Boston; taught *needlework in all its varieties.* M64024

Comment

Every branch of polite learning, as also every refined accomplishment, will be taught.

Taught *Needle and Fancy Work*.

Name	Location	Date(s)
Archer, Mrs.	Large room, 7th St., in Mr. McDuell's new house.	1820
Bage, Mrs.	Between Jacob Leonard's and Elliott's Printing Office, Pennsylvania Ave.	1821
Beams, Charlotte	I St. N, between 4th and 5th West.	1850
Bell, Mrs.	On L, between 9th and 10th Sts.	1850-59
Billings, Mrs. Mary	H St. near the Foundry church.	1820-23
Bonfils, Mrs.	SW corner F and 12th Sts.	1825-27
Browns, Mrs. & Miss [daughter]	Six Buildings, Pennsylvania Ave.	1829
Capitol Hill Seminary/Maria E. Cox, Principal	New Jersey Ave., south side of the Capitol.	1833-1834
Central Female Free School, Margaret Wannall, Principal		1835-45
Chalmers, Miss	One door from the corner of 12th and E Sts.	1829
Colfax Industrial Mission	7th and O Sts. N.W.	1867
Connor, Mrs. M. A.	Corner of 10th and D St., near Pennsylvania Ave.	1829
Cook, Eliza Anne	16th St. between K and L Sts.	1854-68
Cook, John F./**Union Seminary**		1834-55
Cook, Mrs. T.	On north side of F St. between 12th and 13th Sts.	1827
Corbet, Mrs.	G between 6th and 7th.	1822
Costin, Louisa Parke	father's house on Capitol Hill, on A St.	1823-31
Costin, Martha	father's house on Capitol Hill, on A St.	1832-39
Cottage Grammar School	Room on G St., west of the War Office.	1820
Cottringer, Mrs.	13th St., between E and F Sts.	1822-25
Cutts, Mrs. L. Henry	Corner of D and 12th St.	1835
Davis, Mrs.& Miss [daughter]	F St., near Col. Tayloe's.	1820-24
De Lee Ree, Mr. J.	6th St., near the Unitarian Church.	1824
Dodson, Ann	House occupied by J. H. Dodson on Pennsylvania Ave., between 9th and 10th Sts.	1829
Dorman, Madame	Pennsylvania Ave. between 8th and 9th Sts.	1835-41
Durang, Mrs.	New Jersey Ave., house lately occupied by Mrs. Lee.	1810
Dyson, Mrs.	Corner of G and 9th Sts.	1840
Elvans, Miss Frances/**Female Charity School**	On Capitol Hill.	1834-1848
Evans, Miss	1814 - Near to Col. Wharton's, on 8th St. East, opposite the Marine Barrack; 1818 - next door to Judge Thruston's, Capitol Hill.	1814-18
Evans, Miss S.	In the house belonging to Daniel Carroll, fourth door north of Dr. Thomas Ewell's and opposite the Capitol.	1813
Evans, Mrs. Mary Ann & Mrs. Mary Brush, her mother	Near the General Post Office.	1821

Comment
Taught with Miss Shanks; *plain Sewing, Marking, Needle Work*. M66792
Taught *embroidery, card work, and various other fashionable fancy works*.
African American; *sewing* assumed.
Taught *Needle-work*.
From England and Georgetown; white teacher; taught African American children; *sewing* assumed.
From France, New York, Rhode Island; operated school with Mr. Bonfils; taught *Ornamental branches*.
Taught *Lace Work, Fancy Work of different descriptions*.
The ornamental branches form a separate charge.
For orphans; taught *needlework and sewing*.
Taught with Mrs. Gilder; *Plain and Ornamental Needlework*.
African American; classes held every Saturday for 200 girls; taught *various kinds of work upon cloth*.
Taught *Lace and Ornamental Needle Work*.
African American; also taught for three years in a free Catholic school supported by the St. Vincent de Paul Society; *sewing* assumed.
African American; Miss Catharine Costin at one time in charge of female department; *sewing* assumed.
Taught *Needlework*.
Needlework assumed.
African American; *sewing* assumed.
African American; sister of Louisa Costin, took over after her death; *sewing* assumed.
Needle work taught, if desired.
Taught *Plain and Ornamental Needle Work*.
Taught *plain sewing, including dress-making; A French lady will give instruction in all the delicate varieties of Needle and Fancy Work*.
From Massachusetts; taught *Needle work, useful and ornamental; Embroidery, Rug and Print Work*. M69576, 96577
A Female Teacher of superior talents, attends the Female Department, for Plain, Ornamental, Rug, and other Needle Work.
Taught *Needle Work, Plain and Ornamental, $1 extra*.
Taught *Embroidery, Tapestry of different kinds, Bead Work, Plain Sewing of any description, and Cotton Work*.
Taught *plain and fancy Needle Work*. M76986
Taught *all the branches necessary to a polite and useful education*.
From England; established by members of 1st Presbyterian Church; taught *needlework, sewing, and knitting*; Miss Elvans taught in the public school system after 1848.
Taught *Needle Work in its various branches*. M65096
Taught *all kinds of Plain Sewing, Marking, Muslin-Work, Embroidery and Print-Work*. M77025
Taught *Plain Needle Work*.

Name	Location	Date(s)
Fales, Mrs./**Mrs. Fales Boarding School for Young Ladies**	On 13th St, between Pennsylvania Ave. and F St.	1820
Fill, Mr. J./**City Academy and Ladies' Seminary**	Central Masonic Hall.	1833-35
Fletcher, Mrs.	I near 22nd St.	1854-58
Ford, [Rebecca] Mrs. [John G.]	Residence of the late General Brown.	1828
Ford, Mrs. George	New Jersey between K and L.	1818
French, Mrs.	Pennsylvania Ave., nearly opposite to Brown's Hotel.	1824
Gardiner, Mrs.	12th St. West, opposite to Mr. King's Painting Rooms.	1832
Gardiner, Mrs. John	1803 - Pennsylvania Ave. N. near President's Square; 1821 - on Pennsylvania Ave., near the old Theatre.	1803-07 1821
Gilder, Mrs.	One door from the corner of 12th and E Sts.	1829
Godfrey, Ann	Mr. Stuart Williams', near the President's Square.	1800
Good Hope School	Bowen Rd.	1866+
Goodrich, Mrs. and Miss [daughter]	5th St., between D and E.	1859
Gordon, Mrs. Charlotte, Miss Rebecca T. Gordon	1846 - I near 11th St. West, 1852 - New York Ave. near 13th, 1858 - 8th between N and O, northern section of the city, 1861- outside city limits for slave children.	1846-65
Gray, Miss	11th St. West, between G and H Sts. North.	1831-32
Gray, Mrs.	G St. nearly opposite to Mr. G. Duval's.	1809-11
Greentree, Mrs.	New buildings of Mr. McLane on E St. near Rhodes's hotel.	1811-13
Haley, Mrs. Maria	Capitol Hill.	1810
Hall, Mrs. Anne Maria [Mary Ann]	1810 - Capitol Hill, 1820 - A St. near the Capitol; later - E St. North between 11th and 12th.	1810-35
Hampton, Fanny	Northwest corner of K and 19th.	1833-42
Hauel, Miss	1818 - 7th St. near Mr. M'Ewen's North E St., Capitol Hill, 1819 - South B St., Capitol Hill next door to Mr. Thruston's.	1818-19
Hawley, Miss E.	Formerly occupied by Mrs. Howard, and recently by Mr. McLeod, 10th St.	1816-17
Hays, Mrs. Matilda (Alexander)	9th St. West, near New York Ave.	1841-57
Heaney, Miss [Ann]	1831 - House late seminary of Madame Bonfils, F and 12th Sts; 1844 - I St. opposite President's square; 1846 - house adjacent to the residence of Colonel Gardner; 1852 - until accommodations are obtained will give instruction in Mr. S. Carusi's Music Academy.	1831-34 1844-52
Hebb, Mrs.	Capitol Hill.	1830
Henderson, Mrs.		1828-33
Herbert, Miss J.	1826 - 8th St., three doors north Mr. R. Jones's store; 1827 - 6th St., near the Unitarian Church; 1829 - at her residence 8th St. north of Pennsylvania Ave.	1826-29
Hogan, Miss S.	F St., between 13th and 14th.	1852-55
Hohne, Mrs. Ann Sophia	B St., nearly opposite Mr. Edward Ingle's.	1827

Comment

From Philadelphia and Marietta, PA.; taught *Tambouring on lace and muslin, Embroidery in silk, Rug Work, Cotton Work, Plain Sewing.* M69580

Plain and fancy Needlework was taught.

From England; operated school with Mr. Fletcher; white teacher, taught African American children; *sewing* assumed.

From Baltimore; operated school with Mr. Ford; taught *Ornamental Work.*

From Virginia; white teacher; taught African American children; *sewing* assumed.

From Baltimore; taught *Plain and Ornamental Needle Work.*

Taught plain and *ornamental Needlework.*

Operated school with Mr. Gardiner; taught *Needle Work, tambouring, &c.*; in 1821 resumed school and taught *plain and ornamental Needle Work, Embroidery.* M76167

Taught with Miss Chalmers; *Plain and Ornamental Needlework.*

Taught *plain needlework, tambour, and marking.* M67274

African American; *sewing school.*

Taught *Sewing.*

African American; assisted by her daughter Rebecca T. Gordon; *sewing* assumed.

Operated school with Mr. Gray; taught *Plain and Ornamental Needlework.*

Operated school with Mr. Gray; taught *all kinds of Needle work.* M76166; assoc. sampler: **Mary Ann Borrows 1811**.

From Georgetown; taught *useful and ornamental Needful Work.* M68762

White teacher; taught African American children; *sewing* assumed.

African American; *sewing* assumed.

African American; *sewing* assumed.

From Paris; taught *plain and ornamental needle work.* M70595

From the state of New York; taught *Needlework.* M67399

African American; *sewing* assumed.

From Boston; taught *Needlework, plain or the varieties of taste.*

Taught *Needle Work.*

Taught *Needlework.*

Taught *Lace and Ornamental Needle Work, Plain Sewing.*

Taught *Needlework.*

Taught *Needle-work, plain and ornamental.*

APPENDIX II

Name	Location	Date(s)
Hore, Mrs. Maurice	1828 - 14th, between Pennsylvania Ave. and F St.; 1830 - 12th near F St.	1828-30
Howard, Mrs.	1815 - a few yards north of the new Methodist meeting house; 1816 - moved to 10th St., near the Rev. Mr. Matthew's Church. 1817 - moved to Lexington, KY	1815-16
Hyde, Mrs.	25th St., below I and K Sts.	1832
Jackson, Miss	Capitol Hill.	1852
Jones, Miss Arabella/**St. Agnes' Academy**	On "the island," (A canal built in 1815 formed a barrier between most of Washington's southwest quadrant and the rest of the city. This section was called "the island.")	1851
Kesley, Mrs.	On Pennsylvania Ave.	1835-36
Lancasterian School/Mr. Henry Ould, Principal		1812+
Lee, Mrs.	1805 - Pennsylvania Ave., 3 doors west of President's Square; 1809 - house near the Capitol.	1805-09
Lewis, Miss S. E.	Near the west market, adjoining Mrs. S. Hutchinson's	1832
Maguire, Misses	Near the Seven Buildings.	1819-24
McArann, Misses	18th St., between I and K Sts.	1848
McCormick, Miss	Capitol Hill.	1827-28
McCurdy, Mrs. D. [Dennis]	Navy Yard Hill.	1819
McLeod, Mr. John	G and 10th Sts.	1821
McLeod's, Mrs. C.C.	11th St., between F and G.	1841-51
Metherall, Miss	8th St., near the General Post.	1827
Metropolitan Collegiate Institute/Mr. and Mrs. T. H. Havenner, principals	Between 7th and 8th Sts.	1854-60
Middleton, Miss Mary P.	Corner of H and 11th Sts.	1850
Middleton, Mr. Charles H.	Corner of 22nd St. West and I North.	1849+
Mills, Mrs. Eliza B.	Her residence, E St., West of the General Post Office.	1832
Miner, Miss Myrtilla/**Normal School for Colored Girls**		1851-64
Moulton, Miss	Maryland Avenue, Capitol Hill.	1824
Mount, Mrs.	Opposite the City Hall.	1829
Nesmith, Ann	East side 7th E btw L and M St., Navy Yard	1822-27
Nevitte, Charlotte L.	North side of Louisiana Ave., between 8th and 7th Sts.	1839-41
Nichols, Sarah	New Jersey Ave.	1822
Noel, Angela/**St. Martin's School/St. Augustine School**	L St. North and Vermont Ave.	1867
Noyes, Mrs. [Catherine]	1816 - South B St., three doors west of The Revd. M. McCormick's; 1818 - Capitol Hill.	1816-18
O'Brien, Miss	1835 - near St. Peter's Church, Capitol Hill; 1836 - near corner of 7th St. and Louisiana Ave., opposite the bank of Washington; 1837 - nearly opposite the Masonic Hall.	1835-37

Comment

Operated school with Mr. Hore; taught *plain and ornamental needle work*.

Taught *Plain, embossed and open Cotton work, Netting and Tetting, fancy Crewel Works, Embroidery in Gold, Silver, Silk and Worsted, Tambour*. M66584

Taught with Miss Turner; *Plain and Ornamental Needlework*.

African American; *sewing* assumed.

Catholic; African American; *sewing and needlework* assumed.

Operated school with Mr. Kesley; taught *plain and ornamental Needlework*.

Plain needlework, knitting, and mantua making assumed.

Taught *Needle and Fancy work*. M76165

Taught *plain sewing, marking, lace work, and fancy bead*.

From Baltimore; school operated by their father Hugh Maguire; taught *Plain and Ornamental Needle Work*. M70793

Taught *all the varieties of Plain and Ornamental Needlework*.

From Virginia; taught *Needle and Fancy work*.

Operated school with Mr. McCurdy; *taught needle-work*. M70796

Excellent teachers in every department will be immediately employed . . . Plain and ornamental Needle Work taught.

Taught *the useful and ornamental branches*.

Taught *Lace*.

Ornamental Needlework taught.

Taught *Needlework*.

African American; assisted by his wife the former Margaret Thompson; *sewing* assumed.

From the South; taught *Ornamental branches as desired*.

White teacher; taught classes *in domestic skills* for African American children.

Taught *Plain and Ornamental Needlework*.

Taught *Needle Work*.

Needlework assumed.

Sewing assumed.

Needlework assumed.

Catholic; African American; assisted by Miss Julia Smith; **St. Martin's** later became **St. Augustine School**; *Needlework and sewing* assumed.

Taught *various branches of female education*.

Taught *plain and ornamental Needlework*.

APPENDIX II   245

Name	Location	Date(s)
Orris, Mrs.	Large room on 10th St., near Pennsylvania Ave., opposite the Threatre.	1818-19
Peters, Mrs. H. A.	E St. between 8th and 9th.	1847
Phillips, Mrs.	Above M. Dalton's, near Lear's wharf.	1799
Plant, Mrs. Martha W.	12th St., opposite King's Painting establishment.	1838
Pratt, Miss E. & M.	Corner of L St. South and 4th St. East.	1832
Public schools of the city of Washington		1806
Reagan, Miss	House next to the one lately occupied by Mr. Elliott on the Capitol Hill.	1807
Reagan, Mrs.	1806 - house F St. between Capt. James Hoban and Josiah W. King; 1807 - F St. near Mr. Semme's tavern.	1806-07
Resolute Beneficial Society	near the Eastern public school	1818
Rooker, Misses	1845 -12th St., near the corner of Maryland Ave., in the southern section of the city, known as "the Island;" 1852 - corner of 6th and F Sts; 1853 - E St., between 6th and 7th.	1845-53
Russ, Rebecca	East side 7th E btw L and M St., Navy Yard	1822-27
Sawkins, Misses	Southwest corner of 12th and F Sts.	1834
Sawkins, Mrs. & Miss	Between 12th and 13th Sts., Pennsylvania Ave.	1823
Shanks, Miss	Large room, 7th St., in Mr. McDuell's new house.	1820
Sinnott, Miss Margaret	1808 - fronting North G St., near the Treasury Office; 1810 - 14th near F st.; 1821 - contiguous to the residence of the British Minister; 1822 - removed from the Seven Buildings to 11th St., nearly opposite Mr. J. McLeod's new building; 1826 - Varnums's Row, D St.; 1827 - F St., next house but one to 7th St., 1842 - moved from Capitol Hill to I St., between 14th St. and St. Matthew's Church.	1808-16 1820-42
Smith, Elizabeth	On "the island," later Capitol hill.	1843-60
Smith, Miss Julia/**St. Martin's School**	L St. North and Vermont Ave.	1867
Smith, Mrs. Isabella and daughters	1830 - K St. north and 13th St. West; 1831 - F St. near 13th.	1830-32
Squire, Miss Maria	1812 - 19th St. West, between F and G Sts.; 1819 - Pennsylvania Ave., opposite the Seven Buildings	1812-19
St. Matthew's School	The Octagon House; 1799 New York Ave., NW.	1860-65
St. Joseph's School for Young Ladies	E St. between 6th and 7th Sts.	1847-50
St. Paul's Female Academy	Capitol Hill.	1831-34
St. Rose's Industrial School	2023 G St.	1868-1947
St. Vincent de Paul Society	1858 - Corner of 14th and H Sts., 1860 - L St., between 12th and 13th.	1858-61
St. Vincent's Orphan and Day School	House of late Marshal Boyd, in F St.	1825-1968
Stone, Anna Maria (Mrs. Henry)	North side F St. between 19th and 20th Sts. West.	1816-22
Tastet, Mrs.	House lately occupied by Miss Hawley as a Seminary, near the Catholic Church.	1817

Comment

Taught *plain and fancy needle work*. M70728

Taught *all the branches of Fancy Needlework, Worsted Flowers, Embroidery, &c.*

From England; moved to Georgetown in 1800; taught *plain work, flowering and marking*. M67290

Taught *plain and fancy Needlework*. M76986

Taught *Plain and Fancy Work*.

Assoc. sampler: **Ella Hancock 1853**.

Taught *Tambouring, embroidery, open work, queen's work, marking, all kinds of plain sewing*. M76164

From Baltimore; also taught in Hagerstown and Frederick, MD; taught *Tambouring, embroidery, open work, queen's work, marking, all kinds of plain sewing*. M76996

Taught *other branches of education*.

From Baltimore; taught *Plain and Ornamental Needlework*.

Needlework assumed.

Taught *ornamental acquirements*.

From Baltimore; taught *plain and fancy Needle Work*.

Taught with Mrs. Archer; plain *Sewing, Marking, Needle Work*. M66792

From Baltimore; taught *different branches of plain and ornamental Needle Work*. M76163

African American; *sewing* assumed; went to Georgetown in 1860.

Catholic; African American; assisted Angela Noel; *sewing and needlework* assumed.

From New York; taught in Georgetown 1829 - 1830; taught *all the branches of useful and ornamental education*.

Taught *plain and ornamental Needle Work, Card work of various descriptions*. M57865

Catholic; Sisters of Charity; *sewing* assumed.

Catholic; Sisters of Charity; taught *Cotton Embroidery, Plain and Ornamental Needlework*; extra charge for *Cheneille and Silk Embroidery*; assoc. sampler: **Caroline R. Masi 1847**.

Catholic; Sisters of Charity; taught *plain and fancy Needle work, Lace Work*.

Catholic; *Sewing, dressmaking* taught.

Catholic; African American; girls taught under Eliza Ann Cook; *sewing* assumed.

Catholic; Sisters of Charity; *taught plain and fancy needlework, tapestry*; assoc. samplers: **Catharine Vonderlehr 1837, Julia Winona Lacey 1848, Mary Ridgway, n.d.**

Operated school with Mr. Stone; taught *Needlework both plain and ornamental*. M38211

Taught Embroidery. M71774

APPENDIX II 247

Name	Location	Date(s)
Taylor, Miss Charlotte Ann/**Female Academy and Boarding School**	1813 - At the house of General Van Ness near Pennsylvania Ave.; 1818 - G St., a little to the westward of Dr. Elzy's dwelling house.	1813-1818
The Colored Orphans' Home/School	8th St.	1863-71+
Thompson, Margaret	26th near Pennsylvania Ave.	1842-46
Thompson, Mrs.	Louisiana Ave., nearly opposite the City Hall.	1829-36
Trinity Institute for Young Ladies/The Young Ladies Institute, Mrs. J. A. Davis, Principal	4 1/2 St., between C St. and Pennsylvania Ave.	1848-51
Turnbul, Mrs. Elizabeth	Pennsylvania Ave., next door to Mrs. Byrne.	1819-22
Turner, Miss	25th St., below I and K Sts.	1832
Tyson, Mary A. & Sisters /**Mary A. Tyson and Sisters' Seminary For Young Ladies**	F St., north side, between 12th and 13th.	1840-55
Union Institute, Miss E. A King, Principal of Female department	E St., between 9th and 10th Sts.	1849
Vidler, Ann	Greenleaf-Point; at 9th and K Sts. S.E. (Navy Yard Hill).	1797
Walker, Miss Susan/**Industrial School**	Campbell barracks, near the terminus of the 7th St. railroad.	1865
Wall, Mary	15th St., NW	1824
Wall, Miss Sarah E. /**New England Friends' Mission**	Government buildings.	1865
Wallace, Mrs.	10th St., adjacent to Pennsylvania Ave.	1820
Washington Female Orphan Asylum School	Northwest corner of 10 St. NW, near Pennsylvania Ave.	1815-1824+
Washington, Annie E	1857 - K between 17th and 18th Sts West; 1858 - L street; 1864 - corner of 19th and I Sts.	1857-67
Western Academy/Miss Young, Principal	Corner of 17th St.	1831-32
Wheat, Mrs.	On 11th St., between G and H Sts.	1832
White, Mrs. Richard		1806
Wolfenden, Mrs. B.	Corner of 4th St. and Virginia Ave.	1823
Wood, Miss/**Washington Eastern Academy**/J. Sterns, Principal		1822
Wood, Miss	13th St., between E and F Sts.	1835
Wood, Mrs. Ellen B./**St. Aloysius School for Girls**	1863 - 15th; 1864 - E St. North; 1867 - Third St. West and G St. North.	1863-67+
Wormley, Mary	Near corner of Vermont Ave. and I St.	1830-32
Wright, Miss Mary F.	House of Mrs. Glover, in 10th St.	1830
Young, Miss Ann	18th St., first door from Pennsylvania Ave.	1845-49

Comment

From England; taught *Plain Sewing, Marking & Muslin work, Fine and Plain Needle-Work.* M57870

African American; Children taught *sewing, knitting, and straw-braiding.*

African American; *sewing* assumed; took over from Fanny Hampton; later married Charles H. Middleton and assisted in his school.

Operated school with Mr. Thompson; taught *Needlework.*

Needlework taught.

Tambour-work taught by lessons if required. M70750

Taught with Mrs. Hyde; *Plain and Ornamental Needlework.*

From Baltimore; taught *Worsted and Ornamental Needlework in all its various branches;* assoc. sampler: **Mary M. Bryant 1848**.

Instruction is given in plain and ornamental needlework.

Taught plain, open and Tambour Work. M64525

Taught *various kinds of plain sewing.*

Quaker; from Virginia; white teacher; taught African American children; *sewing* assumed.

From Massachusetts; white teacher; taught *sewing* to African American children.

Taught *plain needlework, fancy muslin work.* M70753

Sewing taught; Dolley Madison one of the original founders and volunteer seamstress.

African American; *sewing* assumed; later taught in the public schools.

Needlework taught.

Operated school with Mr. Wheat; *taught Ornamental Needle Work.*

Taught various *useful and ornamental kinds of works.*

From Baltimore; taught *plain Sewing and Marking, Embroidery and other ornamental Needle work.*

From Newburyport, MA; taught *Needle-work.*

Taught *Needle Work.*

Born in Hayti [Haiti]; from Philadelphia; for African American girls; *sewing and needlework* assumed.

African American; *sewing* assumed.

From Georgetown; taught *Plain and Ornamental Needle Work.*

A proportionate time will be allotted to the ornamental studies.

Miss Matilda Flanigan Dr. to Convent of the Visitation of St. Mary

1817 Nov.	7	To 6 Months Board, Tuition & washing in advance, at $124 per Ann.	62.00	
"	"	6 ditto Doctors fee	1.50	
"	"	6 do fire for Schools	2.00	
"	"	6 do Ink quills & paper	2.00	
"	"	6 do Slate & pencils	0.25	
"	"	6 do use of bed & Cot	2.00	69.75
1818 May	7	To 6 Months in advance as above	69.75	
"	"	1 pair striped & 1 rose blanket	7.50	
"	"	1 Cloth shawl & 1½ yd flannel	2.84½	
"	"	¾ yd Jaconet muslin & 1½ yd Cambric	1.59½	
"	"	2½ yds Cotton & 2 linen	7.75	89.44
"	"	1 pair Scissors, Canvass & Silks	4.75	
"	"	1 do Shoes & Stockings, Pot & Bason	2.75	
"	"	2 pocket handk. & 2 pieces of tape	00.75	
"	"	2 Combs, 1 paste board & box	00.68½	8.93½
"	"	Thread, Cotton, pins & needles	1.75	
"	"	7 yds Calico for coverlid	1.54	
"	"	½ yd satin ½ do lawn, drawing stand, frame & silk	6.08½	
"	"	1½ yd India Cotton & 6 yds Calico	2.62½	12.00
			Amount	180.12½
1817 Nov.	7	By cash rec'd for one quarters expence	31.00	
1818	"	By do to purchase sundries	30.00	
July	8	By Do — Do — Do —	20.00	$81.00
			Bal. due	$99.12½

APPENDIX III

YOUNG LADIES' ACADEMY, GEORGETOWN, STUDENT RECORDS

Compiled by Susi B. Slocum

The Young Ladies' Academy in Georgetown, administered by the sisters of the Order of the Visitation, was established in 1799. However, very few records earlier than 1816 have survived. A notable exception is the 1800 receipt, signed by Maria Sharpe, the school's first teacher (Figure 6-3). In the receipt, Sharpe wrote the name of the school as George Town Ladies Academy. Later ledgers record the name as Ladies' Academy of the Visitation, which is also found on various annual prizes awarded to students (Figures 6-9, 6-10, 6-11). The name Young Ladies' Academy only appears on needlework produced at the school.

The school kept various account books for their students, and four were researched for this study:

- Entrance Book (1816–1842) — Chronological by student recording the per annum tuition as a day scholar or boarder; certain common expenses; extra fee classes chosen; party responsible for the account; and the home location, if provided.

- Letter Book (1817–1837) — Copies of correspondence concerning the student's account, academic progress, and well-being. Sections of this book were also used to create a chronological summary of journal entries for each student (like the Student Ledger).

- Journal (1818–1830, 1830–1835, 1835–1845) — Record of specific transactions (expenses and payments) in chronological sequence for all students. Composite journal entries were posted to the Student Ledger.

- Student Ledger (1817–1836) — Account book of debits and credits by student name, being a chronological summary by year of journal entries and showing that the account balanced over the period of enrollment or until it was paid in full.

The earliest embroidery charges found in the available account books occurred in May 1818 for Matilda Flanigan (Figure III-1) and followed on through 1820 for other students.

Journal entries disclose silk work on canvas, silk for sampler, and silk and chenille on satin. A total of nine distinct needlework charges, each with individual costs, were listed in an entry for Eliza Neale in November 1819.

The ledgers also reveal subsequent embroidery instruction for some of the girls known to have stitched samplers. Eleanor Waring, for example, began a more advanced satin embroidery in 1820, following her 1819 sampler (Figure 6-25). The last expense for "drawing a piece" (of embroidery) was in December 1823. To date, no satin or silk embroideries from the 1818–1823 period have been discovered.

In November 1818, the first flat fee "piece of embroidery" at $12 was charged to Elizabeth Lancaster (Figure III-2). Her entry also shows "Silks for Sampler" at $2. The flat fee pricing was not consistently used until 1821 and then only through 1824. The later "piece of embroidery" entries probably recall the earlier designation and were most likely tapestry to stitch covers for a footstool, music stand, lamp stand, or pitcher stand. The fee ranged between $7 and $12.

The dearth of embroidery entries after 1821 is evident in the records. Besides the ongoing economic depression, it probably reflects the change in curricular focus engendered by Father Clorivière's more academic 1822 prospectus, followed by Father Wheeler's emphasis on modern science, with "Philosophical and Chemical apparatus," as of 1827.

By June 1825, recorded costs changed from embroidery to "tapestry." The tapestry fees ranged from 50 cents to $10. The 1833 charge for Ellen Jenkins specified, "materials for a large piece of tapestry," probably signaling the arrival of more advanced Berlin wool work patterns that fostered some student canvas work of religious subjects. Tapestry entries are noted up through 1837 for the period studied.

The interest in tapestry waxed and waned as other types of handwork became popular, such as hand-size fire screens from 1829 to 1830. Fancy work also competed with tapestry during 1830 and especially in 1831. The average cost of the screen or the fancy work was $5. More importantly, the students were dwelling on their scientific course work and spending $5 on "use of apparatus."

In summary, extant student records for the Young Ladies' Academy of Georgetown show charges for needlework materials, patterns, and equipment from 1818 until the late 1880s.

Student(s) First Name	Student(s) Last Name	Date of Entry	Embroidery Charges	Cost
Matilda	Flanigan	May 1818	Canvass & Silks; tape; satin, lawn, drawing, stand, frame & silk; India Cotton	$10.84
Elizabeth	Lancaster	7/8/1818	White satin; drawing satin; linen, India Cotton & tape; use of stand & frame	$4.56
Mary	Byrne	10/1/1818	Satin; linen; Cotton; tape; drawing Satin; use of stand & frame	$4.75
Elizabeth	Lancaster	Nov 1818	Silks for Sampler; piece of embroidery	$14.00
Rebecca	Boarman	2/10/1819	Drawing a piece for embroidery; use of stand & frame; Shenille; spool floss; Card floss	$6.58
Matilda	Flanigan	5/7/1819	Silk for sampler; spool floss silk; card floss silk; shenelle	$14.52
Elizabeth	Lancaster	8/8/1819	Silks for sampler; spool floss silk; card floss silk; shenille	$14.52
Adeline	Posey	8/9/1819	Satin; linen; india cotton	$1.63
Catharine	Cleary	8/22/1819	Satin & materials for embroidery	$6.00
Rebecca	Boarman	9/10/1819	Piece of embroidery	$8.00
Eliza	Neale	11/23/1819	Satin for embroidery; fine linen; tape; Shenille; spool floss; card floss; drawing piece for embroidery; use of stand & frame for embroidery	$11.44
Harriott	Yost	12/16/1819	Drawing & materials for embroidery	$10.00
Mary A.	Fenwick	4/5/1820	Piece of embroidery	$10.00
Eleanor & Henrietta	**Waring**	4/5/1820	Satin; fine linen; india cotton; tape; drawing two pieces for embroidery; use of stands & frames for embroidery; Shenille; card floss; spool floss	$22.79
Mary	Burns	8/16/1820	Satin, linen; india cotton, tape; drawing her piece, use of stand & frame; Spool floss; card floss	$10.01
Mary A.	Fenwick	9/1/1820	Lutestring; linen; india cotton; tape; drawing her piece; use of stand & frame; card floss	$4.88
Elizabeth	Spalding	3/7/1821	Piece of embroidery	$10.00
Henrietta	Thompson	5/2/1821	Piece of embroidery	$10.00
Elizabeth	Spalding	12/20/1821	Piece of embroidery	$8.00
Adelaide	Jullien	6/1/1822	Piece of Embroidery	$7.00
Ann Delia	Myers	12/11/1823	Drawing a piece of Embroidery & the Use of a stand & frame	$3.50
Eleanora	**Neale**	1823	Board and tuition expenses but no charges recorded for 1823 sampler	
Margaret	Barry	1/9/1824	Piece of Embroidery	$8.00
Mary E.	Boothe	4/2/1824	Piece of Embroidery	$8.00
Ann Eliza & Henrietta	Tarbell	12/12/1824	Piece of embroidery	$8.00

Student(s) First Name	Student(s) Last Name	Date of Entry	Embroidery Charges	Cost
Maria & Elizabeth	Carroll	6/22/1825	2 Covers in Tapestry for Musick Stools; 2 Covers in Tapestry for foot stools	$10.00
Elizabeth	Threlkeld	7/11/1825	Materials for working a musick stool Cover	$3.00
Catharine	McSherry	3/29/1826	Two musick stools	$6.00
Misses (Ann)	Cassin	7/1/1827	1 music stand cover	$5.00
Eliza & Julia	Garesche	5/5/1828	1 piece of tapestry	$4.00
Henrietta	Dunlop	7/24/1828	Piece of tapestry	$3.00
Misses	Smith	9/18/1828	2 pieces of tapestry	$6.00
Mary	**Laurence**	1829	Day scholar tuition expenses but no charges recorded for sampler dated 1829	
Misses	Lasala	10/2/1829	Fire screens & tapestry	$10.50
Elizabeth	Cox	9/21/1830	Tapestry	$2.50
M. (Mary) O. (Olivia)	Stonestreet	10/6/1830	Music stool (amount combined with unrelated expenses)	$10.96
M. (Mary) E.	Mahoney	1/24/1831	Mat(erials) for Tapestry & pieces of music	$3.75
Frances	Helm	4/16/1831	Piece of tapestry	Blank
E. (Ellen) A. (Ann)	Hill	7/11/1831	Materials for tapestry	$4.00
Robina	Hillen	7/27/1831	Materials for tapestry	$4.00
Clementina	Graham	9/1/1831	Materials of tapestry	$4.00
Alicia	Freeman	9/8/1831	Materials for tapestry	$4.00
Misses	Nicholson	9/16/1831	Materials for tapestry	$4.00
Frederica	Bonford	9/17/1831	Materials for tapestry	$1.00
Mary	Fitzgerald	9/20/1831	Materials for tapestry	$4.00
A. (Ann)	Brooks	10/5/1831	Materials for tapestry	$4.00
Mary	Coursey	10/5/1831	Materials for tapestry	$3.00
Maria	Brent	10/5/1831	Materials for tapestry	$4.25
E. (Ellen) A. (Ann)	Hill	10/5/1831	Materials for tapestry	$4.00
E. (Emily)	Long	10/5/1831	Materials for tapestry	$4.00
E. (Elizabeth)	Reilly	10/5/1831	Materials for tapestry (lamp); materials for tapestry (foot stool)	$7.00
F.	High	10/5/1831	Materials for tapestry	$3.00
E.	Jenkins	10/5/1831	Materials for tapestry	$3.00
[Emily]	O'Donnell	10/5/1831	Materials for tapestry	$4.00
Misses	Pearson	10/5/1831	Materials for tapestry	$4.00
E.	Rodgers	10/5/1831	Materials for tapestry	$4.50
E. (Elizabeth)	Beall	10/5/1831	Materials for tapestry	$3.00
Elizabeth	Reilly	10/20/1831	Materials for tapestry	$7.00
Mary	Reilly	4/13/1832	Books, tapestry & shoes	$8.39
Camilla	Brette	7/5/1832	Materials for tapestry	$5.00
Mary	Fitzgerald	7/5/1832	Materials for tapestry	$5.00

Student(s) First Name	Student(s) Last Name	Date of Entry	Embroidery Charges	Cost
Ellen Ann	Hill	7/5/1832	Materials for tapestry	$4.00
Robina	Hillen	7/5/1832	Materials for lamp stands	$5.00
Mary	Neally	7/8/1832	Materials for Embroidery	$7.00
Camilla	Brette	9/15/1832	Materials for tapestry	$5.00
M. Louisa	Smith	June 1833	Tapestry	$1.50
Elizabeth	Cox	6/26/1833	Materials for tapestry	$4.50
Abby	Clark	7/9/1833	Materials for tapestry	$10.00
R. (Robina) F.	Hillen	7/9/1833	1 pr foot stools in tapestry	$4.50
M. (Mary) L. (Louisa)	Hobby	7/9/1833	Materials for tapestry	$5.00
Ellen	Jenkins	7/9/1833	Materials for a large piece of tapestry	$6.50
Misses	Nicholson	7/9/1833	5 pieces of tapestry	$12.00
R. (Rosetta)	Worthington	7/9/1833	Pitcher stands in tapestry	$4.00
Mary	Fitzgerald	7/10/1833	Materials for tapestry	$3.00
E. (Ellen) A. (Ann)	Hill	7/11/1833	Piece of emb 8.00, framed velvet samp 9.00	$17.00
R. (Rosetta)	Worthington	7/11/1833	Piece of embroidery & frame	$18.00
Elizabeth	Bromwell	7/24/1833	Materials for tapestry	$2.50
Elizabeth T.	Cox	10/15/1833	Tapestry	$2.00
V. (Virginia)	Edwards	11/4/1833	Frames for painting and embroidery	$14.50
Margaret	Clinton	11/22/1833	Piece of embroidery	$10.00
H. (Hellen)	Mason	11/26/1833	Tapestry	$2.50
Misses	Ewing	12/17/1833	Tapestry	$4.00
Mary	Hunter	1/2/1834	Tapestry	$2.00
E.	Jenkins	1/2/1834	Tapestry	$8.00
Maria L.	Hobby	2/28/1834	Tapestry	$2.00
Henria	Clayton	3/18/1834	Tapestry	$1.00
Louisa	Fenwick	4/5/1834	Tapestry	$1.50
Elizabeth	Bromwell	5/22/1834	Tapestry	$2.00
Jane	Whyte	5/26/1834	Tapestry	$0.50
Leonide	Duperu	5/27/1834	Tapestry	$0.50
Mary	Jones	5/27/1834	Tapestry	$0.50
Charlotte	Coad	7/10/1834	Tapestry	$2.00
Mary	Hunter	7/18/1834	Tapestry	$2.00
Eliza	Smith	7/23/1834	Tapestry	$1.50
Rosey	Spence	7/23/1834	Tapestry	$1.10
Abossinon?	Clay	Sept 1834	Tapestry	$1.00
Elizabeth	Cox	10/1/1834	Tapestry	$2.00
Mary	Villard	10/13/1834	Tapestry	$1.00
Jo. (Josephine)	Warring	10/24/1834	Tapestry	$1.00
Mary	Villard	12/2/1834	Tapestry	$5.00

Student(s) First Name	Student(s) Last Name	Date of Entry	Embroidery Charges	Cost
Eliza	Durkin	1/7/1835	Tapestry	$2.50
Martha	Duvall	1/7/1835	Tapestry	$2.50
Eliza	Ewing	2/14/1835	Tapestry	$6.00
Ann & E. (Emma)	Norvell	3/4/1835	Pieces of tapestry	$3.00
Josephine	Warring	3/24/1835	Piece of tapestry	$1.00
Maria	Mitchell	April 1835	Piece of tapestry	$1.00
Lucretia	Thompson	5/1/1835	Tapestry	$5.00
Mary	MaGruder	5/20/1835	Piece of tapestry	$2.00
Maria	Mitchell	7/3/1835	Piece of tapestry	$1.00
Mary	MaGruder	7/6/1835	Piece of tapestry	$5.00
Lucretia	Thompson	7/6/1835	Piece of tapestry	$5.00
Celestia	Reardon	8/19/1835	Piece of tapestry	$1.00
Ellen	McDonnell	10/15/1835	Piece of tapestry	$5.00
Louisa	Villard	10/15/1835	Tapestry	$1.00
Martha	Pearson	10/24/1835	Tapestry	$5.00
Mary	Liggat	11/9/1835	Piece of tapestry	$1.00
Henrietta	DeCousey	April 1836	Tapestry	$4.00
May	Coyle	4/16/1836	Piece of tapestry	$1.00
Ellen	McDonnell	5/4/1836	Piece tapestry	$3.00
Emily	Gardiner	5/8/1836	Tapestry	$1.50
Eliz. & Ann	Jewel	7/22/1836	1 Foot stool (Tapestry)	$4.00
Adelle	Cochran	Sept 1836	Piece of tapestry	$2.00
Virginia	Semmes	9/17/1836	Piece of Tapestry	$2.50
Rebecca	Alford	2/2/1837	Tapestry	$4.00
Elizabeth	Thompson	2/6/1837	Piece of Tapestry	$4.00
Camilla	Calhoon	2/13/1837	Tapestry	$4.00
Sarah	Williams	3/1/1837	Materials for Tapestry	$2.00
Ellen	McDonnell	5/11/1837	Books, music, tapestry etc.	$11.68
Matilda	Waring	6/3/1837	Tapestry	$1.50

NOTE: This list based on available account books at the Georgetown Visitation Monastery Archives.
Name in bold designates a student whose needlework is extant.

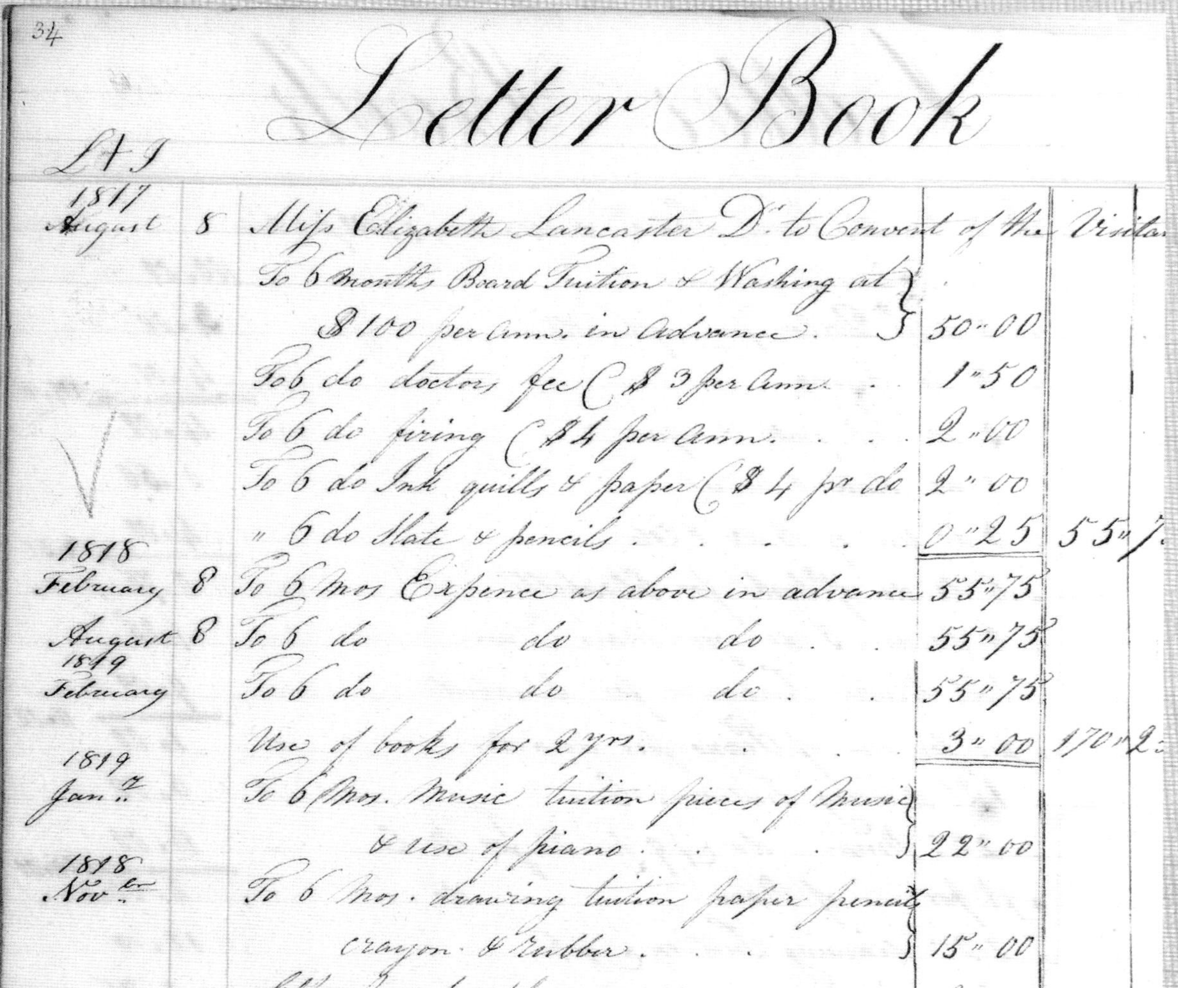

Letter Book

34

L+S

1817 August 8		Miss Elizabeth Lancaster D.r to Convent of the Visita[tion]		
		To 6 months Board Tuition & Washing at $100 per Ann. in Advance	50"00	
		To 6 do doctors fee @ $3 per Ann.	1"50	
		To 6 do firing @ $4 per Ann.	2"00	
		To 6 do Ink quills & paper @ $4 pr do	2"00	
		" 6 do Slate & pencils	0"25	55"75
1818 February 8		To 6 Mos Expence as above in advance	55"75	
August 8		To 6 do do do	55"75	
1819 February		To 6 do do do	55"75	
1819 Jan.y		Use of books for 2 yrs.	3"00	170"25
		To 6 Mos. Music tuition pieces of Music & use of piano	22"00	
1818 Nov.r		To 6 Mos. drawing tuition paper pencils crayon & rubber	15"00	
		Silks for Sampler	2"00	
		On account of her piece of embroidery	12"00	51"00
1819 May 27		To 6 Mos. drawing &c. in advance as above	15"00	
July		To 6 do Music &c as above	22"00	
August 8		To 6 Mos Board. Tuition. Washing & other expenses as above in advance	55"75	92"75
		Supra C.r		$369"75
		By Cash rec.d from her brother	50"00	
		By do p.r Rev.d Charles Neale	50"00	
		By do p.r Miss C Lancaster	100"00	200
		Bal.ce due		$169

Figure III-2. Letter Book entries for Elizabeth Lancaster. 1817-1819.
Georgetown Visitation Monastery Archives

SELECT BIBLIOGRAPHY

Allen, Gloria Seaman. *A Maryland Sampling: Girlhood Embroidery, 1738–1860.* Baltimore: Maryland Historical Society, 2007.

———. "'Plain and Ornamental Needle-Work' from the Young Ladies' Academy of Georgetown: Recent Attributions." *The 43rd Washington Antiques Show Catalogue.* Washington, DC, 1998.

———. "Needlework Education in Antebellum Alexandria, Virginia." *The Magazine Antiques* 159, no. 2 (February 2001): 332–41.

———. "Pictorial Embroideries from Antebellum Alexandria: The Students of Sarah Eliza Edmonds." *Sampler and Antique Needlework Quarterly* 17, no. 3 (2011): 40–46.

———. "Embroidered Maps from Alexandria, District of Columbia." *Sampler and Antique Needlework Quarterly* 17, no. 4 (2011): 42–46.

Atlee, Samuel Yorke. *History of the Public Schools of the City of Georgetown.* Georgetown, DC: Board of Trustees, for the National Centennial Year, 1876.

Barnard, Henry. *Special Report of the Commissioner of Education on the Condition and Improvement of Public Schools in the District of Columbia.* Washington, DC: Government Printing Office, 1871.

Barnes, Robert. *Marriages and Deaths from Baltimore Newspapers 1796–1816.* Baltimore: Genealogical Publishing Co., Inc., 1978.

Bivins, John and Forsyth Alexander. *The Regional Arts of the Early South.* Winston-Salem, NC: MESDA, 1991.

Bolton, Ethel Stanwood, and Eva Johnston Coe. *American Samplers.* New York: Dover Publications, Inc. 1973.

Bowie, Effie Gwynn. *Across the Years in Prince George's County.* 1947; repr., Baltimore: Genealogical Publishing Co., Inc., 1975.

Bryan, Wilhelmus Bogart. *A History of the National Capital: From Its Foundations through the Period of the Adoption of the Organic Act.* New York: Macmillan, 1916.

Caemmerer, H. Paul. *A Manual on the Origin and Development of Washington.* Washington, DC: United States Government Printing Office, 1939.

Catalogue of the Members of the Female Seminary, for the Year Commencing September 1, 1834 . . . Georgetown, DC: W. A. Rind, Senior, 1835.

Catalogue of the Members of the Female Seminary, for the Year Commencing September 1, 1835 . . . Washington, DC: Duff Green, 1836.

Catalogue of the Members of the Female Seminary, for the Year Commencing September 1, 1847 . . . Washington, DC, 1848.

Catalogue of the Female Seminary, Georgetown, D.C. for the session 1854–1855 . . . Washington, DC: R. A. Waters, 1855.

Crew, Harvey W., ed., *Centennial History of the City of Washington, D.C.* Dayton, OH: Published for H. W. Crew by the United Brethren Publishing House, 1892.

Curry, Mary E. "The Georgetown Female Seminary and the National Park Seminary." Unpublished research paper, American University, spring 1970.

Darwin, Erasmus. *A Plan for the Conduct of Female Education in Boarding Schools, Private Families, and Public Seminaries.* Philadelphia, John Ormrod, 1798.

Davis, Madison. "The Navy Yard Section during the Life of the Rev. William Ryland." *Records of the Columbia Historical Society* 4 (1901): 200.

Deutsch, Davida Tenenbaum. "Needlework Patterns and Their Use in America." *The Magazine Antiques* 139, no. 2 (February 1991): 368–81.

———. "Samuel Folwell of Philadelphia: An Artist for the Needleworker." *The Magazine Antiques* 119, no. 2 (February, 1981): 420–23.

——— and Betty Ring. "Homage to Washington in Needlework and Prints." *The Magazine Antiques* 119, no. 2 (February 1981): 402–19.

Dixon, Joan M. *National Intelligencer & Washington Advertiser Newspaper Abstracts 1806–1810*. Bowie, MD: Heritage Books, Inc., 1996.

———. *National Intelligencer Newspaper Abstracts 1824–1826*. Bowie, MD: Heritage Books, Inc., 1997, 1999. [and subsequent]

Donnelly, Mary Louise. *Major William Boarman, Charles County, Maryland (1630–1709) His Descendants*. Ennis, TX: The author, 1990.

Downing, Margaret Brent. "The Development of the Catholic Church in the District of Columbia from Colonial Times to the Present." *Records of the Columbia Historical Society* 15 (1912): 39–43.

Ecker, Grace. *A Portrait of Old Georgetown*. Richmond: Dietz Press, 1951.

Elliot, Jonathan. *Historical Sketches of the Ten Miles Square*. Washington: J. Elliot Jr., 1830.

Ferguson, George. *Signs and Symbols in Christian Art*. New York: Oxford University Press, 1958.

Finkel, M. & Daughter. *Samplings: A Selected Offering of Antique Samplers and Needlework*. Philadelphia: M. Finkel & Daughter, Inc., 1992–2012.

Garrett, Elisabeth Donaghy. "American Samplers and Needlework Pictures in the DAR Museum, Part II: 1806–1840." *The Magazine Antiques* 107, no. 4 (April 1975), 694–98.

Gell, Mada-anne. "A History of the Development of Curriculum, Georgetown Visitation Preparatory School 1865–1965." Ph.D. diss., Catholic University, 1983.

———. "Georgetown Visitation: The Myth of the Finishing School." *Salesian Living Heritage*, 1 (1986), 31–38.

Genealogical Research Committee Report, New Jersey, Series 1, Volume 67. *Tombstone Inscriptions of Persons Born before 1820 and Buried in the Western Half of Riverview Cemetery Trenton, New Jersey*. Submitted by General David Forman Chapter. National Society of the Daughters of the American Revolution, 1929; repr., Hazelwood, MO: Elizabeth Jones Leighton, 1997.

Genealogical Research Committee Report, Pennsylvania, Series 1, Volume 153. *Marriage Register from 1787 to 1799 St. Joseph's Church Philadelphia Pennsylvania*. Compiled by Rev. Robert A. Parsons S.J. Submitted by Judge Lynn Chapter. Washington, DC: National Society Daughters of the American Revolution, 1952.

Genealogical Research Committee Report, Virginia, Series 1, Volume 66. *Register of Baptisms, Marriages and Funerals During the Ministry of the Revd Doct^r James Muir in the Presbyterian Church of Alexandria, D.C.* Submitted by Fairfax County Chapter. Washington, DC: National Society Daughters of the American Revolution, 1953.

Georgetown Visitation Monastery Archives, Entrance Book, 1816–1842.

Georgetown Visitation Monastery Archives, Ledgers, 1817–1845.

Georgetown Visitation Monastery Archives, Letter Book, 1817–1837.

Graffam, Olive Blair. *"Youth Is the Time for Progress": The Importance of American Schoolgirl Art, 1780–1860*. Washington, DC: DAR Museum, 1998.

Herr, Patricia T. *"The Ornamental Branches": Needlework and Arts from the Lititz Moravian Girls' School between 1800 and 1865*. Lancaster, PA: The Heritage Center Museum of Lancaster County, 1996.

Hibben, Henry B. *Navy Yard, Washington: History from Organization, 1799 to Present Date*. Washington: Government Printing Office, 1890.

Hinshaw, William Wade. *Encyclopedia of American Quaker Genealogy*. Vol. 6. 1950; repr., Baltimore: Genealogical Publishing Co., Inc., 1973, 1993.

Hollan, Catherine B. *In the Neatest, Most Fashionable Manner: Three Centuries of Alexandria Silver*. Alexandria, VA: The Lyceum, 1994.

Hollowak, Thomas L. *Index to Marriages and Deaths in The [Baltimore] Sun, 1837–1850.* Baltimore: Genealogical Publishing Co., Inc., 1978.

Huber, Carol. "What Were They Thinking? Silk Embroideries Give Us a Clue." *Antiques & Fine Art* 9, no.2 (Winter–Spring 2009): 244–49.

Huber, Stephen and Carol Huber, compilers. *The Sampler Engagement Calendar and Reference Guide 1999.* Old Saybrook, CT, 1992–2003.

Ivey, Kimberly Smith. *In the Neatest Manner: The Making of the Virginia Sampler Tradition.* Austin, TX: Curious Works Press; Williamsburg, VA: The Colonial Williamsburg Foundation, 1997.

Jackson, Richard P. *The Chronicles of Georgetown, D.C. from 1751 to 1878.* Washington: R. O. Polkinhorn, printer, 1878.

Johansen, Mary Carroll. "All Useful, Plain Branches of Education: Educating Non-Elite Women in Antebellum Virginia." *Virginia Cavalcade* 49 (Spring 2000): 76–83.

———. "'Intelligence, Though Overlooked': Education for Black Women in the Upper South, 1800–1840." *Maryland Historical Magazine* 93 (1998): 443–66.

Johnston, Christopher. "The Brooke Family." *Maryland Genealogies: From the Maryland Historical Magazine*, Volume 1. Baltimore: Genealogical Publishing Co., Inc., 1980.

———. "Neale Family of Charles County." *Maryland Genealogies: A Consolidation of Articles from the Maryland Historical Magazine*, Volume 2. Baltimore: Genealogical Publishing Co., Inc., 1980.

The Junior League of Washington. *The City of Washington: An Illustrated History*, edited by Thomas Froncek. New York: Alfred A. Knopf, 1977.

Kaestle, Carl F. *Joseph Lancaster and the Monitorial School Movement: A Documentary History.* New York: Teachers College Press, 1973.

Krueger, Glee F. *A Gallery of American Samplers: The Theodore H. Kapnek Collection.* New York: E. P. Dutton, in association with the Museum of American Folk Art, 1978.

Lancaster, Joseph. *An Account of the Lancasterian Method of Teaching Needlework.* Baltimore, ca. 1821.

———. *The British System of Education: Being a Complete Epitome of the Improvements and Inventions . . .* Washington: Joseph Milligan, 1812.

Lathrop, George Parsons and Ruth Hawthorne Lathrop. *A Story of Courage: Annals of the Georgetown Convent of the Visitation of the Blessed Virgin Mary.* Cambridge, MA: Riverside Press, 1895.

Love, Ellen Lane and Frank Earl Cooley Jr. "The Family of Thomas Love of Truro Parish, Fairfax County, Virginia." Unpublished manuscript, 1965.

Mackall, S. Somervell. *Early Days of Washington.* Washington, DC: The Neale Co., 1899.

Mapping Maryland: The Willard Hackerman Collection. Baltimore: Maryland Historical Society, 1998.

McGroarty, William Buckner. "Elizabeth Washington of Hayfield." *Virginia Magazine of History and Biography* 33 (1925): 154–65.

———. *The Old Presbyterian Meeting House at Alexandria Virginia 1774–1874.* Richmond: Wm. Byrd Press, 1940.

Melish, John. *Travels through the United States of America, in the years 1806 & 1807, and 1809, 1810, & 1811; including an account of passages betwixt America and Britain, and travels through various parts of Britain, Ireland, & Canada.* London and Dublin: Melish, Cowie and Cumming, 1818.

Miller, T. Michael. *Artisans and Merchants of Alexandria, Virginia 1780–1820.* Vols. 1 & 2. Bowie, MD: Heritage Books, 1991–1992.

———. *Portrait of a Town: Alexandria, District of Columbia 1820–1830.* Bowie, MD: Heritage Books, 1995.

Mitchell, Mary. *Divided Town.* Barre, MA: Barre Publishers, 1968.

Moore, Gay Montague. *Seaport in Virginia: George Washington's Alexandria.* Richmond, VA: Garrett and Massie, Inc., 1949.

Morrow, Diane Batts. *Persons of Color and Religious at the Same Time: The Oblate Sisters of Providence, 1828–1860.* Chapel Hill: University of North Carolina Press, 2002.

New Advent Catholic Encyclopedia.

Newman, Harry Wright. *Charles County Gentry.* 1940; repr., Baltimore: Genealogical Publishing Co., Inc., 1971.

"Notices of Marriages and Deaths in *Poulson's American Daily Advertiser, 1811–1825.*" *Collections of the Genealogical Society of Pennsylvania.* Vol. 61. Philadelphia: The Genealogical Society of Pennsylvania, 1901.

O'Neill, Francis P. *Index of Obituaries and Marriages in The [Baltimore] Sun 1871–1875.* Vol. 1. Westminster, MD: Family Line Publications, 1995.

Our Town, 1749–1865: Likenesses of this Place & Its People Taken from Life, by Artists Known and Unknown. Alexandria, VA: Alexandria Association, 1956.

Parran, Alice Norris. *Series II of "Register of Maryland's Heraldic Families."* Baltimore: The Southern Maryland Society of Colonial Dames, 1938.

Peden, Henry C. Jr. *Baltimore City Deaths and Burials 1834–1840.* Westminster, MD: Family Line Publications, 1998.

———. *Bastardy Cases in Harford County, Maryland, 1774–1844.* Bowie MD: Willow Bend Books, 2001.

———. *Revolutionary Patriots of Charles County, Maryland 1775–1783.* Westminster, MD: Family Line Publications, 1997.

Piet, Mary A., and Stanley G. Piet, compilers. *Early Catholic Church Records in Baltimore, Maryland 1782 through 1800.* Westminster, MD: Family Line Publications, 1989.

Pippenger, Wesley E. *Dead People on the Move! Reconstruction of the Georgetown Presbyterian Burying Ground, Holmead's (Western) Burying Ground, and Other Removals in the District of Columbia.* Westminster, MD: Willow Bend Books, 2004.

———. *District of Columbia Marriage Licenses Register 1, 1811–1858.* Westminster, MD: Family Line Publications, 1994.

———. *District of Columbia Probate Records, Will Books 1 through 6, 1801–1852 and Estate Files 1801–1852.* Westminster, MD: *Family Line Publications, 1996.*

———. *Georgetown District of Columbia Marriage and Death Notices 1801–1838.* Bowie MD: Willow Bend Books, 2004.

———. *Tombstone Inscriptions of Alexandria, Virginia.* Vol. 1. Westminster, MD: Family Line Publications, 1992, rev. 1993.

Powell, Mary G. *The History of Old Alexandria, Virginia.* Westminster, MD: Family Line Publications, 1995.

Preston, Emmett D. Jr. "The Development of Negro Education in the District of Columbia." *Journal of Negro Education* 9 (1940): 595–603.

Proctor, J. C. "Joseph Lancaster and the Lancasterian Schools in the District of Columbia." *Records of the Columbia Historical Society,* 25 (1921).

Reps, John W. *Washington on View: The Nation's Capital Since 1790.* Chapel Hill: The University of North Carolina Press, 1991.

Ring, Betty. *Girlhood Embroidery: American Samplers & Pictorial Needlework 1650–1850.* 2 vols. New York: Alfred A. Knopf, 1993.

———. "Maryland Map Samplers." *Maryland Antiques Show and Sale.* Baltimore: Maryland Historical Society, 1986, 105–9.

Robare, Mary Holton. *When This You See Remember Me. . . . Schoolgirl Samplers of Winchester and Frederick County, Virginia.* Harrisonburg, VA Winchester-Frederick County Historical Society, 2010.

Robertson, Ann Bigley. *An Enduring Legacy: The Painting Collection of Georgetown Visitation.* Washington, DC: Georgetown Visitation Monastery, 2000.

Royall, Anne Newport. *Sketches of History, Life, and Manners in the United States.* New Haven, CT, 1826.

Sargent, Jean A., ed. *Stones and Bones: Cemetery Records of Prince George's County Maryland.* Bowie, MD: Prince George's County Genealogical Society, Inc., 1984.

Schiffer, Margaret B. *Historical Needlework of Pennsylvania.* New York: Charles Scribner's Sons, 1968.

Sharp, John G. *History of the Early Washington Navy Yard, 1799–1860.* Washington, DC: Naval District Washington, 2005.

Sizer, Theodore, Nancy Sizer, et al. *To Ornament Their Minds: Sarah Pierce's Litchfield Female Academy, 1792–1833.* Litchfield, CT: The Litchfield Historical Society, 1993.

Smedley, Susanna, compiler. *Catalog of Westtown Through the Years.* Westtown, PA: Westtown Alumni Association, 1945.

INDEX

Page numbers in *italics* indicate figures and *n* indicates footnotes.

Abbot, Mary Moulder, 98, *99*
Abbott, Martha Duncan, 98, *98* (sampler)
abolition, 31, 46*n*, 206
academies
    Alexandria, 27*n*, 41
    Miss Bootes' Female Academy, 73*n*
    St. Agnes' Academy, 146
    St. Francis Xavier's, 44, *44*
    St. Joseph's, 214
    St. Paul's Female, 148
    Washington Academy East, 143, 169, 177, 187
    Young Ladies' Academy of Georgetown, 49*n*, 73, 74, 77, 101, 103–105, *104*, 106, *107*, 110*n*, 111, 112, 113*n*, 113–114, 116–118, *117*, *118*, 120, 121–122, 124, 127–130, *128*, *129*, *130*, 132–134, *133*, *134*, 137–138, *138*, 157
Adams, John, 50*n*, 167
Adams, John Quincy, 111, 111*n*, 192
African Americans
    Banneker, Benjamin, 58
    Becraft, Maria, 75, 75*n*
    Bell School House, 145
    Cameron, Mrs., 11
    education of, 9*n*, 11, 11*n*, 12, 74–75, 75*n*, 111*n*, 145, 145*n*, 146, 146*n*, 192
    free blacks, 11, 32, 73, 75*n*, 145
    Jones, Arabella, 146
    Morris, Sylvia, 11
    Navy Yard School, 145–146
    needlework instruction, 11–12, 214
    Oblate Sisters of Providence, 146
    Shinner, Michael diary, 146*n*
    Tutten, 11
Alexandria, 141, 213
    apprenticeship and indenture, 19, 203–204
    early history, 7, 7*n*, 8–12, 141
    pictorial embroideries, 49–58
    printed maps, 58–66
    schools
        Alexandria Academy, 27*n*, 41
        Lancasterian, 9–10, 74, 143
        Muir, Mary Lang, 42–43
        St. Francis Xavier's Academy, 44
        teachers and schools in, 191
        Washington Free School, 9*n*
        Young Ladies' Boarding and Day School, 13
    teachers, 12–14, 213
    themes, 50
    View of, by James T. Palmatary, 8–9
Alexandria Advertiser, 12*n*, 13*n*, 18*n*, 20*n*, 192*n*, 200*n*
Alexandria Advertiser and Commercial Intelligencer, 66*n*
Alexandria Daily Advertiser, 25*n*, 31*n*, 64*n*
Alexandria Free School for Girls. *See* Female Lancasterian School.
Alexandria Gazette, 44
American Revolution, 8, 9*n*, 21, 26, 29, 59, 101, 119*n*, 123*n*, 19,
Atkinson, Sarah E., 46, 46*n*, *47* (sampler)

B

Balch, Jane Whann, 79*n*, *216* (embroidered picture)
Balch, Reverend Stephen Bloomer, 79, 216
Baltimore American and Commercial Daily Advertiser, 124*n*
Baltimore Fire Insurance Company, 112*n*
Barber, Jerusha, 105, 107*n*
Barton, Elizabeth, *23* (sampler), 24–25
Beall, Harriet, 80–81, *81* (sampler)
Beall, Margaret, 91
Beall, Ninian, 80, 81, 81*n*
Becraft, Maria, 75
Bell School House, 145
Benton, Jessie Ann, 91
Boarman, Mary Rose, 125, 126, *126* (sampler), *127* (sampler), 129–130, 129*n*, 135
Boarman, Rebecca, 108*n*, *129*, 129
Bohlayer, Mary Christeen, 186, *187* (sampler)
Bontz, Mary Ann, 38–39, *38* (sampler), 40
Boswell, Maria, 152*n*, 175–177, *176* (sampler), 177*n*, 178, 179, 181, 184
Brooke, Mary Rebecca J., *126* (sampler), 128, 128*n*, 129
Brown, William Templeman memorial, *22* (sampler), 23-24, 23*n*,
Bryant, Mary M., 67*n*, 208, *208* (sampler)
Bull Run, battle of, 92*n*
Burr, Aaron, 50, 50*n*

C

Campbell, Anne, 53, 54, 54*n*, *54* (embroidered picture), 55
Carbery, Helen, 163, *163* (sampler)
Carroll, Charles, 121, 121*n*
Carroll, Daniel, 121, 121*n*
Carroll, Henry Hill, 121, 121*n*
Carroll, John, 105, 115*n*, 128*n*, 131*n*
Carroll, Mary Ann, *120* (sampler), 121–122
Carson, Ann, 35–36, 38, 42
Carter, Sarah Ann, 164, *164* (sampler), 165
Cassady, Catherine, 180–181, *181* (sampler), 181*n*
Cassedy, Margaret A., 181–182, *181* (sampler), 182*n*
Catholic Female School, Frederick, Maryland, 157
Centinel of Liberty & Georgetown & Washington Advertiser, 75*n*, 87*n*, 103*n*, 121*n*, 200, 200*n*, 201*n*

Chevalier, Sister Luc, 102
Clemens, Catherine Ann Lavinia, 136, *137* (embroidered picture)
cholera, 88*n*
Cloriviere, Father, *106*, 107, 107*n*, 108*n*, 110, 134, 138
Clubb, Charlotte, *175* (sampler), 175–177, 180, 187
Combs, Celestia Mary, 125, *125* (sampler), 127–128
Conceria, P., *America*, 50, *50*, 50*n*
Copley, Mary, 82, *82* (sampler)
Copper, Christiana, 18, 18*n*
Cox, James, 119
Crowley, Julia Ann, *172* (sampler), 172–174, *178* (sampler), 178–179

D

Daily American Advertiser, 199*n*
De La Marche, Madame Marie, 75, 101, 103–105, 201
De La Rochefoucault, Sister Celeste le Blond, 102, 105
De Limoëlan de Cloriviere, Joseph-Pierre Picot. *See* Father Cloriviere.
Dellaway, Julia Ann, 84–85, *84* (sampler)
Du Bourg, William, 102, 102*n*
Du Cherray, Madame, 76, 192, 197, 198
Durkee, Eleanor, *123* (sampler), 123–125

E

Edmonds, Edmund, 13*n*, 57, 57*n*, 58*n*, 67*n*
Edmonds, Sarah Allison, 13, 13*n*, 14, *14*, 57, 57*n*, 66, 67, 67*n*
Edmonds, Sarah Eliza, 51, 53–58, 58*n*, 67
Eighteenth-century samplers
    Green, Elizabeth (Betsy), 18, 18*n*
    Horwell, Ann May, *20*, 20–21, 22
    Janney, Hannah and Rebecah, 15, 16, *16* (sampler), 17, *17* (sampler), 18
    Leap, Ann, *19* (sampler), 19–20
Ellicott, Andrew, 58, 59
Elliot, Jonathan, 74*n*
Embroidered maps, 58–66
Embroideries, pictorial, 48–56, 54*n*, 55, 113-114
    teachers of, 57–58
    themes, literary, 49–58
    themes, patriotic, 49–50
English, David, 73*n*, 87, 87*n*

English, Lydia Scudder, 73, 79–80, 86–87, *87*, 88, 88*n*, 89, 89*n*, 91–93, 95–99, 195
Ensey, Martha, *179* (sampler), 179*n*, 179–180
Evans, Mary Ann, *195*

F

Fearson, Mary Elizabeth, 85, *85* (sampler), 86
Federal Gazette, 121
Female Seminary of Georgetown, 73, 79, 80, 86–88, 88*n*, 90–91, 93, 94*n*, 95, 99
Fifield, Rebecca Ann, 27, *27* (sampler), 43
Flanigan, Matilda, 108, *108*
Fleming, Margaret, 24–25, *24* (sampler), 56, *57* (embroidered picture)
Folwell, Elizabeth, 114, 118
Folwell, Samuel, 114, 118–119
Fort McHenry, 209
Fowler, Julia Ann Wilmore, 89–90, *90*
French Revolution
  and Order of Saint Clare, 101–102

G

Garrett, Elisabeth Donaghy, 167*n*, 174*n*, 179*n*
Gell, Sister Mada-anne, 105*n*, 107*n*, 111*n*
Georgetown, District of Columbia
  Catholic community, 103, 128*n*
  early history, 69, 71–72, 103, 141*n*
  needlework influences, 213
  variety of styles in, 213
  needlework teachers, 71, 75–77
  Port of Georgetown, 70, 71
Georgetown and Federal City, *140*
Georgetown College, 71, 71*n*, 72–73, 101, 102, *102*, 123, 132, 135*n*
Georgetown Female Seminary, 73, 79, 80, 86, 87, 88, 88*n*, 90, 91, 93, 94*n*, 95, 99. *See also* Female Seminary of Georgetown.
Georgetown Lancasterian School, 10*n*, 73–74
Georgetown Visitation Convent/Monastery, 74, *100*, *106*, 107, 107*n*, 108*n*, 110, 111*n*, *138*
Georgetown Visitation Preparatory School 73, 101, 104*n*, 111*n*. *See also* Young Ladies' Academy of Georgetown.
Graffam, Olive Blair, 50*n*, 98*n*, 144*n*, 158*n*, 167*n*
Graham, Elizabeth, *62* (embroidered map), 63–65
Green, Betsy, 18, 18*n*

H

Hancock, Ella, 144, *144* (sampler), *145*
Harrison, Reverend Elias, 25, 40*n*, 41, 41*n*
Harrison, Mary, 38, 39, *39* (sampler), 40
Harrison, William Henry, 209
Hawley, Miss, 76*n*, 194
Hay, Catharine, *173* (sampler)
Herbert, Eliza Jane, *188* (sampler)
Herr, Patricia T., 53*n*
Highlands, by Caroline Rebecca Nourse Dulany, *194*
Hill, Samuel, 59
Hooff, Julia Maria, *48*, 51, *52* (embroidered picture), 53, 54
Hopkins, Johns, 16
Horwell, Ann May, 20, *20* (sampler), 21, 22
Horwell, Ann, 22, 22*n*
Horwell, Richard, 21, 22
Horwell, Sarah May, 21–22, *21* (sampler), 31
Hunter, Andrew, 145

I

immigrants, 38, 73, 80, 101, 124, 157, 168, 181
Irwin, Hannah, 29*n*
Ivey, Kimberly Smith, 21*n*, 50*n*, 53, 53*n*, 61, 61*n*, 161*n*, 167*n*

J

Jackson, Artridge Priscilla, 81*n*, 94–95, *95* (sampler), 96
Jackson, Emily Mary, 122, *122* (sampler), 123, 123*n*, 124
James, Amelia, *182* (sampler), 182–183
Jameson, Eliza, 113, 116, *116* (embroidered picture)
Janney, Hannah, *16* (sampler), 15–18
Janney, Joseph, 15, 15*n*, 18
Janney, Rebecah, *17* (sampler), 15–18
Jefferson, Thomas, 50, 50*n*, 167
Jones, Arabella, 146
Judge, Margaret, 10*n*, 14, 32, 32*n*, 74, *74*
Judge, Rachel, 10, 10*n*, 14, 74

K

Kemmelmeyer, Frederick, 13, 13*n*
Kurtz, Sarah *78* (sampler), 79–80

L

Laird, Barbara (Lucinda), 80
Laird, Margaret, 80
Lalor, Alice (Mother Teresa), 103–104, 103n, 105, 113, 114, 117
Lalor, Maria Teresa, 113, 117, *117* (embroidered picture), 118, *118* (embroidered picture), 119, 119n, *119* (painted pictures), 120, 120n
Lancaster, Joseph, 10, 10n, 11, 73, 73n
Lancasterian schools, 10n, 73, 74, 74n, 143, 214
Larkin, Mr. and Mrs., *199*
Latrobe, Benjamin Henry, 204, 204n
Laurence, Catherine, *135*
Laurence, Mary Elizabeth, 110, 130, 133–134, *134* (sampler), 135, *135*, 136, 136n, *136*
Leadbeater, Anna, *34* (sampler)
Leadbeater, Lucy, 33n
Leadbeater, Mary Pleasants. *See* Mary Pleasants Stabler.
Leap, Ann, 19–20, *19* (sampler), 50–51, *51* (embroidered picture)
Lemoine, Maria Magdalene, *64* (embroidered map), 65, *65*
L'Enfant, Pierre (Peter) Charles, 59, 141, 195

M

Madison, Dolley, 144
maps, embroidered, 49, 58–66
maps, printed, 58–60
Marechal, Archbishop Ambrose, 109, 134, 134n, 135n
Maryland
    Catholic community, 101, 103, 115n, 129n, 131n
    and education of females, 101
    immigration, 101
    political intolerance of, 103, 115n
    support of independence, 101
    tobacco commerce, 71
Masi, Caroline, 149, *149* (sampler)
Massoletti, Julietta, *x*, 22, 22n
May, Ann, 20–21
McDermott, Maria (Sister Mary Frances), 103, 103n, 104, 105, 114
McFarlane, Elizabeth, 45n
McFarlane, Margaret, *45* (sampler), 45, 45n, 46
McKnight, Martha Bryan, 55 (embroidered picture), 55–56, *56*
McLeod, John, 169, 177, 187, 194, 195, 205n
Meem, Mary Margaret, 96–97, *97* (sampler)
memorial sampler, 22, 23–24
Mitchell, Elizabeth and Maria, 108, *108*
Monroe, James, 192, 209
Muir, Elizabeth Welman, 41, 41n, 42, 42n, 43n
Muir, Reverend Doctor James, 24n, 25, 37, 40n, 41, 41n, 42, 66
Muir, John, 37, 42, 42n, 63
Muir, Mary, 35, *35* (sampler), 37, 38, 39, 39n, 41n, 42, 45
Muir, Mary Lang, 42, *42*, 43
Muir, Misses, 41, 42

N

National Intelligencer and Washington Advertiser, 153n, 169n, 187n, 205, 205n
Navy Yard, 167–170
    architectural samplers, 167–188
    community, 145, 149, 152, 152n, 153, 154n, 157, 163, 164, 213
    trades and crafts, shipbuilding, 143, 163, 168
    and War of 1812, 168
Neale, Eleanora, 109, 111, 130, 132, 132n, *132* (sampler), 133
Neale, Leonard, 73, 103, 103n, 104, 105, 107n, 133, 133n, 137
needlework, teaching of,
    Lancasterian method, 9–10, 10n, 11, 11n, 73–74, 74n, 80, 87, 168–70
needlework, types of
    Dresden, 196
    embroidery, 196
    marking, 196, 214
    open work, 196
    plain and ornamental, 196
    print work, 196
    tambour, 196
    worsted wool, 67
New Academy, 102, *120* (sampler), 121
Nicholls, Elizabeth Rind, 93
Nourse, Caroline Rebecca, *102*, *The Potomac, Analostan Island and Georgetown College*
Nourse, Rosa M., 77, *77*, 194

O

Oblate Sisters of Providence, 75, 146
O'Brien, Julia, *174* (sampler), 174, 174*n*, 175–177, 179, 180
Order of Saint Clare, 101–102, 102*n*, 103, 105, 121, 130
O'Reilly (O'Riley), Robert (Mrs.), *13*, 66-67
Orme, Elizabeth, 79, 96, 97, *97* (sampler), 98
Ould, Paulina, 86, *86* (sampler)
Ould, Robert, 73, 86

P

Painter, Rachel, 29, 29*n*, 32, 200, 200*n*
Palmatary, James T., 8–9, *View of Alexandria Va.*
Panic of 1819, 107*n*, 109, 133, 200, 210*n*
Peale, Charles Willson, 70, *Benjamin Stoddert Children*
Phillips, Mrs., 75, 76, 200, *200*
Plummer, Ann, *30* (sampler), 31
Poor Clares. *See* Order of Saint Clare.
Port of Georgetown, 70, 71
Potomac, Analostan Island and Georgetown College, *102*, by Caroline Rebecca Nourse
Potter, Margaret Ann, 53–55, 55*n*
Poulson's American Daily Advertiser, 119*n*, 120*n*

Q

Quaker samplers, 29–34
Quaker schools
    Nine Partners' Boarding School, 10*n*, 29
    Sandy Spring, Maryland, 31–32, 32*n*
    Westtown Boarding School, 29, 31, 31*n*, 32*n*
    See also Religious Society of Friends.
Queen, Catharine F., 113–114, *115* (embroidered picture), 115, 115*n*, 116, 117

R

Reid, John, 60, 61
Religious orders
    Jesuits (Society of Jesus), 71, 72, 101–102, 114, 115*n*, 124, 131*n*
    Oblate Sisters of Providence, 75, 146
    Order of Saint Clare, 101–102, 102*n*, 103–105, 121, 130
    Order of the Visitation, 74, 105, 105*n*, 138, 149*n*
    Sisters of Charity, 44, *44*, 75*n*, 146, 146*n*, 148, 214
    Ursuline Sisters, 101, 102, 107*n*, 126–127
Religious Society of Friends, 29, 29*n*, 30–33, 74, 200, 207, 213
Resler, Eve, *61* (embroidered map), 61, 61*n*, 62, 62*n*, 63, 64*n*, 67
Resolute Beneficial Society. *See* Bell School House.
Ring, Betty, 30, 31*n*, 53*n*, 58*n*, 113, 113*n*, 121*n*, 123*n*, 125*n*, 132*n*, 167*n*, 173*n*, 177*n*, 179*n*, 180, 192*n*
Ridgway, Mary, 148, *148* (sampler)
Robertson, Willamina, 27–29, *28* (sampler)
Rollinson, William, 60
Roman Catholic Church
    benevolent schools, 74, 75*n*, 107*n*, 110*n*
    Catholic schools in Washington City, 146, 148–49, 157
    community in Maryland, 101, 103, 115*n*, 129*n*, 131*n*
    and education of young women, 101, 103, 105, 110*n*
    influence of, 213
    needlework and pious symbolism, 120, 122–127, *127*, 124*n*, 130, 130*n*, 135, *135*, 137, 138, 213
    political intolerance of, 103, 115*n*
    Trinity Church, 75, 118, 128*n*, 133, 134
    Visitation. *See* Young Ladies' Academy of Georgetown
Royall, Anne
    on education, 143
    on Georgetown, 72
    on Visitation Monastery, 72, 110, 110*n*
    on Washington City, 142, 145, 167
Rudd, Ann Tottington, 25–27, *26* (sampler*)*, 26*n*, 27*n*

S

Saint Agnes' Academy, 146
Saint Francis Xavier's Academy, 44, *44*
Saint John's Female Benevolent School, 75*n*
Saint Joseph's, Georgetown, 74, 107*n*
Saint Joseph's, Washington City, 148, 149*n*
Saint Joseph's Academy, Emmitsburg, 44, 44*n*
Saint Paul's Female Academy, 148, 163

Saint Vincent's Female Orphan Asylum and School, 146, 146n, 147, 157, 168
Saint Rose's Industrial School for Girls, 146n
Scaggs, Ann Lucretia Mayo, 82–84, *83* (sampler)
Scott, Mary Ann, 94–96, *94* (sampler)
Searle, Miss, 77, 197, *197*
Seminary Hospital, *92*
Shaaff, Ann, 89n, 112
Sharpe, Maria, (Sister Ignatia) 103, 103n, 104, *104*, 105, *105*, 105n, 114, 117
Shedden, Matilda Maria Dowdell, 196, 196n, *196*
Simmons, Margaret C., 158, *158* (sampler), 159, 159n, 184, 185, *186* (sampler)
Simpson, Mrs., 76
Sinnott, Margaret, 153, 195, 197, 204, *204*, 205, *205*, 205n, 206, 206n, 207
Slave, slavery, 9, 12, 27, 46n, 75, 88n, 92, 92n, 97, 111n, 123, 145, 179n
Smith, Margaret Bayard, 204
Smith, Mrs., 76
Stabler, Deborah Brooke Pleasants, 31, 31n
Stabler, Elizabeth, 31–32, *32* (sampler)
Stabler, Mary Pleasants, 32–34, 32n, 33, *33* (sampler), 43
Staples, Kathleen, 53n
Studebaker, Sue, 46n
Suter, Rebecca, 35–37, *36* (sampler), 38, 45

T

Tait, Mary Maury, 184, *184* (sampler), 185–186, 188
Taylor, Hester Dashiell, 35, 35n
Teachers of needlework,
    Armstrong, Alfred, 197, *197*
    Bage, Mrs., 198
    Barber (Sister Mary Augustine), Jerusha, 105, 107n
    Becraft, Maria, 75, 75n
    Bell, Mrs., 12, 199
    Bonfils, Mrs., 157, 194, 201
    Boots/Bootes, Miss, 85
    Brush, Mrs. Mary, 193, 198
    Chevalier, Sister Luc, 102, 197
    Cobb, Mary W., *85*, 86
    Cooke, Mrs., 12, 13, 50–51, 67
    Cottringer, Mrs., 156, 200, 201
    Cutts, Mrs. L. Henry, 193, 198
    De La Rochefoucault, Sister Celeste le Blond, 102, 105, 197
    De La Marche, Madame Marie, 75, 101, 103–105, 197, 201
    Dorman, Madame, 196
    Doyle, The Misses, 193
    Du Cherray, Madame, 76, 192, 197, 198
    Dunlap, Maria Anne, 66, 198
    Edmonds, Mrs. Edmund (Sarah Allison), 13, 14, 57, 57n, 58, 66–67, 67n, 196
    Edmonds, Sarah Eliza, 51, 53–57, 57n, 58, 58n, 67
    English, Jane Threlkeld, 87, 91n
    English, Lydia Scudder, 86–93, 93n, 195
    Evans, Miss, 169–170, 174n
    Evans, Mrs. Mary Ann, 193, 195, *195*, 198
    Evans, Miss S., 195
    Fales, Mrs., 192, 198
    Ford, Mrs. Andrew, 20
    Gaither, Mrs., 197
    Godfrey, Ann, 200
    Gray, Mr. & Miss, 193, 195
    Gray, Mr. & Mrs., 152
    Greentree, Mrs., 197
    Hagarty, Mrs., 66
    Hagerty, Mrs., 194
    Hallowell, Mary, 32n
    Hannah, Elizabeth, 12, 15
    Hardester, Mary, 192
    Harrover, Margaret Jain, 91–92
    Hauel, Miss, 192
    Hawley, Miss, 76n, 194
    Healey, Caroline, 88n
    Heaney, Miss, 192, 194, 199
    Hebb, Mrs., 197
    Henderson, Mrs., 199
    Herbert, Miss J., 160, 199
    Hogan, Miss, 198
    Hore, Mr. & Mrs. Maurice P., 192, 193
    Howard, Mrs., 76, 76n, 151, 194
    Jacks, Ann, 25, 25n
    Janney, Mary, 31, 31n
    Janney, Miss, 31, 31n
    Johnston, Miss Mary, 193
    Jones, Miss Arabella, 146
    Judge, Margaret, 10n, 14, 32, 32n, 74
    Judge, Rachel, 10, 10n, 14, 74
    Lalor (Sister Teresa), Alice, 103–105, 103n, 113–114, 117

Larkin, Mr. & Mrs., 194, 199
Lathrop, Mr., 199
Lee, Mrs., 196, 200
Lunt, Betsey, 18, 18*n*
Mark, Mrs. Ann, 193
May, Ann, 20
McCurdy, Mrs. D. (Mary), 170, 188
McDermott (Sister Mary Frances), Maria, 103–105, 103*n*, 114
McLeod, John, 169, 169*n*, 177, 187, 194, 195, 205, 205*n*
Mills, Mrs. Eliza B., 165
Moulton, Miss, 27
Muir, Elizabeth Welman, 41, 42, 42*n*, 43*n*
Muir, Mary Lang, 37, 42, 42*n*, 43, 43*n*
Muir, Misses, 41, 42
Nesmith, Ann, 170, 171*n*
Nourse, Miss Rosa M., 77, 194, 194*n*
O'Brien, Miss, 199
O'Reilly, Mrs. Robert, 13, *13*, 66, 66*n*, 67, 196
Painter, Rachel, 29, 29*n*, 32, 200, 200*n*
Philips, Mrs. E., 191–192
Phillips, Mrs., 75, 76, 200, *200*
Pope, Mrs. Emmeline, 193
Porter, Mrs., 43, 43*n*, 198, 201
Reagan, Mrs., 196
Rowen, Mrs., 201
Russ, Rebecca, 170, 171*n*
Sawkins, The Misses, 194
Searle, Miss, 77*n*, 197, *197*
Sharpe, Maria, (Sister Ignatia), 103–105, 103*n*, 104, 105, 105*n*, 114, 117
Shedden, Mrs., 196, 196*n*, *196*
Simpson, Mr. & Mrs., 76, 209
Simson, Mrs., 12, 12*n*, 199
Sinnott, Miss Margaret, 153, 195, 197, 204–206, *204*, 205*n*, *205*, 206*n*, *207*
Sketchly, Mr. & Mrs., 192
Smith, Mrs., 76, 200
Smith, Miss Ann, 192
Smith, Christian, 12, 15
Smith, Elizabeth, 192
Smith, Mrs. Isabella, 192, 193, 197
Stabler, Deborah Brooke Pleasants, 31, 31*n*
Stone, Mrs. Henry (Maria), 192, 200, 210, 211
Talbot, Mary Anna, 200
Tannent, Mrs. *See* Tennent
Tastet, Mrs., 194
Taylor, Charlotte, 192, 198, 209–210
Tennent, Mrs., 12, 196
Tyson & Sisters, Mary A., 67*n*, 193, 195, 198, 206–208, *207*, *208*
Vidler, Ann, 143*n*, 196
Walker, Miss Susan, 146
Waugh, Mr. & Mrs., 192, 195, 197
Webber, Mrs. & Miss, 192, 198
White, Mrs. Richard, 143
Wiley, Mrs., 76, 200
Winter, Mr. & Mrs., 9
Wright, The Misses, 192
Young, Miss, 143–144

Teaching
    demographics of, 201
    diverse origins of, 191–192
    historical evidence, scarcity of, 204
    itinerancy, 191–192
    marital status, 192–193, 205*n*,

Tyson, Mary A. & Sisters, 67, 67*n*, 193, 195, 198, 206–208, *207*
Teresa, Sister. *See* Alice Lalor.
Tevis, Julia Hieronymous, 76–77, 208–211, *211*
Thackara, James, 59, 60, 63, 65
Thomee, S., *13*
Thompson, Mary Ann Eliza, 163*n*, 183–185, *183* (sampler)
tobacco commerce, 70, 71, 80
Tyson, Mary A., 67, 67*n*, 193, 195, 198, 206, *207*
Tyson Sisters, 67*n*, 206–208

V

Vallance, John, 59, 60, 63, 65
Van Lommel, Father, 75, 135
Verses:
    Addison, Joseph, 172
    Bruce, Michael, 18
    Cennick, John, 39, 39*n*
    Clarke, Adam, 32
    Cowper, William, 183, 183*n*
    Dodsley, Robert, 39
    Gay, John, 79
    Goldsmith, Oliver, 186
    Heber, Bishop Reginald, 165, 165*n*
    Lyttleton, Lord George, 24
    Masters, Mary, 37, 37*n*
    Newton, John, 95
    Paine, Thomas, 21
    Percival, James Gates, 97

Poe, Edgar Allen, 156n
Pope, Alexander, 16, 16n, 46, 96, 164, 181
Pope, Walter, 26
Swift, Jonathan, 22
Thomson, James, 53
Watts, Doctor Isaac, 18, 28, 46, 95, 130, 174
Wesley, John, 82
Virginia Gazette and Alexandria Advertiser, 41n, 66n
Virginia Gazette and General Advertiser, 13n, 14n, 66n
Virginia Journal and Alexandria Advertiser, 12n, 15n
Visitation Academy, See Young Ladies' Academy of Georgetown.
Visitation Monastery. *See* Young Ladies' Academy of Georgetown
    embroideries described, 108–120
    tuition rates, 108–109
Vonderlehr, Catharine, 147, *147* (sampler)
Vowell, Mary Stewart, *43* (sampler), 43–44

W

Waring, Eleanor, 130–131, *131* (sampler), 132
Waring, Henrietta and Eleanor, *109*, 109, 130–131
War of 1812, 11n, 27, 79, 81, 98, 123n, 124, 144, 168, 205, 209, 210n, 214
Washington City, *3*, *140*, *166*, *190*, 201–202
    Catholic schools, 146–147
    early history, 51, 81n
    female education in, 191, 203, 204
    free black community, 145
    Industrial schools, 146
    Lancasterian system, 143
    plan for, *142*
    Plan of Part of the City of Washington, *171* (Nicholas King)
    public schools in, 143–144
Washington, George, 7, 9, 9n, 13n, 26, 26n, 50, 50n, 58, 59, 61, 62, 62n, 63, 65, 71, 141, 198–199
Washington National Intelligencer, 153n
Washington Navy Yard, 151. *See* Navy Yard.
Wheeler, Father Michael, 110–111, 111n, 133
White, Mrs. (Richard), 143

Wiley, Mrs., 76
Women's education
    need debated, 203
Wood, Ann Maria, 45, *46* (sampler)
Wood, Marian, 35, *35* (sampler), 36–39, 42

Y

yellow fever, 63, 63n, 64n, 103, 209
Young Ladies' Academy of Georgetown, 49n, 73, 74, 77, 101, 103, 105, *107*, 110n, 111, 112, 113, 113n, 114, 116, 117, 118, 120, 121, 122, 124, 127, 128, 129, 130, 132, 133, 134, 137, 138, 157
    "Cedar Grove" samplers, *122*, *123*, 123–124, 124n, 137
    curriculum of, 105, 107, 110, 111, 111n, 197
    early embroideries, 113–119
    early history, 74, 101, 102–103, 104, 104n, 105, 111n, 115n
    early teachers, 103–104
        Lalor, Alice, 103–104, 103n, 105, 113, 114, 117
        McDermott, Maria, 103, 103n, 104, 105, 114
        Sharpe, Maria, 103, 103n, 104–105, *104*, 105n, *105*, 114, 117
    embroideries-pictorial, 49n, 104, 113n, 113–114, 116, 117, 137
    enrollment, 111, 111n
    French influence, 101–102, 107, 121, 123, 127
    holy cards, 134–135, *135*
    Maryland Catholics, 101, 103, 115n, 129n, 131n
    merit rewards, 111, 112, *112*, 113, 113n, *113*, 136
    needlework and school ledger records, 104n, 107n, 108, 108n, *108*, 109, *109*, 111, 112n, 129, 130–132, 134, *136*, 250, 257
    needlework, surviving, 214
    plan, *106*
    samplers, parrot, 130–135
    samplers, religious, 101, 122–130, 213, 214
    tuition/boarding, 107–112, 107n, 108n, *108*, *109*, 112n, 133, 134, *136*
    View of Georgetown Visitation, *107*
    wool work samplers, 112n, 136, *137* (embroidered picture), 137n, 138